2015 Valuation Handbook

Guide to Cost of Capital

Market Results Through 2014

Duff & Phelps

WILEY

Cover image: Duff & Phelps
Cover design: Tim Harms

Published by John Wiley & Sons, Inc., Hoboken, New Jersey.

For general information on our other products and services or for technical support, please contact our Customer Care Department within the United States at (800) 762-2974, outside the United States at (317) 572-3993 or fax (317) 572-4002.

Wiley publishes in a variety of print and electronic formats and by print-on-demand. Some material included with standard print versions of this book may not be included in e-books or in print-on-demand. If this book refers to media such as a CD or DVD that is not included in the version you purchased, you may download this material at http://booksupport.wiley.com. For more information about Wiley products, visit www.wiley.com.

ISBN 978-1-119-07022-1 (Hardcover)
ISBN 978-1-119-07036-8 (ebook)

Printed in the United States of America

10 9 8 7 6 5 4 3 2 1

About the Data

The information and data presented in the *2015 Valuation Handbook – Guide to Cost of Capital* and the online *Risk Premium Toolkit* and the online *Cost of Capital Analyzer* has been obtained with the greatest of care from sources believed to be reliable, but is not guaranteed to be complete, accurate or timely. Duff & Phelps, LLC (www.duffandphelps.com) and/or its data providers expressly disclaim any liability, including incidental or consequential damages, arising from the use of the *2015 Valuation Handbook – Guide to Cost of Capital* and/or the online *Risk Premium Toolkit* and/or the Cost of Capital Analyzer or any errors or omissions that may be contained in the *2015 Valuation Handbook – Guide to Cost of Capital* and/or the online *Risk Premium Toolkit* and/or the online *Cost of Capital Analyzer,* or any other product (existing or to be developed) based upon the methodology and/or data published herein. One of the primary sources of raw data used to produce the derived data and information herein is Morningstar, Inc. Use of raw data from Morningstar to produce the derived data and information herein does not necessarily constitute agreement by Morningstar, Inc. of any investment philosophy or strategy presented in this publication.

About Duff & Phelps

Duff & Phelps is the premier global valuation and corporate finance advisor with expertise in complex valuation, dispute consulting, M&A, restructuring, and compliance and regulatory consulting. The firm's more than 1,500 employees serve a diverse range of clients from offices around the world. For more information, visit www.duffandphelps.com.

M&A advisory and capital raising services in the United States are provided by Duff & Phelps Securities, LLC. Member FINRA/SIPC. Pagemill Partners is a Division of Duff & Phelps Securities, LLC. M&A advisory and capital raising services in the United Kingdom and Germany are provided by Duff & Phelps Securities Ltd., which is authorized and regulated by the Financial Conduct Authority.

Additional Resources

To download a free copy of "Developing the Cost of Equity Capital: Risk-Free Rate and ERP During Periods of 'Flight to Quality'" by Roger J. Grabowski, visit: www.duffandphelps.com/CostofCapital.

To learn more about the latest theory and practice in cost of capital estimation, see *Cost of Capital: Applications and Examples* 5th edition, by Shannon P. Pratt and Roger J. Grabowski (John Wiley & Sons, Inc., 2014).

> "*Shannon Pratt and Roger Grabowski have produced a remarkably comprehensive review of the subject…it is a work that valuation practitioners, CFOs, and others will find an invaluable reference.*"
>
> **– Professor Richard Brealey**, London Business School (from the Foreword)
>
> *"Estimating the cost of capital is critical in determining the valuation of assets, in evaluating the capital structure of corporations, and in estimating the long run expected return of investments. Shannon Pratt and Roger Grabowski have the most thorough text on the subject, not only providing various estimation methods, but also numerous ways to use the cost of capital."*
>
> **– Professor Roger G. Ibbotson**, Yale School of Management, former chairman and founder of Ibbotson Associates, chairman, founder, and CIO of Zebra Capital.

Other Duff & Phelps valuation data resources published by John Wiley & Sons include: (i) the *Valuation Handbook – Industry Cost of Capital*, which provides the same type of rigorous industry-level analyses of U.S. industries previously published in the green-cover Morningstar/ Ibbotson Cost of Capital Yearbook (discontinued in 2013), and (ii) *International Valuation Handbook – Guide to Cost of Capital*, which provides country-level equity risk premia (ERPs), relative volatility (RV) factors, and country risk premia (CRPs) which can be used to estimate country-level cost of equity capital globally, for up to 188 countries, from the perspective of investors based in any one of up to 55 countries (depending on data availability). In Fall 2015, we expect to publish a fourth book, *International Valuation Handbook – Industry Cost of Capital*, which will provide global industry analyses.

We welcome reader comments, questions, and suggestions. Your feedback is an important source of information for helping us to constantly improve the *Valuation Handbook – Guide to Cost of Capital*, and our related valuation data resources.

To order additional copies of the *Valuation Handbook – Guide to Cost of Capital*, or other Duff & Phelps valuation data resources published by John Wiley & Sons, please go to:
www.wiley.com/go/ValuationHandbooks

Table of Contents

Acknowledgements

Authors

Roger J. Grabowski, FASA
Managing Director, Duff & Phelps

James P. Harrington
Director, Duff & Phelps

Carla Nunes, CFA
Director, Duff & Phelps

Thank you

The authors give special thanks to Senior Associate Niel Patel and Valuation Intern Kevin Madden of Duff & Phelps for their assistance in assembling the exhibits presented herein, analysis, editing, and quality control. We thank Executive Assistant Michelle Phillips for production assistance and Vice President Tim Harms for design, production and layout design. We also thank Paul Wittman of Wittco Software for updating the software and processing the data. Finally, the authors thank former colleague, David King, for his insights and assistance in prior years.

Introduction

The *Valuation Handbook – Guide to Cost of Capital ("Valuation Handbook")* is not designed to duplicate the contents of comprehensive, learned treatises on estimating the cost of equity capital such as, Shannon P. Pratt and Roger J. Grabowski, *Cost of Capital: Applications and Examples* 5th edition (John Wiley & Sons, Inc., 2014). That book, for example, covers the latest theory and practice in cost of capital estimation, including cost of capital for uses in business valuation, project assessment and capital budgeting, divisional cost of capital, reporting unit valuation and goodwill impairment testing, valuing intangible assets for financial reporting, and transfer pricing.

Rather, the *Valuation Handbook* is designed to complement such works, providing a brief refresher for valuation analyst on the approaches to valuation and estimating the cost of equity capital, but primarily focusing on the data sources commonly available for estimating the cost of equity capital.

Who Should Use the Valuation Handbook – Guide to Cost of Capital

The *Valuation Handbook* is designed to assist financial professionals in estimating the cost of equity capital (k_e) for a subject company. Cost of equity capital is the return necessary to attract funds to an equity investment. The valuation data and methodology in the *Valuation Handbook* can be used to develop cost of equity capital estimates using both the build-up method and the capital asset pricing model (CAPM). In addition to the traditional professional valuation analyst, the *Valuation Handbook*, and the online *Risk Premium Toolkit,* and online *Cost of Capital Analyzer*, are designed to serve the needs of:[i.1]

- Corporate finance officers for pricing or evaluating mergers and acquisitions, raising private or public equity, property taxation, and stakeholder disputes.
- Corporate officers for the evaluation of investments for capital budgeting decisions.
- Investment bankers for pricing public offerings, mergers and acquisitions, and private equity financing.
- CPAs who deal with either valuation for financial reporting or client valuations issues.
- Judges and attorneys who deal with valuation issues in mergers and acquisitions (M&A), shareholder and partner disputes, damage cases, solvency cases, bankruptcy reorganizations, property taxes, rate setting, transfer pricing, and financial reporting.

i.1 The *Risk Premium Toolkit* (previously call the "*Risk Premium Calculator*") and *Cost of Capital Analyzer* are web-based companion applications that are based on the same data and methodology that is published in the *Valuation Handbook – Guide to Cost of Capital.* Both the *Risk Premium Toolkit* and the *Cost of Capital Analyzer* can be used by the valuation analyst to estimate cost of equity capital for a subject company dependent on its size and risk characteristics using multiple models (including the build-up method and CAPM). The *Risk Premium Toolkit* is available from Business Valuation Resources, LLC (BVR) (website: www.bvresources.com/costofcapital; phone: 1 (503) 291-7963 ext. 2). The *Cost of Capital Analyzer* is available from ValuSource, (website: www.valusource.com/vhb; phone: 1 (800) 825-8763).

About the Valuation Handbook – Guide to Cost of Capital

The *2015 Valuation Handbook* includes all of the critical data (i.e., historical long-term ERP, supply-side long-term ERP, size premia, and industry risk premia, etc.) that was previously available in the *SBBI® Valuation Yearbook* and provides users of *SBBI®* valuation data with the same sources of data and methodology.[i.2]

The *2015 Valuation Handbook's "data through" date:*

- The *2015 Valuation Handbook* includes data through December 31, 2014, and is intended to be used for 2015 valuation dates.

The *2015 Valuation Handbook* includes two sets of valuation data:

- Data previously available in the *SBBI® Valuation Yearbook*; and

- Data available in the Duff & Phelps *Risk Premium Report.*

The size premia data previously published in the *SBBI® Valuation Yearbook* is referred to as the "CRSP Deciles Size Premia" exhibits in the *Valuation Handbook,* while the size and risk premia data published in the Duff & Phelps *Risk Premium Report* continues to be titled "Risk Premium Report" exhibits.

The *Risk Premium Report* has been published annually since 1996 and, like the former *SBBI® Yearbook*, provides data and methodology to assist financial professionals in estimating the cost of equity capital for a subject company using various build-up models and the CAPM.

[i.2] Morningstar, Inc. announced in September 2013 that it would no longer publish the Morningstar/Ibbotson *SBBI® Valuation Yearbook* and other valuation publications and products.

Same Data Sources

The same data sources used to produce the data in the former *SBBI® Valuation Yearbook* are used to produce the data in the new *Valuation Handbook*:

- The Center for Research in Security Prices (CRSP) standard market-cap-based NYSE/NYSE MKT/NASDAQ indices. To learn more about the Center for Research in Security Prices at the University of Chicago Booth School of Business, visit www.crsp.com

- Standard & Poor's *Research Insight* database. To learn more about Standard and Poor's, visit www.standardandpoors.com/home/en/us

- *SBBI®* Series from Morningstar's *Direct* database. To learn more about Morningstar's *Direct* database, visit www.corporate.morningstar.com

New in the 2015 Valuation Handbook

The *Valuation Handbook – Guide to Cost of Capital* is in its second year of publication with the release of the 2015 edition (this book). The inaugural 2014 edition was self-published by Duff & Phelps; starting in 2015, the *Valuation Handbook – Guide to Cost of Capital* is published by John Wiley & Sons, marking a significant milestone for the *Valuation Handbook*.

We expanded our discussion in Chapter 3 of the risk-free rate and the equity risk premium with analyses of the effects of flight to quality and massive central bank monetary interventions on these two important cost of capital inputs.

We added a table of debt betas (by credit grade) to Chapter 5. The observed betas by debt rating can be used in conjunction with the equity beta unlevering and levering formulas which require debt beta estimates.

Chapter 11, "Real Estate", has been added. This new chapter introduces a discussion on real estate and associated rates of return, examines volatility characteristics of U.S. real estate compared to other U.S. asset classes, and provides a table of data that can be used as inputs in performing valuations of individual real property investments.

Chapter 12, "Answers to Commonly Asked Questions" has been added in order to share some of the many thoughtful questions we receive from valuation analysts about the *Valuation Handbook – Guide to Cost of Capital*.

In 2015 we produced two additional valuation data resources: the *Valuation Handbook – Industry Cost of Capital*, and the *International Valuation Handbook – Guide to Cost of Capital*. For more information about Duff & Phelps valuation data resources published by John Wiley & Sons, please go to: www.wiley.com/go/ValuationHandbooks

Chapter 1
Cost of Capital Defined

Introduction

"The cost of capital is the expected rate of return that the market requires in order to attract funds to a particular investment."

– Shannon P. Pratt and Roger J. Grabowski, co-authors of *Cost of Capital*, 5th edition[1.1]

"The opportunity cost of capital is one of the most important concepts in finance. For example, if you are a chief finance officer contemplating a possible capital expenditure, you need to know what return you should look to earn from the investment. If you are an investor who needs to plan for future expenditures, you need to ask what return you can expect to earn on your portfolio."

– Richard Brealey, London Business School

"The opportunity cost of capital is equal to the return that could have been earned on alternative investments at a similar level of risk and liquidity."

– Roger Ibbotson, Yale University

"The cost of capital is the price charged by investors for bearing the risk that the company's future cash flows may differ from what they anticipated when they made the investment."

– McKinsey[1.2]

The cost of capital may be described in simple terms as the expected return appropriate for the expected level of risk.[1.3] The cost of capital is also commonly called the *discount rate*, the *expected return*, or the *required return*.[1.4]

Before elaborating on the specifics of estimating cost of capital inputs, we begin the *Valuation Handbook* with a basic framework. In many instances, valuations are performed by applying a combination of three broad valuation approaches: (i) the income approach, (ii) the market approach, or (iii) the asset approach. The market and asset approaches, however, do not generally rely on a cost of capital input. Income-based methods, on the other hand, are highly dependent on the use of an appropriate cost of capital estimate. There are a wide variety of methods within the income approach, but they are not the subject of

1.1 Shannon P. Pratt and Roger J. Grabowski, *Cost of Capital: Applications and Examples* 5th ed. (Hoboken, NJ: John Wiley & Sons, 2014): 2.

1.2 Tim Koller, Marc Goedhart, and David Wessels, *Valuation: Measuring and Managing the Value of Companies*, 5th ed. (Hoboken, NJ: John Wiley & Sons, 2010): 33.

1.3 Investors tend to try to maximize return for a given amount of risk, or minimize risk for a given amount of return.

1.4 When a business uses a given cost of capital to evaluate a commitment of capital to an investment or project, it often refers to that cost of capital as the "hurdle rate". The hurdle rate is the minimum expected rate of return that the business would be willing to accept to justify making the investment.

this text. Instead, we limit our discussion to the broad categories of single period versus multi-period approaches to distinguish between the notions of capitalizing and discounting.

We then proceed to provide an overview of basic cost of capital concepts, outline general sources of capital, and finally conclude by summarizing some general ways to estimate the cost of typical capital structure components.

Income Approach Overview

Broadly speaking, the income approach can be defined as a way of determining a value indication of an investment (e.g., business, business ownership interest, security, or intangible asset) using one or more methods that convert expected future economic benefits associated with that investment into a single "present value" amount. The basic steps of valuing a business are summarized in Exhibit 1.1.

Exhibit 1.1: Basic Steps in Valuing a Business

Step 1 Estimate expected future cash flows. This is the *numerator* in a discounting and capitalization formula.

Step 2 Estimate the cost of capital (i.e., the "discount rate"). This is a key input in the *denominator* in a discounting and capitalization formula.

Step 3 Use the *cost of capital* to "discount" the expected future cash flows back to present value.

Throughout this book, the terms "business" or "entity" are used to generically represent the subject investment being valued. In reality, the subject investment could include a wholly-owned business, a business ownership interest, a security, or an intangible asset, among many others.

Discounting versus Capitalizing Concepts

Income approaches, in general, derive the present value of expected future economic benefits by either capitalizing a single period benefit amount or discounting to present value a multi-period projection. Depending on the nature of the projections and the subject investment being valued, both methods can be acceptable. The single period and multi-period approaches are summarized as follows:

- **Single Period:** When expected benefits are capitalized, a *single* (representative or normalized) benefit level is divided by an appropriate capitalization factor to convert the benefit to present value. This method would be appropriate when the economic benefits are expected to increase (or decline) at a *constant* rate into the future (i.e., akin to a constant-growth annuity). As such, capitalization is a simplified version of a multi-period analysis.

- **Multi-period:** When expected benefits are discounted, annual benefits are estimated for *each* of the future periods in which they are expected to occur. This stream of economic benefits is converted to present value by applying an appropriate discount rate (or cost of capital) and using present value techniques. Discounting tends to be more appropriate in situations where the economic benefits are expected to increase (or decrease) at *varying* rates into the future.

In its most basic form, the present value concept embedded in the income approach may be represented in equation format as:

Formula 1.1

$$PV = \frac{NCF_0(1+g)^1}{(1+k)^1} + \frac{NCF_0(1+g)^2}{(1+k)^2} + \ldots + \frac{NCF_0(1+g)^n}{(1+k)^n}$$

where:

PV	=	Present value
NCF_0	=	Net cash flow at "time zero" (i.e., "now" or the most recently completed period as of the valuation date)
k	=	Discount rate
g	=	Expected rate of change (growth) in net cash flows
n	=	Total number of periods

Expected future economic benefits are typically measured by net cash flows (sometimes called free cash flows, or simply, cash flows). Net cash flow represents discretionary cash available to be paid out to stakeholders (providers of capital) of an entity or project (e.g., interest, debt payments, dividends, withdrawals) without jeopardizing the projected ongoing operations of the entity or project. Net cash flow is typically defined as an after-tax concept (specifically, *after* corporate income taxes and *before* investor income taxes) because the sources of the discount rate measures are typically drawn from rates of return after corporate income taxes and before investor income taxes.

Capitalization Rates versus Discount Rates

These terms are sometimes confused with each other, but the process of capitalizing is really just a shorthand form of discounting. The data in this book can be used to develop both capitalization rates and discount rates.

As discussed in the previous section, with capitalization rates, we focus on the expected benefit of just a *single* period, usually the expected net cash flow projected for the first year immediately following the valuation date. This amount represents the long-term normalized base level of net cash flows or a base from which the level of cash flows is expected to increase or decline at a more or less *constant* rate. This single-year net cash flow is then divided by the capitalization rate.

A challenge with capitalizing is that for most investments, expected net cash flows are rarely projected to increase at a constant rate into perpetuity from either the year preceding or the year following the valuation date. We do note that such a simplifying assumption is commonly used to estimate the residual year value (sometimes called terminal year value or continuing value) in a multi-period analysis; however, that residual year net cash flow is intended to represent the sustainable or normalized level of cash flows into perpetuity.

Alternatively, discount rates are applied in the context of a *multi*-period analysis. There, annual expected net cash flows from the subject investment are projected over the life of that investment. Again, this is appropriate when the expected cash flows are *not* constant, or are not changing at a constant growth rate. In these cases, the expected cash flows are divided by a present value factor (the terms $(1 + k)^1$ through $(1 + k)^n$ in Formula 1.1), which includes a discount rate (k) estimate. Common practice in business valuation is to assume that the net cash flows are received on average continuously throughout the year (approximately equivalent to receiving the net cash flows in the middle of the year), in which case the present value factor is generally based on a mid-year convention (e.g., $(1+k)^{0.5}$).

A challenge associated with discounting (for most investments) is the accuracy of the projection of expected net cash flows for each specific projection period several years into the future. Nevertheless, since the future cash flows of businesses (and capital projects) are typically not constant, and in some cases, vary significantly from period to period, these types of investments lend themselves to discounting, more so than capitalizing.

Relationship Between Capitalization Rates and Discount Rates

If the expected increase or decrease (i.e., growth) in net cash flows for the investment is stable and sustainable over a long period of time, then a discount rate (cost of capital) can reasonably be converted into a capitalization rate. We could even say that the capitalization rate is a function of the discount rate and growth rate under these conditions. The relationship between the discount rate and the capitalization rate can be put into equation form as shown in Formula 1.2:[1.5]

Formula 1.2

Capitalization Rate = Discount Rate – Expected Growth Rate

Can the discount rate and capitalization rate ever be the same value? Yes – the discount rate and capitalization rate are equivalent when the expected growth rate is equal to zero.[1.6]

1.5 A critical assumption in Formula 1.2 is that the expected rate of increase (growth) in the net cash flow from the investment is reasonably constant over the long term (technically into perpetuity).

1.6 A simple example of when the growth rate could be equal to zero is a preferred stock that is issued in perpetuity, is not callable, for which there is not prospect of liquidation, and which pays a set dividend at the end of each year.

Lastly, notable to Formula 1.1 is its use of *g*, a constant expected rate of growth in net cash flows. This formula can be extended to include different variations of growth stages (e.g. multi-stage growth model), but this level of detail is beyond the scope of this book. For greater detail, see Chapter 4, "Discounting versus Capitalizing" in the *Cost of Capital*, 5th Edition.

As presented in Formula 1.1, a series of annual net cash flows (expected to increase at a constant annual rate *g*) are individually discounted to present value. A constant growth rate enables this formula to be simplified to a single period capitalization. This constant growth capitalization formula is commonly known as the Gordon Growth Model:

$$PV = \frac{NCF_0(1+g)}{(k-g)}$$

Note that for this model to make economic sense, NCF_0 must represent a normalized amount of net cash flow from the investment for the previous year, from which a steady rate of growth is expected to proceed. Therefore, NCF_0 may not need to be the actual net cash flow for period 0 but may reflect certain normalization adjustments, such as elimination of the effect of one or more non-recurring factors.

This capitalization formula serves as the basis for estimation of the residual value in many multi-stage growth models. Often the residual value represents a significant portion of the estimated value of the investment. But because the inputs to the discount rates are imprecise, the goal is to obtain an unbiased estimate of the discount rate. But research has shown that this commonly used formula does not provide an unbiased estimate of the residual value and an adjustment is needed. We discuss this adjustment in section entitled "Estimates of Cost of Capital are Imprecise" at the end of Chapter 1.

Valuation Date

The valuation date is the specific point in time as of which the valuation analyst's opinion of value applies. The valuation date is sometimes referred to as the "effective date" or "appraisal date".

A guiding principle in conducting valuations is that you should incorporate facts that are known or reasonably knowable at the time of the valuation date.

The *2015 Valuation Handbook – Guide to Cost of Capital* includes data through December 31, 2014, and is intended to be used for 2015 valuation dates.

Basic Cost of Capital Concepts

Cost of Capital is Forward-Looking

The cost of capital (like valuation itself) is based on investors' expectations of what will happen in the future, and it is therefore "forward-looking". Cost of capital is used to discount the expected future economic benefits (or income) associated with the ownership of an investment to their present value. The term "expected" represents the average of probability-weighted possible economic benefits (or income) that are usually measured in terms of expected future cash flows.

Exhibit 1.2: Valuation is Equating Expected Future Economic Benefits (Cash Flows) to Present Value

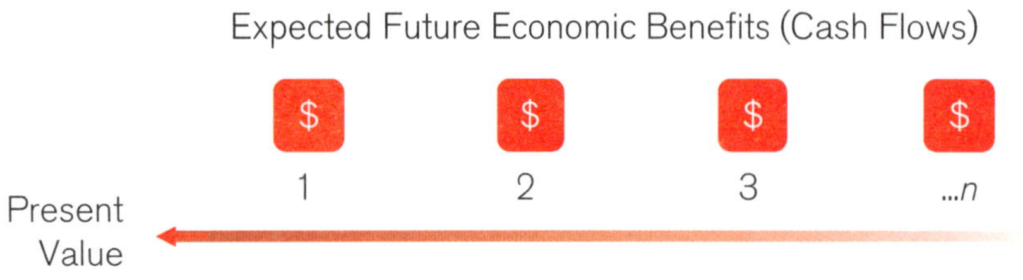

Does History Repeat Itself?

Uncertainty about what is going to happen in the future is the very nature of risk. In the absence of being able to tell the future with anything approaching certainty, we naturally oftentimes look to the past (e.g., analyzing historical market data) in an attempt to gauge what may happen in the future.

For example, the equity risk premium (ERP) – a key variable in estimating the cost of equity capital – is defined as the incremental return that investors demand for investing in equities (stocks) rather than investing in a risk-free asset. As discussed in Chapter 3, one common method for estimating the ERP is to examine the historical differences between equity returns and risk-free returns, and make an assumption that this historical relationship will hold in the future. This method of estimating the ERP "works" only to the extent that history does repeat itself, which is by no means guaranteed.

Past returns may provide, at best, some guidance as to what returns in the future will be (given an expected level of risk). This is not to say that analyzing what happened in the past for hints of what may happen in the future is unhelpful – it generally *is* helpful – especially when compared to the alternative of trying to guess the future without the benefit of learning from the past.

The use of historical data in the formulation of cost of capital inputs is discussed in greater detail in Chapter 3, "Basic Building Blocks of the Cost of Equity Capital – Risk-free Rate and ERP".

Cost of Capital is a Function of the Investment, Not the Investor

The cost of capital is a function of the investment, not the investor.[1.7] In other words, the characteristics of a particular investor does not directly change the characteristics of the investment being analyzed.

The cost of capital comes from the marketplace, and the marketplace is comprised of a pool of investors "pricing" the risk of a particular asset. It therefore represents the consensus assessment of the pool of investors that are participants in a particular market. The term "market" refers to the universe of investors who are reasonable candidates to fund a particular investment.

[1.7] Ibbotson Associates, "What Is the Cost of Capital?" *1999 Cost of Capital Workshop* (Chicago: Ibbotson Associates, 1999).

Cost of Capital is Based on Market Value

When estimating the value of an investment – as defined under a particular standard of value (i.e., fair market value, fair value, etc.) – the measurement is performed using market-based concepts, rather than by relying on the book value, par value, or carrying value of that investment. Although not directly observable, the cost of capital is also estimated by using market data. As stated earlier, the cost of capital is the expected rate of return on alternative investments with similar levels of risk. Investors will compare these alternative investments based on their market value, not their book or carrying amounts.

For example, the yield to maturity shown in the bond quotations in the financial press is based on the closing market price of a bond, not on its face value. Similarly, the implied cost of equity capital for a company's stock is based on the share price at which it trades, and not on the company's book value per share.

Cost of Capital is Usually Stated in Nominal Terms

The data for developing discount and capitalization rates described in this book are expressed in nominal terms. Estimating cost of capital in "nominal" terms means that it includes investors' expectations of future inflation. Conversely, estimating cost of capital in "real" terms means that it does not include investors' inflation expectations.

Cost of capital is usually stated in nominal terms because the return that investors demand is typically going to be at least enough to keep up with what they expect future inflation to be. In other words, investors will require compensation for the expected future erosion of an asset's value due to inflation.

Cost of Capital is Usually Stated in Terms of After-tax Returns

Just as net cash flow is an after-tax concept (i.e., measured after entity-level income taxes), the discount and capitalization rates as developed in this book are also after-tax (specifically, after entity level or corporate income taxes, but before individual investor taxes). The equity "total returns" published in the financial press include both dividends (income) and price (i.e., capital appreciation) returns (reflecting *after*-tax performance at the corporate level), but are *before* taxation at individual investor level.[1.8]

As-if Publicly-traded

The discount and capitalization rates as developed in this book are "as-if publicly-traded". The data used in the *Valuation Handbook* are drawn from information on public companies and, therefore, the resulting cost of capital estimates using the data are "as if public".

Discounting expected future expected cash flows for a non-publicly traded investment (e.g., a closely held business) using an "as if publicly-traded" cost of capital may not provide an accurate estimate of value to the extent that market participants would consider other risks associated with non-publicly traded investments. For example, when estimating the cost of equity capital for a closely held company,

[1.8] Total return consists of three components: (i) price (i.e., capital appreciation) returns, (ii) income returns (e.g., dividends), and (iii) reinvestment (e.g., of dividends) returns.

the risks will more than likely differ from the risks of the sample of guideline public companies to which it is being compared (i.e., the "peer group"), and valuation analysts may therefore deem additional adjustments to the cost of capital estimate necessary.

Minority Interest

Some valuation analysts argue that the income approach always produces a publicly-traded minority basis of value because the build-up method and the capital asset pricing model (CAPM) develop discount and capitalization rates from minority transaction data in the public markets. This is not correct. The discount and capitalization rates as developed in this book do not include an implied "minority interest" discount in them. There is little or no difference in the rate of return that most investors require for investing in a public, freely tradable minority interest versus a controlling interest.[1.9]

The Delaware Court of Chancery recognizes that discount rates derived from public company data should not be adjusted for an implied minority discount.[1.10] The Court of Chancery first rejected this adjustment in 1991[1.11] and, except for one anomalous exception, it has continued to reject adding a control premium to valuations where the valuation experts used the discounted cash flow method, a form of the income approach.

Controlling Interest

Investors typically do not reduce their required rate of return because they are buying a controlling interest in an investment, rather than a minority interest.

Generally, the cost of capital is the same for minority interest investments as for controlling interest investments. While a premium above current market trading prices is often paid to acquire a controlling equity interest, this premium is typically paid because buyers expect to implement some measures to increase future cash flows of the target investment, not because of a lower cost of capital associated with control.

Varying Cost of Capital

When we value an investment, we are estimating the present value of the expected future economic benefits or income associated with that investment. Like all valuation inputs, the cost of capital should also reflect future expectations. In theory, when dealing with multiple periods in the forecast period, the risk profile of the annual future cash flows will likely differ from period to period. As a result, the cost of capital associated with any investment would arguably also change from period to period. This can quickly become a very complex exercise.

1.9 Pratt, *Business Valuation Discounts and Premiums* (Hoboken, NJ: John Wiley & Sons, 2001): 30, cited in Lane, 2004 Del. Ch. LEXIS 108.

1.10 Valuation analysts should be aware of the influence that the Delaware Court of Chancery has on other courts, such as the U.S. Tax Court. The Delaware Court of Chancery hears more valuation-related cases than any other court, and many courts look, even informally, at the decisions of that court for guidance. To learn more, visit: www.courts.delaware.gov/chancery

1.11 *In re Radiology Associates*, 611 A.2d 485, 494 ("The discounted cash flow method purports to represent the present value of Radiology's cash flow. . .The discounted cash flow analysis, as employed in this case, fully reflects this value without need for an adjustment").

As a simplification, valuation analysts generally estimate a single cost of capital and apply it to each of the periods in the forecast.

Sources of Capital

Thus far the term cost of capital has been used in generic terms. As stated earlier, the cost of capital is the expected rate of return required to attract funds to a particular investment. The word "capital" in "cost of capital" refers to the components of an entity's capital structure. The capital structure is a function of how the entity raises capital to fund its business operations (i.e. the funding sources). Businesses typically raise capital by issuing (i) common equity, (ii) preferred equity, and/or (iii) debt.[1.12, 1.13]

The capital structure can include a combination of these three components, each of which has its own cost of capital.[1.14] When valuing the overall business enterprise, these three types of cost of capital are "blended" together to form a "weighted average cost of capital", or WACC.

The basic forms of cost of capital when referring to an entity's capital structure are defined as follows:

- **Common equity capital:** The cost of equity capital is the expected return to common equity (i.e., stock) investors. Often referred to as simply the cost of equity. Common stocks are the most widely-held form of equity, and thus the most familiar type of equity investment for most people. Common stock owners hope to gain from rising share prices, and from dividend distributions. Dividends to common equity investors are typically paid after dividends to preferred equity investors have already been paid. Also, common equity investors are typically "last in line" in the case of liquidation or bankruptcy. Common equity is generally *riskier* than either preferred equity or debt instruments, but over the long-term may provide a higher return. (Note that the higher the risk of an investment, the higher the expected return.)

- **Preferred equity capital:** The cost of preferred equity capital is the expected return to preferred equity (i.e., stock) investors. Usually referred to as the cost of preferred equity. Preferred shares often pay a fixed dividend, and this dividend is typically paid prior to any dividend payments to common equity shareholders. Because the preferred equity's dividend is often fixed, it often trades like a bond with a coupon and its price will fluctuate (inversely) with market interest rates.[1.15] However, certain forms of preferred stock (e.g. convertible preferred) have features that resemble common equity. Preferred equity is generally *less* risky than common equity, but *riskier* than debt instruments.

1.12 There may be more than one subcategory in any or all of the listed categories of capital. Also, there may be related forms of capital, such as warrants or options.

1.13 Equity securities are generically referred to as "stocks", and debt securities are generically referred to as "bonds".

1.14 The cost of raising capital should include the costs of raising capital from external capital sources. These costs, commonly termed flotation or transaction costs, reduce the actual proceeds received by the firm. Some of these are direct out-of-pocket outlays, such as fees paid to underwriters, legal expenses, and prospectus preparation costs. Because of this *reduction* in proceeds, the business's required returns must be *greater* to compensate for the additional costs.

1.15 The price of preferred equity will fluctuate as similar-risk investments' yields vary. Because of the similarities of certain preferred equities and bonds, these preferred equities' prices will tend to fluctuate with the generic concept of "interest rates".

- **Debt capital:** The cost of debt capital is the expected return to debt (e.g., bond) investors. Usually referred to simply as cost of debt. Note that the cost of debt is estimated prior to the tax effect (without regard to the tax shield). Debt capital is generally *less* risky than preferred equity and common equity.

- **Weighted average cost of capital (WACC):** The cost of capital to the overall business is commonly called the WACC. WACC represents the market-capitalization-weighted cost of capital for both equity holders (both common and preferred) and debt holders. WACC is sometimes referred to as "blended cost of capital", or simply "overall cost of capital". WACC is typically estimated on an after-tax basis, as explained later in this chapter.

Cost of Capital Input Assumptions

Data and methodology in the Valuation Handbook can be used to estimate the cost of common equity capital. Estimating the costs of the other components of the capital structure – preferred equity capital and debt capital – is typically more straightforward than estimating the cost of common equity capital. This is because the cost of capital (risk) of fixed-income securities (bonds) and fixed-income-like securities (preferred stocks) are usually directly observable in the market, while the cost of equity capital is not. We discuss these components only briefly here.[1.16]

Estimating the Cost of Preferred Equity Capital

If the capital structure includes preferred equity capital and it is publicly traded, the market yield (dividend ÷ market price) can be used as the cost of that component. If the preferred security does not trade publically or trades infrequently, the current market yield for preferred stocks with comparable features and risk can be used as a proxy. Standard & Poor's publishes preferred stock rating criteria along with the Standard & Poor's *Stock Guide*. Using this publication, valuation analysts can see where the business's preferred stock would fit within the preferred stock rating system given the financial metrics of the subject entity, and then check the financial press to find the yields for preferred stocks with similar features and estimated ratings.

Estimating the Cost of Debt Capital

If the capital structure includes debt capital, valuation analysts should estimate a current market rate for that component of the entity's capital structure. The interest rate should be consistent with the financial condition of the subject business, based on a comparative analysis of the subject business's operating ratios.

If the entity has been assigned a credit rating, one can estimate the cost of debt using a yield curve analysis. If the entity is not formally rated, one can estimate a credit rating (often called a "synthetic" rating). Major rating agencies such as Standard & Poor's publish their credit rating criteria, making it generally available to investors. For example, the Standard & Poor's *Global Credit Portal®* provides

[1.16] To learn more about the cost of preferred capital and debt capital, see Pratt and Roger J. Grabowski, op.cit.: Chapter 20, "Other Components of a Business's Capital Structure".

median ratios by rating category for a few major industries. *RatingsDirect®* is a Standard & Poor's application that gives a hypothetical credit rating based on the financial metrics of a subject entity. Valuation analysts can see where the investment would fit within the credit rating system and then check the financial press to find the market yields corresponding to the estimated rating.

Debt capital can also include forms of off-balance sheet liabilities such as operating leases and unfunded pension liabilities. Estimating the cost of debt associated with these off-balance items is outside the scope of this book, which focuses primarily on estimating cost of equity capital.

An excellent source of statistics that enable the valuation analyst to gauge the impact of debt-like off-balance sheet items on the capital structure of the subject industry is the *Valuation Handbook – Industry Cost of Capital.*[1.17] These debt-equivalent liabilities (specifically, operating leases and unfunded pension obligations) are not only taken into account by credit rating agencies when assigning a debt rating for a company, but should likely be considered as well when ascertaining the true financial (and equity) risk of the subject company.

For example, in Exhibit 1.3 an abbreviated section of Appendix A from the *2014 Valuation Handbook – Industry Cost of Capital* is shown. Appendix A in the industry book lists the "Latest" debt to-total-capital ratios of all U.S. industries analyzed therein (over 200) *before* and *after* adjusting for capitalized operating leases and unfunded liabilities. For example, when debt-to-total-capital is calculated using "Book Debt" (i.e., *unadjusted* debt), the "Latest" debt-to-total-capital ratio for SIC 57 (Home Furnishings, Furnishing, and Equipment Stores) is 5.8%, but when debt-to-total-capital is calculated using "Book Debt + Off-Balance-Sheet Debt" (i.e., debt *adjusted* to include capitalized operating leases and unfunded pensions), the "Latest" debt-to-total capital ratio for SIC 57 is 21.7%, a difference of 15.9% (21.7% – 5.8%).

[1.17] The *2014 Valuation Handbook – Industry Cost of Capital* (with data through March 2014) was published in October 2014 by Duff and Phelps. The 2015 version of the "industry" book is scheduled for release in late May 2015 (with data through March 2015), and will be published by John Wiley and Sons. The *Valuation Handbook – Industry Cost of Capital* provides the same type of rigorous industry-level analysis previously published in the green-cover Morningstar/ Ibbotson *Cost of Capital Yearbook* (discontinued in 2013). Like the previous Morningstar/Ibbotson *Cost of Capital Yearbook*, the *Valuation Handbook – Industry Cost of Capital* is published with data through March, and includes three intra-year quarterly updates (June, September, and December; updates are not sold separately, and only as a group). And, like the previous Morningstar/Ibbotson *Cost of Capital Yearbook*, the new *Valuation Handbook – Industry Cost of Capital* analyzes over 200 U.S. industries identified by their Standard Industrial Classification (SIC) code. To order copies of the *Valuation Handbook – Industry Cost of Capital* and its quarterly updates, please go to www.wiley.com/go/ValuationHandbooks

Exhibit 1.3: Abbreviated Section of Appendix A from the *2014 Valuation Handbook – Industry Cost of Capital*

		Calculated Using Book Debt	Calculated Using Book Debt + Off-Balance-Sheet Debt
SIC	**Industry Description**	**Debt-to-total Capital (%)**	**Debt-to-total Capital (%)**
57	Home Furnishings, Furnishing, and Equipment Stores	5.8	21.7
591	Drug Stores and Proprietory Stores	13.9	27.7
3711	Motor Vehicles and Passenger Car Bodies	37.0	45.8

		Relative Impact: Operating Leases versus Unfunded Pension Liabilies		
SIC	**Industry Description**	**Primary Driver of Change in Capital Structure**	**Operating Leases (%)**	**Unfunded Pension Liabilities (%)**
57	Home Furnishings, Furnishing, and Equipment Stores	Operating Leases	99.6	0.4
591	Drug Stores and Proprietory Stores	Operating Leases	99.7	0.3
3711	Motor Vehicles and Passenger Car Bodies	Unfunded Pension Liabilities	7.3	92.7

Note that for each industry in Exhibit 1.3, the off-balance-sheet debt item (capitalized operating leases or unfunded pensions) that is the "primary driver" of the change in capital structure is *identified*, and its relative impact *quantified*. For example, the primary driver of the change in capital structure of SIC 591 (Drug Stores and Proprietary Stores) is "Operating Leases", which accounted for 99.7% of the change. Alternatively, the primary driver of the change in capital structure of SIC 3711 (Motor Vehicles and Passenger Car Bodies) was "Unfunded Pension Liabilities", which accounted for 92.7% of the change.

Appendix B of the in the *Valuation Handbook – Industry Cost of Capital* builds on the statistics provided in Appendix A. In Appendix B, the "unlevered" (i) Raw (OLS) betas, (ii) Blume-Adjusted betas, (iii) Peer Group betas, (iv) Vasicek-Adjusted betas, (v) Sum betas, and (vi) Downside betas of each industry are calculated two ways: (i) *with* and (ii) *without* capitalized operating leases and unfunded pension liabilities being considered in the unlevering formula. In the analyses presented in *Valuation Handbook – Industry Cost of Capital*, the "Miles-Ezzell" formulas are used to unlever all beta estimates.[1.18]

In addition to the aforementioned statistics, the *Valuation Handbook – Industry Cost of Capital* provides eight (8) cost of equity capital estimates for each of the industries covered in the book, cost of debt capital and weighted average cost of capital (WACC) estimates, plus capital structure, valuation multiples, industry betas, and more (depending on data availability). Exhibit 1.4 is a sample industry analysis page from the *2014 Valuation Handbook – Industry Cost of Capital.*

[1.18] See James A. Miles and John R. Ezzell, "The Weighted Average Cost of Capital, Perfect Capital Markets and Project Life: A Clarification," *Journal of Financial and Quantitative Analysis* (1980): 719–730.

Exhibit 1.4: Sample Industry Analysis Page from the *2014 Valuation Handbook – Industry Cost of Capital*

Data Updated Through March 31, 2014

4

Number of Companies: 178

Transportation, Communications, Electric, Gas, and Sanitary Services

Industry Description

This division includes establishments providing, to the general public or to other business enterprises, passenger and freight transportation, communications services, or electricity, gas, steam, water or sanitary services.

Sales (in millions)

Three Largest Companies	
AT&T Inc.	$128,752.0
Verizon Communications Inc.	120,550.0
Comcast Corp.	64,657.0

Three Smallest Companies	
York Water Co.	$42.4
Providence And Worcester Railroad	33.3
Sharps Compliance Corp.	21.5

Total Assets (in millions)

Three Largest Companies	
AT&T Inc.	$277,787.0
Verizon Communications Inc.	274,098.0
Comcast Corp.	158,813.0

Three Smallest Companies	
Ambassadors Group Inc.	$88.4
Hudson Technologies Inc.	52.4
Sharps Compliance Corp.	25.5

Annualized Monthly Performance Statistics (%)

Industry	Geometric Mean	Arithmetic Mean	Standard Deviation
1-year	12.8	13.3	10.8
3-year	14.9	15.4	11.0
5-year	20.5	21.2	13.6

S&P 500 Index	Geometric Mean	Arithmetic Mean	Standard Deviation
1-year	21.9	22.4	12.0
3-year	14.7	15.5	14.3
5-year	21.2	22.3	16.9

Return Ratios (%) / **Liquidity Ratio** / **Profitability Ratio** (%) / **Growth Rates** (%)

	Return on Assets		Return on Equity		Dividend Yield		Current Ratio		Operating Margin		Long-term EPS
	Latest	5-Yr Avg	Latest	5-Yr Avg	Latest	5-Yr Avg	Latest	5-Yr Avg	Latest	5-Yr Avg	Analyst Estimates
Median (178)	3.1	3.4	7.3	7.7	2.9	3.2	1.1	1.2	16.3	16.6	7.3
SIC Composite (178)	3.6	3.3	5.4	5.8	3.3	3.7	1.1	1.0	18.2	16.5	9.1
Large Composite (17)	4.2	3.3	6.3	5.7	3.6	4.1	1.2	1.0	19.2	16.3	9.5
Small Composite (17)	3.5	4.1	3.1	5.1	2.4	3.0	1.9	1.6	19.1	19.3	7.4
High-Financial Risk (41)	2.5	-0.4	4.4	-1.0	0.5	0.4	1.1	1.0	7.6	6.3	22.0

Betas (Levered) / **Betas** (Unlevered)

	Levered Raw (OLS)	Blume Adjusted	Peer Group	Vasicek Adjusted	Sum	Downside	Unlevered Raw (OLS)	Blume Adjusted	Peer Group	Vasicek Adjusted	Sum	Downside
Median	0.7	0.8	0.7	0.7	0.7	0.8	0.5	0.6	0.6	0.5	0.5	0.6
SIC Composite	0.7	0.8	0.7	0.7	0.6	0.7	0.5	0.6	0.5	0.5	0.5	0.5
Large Composite	0.6	0.8	0.8	0.6	0.6	0.6	0.5	0.6	0.6	0.5	0.4	0.5
Small Composite	0.8	0.9	0.7	0.8	0.9	0.8	0.7	0.8	0.6	0.7	0.8	0.7
High Financial Risk	1.1	1.1	1.1	1.1	1.2	1.2	0.7	0.7	0.8	0.7	0.8	0.8

Equity Valuation Multiples / **Enterprise Valuation (EV) Multiples**

	Price/Sales		Price/Earnings		Market/Book		EV/Sales		EV/EBITDA	
	Latest	5-Yr Avg	Latest	5-Yr Avg	Latest	5-Yr Avg	Latest	5-Yr Avg	Latest	5-Yr Avg
Median	1.7	1.3	21.1	18.6	1.5	1.3	2.6	2.2	9.6	8.4
SIC Composite	1.6	1.3	18.6	17.2	1.6	1.4	2.3	2.0	8.0	7.3
Large Composite	1.4	1.2	16.0	17.7	1.6	1.4	2.0	1.8	6.5	6.4
Small Composite	3.3	2.3	32.1	19.7	1.9	1.5	3.8	2.9	13.4	10.1
High Financial Risk	0.9	0.5	22.7	–	3.3	3.6	1.4	1.0	9.0	6.8

Enterprise Valuation
SIC Composite

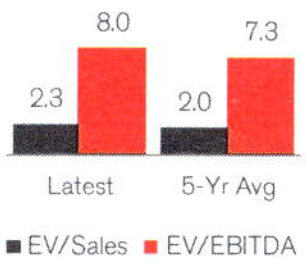

Fama-French (F-F) 3-Factor Model / **Cost of Debt** / **Leverage Ratios** (%)

	Fama-French (F-F) Components			Cost of Debt (%)	Debt/MV Equity		Debt/Total Capital	
	F-F Beta	SMB Premium	HML Premium	Latest	Latest	5-Yr Avg	Latest	5-Yr Avg
Median	0.6	3.9	-3.2	5.4	53.7	58.4	34.9	36.9
SIC Composite	0.7	0.3	-0.6	5.3	52.4	60.0	34.4	37.5
Large Composite	0.7	0.2	-0.8	5.2	48.3	52.1	32.6	34.2
Small Composite	0.6	1.3	1.4	5.2	21.4	33.5	17.6	25.1
High Financial Risk	–	–	–	6.6	79.8	121.7	44.4	54.9

Latest Capital Structure (%)
SIC Composite

Cost of Equity Capital (%)

	CAPM	CRSP Deciles CAPM +Size Prem	CRSP Deciles Build-Up	Risk Premium Report CAPM +Size Prem	Risk Premium Report Build-Up	Discounted Cash Flow 1-Stage	Discounted Cash Flow 3-Stage	Fama-French 3-Factor Model
Median	7.4	9.0	8.4	10.9	13.2	10.5	8.7	7.8
SIC Composite	7.3	7.4	7.8	9.1	10.7	12.6	9.8	7.1
Large Composite	7.2	6.9	7.9	8.0	9.6	13.3	10.7	6.9
Small Composite	8.1	11.8	11.0	14.4	16.3	9.7	7.9	9.8
High Financial Risk	–	–	–	29.6	32.1	–	–	–

Cost of Equity Capital (%)
SIC Composite

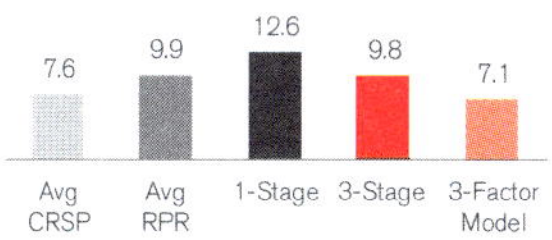

Weighted Average Cost of Capital (WACC) (%)

	CAPM	CRSP Deciles CAPM +Size Prem	CRSP Deciles Build-Up	Risk Premium Report CAPM +Size Prem	Risk Premium Report Build-Up	Discounted Cash Flow 1-Stage	Discounted Cash Flow 3-Stage	Fama-French 3-Factor Model
Median	6.5	7.6	7.3	9.1	10.2	8.5	7.3	7.1
SIC Composite	6.2	6.3	6.6	7.4	8.5	9.7	7.9	6.1
Large Composite	6.2	6.0	6.7	6.8	7.8	10.3	8.6	6.0
Small Composite	7.4	10.5	9.8	12.6	14.1	8.7	7.2	8.8
High Financial Risk	–	–	–	19.3	20.7	–	–	–

WACC (%)
SIC Composite

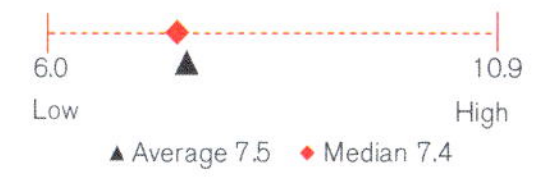

Calculating the Weight of Capital Structure Components

By definition, the WACC formulation requires us to calculate the weight (i.e. percentage of the total) for each component within the capital structure. In theory, the relative weightings of debt and equity or other capital structure components are based on the market values of each of those components, not on their book values. In practice, most valuation analysts tend to assume that the carrying value of debt capital on the balance sheet is a reasonable proxy for its market value. While this is a common practice, doing so when book values differ significantly from market values can distort cost of capital calculations.

The weight of each component of the capital structure is calculated as follows:

Formula 1.3

$$W_e = \frac{M_e}{M_e + M_p + M_d}, \quad W_p = \frac{M_p}{M_e + M_p + M_d}, \quad W_d = \frac{M_d}{M_e + M_p + M_d}$$

where:

W_e = Weight of common equity capital in the capital structure

W_p = Weight of preferred equity capital in the capital structure

W_d = Weight of debt capital in the capital structure

M_e = Market value of common equity capital

M_p = Market value of preferred equity capital

M_d = Market value of debt capital

For example, if M_e = \$90, M_p = \$15, and M_d = \$60, the weight of each of the capital structure components is calculated as follows:[1.19]

$$W_e = \frac{M_e}{M_e + M_p + M_d} = \frac{\$90}{\$90 + \$15 + \$60} = 0.55 \; or \; 55\%$$

$$W_p = \frac{M_p}{M_e + M_p + M_d} = \frac{\$15}{\$90 + \$15 + \$60} = 0.09 \; or \; 9\%$$

$$W_d = \frac{M_d}{M_e + M_p + M_d} = \frac{\$60}{\$90 + \$15 + \$60} = 0.36 \; or \; 36\%$$

[1.19] The weights of the capital structure should add up to 100% (in this example, 55% + 9% + 36% = 100%).

Capital Structure Considerations

The traditional view of the optimal capital structure is that a firm should increase the proportion of debt until its WACC is minimized, and therefore its enterprise value is maximized. However, there is a trade-off between the incremental tax benefits of additional debt and increasing bankruptcy risks.

The ability to carry and service debt (also known as "debt capacity") can vary significantly among firms. For example, as operational profitability increases, debt capacity will tend to increase (and vice versa). In addition, entities with high corporate-level taxes tend to carry more debt, presumably because the "tax effect" (the interest tax shield) associated with their debt is worth more to them relative to entities paying lower tax rates.[1.20]

The mechanical application of the WACC formula ignores the cost of financial distress, thereby systematically underestimating WACC for highly levered companies. As the proportion of debt is increased in the capital structure, the formulas commonly used for levering equity betas (and increasing the cost of equity capital as debt increases) are linear, and therefore likely to *understate* the cost of equity capital at high amounts of leverage. Similarly, the traditional depiction of the cost of debt capital fails to consider the gradually increasing cost of debt as debt is added to the capital structure due to a potential decrease in ability to service.

Many valuation analysts' WACC templates are especially prone to error when leverage is high. WACC templates often give results that do not increase with increases in leverage, which cannot be true when debt exceeds certain thresholds. One possible solution is to migrate the capital structure over time from the current leverage level to the optimal or target level. The inputs (e.g. cost of debt) would have to be internally consistent with the leverage assumption in each forecast period.

Varying Capital Structure Assumptions

Again, when we value something, we are valuing the present value of the expected future economic benefits or income associated with the investment. It follows that the capital structure used in the valuation analysis (like all valuation inputs) should also reflect future expectations. In other words, "the relevant weights should be based on the proportions of debt and equity that the firm targets for its capital structure over the long-term planning period".[1.21] The target capital structure is the mix of debt, preferred equity, and common equity the firm plans to use over the long-run to finance its operations.

Two questions often arise when selecting the capital structure assumption: (i) whether an actual or a hypothetical capital structure should be used, and (ii) whether to assume a constant or a variable capital structure.

1.20 Interest payments to service debt capital are typically tax deductible. This "tax shield" effect results in a *lower* net cost of debt. The *greater* the tax rate, the *greater* the value of the "shield".

1.21 Alfred Rappaport, *Creating Shareholder Value: A Guide for Managers and Investors*, revised ed. (New York: Free Press, 1997): 37.

In answer to the first question, if an entity (or an interest in that entity) is required to be valued as is, assuming the capital structure will remain intact, then the amount of debt in the entity's actual capital structure should be used. One simple example might be the case of a non-controlling (or minority) equity interest versus a controlling equity interest. If a non-controlling interest is to be valued, the entity's existing level of debt as of the valuation date may be appropriate because it might be beyond the power of a minority stockholder to change the capital structure. Alternatively, if a controlling interest is being valued, an argument could be made that a hypothetical capital structure may be used because a controlling owner would presumably have the power to alter the capital structure. Facts and circumstances specific to the valuation will dictate which of these arguments is appropriate.

In answer to the second question, as a simplification most valuation analysts develop a single discount rate (e.g. WACC) when applying the income approach. This means that a single capital structure assumption is generally used (either the current capital structure or a target capital structure) when computing a WACC. When relying on a single point estimate, valuation analysts frequently adopt the average or median capital structure of guideline companies in the subject company's industry with the assumption that the subject company would finance its operations over the long term in a similar fashion as the guideline companies.

Notwithstanding this general practice, there may be circumstances when a migrating or varying capital structure is considered appropriate, as suggested above. To the extent that an entity's capital structure (at market value weights) varies over time, using a constant capital structure and constant WACC to discount the projected cash flows in each period will misstate the value of the entity. When dealing with overlevered entities, to the extent that the proportion of debt is expected to migrate downwards over time, using a constant WACC with the initial capital structure would likely undervalue the business (assuming that appropriate adjustments had been made to increase the cost of debt and equity to reflect current excess debt levels, which would result in the current WACC being greater than the optimal target WACC). WACC in this case would likely *decline* over time because the cost of debt would arguably decrease as the proportion of debt drops and the influence of financial distress is mitigated in the cost of equity.

Calculating WACC

WACC is based on the cost of each capital structure component net of any corporate-level tax effect of that component. Because we are interested in cash flows after entity-level taxes, literature and valuation analysts typically refer to this formulation of the WACC as an after-tax WACC.

The basic formula for computing the after-tax WACC for an entity with three capital structure components is:

Formula 1.4

$$WACC = (k_e \times W_e) + (k_p \times W_p) + (k_{d(pt)}[1-t] \times W_d)$$

where:

$WACC$	=	Weighted average cost of capital (after-tax)
k_e	=	Cost of common equity capital
W_e	=	Weight of common equity capital in the capital structure
k_p	=	Cost of preferred equity capital
W_p	=	Weight of preferred equity capital in the capital structure
$k_{d(pt)}$	=	Cost of debt capital (pre-tax)
t	=	Income tax rate
W_d	=	Weight of debt capital in the capital structure

For example, using the weight of capital structure components calculated in the previous example (W_e = 55%, W_p = 9%, W_d = 36%), and assuming a hypothetical cost of equity capital of 16%, a cost of preferred equity capital of 10%, a (pre-tax) cost of debt capital of 6%, and a tax rate of 39%, WACC is calculated as follows:

$$WACC = (k_e \times W_e) + (k_p \times W_p) + (k_{d(pt)}[1-t] \times W_d)$$

$$WACC = (16\% \times 55\%) + (10\% \times 9\%) + (6\%[1-39\%] \times 36\%)$$

$$WACC = (8.8\%) + (0.9\%) + (1.3\%) = 11.0\%$$

If the capital structure varies significantly over time, using a constant WACC will probably result in the incorrect value of the company or project. While Formula 1.4 is by far the most widely used discount rate for valuing the business enterprise, it is based on certain simplifying assumptions that may or may not be true in specific circumstances. For example, the formula assumes that the income tax deductions from interest expense (i.e., the interest tax shield) results in reduced cash income taxes in the period in which the interest is paid. The formula should not be used when the interest tax shields do not result in reduced cash taxes. Nor should the constant WACC formula be used when the ratio of equity to invested capital is not expected to be constant over time in market value terms (though the varying WACC method can adjust for this error).

For entities with publicly-traded common stock, preferred stock and debt, the weights can be derived from observed market values. For entities for which some or all of their preferred stock and debt are not publicly-traded, the market values must be estimated (after estimating the cost of preferred equity or the cost of debt, as outlined earlier in the chapter). But when dealing with closely-held common stock, the weights for the common equity can only be determined at the end of the valuation process. That methodology requires using an iterative calculation process.[1.22]

Estimates of Cost of Capital are Imprecise

The cost of capital is used to discount expected net cash flows of a business, business ownership interest, security, or intangible asset to present value, and as such represents the expected (i.e., *future*) rate of return of an investment. Cost of capital is therefore (by definition) a forward-looking concept, and is an *imprecise* measure with regard to its exact value. After all, the future cannot be predicted with anything approaching certainty. Because the true (future) returns are not observable, they are typically estimated by looking to historical data, with the expectation that the past will repeat itself (which is not always true).

Even if the estimate of the cost of capital is unbiased, the resulting estimated investment or firm value (which is, at least in part, a function of the cost of capital) will be biased (i.e., under- or over-stated) in the presence of estimation errors associated with the cost of capital. These have to be adjusted to enable an unbiased estimation of the investment or firm value. These considerations are particularly important when estimating terminal values consisting of the net cash flows generated after a period of detailed forecast that typically ends after 5–10 years. This terminal value is in most cases a significant portion of the investment or firm value, thus an unbiased estimation is essential.

Various authors have tackled the problem of imprecise estimation and methods to adjust the discount rates to obtain an unbiased estimate of the terminal value. In one recent paper the authors derive adjustments to the cost of capital that account for estimation uncertainty as to the cost of capital inputs.[1.23] Using their estimation risk-adjusted cost of capital, the authors obtain unbiased investment or firm values when applying the terminal value formulae. Their adjustment is a function of the uncertainty as to the cost of capital.

For example, assume the analyst estimates the cost of capital for Business A to be equal to 10%. In this case, assume that the analyst is highly certain of the cost of capital inputs (e.g., the beta estimate has a small standard error and has been relatively constant over the recent past). The authors calculate that the bias-corrected discount rate would be as close as 10.113%. But assume that the analyst estimates the cost of capital for Business B to be 10% but due to the relatively uncertain as to the accuracy of the inputs (e.g., the beta estimate has a large standard error and has fluctuated in recent periods) as of the valuation date there is greater uncertainty as to the correct cost of capital. The authors calculate that the bias-corrected discount rate under those circumstances could be as different as 12.136%. We refer the reader to that paper for a discussion of the theory and their Table 3 of adjusted costs of capital. The authors point out that their work deals with the uncertainty of the discount rate estimation and not the uncertainty of the expected net cash flow estimates.

1.22 Pratt and Grabowski, op.cit., Chapter 21, "Weighted Average Cost of Capital."

1.23 Simon Elsner and Hans-Christian Krumholz, "Corporate valuation using imprecise cost of capital," *Journal of Business Economics*, Vol. 83 (9): 985-1014.

Key Things to Remember about Cost of Capital

- The cost of capital is the expected rate of return that market participants require in order to attract funds to a particular investment. The cost of capital is an opportunity cost.

- The cost of capital is also commonly called the discount rate, the expected return, or the required return.

- There are three broad valuation approaches: the (i) income approach, (ii) the market approach, and (iii) the asset-based approach. We focus on income-based methods in this book, since these are the methodologies that require cost of capital estimates.

- Capitalizing and discounting are two ways to bring expected cash flows back to present value under the income approach. In capitalizing, we focus on the cash flow of just a single normalized period. In discounting, we project the annual expected cash flows from the subject investment over the life of that investment.

- The cost of capital (like all valuation inputs) is forward-looking. Cost of capital is used to discount expected *future* cash flows to present value. Because the future cannot be predicted with anything approaching certainty, estimates of cost of capital are inherently imprecise.

- Past returns may provide some guidance as to what returns in the future will be, but there is no guarantee that the past will "repeat itself".

- Cost of capital is a function of the investment, not the investor.

- Cost of capital is based on market value, and is usually stated in nominal, after-tax terms (after corporate taxes, but before individual investor taxes).

- The data used in the *Valuation Handbook* are drawn from information on public companies and, therefore, the resulting cost of capital estimates developed using this book are "as if public". Valuation analysts may deem additional adjustments to be necessary.

- The cost of capital to the overall business is commonly called the WACC. WACC represents the market-capitalization-weighted cost of capital for both equity holders (both common and preferred) and debt holders.

- The data and methodology in the *Valuation Handbook* can be used to estimate cost of common equity capital.

Chapter 2
Methods for Estimating the Cost of Equity Capital

Basic Framework[2.1]

All of the methods commonly used to estimate the cost of equity capital have the same basic framework: they start with a "risk-free" rate, and then add a premium for "risk", as summarized in Exhibit 2.1.

Exhibit 2.1: The Basic Framework of the Models Used to Estimate the Cost of Equity Capital

Cost of Equity Capital = Risk-free Rate (R_f) + Risk Premium (RP)

Two of the most widely used methods of estimating the cost of equity capital are the build-up method and the capital asset pricing model (CAPM). Both methods are predicated on this basic framework. In this book we focus on how to use the two valuation data sets (CRSP Deciles Size Premia exhibits and Risk Premium Report exhibits) contained herein to estimate the cost of equity capital using these two methods.

The nominal risk-free rate (R_f) is in theory a function of the real (risk-free) rate of interest plus expected inflation. The risk-free rate is the return available on a security that the market generally regards as free of the risk of default.[2.2] The nominal risk-free rate serves as an inflation adjustment mechanism, increasing or decreasing the cost of equity capital as inflation estimates change. During periods of increased inflation expectations, nominal risk-free rates increase, thereby increasing the expected returns estimated through cost of equity capital models. Similarly, during periods of decreased inflation expectations, nominal risk-free rates decrease, thereby decreasing the expected returns estimated through cost of equity capital models.

As the market's perception of an investment's riskiness increases, the risk premium, *RP*, also increases; accordingly, the rate of return that the market requires (the discount rate) will likewise increase for a given set of expected cash flows. The *greater* the market's required rate of return, the *lower* the present value of the investment, and the *lower* the market's required rate of return, the *greater* the present value of the investment.

[2.1] This chapter is excerpted in part from Shannon P. Pratt and Roger J. Grabowski, *Cost of Capital: Applications and Examples* 5th ed. (Hoboken, NJ: John Wiley & Sons, 2014)

[2.2] The yield on a 20-year constant maturity U.S. government bond is used as a proxy for the risk-free rate in the *2015 Valuation Handbook - Guide to Cost of Capital*, unless otherwise noted.

Defining Risk

Probably the most widely accepted definition of risk in the context of investment valuations is the degree of uncertainty of achieving future expectations at the times and in the amounts expected.[2.3] The definition implies uncertainty as to both the *amounts* and the *timing* of expected economic income. By expected economic income, in a technical sense, we mean the expected value (i.e., weighted mean/average) of the probability distribution of possible economic income for each forecast period.

In Chapter 1, we discussed the valuation process of present value as applied to expected cash flows. Any one year's distribution of possible net cash flows can be thought of as a bundle of possible outcomes. The present value of this series of expected cash flows can be depicted in the following formula (assuming a constant growth rate g):

Formula 2.1

$$PV = \frac{NCF_0(1+g)^1}{(1+k)^1} + \frac{NCF_0(1+g)^2}{(1+k)^2} + \ldots + \frac{NCF_0(1+g)^n}{(1+k)^n}$$

where:

PV = Present value

NCF_0 = Net cash flow at "time zero" (i.e., "now" or the most recently completed period as of the valuation date)

k = Discount rate

g = Expected rate of change (growth) of net cash flows

n = Total number of periods

This can also be written as:

$$PV = \frac{NCF_1}{(1+k)^1} + \frac{NCF_2}{(1+k)^2} + \ldots + \frac{NCF_n}{(1+k)^n}$$

where:

NCF_n = Expected net cash flow at the end of period n (implicitly, the NCF in each period may be growing at a constant or at a varying growth rate from the prior period)

2.3 David Laro and Shannon P. Pratt, *Business Valuation and Federal Taxes: Procedure, Law, and Perspective*, 2nd ed. (Hoboken, NJ: John Wiley & Sons, 2010), Chapter 12.

Market Returns Increase as Risk Increases by Asset Class

In finance theory, investors are generally assumed to be risk averse. Risk aversion can be measured by the amount of additional expected payoff an investor requires to accept additional risk.

If we plot the observed relationship of risk and return over time, we observe a strong linear relationship between risk and return, which is referred to as the capital market line (CML). The CML is defined as a line used in the capital asset pricing model that plots the rates of return for efficient portfolios,[2.4] depending on the rate of return and the level of risk (as measured by standard deviation) for a particular portfolio (see Exhibit 2.2). The empirical estimate of the CML shows the market's pricing of portfolios of assets over the period 1926 through 2014. As the risk (as measured by the standard deviation of returns) increases, the realized return increases.

Exhibit 2.2: Capital Market Line – Empirical Estimate based on Realized Total Returns by Asset Class 1926–2014

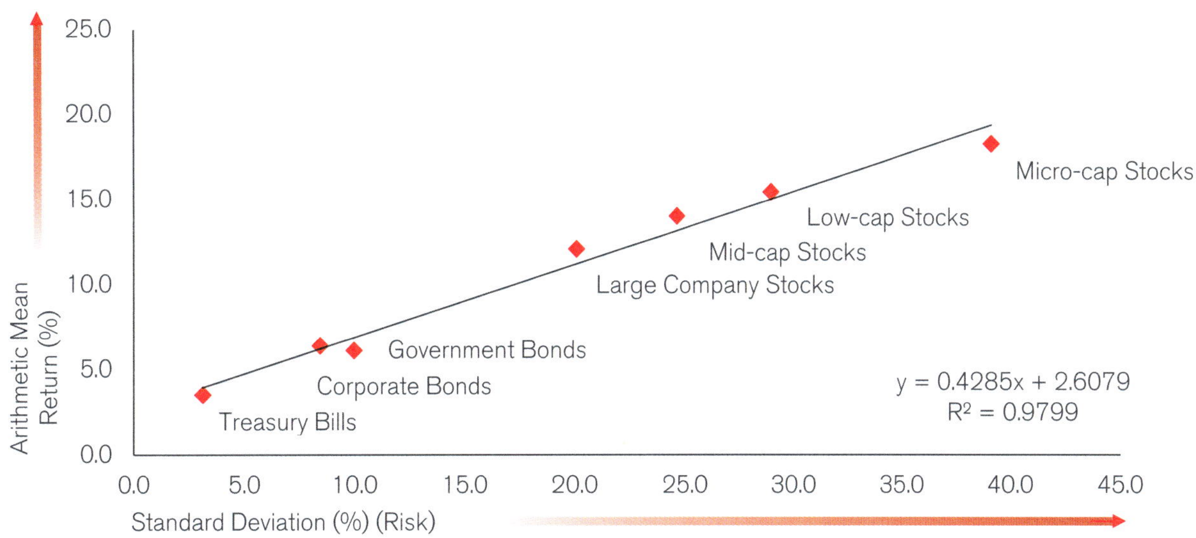

Source of underlying data: Morningstar *Direct* database. Copyright © 2015 Morningstar, Inc. All rights reserved. Used with permission. Calculated by Duff & Phelps.

Because investors are risk averse, the market requires an increasing rate of return as the risk of a bad outcome increases. How do we know the market demands and receives greater returns for taking on greater risk? If we look at arithmetic mean returns and risk (as measured by the standard deviation of returns) realized over time across asset classes, we observe that greater returns seem closely related to greater risk (see Exhibit 2.3).

2.4 CML is the tangent line drawn from the risk-free point to the feasible region for risky assets. This line shows the relationship between the return and total risk for efficient portfolios. Efficient portfolios are a combination of risky assets plus the risk-free asset, which minimizes risk for a given level of return (i.e., the lowest-risk highest-reward set of portfolios), or maximizes return for a given level of risk.

Exhibit 2.3: Summary Statistics of Total Returns, Income Returns, and Capital Appreciation Returns of Basic U.S. Asset Classes
1926–2014

1926–2014	Geometric Mean Returns (%)	Arithmetic Mean Returns (%)	Standard Deviation of Returns (%)
Large Company Stocks			
Total Return	10.1	12.1	20.1
Income Return	4.0	4.0	1.6
Capital Appreciation Return	5.9	7.8	19.4
Small Company Stocks			
Total Return	12.2	16.7	32.1
Mid-cap Stocks (Decile 3-5)			
Total Return	11.2	14.0	24.6
Income Return	3.8	3.8	1.8
Capital Appreciation Return	7.2	10.0	23.9
Low-cap Stocks (Decile 6-8)			
Total Return	11.6	15.4	28.9
Income Return	3.5	3.5	2.0
Capital Appreciation Return	8.0	11.8	28.3
Micro-cap Stocks (Decile 9-10)			
Total Return	12.3	18.3	39.1
Income Return	2.5	2.5	1.7
Capital Appreciation Return	9.8	15.6	38.3
Long-term Corporate Bonds			
Total Return	6.1	6.4	8.4
Long-term Government Bonds			
Total Return	5.7	6.1	10.0
Income Return	5.0	5.1	2.6
Capital Appreciation Return	0.4	0.8	9.0
Intermediate-term Government Bonds			
Total Return	5.3	5.4	5.6
Income Return	4.5	4.5	2.9
Capital Appreciation Return	0.6	0.7	4.5
US Treasury Bills			
Total Return	3.5	3.5	3.1
Inflation	2.9	3.0	4.1

Data from 1926–2014. Total return is equal to sum of three components returns: income return, capital appreciation, and reinvestment return.

Source of underlying data: (i) Stocks, Bonds, Bills, and Inflation® (SBBI®) return series from the Morningstar *Direct* database. Series used: Large Company Stocks (IA SBBI US Large Stock TR USD Ext). The "SBBI US Large Stock" return series is essentially the S&P 500 index; Small Company Stocks (IA SBBI US Small Stock TR USD); Long-term Corp. Bonds (IA SBBI US LT Corp TR USD); Long-term Gov't Bonds (IA SBBI US LT Govt TR USD); Intermediate-term Gov't Bonds (IA SBBI US IT Govt TR USD); T-bills (IA SBBI US 30 Day TBill TR USD); Inflation (IA SBBI US Inflation). All rights reserved. Used with permission. (ii) CRSP U.S. Stock Database and CRSP U.S. Indices Database © 2015 Center for Research in Security Prices (CRSP®), University of Chicago Booth School of Business. CRSP standard market-cap-weighted NYSE/NYSE MKT/NASDAQ deciles 1–10. Mid-cap stocks represented by a market-capitalization weighted portfolio comprised of CRSP deciles 3-5; Low-cap stocks represented by a market-capitalization weighted portfolio comprised of CRSP deciles 6-8; Micro-cap stocks represented by a market-capitalization weighted portfolio comprised of CRSP deciles 9-10. Used with permission. All rights reserved. Calculations performed by Duff & Phelps LLC.

Types of Risk

Although risk arises from many sources, this chapter addresses risk in the economic sense, as generally used in the conventional methods of estimating cost of capital. In this context, capital market theory divides risk into four components:

1. Maturity risk
2. Market risk
3. Company-specific risk
4. Liquidity and marketability risk

Maturity Risk

Maturity risk (also called horizon risk, interest rate risk, or term risk) is the risk that the value of the investment may increase or decrease because of changes in the level of interest rates. The longer the term of an investment, the greater the maturity risk. For example, market prices of long-term bonds fluctuate much more in response to changes in levels of interest rates than do market prices of short-term bonds or notes. When we refer to the yields on long-term U.S. government bonds as risk-free rates, we mean that we regard them as free from the prospect of default. We recognize that they do incorporate maturity risk: the only part of the yield that is arguably risk-free is the income return component. That is, the interest payments promised are risk-free, or so we assume. But the market price or value of the bonds move up or down as interest rates move, creating a capital gain or loss. Thus, there is a risk (i.e., an opportunity cost) to capital embedded in these bonds.

The longer the maturity, the greater the susceptibility to changes in market price in response to changes in market rates of interest. With regard to interest rates, much of the uncertainty derives from the uncertainty of future inflation levels.

Market Risk

Market risk (also called systematic or undiversifiable risk in the context of the pure textbook CAPM) is the uncertainty of future returns due to the sensitivity of the return on a subject investment to variability in returns for the investment market as a whole. Although this is a broad conceptual definition, for many U.S. companies, the investment market as a whole is generally limited to the U.S. equity markets, and typically returns are measured on either the New York Stock Exchange (NYSE) Composite Index or the Standard & Poor's (S&P) 500 Index. For multinational companies, the investment market may be more appropriately considered the world equity markets with returns measured on the S&P Global 1200 Index or one of the MSCI Global Standard indices.

The term that is commonly used for sensitivity to market risk is beta. In the context of the CAPM, beta measures the expected sensitivity of changes in returns of a security (either an individual company or a portfolio of companies) to changes in returns of the "market". In the U.S., the market proxy, or benchmark, is often the S&P 500 Index or the NYSE Composite Index.

While beta has come to have a specific meaning in the context of the CAPM, beta is used in finance literature as a more general term meaning the sensitivity of an investment to any of a variety of risk factors. Bonds have beta risks (e.g., risks to changes in interest rates and to general economic conditions as reflected in the broad stock market). Individual stocks have beta risks (e.g., to general economic conditions as reflected in the broad stock market and to the relative risks of large company stocks to small company stocks).

Some theorists hold that the only risk that capital markets reward with an expected premium rate of return (over the risk-free asset) is market risk, because other company-specific risks can be eliminated by holding a well-diversified portfolio of investments. Recent research increasingly shows that the market prices other risks as well (i.e., other risks are systematic).

For example, the size premium is a risk factor that is systematic (priced by the market) and is an adjustment to pure CAPM. Empirical evidence indicates that beta alone does not measure the risk of smaller companies. We discuss the size premium in Chapter 4.

Company-specific Risk

Company-specific risk (sometimes called unique or idiosyncratic risk) is the uncertainty of expected returns arising from factors other than those factors correlated with the investment market as a whole. These factors may include characteristics of the industry and/or the individual company. In international investing, they also can include characteristics of a particular country.

Some of the unique risk of an investment may be captured in systematic risk factors priced by the market such as the size premium. Fully capturing company-specific risk in the discount rate requires analysis of the company in comparison with other companies. However, while the size premium captures many risk factors, valuation analysts must be careful to capture all the risk factors and at the same time avoid double-counting of risk.

Capital market theory assumes efficient markets. That is, it assumes prices change concurrent with changes in the economic fundamentals (economy, industry, or company factors) such that the market prices of public stocks represent the consensus of investors as to the present value of cash flows and that changes in such fundamentals are "instantly" recognized in market prices. One study supports the rationality of stock prices where data on expected cash flows are available to investors.[2.5]

But market inefficiency can (and does) occur for public stocks, particularly for smaller company stocks that do not have sufficient investor following such that their prices react to changes in fundamentals in a timely fashion. We do recognize that market prices may not correctly or fully account for the fundamentals of a smaller, thinly traded public company at particular points in time. Studies on returns of

2.5 Aharon R. Ofer, Oded Sarig, and Keren Bar-Hava, "New Tests of Market Efficiency Using Fully Identifiable Equity Cash Flows" Working paper, February 2007. Available at http://www.ssrn .com/abstract=965242

small public companies that quantify the size premium, capture the average effect. A company-specific adjustment may still be appropriate (either positive or negative) even if size is already considered.

While the pure CAPM holds that any risk beyond market or beta risk can be diversified away (hence the term diversifiable risk often being equated with company-specific risk) researchers have found other risk factors are priced by the market (i.e., other risk factors are also systematic risk factors). We discuss the company-specific risk premium in Chapter 6.

Liquidity and Marketability Risk

Discussions of capital market theory generally assume that investments are "liquid", and many of the observations about risk and return are drawn from information about liquid investments. Liquidity generally refers to the ability to readily convert an investment into cash without significant loss of principal – the *less* liquid an investment is, the *riskier* it is, and vice-versa. In other words, investors *like* liquidity, and *dislike* illiquidity, and will therefore demand more compensation for investing in illiquid investments. These risks, while listed here separately, are systematic risks in that the pricing of these risks for a particular investment moves with the overall market pricing of liquidity and marketability risks. The risk premiums for lack of liquidity and marketability can be embedded in the discount rate or as a separate adjustment from an "as if liquid" ("as if freely traded") estimate of value.

Marketability and liquidity are major risks facing closely held companies (both minority and controlling interests), and can have a significant impact on the ultimate value. However, valuation analysts (except for venture capitalists) typically do not factor these risks into the discount rate. Instead, the common approach is to value the closely held company or interest in the company "as if freely traded" and then subtract a discount that incorporates a discount for lack of marketability and a discount for lack of liquidity because most of the valuation metrics that we use are drawn from the public markets.

Cost of Equity Capital Estimation Methods

In practice, the build-up method and CAPM are the most frequently used methods to estimate the cost of equity capital. The risk premia and size premia presented in the *Valuation Handbook's* data exhibits can be used to develop cost of equity capital estimates using build-up and CAPM, and so we focus on these two methods here.

The *Valuation Handbook* provides two sets of valuation data that analysts can use to estimate the cost of equity capital:

- **CRSP Deciles Size Premia Exhibits:** These exhibits provide the size premia and other valuation data previously published in the Morningstar/Ibbotson *SBBI® Valuation Yearbook*.

- **Risk Premium Report Exhibits:** These exhibits provide the size premia and other valuation data previously published in the Duff & Phelps *Risk Premium Report*.

The build-up method and the CAPM method are the most frequently used methods for estimating cost of equity capital. These methods are summarized in Exhibit 2.4. All of the methods start with a risk-free rate (R_f), and then add various premia for risk.[2.6]

Exhibit 2.4: The Build-up Methods and CAPM Models

CRSP Decile Size Premia Exhibits

Build-Up

$$k_e = R_f + RP_m + RP_i + RP_s$$

CAPM

$$k_e = R_f + \beta \times (RP_m) + RP_s$$

Risk Premium Report Exhibits

Build-Up

$$k_e = R_f + RP_{m+s} + ERP\ Adjustment$$

CAPM

$$k_e = R_f + \beta \times (RP_m) + RP_s$$

NOTE: *All cost of equity estimates developed using the Valuation Handbook – Guide to Cost of Capital are prior to the addition of any company-specific risks (RP_c) that the individual analyst deems appropriate.*

where:

k_e	= Cost of equity capital
R_f	= Risk-free rate
RP_m	= Equity risk premium (also referred as ERP)
RP_s	= Size premium
RP_i	= Industry risk premium
RP_c	= Company-specific risk premium
β	= Beta
RP_{m+s}	= Equity (market) risk premium plus size premium combined
ERP Adjustment	= An adjustment to account for the difference between the forward-looking ERP that the analyst has selected and the historical (1963–present) ERP that was used as a *convention* in the calculations performed to create the Risk Premium Report exhibits. Used only when using the Risk Premium Report exhibits. See Chapter 9, "Risk Premium Report – General Information".

2.6 The Risk Premium Report exhibits provides eight methods of estimating the cost of equity capital, including unlevered cost of equity capital and high-financial-risk cost of equity capital. For detailed examples of these cost of equity capital methods, see Chapter 10.

Build-up

The build-up method is an additive model commonly used for calculating the cost of equity capital. As the name implies, successive "building blocks" are summed, each representing the additional risk inherent to investing in alternative assets. Both of the sets of valuation data presented in the *2015 Valuation Handbook – Guide to Cost of Capital* (CRSP Deciles Size Premia exhibits and Risk Premium Report exhibits) can be used to develop cost of equity capital estimates using the build-up method.

CRSP Deciles Size Premia – Build-up Method

The first set of valuation data in the *Valuation Handbook – Guide to Cost of Capital* that valuation analysts can use to estimate the cost of equity capital is the CRSP Deciles Size Premia exhibits. These exhibits provide the size premia and other valuation data previously published in the *SBBI® Valuation Yearbook*. Formula 2.2 presents the CRSP Deciles Size Premia build-up method.

Formula 2.2

$$k_e = R_f + RP_m + RP_i + RP_s$$

The CRSP Deciles Size Premia build-up method follows the basic framework of all cost of equity capital estimation models: a premium for risk is added to the risk-free rate. In this case, the "premium for risk" is deconstructed into three components:

- **Equity risk premium (RP_m):** The equity risk premium is the extra return that investors demand to compensate them for investing in a diversified portfolio of large common stocks rather than investing in risk-free securities. The equity risk premium is sometimes referred to as the "market" risk premium.

- **Size premium (RP_s):** The size premium represents the difference between actual historical excess return and the excess return predicted by beta. The "size effect" is based on the empirical observation that companies of smaller size are associated with greater risk and, therefore, have greater cost of capital. All size premia in the *Valuation Handbook* are "beta-adjusted", meaning that they have been adjusted to remove the portion of excess return that is attributable to beta, leaving only the size effect's contribution to excess return.

- **Industry risk premium (RP_i):** A measure of beta risk scaled around 0. An $RP_i < 0$ implies that the industry is *less* risky than the market, an $RP_i = 0$ implies that the industry has the *same* risk as the market, and an $RP_i > 0$ implies that the industry is *riskier* than the market. RP_i are not appropriate for use with CAPM, but are only appropriately used in "build-up" methods of estimating cost of equity capital that do not already have a measure of beta. An RP_i is used solely within the context of a build-up method. RP_i are a necessary cost of capital ingredient for those valuation analysts who like to use a build-up method in their valuation analysis (alone, or in addition to the CAPM).

Risk Premium Report – Build-up Method

The second set of valuation data in the *Valuation Handbook* that valuation analysts can use to estimate the cost of equity capital is the Risk Premium Report exhibits. These exhibits provide the size premia and other valuation data previously published in the Duff & Phelps *Risk Premium Report*. Formula 2.3 presents the Risk Premium Report build-up 1 method.

Formula 2.3

$$k_e = R_f + RP_{m+s} + ERP\ Adjustment$$

The Risk Premium Report build-up 1 method, just like the CRSP Deciles Size Premia build-up method, follows the basic framework of all cost of equity capital estimation models: a premium for risk is added to the risk-free rate. In this case, the "premium for risk" is deconstructed into two components:

- **Risk Premia over the Risk-free Rate (RP_{m+s}):** Risk premia over the risk-free rate represents the difference between the historical (observed) return of equities over the risk-free rate, and are a measure of risk in terms of the combined effect of *market* risk and *size* risk.

- **ERP Adjustment:** The ERP Adjustment is needed to account for the difference between the forward-looking ERP as of the valuation date that the analyst has selected to use in his or her cost of equity capital calculations, and the historical (in this case, 1963–present) ERP that was used as a *convention* in the calculations performed to create the Risk Premium Report exhibits. See chapter 9 for detailed discussion of the ERP adjustment.

The Risk Premium Report exhibits provide valuation analysts with eight methods of estimating the cost of equity capital. The Build-up 1 and the CAPM are the most commonly used in practice. For detailed examples on the various methods of estimating the cost of equity capital using the Risk Premium Report exhibits, see Chapter 9.

CAPM

The CAPM has served as the foundation for pricing risk for nearly fifty years. Financial theorists generally have favored using the CAPM as the preferred method to estimate the cost of equity capital and the CAPM has become the most widely used method for estimating the cost of equity capital.

As with any model, certain assumptions are made in developing CAPM, and those assumptions also represent limitations. Outlining the CAPM's several assumptions and criticisms is beyond the scope of this book. Despite its many criticisms, the CAPM is still one of the most widely used models for estimating the cost of equity capital, especially for larger companies in its pure textbook form, and even for smaller companies and closely held companies in its expanded or adjusted form (a.k.a. modified CAPM). The pure textbook CAPM formula is shown in Formula 2.4:

Formula 2.4

$$k_e = R_f + \beta \times (RP_m)$$

where:

k_e	=	Cost of equity capital
R_f	=	Risk-free rate
β	=	Beta
RP_m	=	Equity risk premium (also referred as ERP)

The primary difference between the CAPM and the (basic) build-up method is the introduction of a market or systematic risk factor for a specific stock, which acts as a modifier to the general equity risk premium. In the context of the CAPM, market risk is measured by a risk factor called beta. Beta measures the sensitivity of excess total returns (total returns over the risk-free rate of return) on any individual security (or portfolio of securities) to the excess total returns on some measure of the market, such as the Standard & Poor's (S&P) 500 Index or the New York Stock Exchange (NYSE) Composite Index.

In theory, beta can be defined as:

Formula 2.5

$$\beta = \frac{cov(R_i, R_m)}{var(R_m)}$$

where:

β	=	Beta
R_i	=	Return on security
R_m	=	Return on market portfolio
$Cov(R_i, R_m)$	=	Expected covariance between the return on security i and the market return R_m. Can also be measured in terms of excess returns of security i (R_i-R_f) and the excess market return (R_m-R_f)
$Var(R_m)$	=	Expected variance of excess return on the overall stock market

Covariance measures the degree to which the return on a particular security and the overall market's return move together. Covariance is not volatility. Covariance is a measure of the two variables' tendency to vary in the same direction and in the same relative amounts.

Estimation of Equity Beta

Beta is a forward-looking concept. However, the most widely used techniques for estimating beta generally use historical data over a sample or look-back period and assume that the future will be sufficiently similar.

Research shows that betas are time-varying (i.e., sensitive to market changes as the economy changes; betas differ during improving economic conditions compared with periods when economic conditions are declining). Using a historical method based on a sample period may not provide a reliable indication of expected beta when economic conditions are changing. The current and expected future economic conditions may differ from the economic conditions during the look-back period. Therefore, the beta estimated using the data for the look-back period may not reflect the future.

Academics prefer to estimate beta by comparing the excess returns on an individual security relative to the excess returns on the relevant market index. By *excess return*, we mean the total return (which includes both dividends and capital gains and losses) over and above the return available on a risk-free investment (e.g., U.S. government securities). Use of excess returns allows for normalizing changes in returns for changes in inflation during the look-back period.

For publicly traded securities, valuation analysts can estimate beta via regression (ordinary least squares (OLS) regression), by regressing the excess returns on the individual stock ($R_i - R_f$) against the excess returns on the market ($R_m - R_f$) during the look-back period. The resulting slope of the best-fit line is the beta estimate.

On a final note, because closely held companies, divisions, and reporting units have generally no market price, their betas cannot be measured directly. Thus, to use the CAPM to estimate the cost of capital for a closely held company, division, or reporting unit, it is necessary to estimate a proxy beta for that business. This is often accomplished by using an average or median beta for the industry group or by selecting specific guideline public companies and using some composite of their betas. The goal is to match the risk of that subject business to the risks of the guideline public companies.[2.7]

[2.7] An excellent source of industry and peer group beta statistics for use in CAPM estimates of cost of equity capital is the *Valuation Handbook – Industry Cost of Capital.* The *2014 Valuation Handbook – Industry Cost of Capital* (with data through March 2014) was published in October 2014 by Duff and Phelps. The 2015 version of the "industry" book is scheduled for release in late May 2015 (with data through March 2015), and will be published by John Wiley and Sons. In addition to levered and unlevered industry and peer group betas, the *Valuation Handbook – Industry Cost of Capital* provides eight (8) cost of equity capital estimates for each of the U.S. industries covered in the book, cost of debt capital and weighted average cost of capital (WACC) estimates, plus capital structure, valuation multiples, industry betas, and more (depending on data availability). See Exhibit 1.4 for a sample industry analysis page from the *2014 Valuation Handbook – Industry Cost of Capital.* To order copies of the *Valuation Handbook – Industry Cost of Capital* and its optional quarterly updates, please go to www.wiley.com/go/ValuationHandbooks

Modified CAPM

If we modify the CAPM to also reflect the size effect (RP_s), we can expand the cost of equity capital formula as follows:[2.8]

Formula 2.6

$$k_e = R_f + \beta \times (RP_m) + RP_s$$

where:

k_e	=	Cost of equity capital
R_f	=	Risk-free rate
β	=	Beta
RP_m	=	Equity risk premium (also referred as ERP)
RP_s	=	Size premium

CRSP Deciles Size Premia and Risk Premium Report – CAPM

Both sets of valuation data (CRSP Deciles Size Premia exhibits and Risk Premium Report exhibits) presented herein can be used to develop cost of equity capital estimates using the CAPM and share the same variables (see Formula 2.6). A premium for risk is added to the risk-free rate. In this case, the "premium for risk" is deconstructed into three components:

- **Equity risk premium (*RP_m*):** The equity risk premium is the extra return that investors demand to compensate them for investing in a diversified portfolio of large common stocks rather than investing in risk-free securities. The equity risk premium is sometimes referred to as the "market" risk premium.

- **Size premium (*RP_s*):** The size premium represents the difference between actual historical excess returns and the excess return predicted by beta. The "size effect" is based on the empirical observation that companies of smaller size are associated with greater risk and, therefore, have greater cost of capital. All size premia in the *Valuation Handbook* are "beta-adjusted", meaning that they have been adjusted to remove the portion of excess return that is attributable to beta, leaving only the size effect's contribution to excess return.

2.8 Formula 2.6 represents textbook CAPM *after* the addition of a size premium (RP_s), but prior to any additional "company-specific" risk premiums (RP_c) that may be deemed applicable by the individual valuation analyst.

- **Beta (β):** Measure of the systematic risk of a stock; the tendency of a stock's price to correlate with changes in the market. It is used as a modifier to the equity risk premium (ERP) in the context of the CAPM. Beta is the sole risk measure of equity capital of the pure CAPM, the form of the CAPM most often shown in textbooks. The combination of equity beta for the subject business multiplied by the ERP for the market equals the estimated risk premium for the subject business.

Other Cost of Equity Capital Estimation Methods

The pure "textbook" CAPM (see Formula 2.4) provides fundamental insights about risk and return. Textbook CAPM (i) provides a framework to fundamental concepts of asset pricing and portfolio theory and (ii) is simple to understand and easy to apply. However, textbook CAPM is fraught with empirical problems, and its empirical record is poor.[2.9]

Because of that poor record, a number of alternative models have been developed that better explain differences in rates of return among stocks of companies. Many of these models are multifactor models; they include risk factors that have been shown to be priced by the market, other than simple market beta. Generally, the multifactor models begin with a risk-free rate of return and add one or more factors based on the risks of the investment.[2.10] For example, the "modified" CAPM introduces a size premium and a company-specific risk premium to the pure CAPM (see Formula 2.6).

Alternatively, the valuation analyst can estimate the expected rate of return *implied* by the existing price for publicly traded securities. In this approach, the analyst typically uses the income approach to reverse-engineer the cost of capital given (i) estimates of expected future net cash flows of the subject company, and (ii) the observable market price of the company.

In any case, these methods are designed to help us understand how the market prices *risk*. But defining the relationship among risk measures and returns is not an easy task, and researchers often observe what they term anomalies (i.e., a result that differs from what is expected). For example, Ibbotson and Idzorek discuss the concepts of risk in a recent paper:[2.11]

"We believe that most of the best-known market premiums and anomalies can be explained by an intuitive and naturally occurring (social or behavioral) phenomenon observed in countless settings: popularity. Popularity is often defined as a social phenomenon associated with being admired, sought after, well known, and/or accepted...How can we apply popularity to the relative performance of different asset classes and different securities? Asset pricing theories have long recognized that expected returns should not be the same for the various instruments in the marketplace. The primary explanation for these differences has been differences in risk. Of course, risk is unpopular – investors do not like risk and want to be compensated for it."

2.9 Pratt and Grabowski, op.cit., Chapter 13, "Criticism of CAPM and Beta versus Other Risk Measures." See also: Mike Dempsey, "The Capital Asset Pricing Model (CAPM): The History of a Failed Revolutionary Idea in Finance," *Abacus* Vol. 49 (Supplement) and Pablo Fernandez, "CAPM: An Absurd Model," working paper (January 8, 2015). Available at SSRN: http://ssrn.com/abstract=2505597

2.10 Pratt and Grabowski, op.cit., Chapter 18, "Other Methods of Estimating the Cost of Equity Capital."

2.11 Roger G. Ibbotson and Thomas M. Idzorek, "Dimensions of Popularity," *The Journal of Portfolio Management* Vol 40 (5):68-74.

Ibbotson and Idzorek continue: "Although risk is clearly unpopular, it is only one dimension of popularity. Popularity can include all sorts of other characteristics that do not fit well into the risk and return paradigm." One example of this is "liquidity", or the risk of not being able to turn your investment into cash extremely quickly without a price concession. Liquidity cannot easily be squeezed into a traditional risk and return paradigm since *less* liquid assets are not necessarily *more* volatile, nor do they necessarily have *higher* betas.

Studies have shown that although risk may be the main driver of return differences *across* asset classes, there is increasing evidence that risk is not the primary driver *within* asset classes in that within the stock market, the lower-risk characteristics are often associated with higher returns – the *opposite* of underlying capital market theory. The term "risk" has become synonymous for the sum total of all attributes investors do not like. In Chapter 4 we further discuss the relationship between liquidity, size and returns, as illiquidity is one of those attributes that is "unpopular".

The authors conclude: "academics have sought to explain and understand asset prices, with a strong emphasis on market premiums and market anomalies. Generally, these academics end up falling into one of two camps: the equilibrium efficient market camp or the behavioral economics camp. Popularity offers an explanation that is consistent with both approaches."

This paper shows that we are in the relative infancy of understanding how the market prices risk. We provide in this book multiple sources of data so the user can develop cost of equity capital estimates using several models and then check the results of applying these models with observed returns.

Key Things to Remember about the Methods for Estimating the Cost of Equity Capital

- The build-up method for estimating the cost of equity capital has the following five components:

  1. A risk-free rate

  2. A general equity risk premium (ERP)

  3. A size premium

  4. An industry adjustment factor

  5. A company-specific risk adjustment (which can be either positive or negative, depending on the differences in risks comparing the subject company to the guideline companies from which the size premium was derived)

- The CAPM differs from the build-up method by introducing the beta coefficient, β, the sensitivity of excess returns for the subject company stock to excess returns for the market.

- The CAPM, like most economic models, offers a theoretical framework for how certain relationships would exist subject to certain assumptions.

- The pure textbook CAPM has several underlying assumptions, which may be met to a greater or lesser extent for the market as a whole or for any particular company or investment. While some question whether empirical evidence is consistent with the predictions resulting from the theory, CAPM is widely used today.

- All cost of equity estimates developed using the *Valuation Handbook* are prior to the addition of any company-specific risks (RP_c) that the individual analyst deems appropriate.

- There are all sorts of other characteristics that do not fit well into the risk and return paradigm. We are in the relative *infancy* of understanding how the market prices risk. Generally, academics end up falling into one of two camps: the equilibrium efficient market camp or the behavioral economics camp. "Popularity" may offer an explanation that is consistent with both approaches.

Chapter 3
Basic Building Blocks of the Cost of Equity Capital – Risk-free Rate and Equity Risk Premium

The basic building blocks for the build-up methods and the modified capital asset pricing model (CAPM) are:

- Risk-free rate
- Equity risk premium
- Size premium
- Beta (in CAPM) or industry risk premium (in build-up method)
- Company-specific risk premium

We will discuss the risk-free rate (R_f) and the equity risk premium (ERP) in this chapter. We will discuss the remaining building blocks in later chapters.

The Risk-free Rate and Equity Risk Premium: Interrelated Concepts

A risk-free rate is the return available, as of the valuation date, on a security that the market generally regards as free of the risk of default.

For valuations denominated in U.S. dollars, valuation analysts have typically used the spot yield to maturity (as of the valuation date) on U.S. government securities as a proxy for the risk-free rate. The two most commonly used risk-free bond maturities have been the 10- and 20-year U.S. government bond yields.

The use of (i) long-term U.S. government bonds, and (ii) an ERP estimated relative to yields on long-term bonds most closely match the investment horizon and risks that confront business managers who are making capital allocation decisions and valuation analysts who are applying valuation methods to value a "going concern" business.

The risk-free rate and the ERP are interrelated concepts. All ERP estimates are, by definition, developed *in relation* to the risk-free rate. Specifically, the ERP is the extra return investors expect as compensation for assuming the additional risk associated with an investment in a diversified portfolio of common stocks, compared to the return they would expect from an investment in risk-free securities.

This brings us to an important concept. When developing cost of capital estimates, the valuation analyst should match the term of the risk-free rate used in the CAPM or build-up formulas with the duration of the expected net cash flows of the business, asset, or project being evaluated.[3.1] Further, the term of the risk-free rate should *also* match the term of the risk-free rate used to develop the ERP, as illustrated in Exhibit 3.1.

Exhibit 3.1: The Risk-free Rate and ERP Should be Consistent with the Duration of the Net Cash Flows of the Business, Asset, or Project Being Evaluated

Term of risk-free rate used in CAPM or Build-up equation	=	Expected duration of the net cash flows of the business, asset, or project being evaluated	=	Term of risk-free rate used to develop the ERP

In many of the cases in which one is valuing a business, a "going concern" assumption is made (the life of the business is assumed to be indefinite), and therefore selecting longer-term U.S. government bond yields (e.g. 20 years) as the proxy for the risk-free rate is appropriate.

The risk-free rate and the ERP, like all components of the cost of equity capital (and the cost of equity capital itself), are *forward-looking* concepts. The reason that cost of capital is a forward-looking concept is straightforward: when we value a company (for instance), we are trying to value how much we would pay (now) for the *future* economic benefits associated owning with the company. Since we will ultimately use the cost of capital to discount these future economic benefits (usually measured as *expected* cash flows) back to their present value, the cost of capital itself must *also* be forward-looking.

Spot Risk-free Rates versus Normalized Risk-free Rates

Beginning with the financial crisis of 2008 (the "Financial Crisis"), analysts have had to reexamine whether the "spot" rate is still a reliable building block upon which to base their cost of equity capital estimates. The Financial Crisis challenged long-accepted practices and highlighted potential problems of simply continuing to use the spot yield-to-maturity on a safe government security as the risk-free rate, without any further adjustments.

During periods in which risk-free rates appear to be abnormally low due to flight to quality or massive central bank monetary interventions, valuation analysts may want to consider normalizing the risk-free rate. By "normalization" we mean estimating a risk-free rate that more likely reflects the *sustainable* average return of long-term U.S. Treasuries.

[3.1] This chapter is excerpted in part from Shannon P. Pratt and Roger J. Grabowski, *Cost of Capital: Applications and Examples* 5th ed. (Hoboken, NJ: John Wiley & Sons, 2014)

Why Normalize the Risk-free Rate?

The yields of U.S. government bonds in certain periods during and after the Financial Crisis may have been *artificially* repressed, and therefore likely unsustainable. Many market participants will agree that nominal U.S. government bond yields in recent periods have been artificially low. Even members of the Federal Open Market Committee (FOMC), have recently discussed the need to "normalize" interest rates.[3.2] In a recent interview to the Wall Street Journal, James Bullard, President of the Federal Reserve Bank of St. Louis, said that:[3.3]

> *"I think it is important to get started and to start normalizing policy."*

He also acknowledged that rates were still very low by historical standards:

> *"Even once we start to normalize, interest rates would be extraordinarily low."*

While the views of one FOMC member do not reflect the official positions of the committee, the reality is that the minutes of recent meetings repeat the term "policy normalization" several times, in the context of deciding if and when to raise interest rates.[3.4] It is true that Federal Reserve Bank ("Fed") officials are very cautious on how to characterize the timing of nominalization policies. For example, at the December 16-17, 2014 meeting, the FOMC issued the following statement:

> *"Based on its current assessment, the Committee judges that it* ***can be patient in beginning to normalize the stance of monetary policy****. The Committee sees this guidance as consistent with its previous statement that it likely will be appropriate to maintain the 0 to 1/4 percent target range for the federal funds rate for a* ***considerable time*** *following the end of its asset purchase program in October..." [Emphasis added]*

However, in conjunction with the December 16–17, 2014 meeting, FOMC members also submitted their projections of the most likely outcomes for real GDP growth, unemployment rate, inflation, and the federal funds rate for each year from 2014 to 2017 and over the longer run.[3.5] Fifteen out of the 17 submissions believed that the target level for the federal funds rate should be increased during 2015.[3.6]

3.2 The FOMC is a committee within the Federal Reserve System ("Fed"), charged under U.S. law with overseeing the nation's open market operations (i.e., the Fed's buying and selling of U.S. Treasury securities).

3.3 Hilsenrath, J., Blackstone, B. (2015, January 19). Fed Officials on Track to Raise Short-Term Rates Later in the Year. *The Wall Street Journal*. Retrieved from: http://www.wsj.com/articles/fed-officials-on-track-to-raise-short-term-rates-later-in-the-year-1421694861

3.4 For example, the term "normal" or variations on the word "normalize" were mentioned 32 times in the minutes of the FOMC meeting held on December 16–17, 2014. To access minutes of FOMC meetings visit: http://www.federalreserve.gov/monetarypolicy/fomccalendars.htm

3.5 The federal funds rate is the interest rate at which depository institutions lend balances to each other overnight. The target federal funds rate is used as the benchmark interest rate to implement U.S. monetary policies, such as raising or reducing interest rates.

3.6 "Minutes of the Federal Open Market Committee December 16–17, 2014", Board of Governors of the Federal Reserve System. For details visit: http://www.federalreserve.gov/monetarypolicy/fomccalendars.htm

So what does it mean when someone says the current U.S. Treasury yields are not "normal"? And even if interest rates are not considered "normal", why is that any different from other periods in history? Remember, the risk-free rate is intended to adjust the cost of equity capital for expected future inflation. Typically, valuation analysts use a 20-year U.S. government bond yield when developing a U.S. dollar-denominated cost of equity capital. Therefore, the risk-free rate should reflect an average expected return over those years.

To be clear, in most circumstances we would prefer using the "spot" yield (i.e., the yield available in the market) on a safe government security as a proxy for the risk-free rate.[3.7] However, during times of flight to quality and/or high levels of central bank intervention (such as the period beginning with the Financial Crisis) those *lower* observed yields imply a *lower* cost of capital (all other factors held the same), just the opposite of what one would expect in times of relative economy-wide distress and uncertainty. During these periods, using a non-normalized risk-free rate (with no corresponding adjustments to the ERP) would likely lead to an *underestimated* cost of equity capital, and so a "normalization" adjustment may be a reasonable approach to address the apparent inconsistency.

Why isn't the Current Spot Risk-Free Rate Considered "Normal"?

Part of the reason that U.S. Treasury yields are likely "artificially repressed" is that the "Fed" has been *telling* us that its actions are intended to push rates down, and thus boost asset prices (e.g., stocks, housing). For example, at the September 13, 2012 FOMC press conference, the Fed Chairman at the time, Ben Bernanke, stated:

> *"...the tools we have involve affecting financial asset prices...To the extent that home prices begin to rise, consumers will feel wealthier, they'll feel more disposed to spend ... So house prices is one vehicle. Stock prices – many people own stocks directly or indirectly...and if people feel that their financial situation is better because their 401(k) looks better or for whatever reason, their house is worth more, they are more willing to go out and spend, and that's going to provide the demand that firms need in order to be willing to hire and to invest."*

[3.7] Government bond yields can be found at Board of Governors of the Federal Reserve System website at: http://www.federalreserve.gov/releases/h15/data.htm

In Exhibit 3.2, the balance sheet of the U.S. Federal Reserve is shown over time. Since the Financial Crisis, the Fed has been purchasing massive quantities of U.S. Treasuries and mortgage backed securities (MBS) through a series of so-called quantitative easing (QE) measures. At the end of December 2014, the Fed's balance sheet summed to $4,499,581 million ($4.5 *trillion*).

Exhibit 3.2: Balance Sheet of the Federal Reserve (vis-à-vis Credit Easing Policy Tools)
January 2007–December 2014

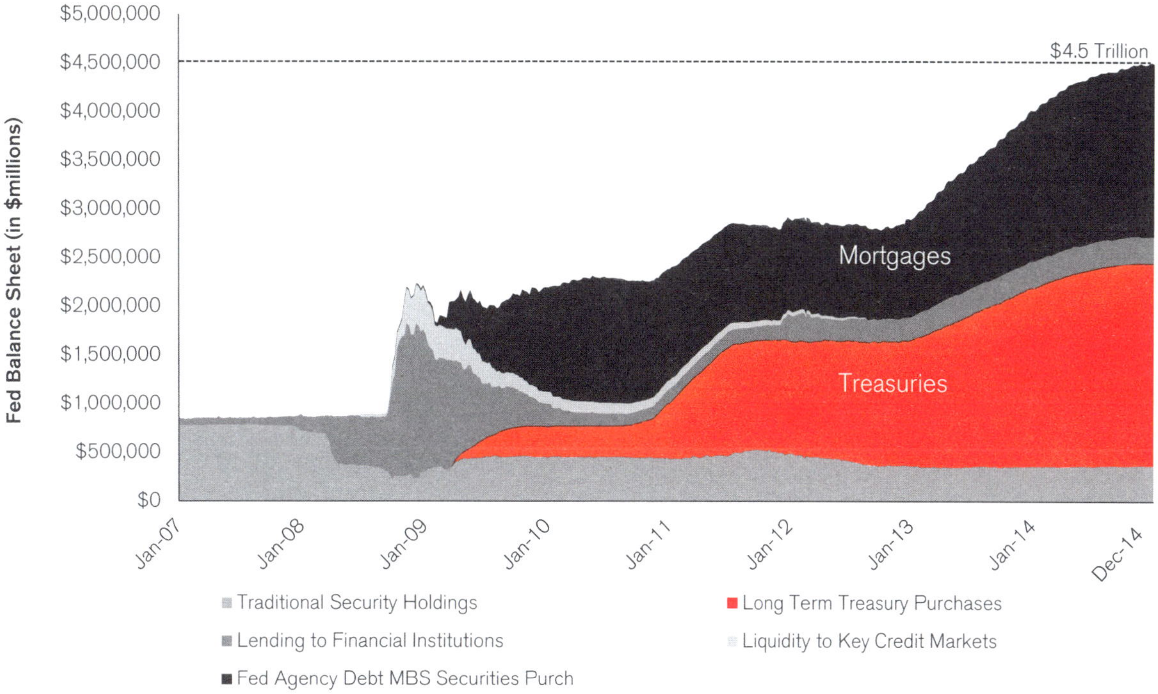

Source of underlying data: Federal Reserve Bank of Cleveland. To learn more, visit: https://www.clevelandfed.org

In the post-crisis period, some analysts estimated that the Fed's purchases accounted for a growing majority of new Treasury issuance. In early 2013 in the online version of the *Financial Times*, one analyst wrote, *"The Fed, the biggest buyer in the market, has been the driver of artificially low Treasury yields*[3.8]. In Exhibit 3.3 we show the aggregate dollar amount of marketable securities issued by the U.S. Department of Treasury (e.g., bills, notes, bonds, inflation-indexed securities, etc.) from 2003 through November 2014. We also display how much of the U.S. public debt is being held by the Fed, foreign investors (including official foreign institutions), and other investors.

[3.8] Michael Mackenzie, "Fed injects new sell-off risk into Treasuries", FT.com, January 8, 2013.

Exhibit 3.3: Marketable U.S. Treasury Securities Held by the Public
December 2003–November 2014

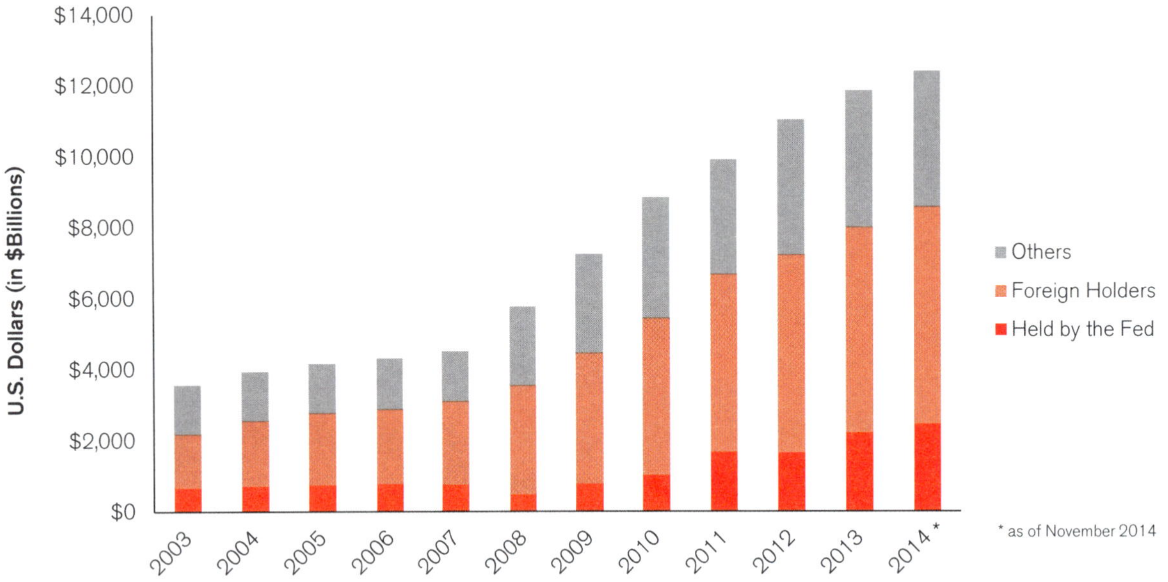

Source of underlying data: Federal Reserve Bank of St. Louis Economic Research; U.S. Department of the Treasury. Compiled by Duff & Phelps LLC.[3.9]

Notably, the issuance of marketable interest-bearing debt by the U.S. government to the public increased almost threefold between the end of 2007 and November 2014. Keeping everything else constant (*ceteris paribus*), the law of supply and demand would tell us that the dramatic increase in supply would lead to a significant decline in government bond prices, which would translate into a surge in yields. But that is not what happened. During the same period, the Fed more than tripled its purchases of U.S. Treasury securities, representing an 18% compound annual growth rate.[3.10] Between 2003 and 2008, the Fed's holdings of U.S. Treasuries had held fairly constant in the vicinity of $700 to $800 billion, with December 2008 being the significant exception, when holdings dropped to approximately $476 billion. The first QE program was announced by the FOMC in November 2008, and formally launched in mid-December 2008. After that period, the various QE programs implemented by the Fed have contributed to absorb a sizable portion of the increase in U.S. Treasuries issuance.

Similarly, broad demand for safe government debt by foreign investors, amid the global turmoil that followed the Financial Crisis, has absorbed another considerable fraction of new U.S. Treasuries issuance. How significant are these purchases by the Fed and foreign investors? Exhibit 3.4 shows the same information as in Exhibit 3.3, but displays the relative share of each major holder of marketable U.S. Treasuries since 2003 until November 2014.

3.9 Sources included: (i) Board of Governors of the Federal Reserve System (US), U.S. Treasury securities held by the Federal Reserve: All Maturities [TREAST], retrieved from FRED, Federal Reserve Bank of St. Louis https://research.stlouisfed.org/fred2/series/TREAST/, February 5, 2015; (ii) Monthly Statements of the Public Debt (MSPD) retrieved from http://www.treasurydirect.gov/govt/reports/pd/mspd/mspd.htm, February 5, 2015; and (iii) U.S. Department of the Treasury International Capital (TIC) System's Portfolio Holdings of U.S. and Foreign Securities – A. Major Foreign Holders of U.S. Treasury Securities retrieved from http://www.treasury.gov/resource-center/data-chart-center/tic/Pages/ticsec2.aspx, February 5, 2015.

3.10 If the comparison had been made between 2008 and 2014, the increase would be even more staggering: holdings by the Fed increased 417%, or a 32% compound annual growth rate.

Exhibit 3.4: Relative Holdings of Marketable U.S. Treasury Securities Held by the Public (in percentage terms) December 2003–November 2014

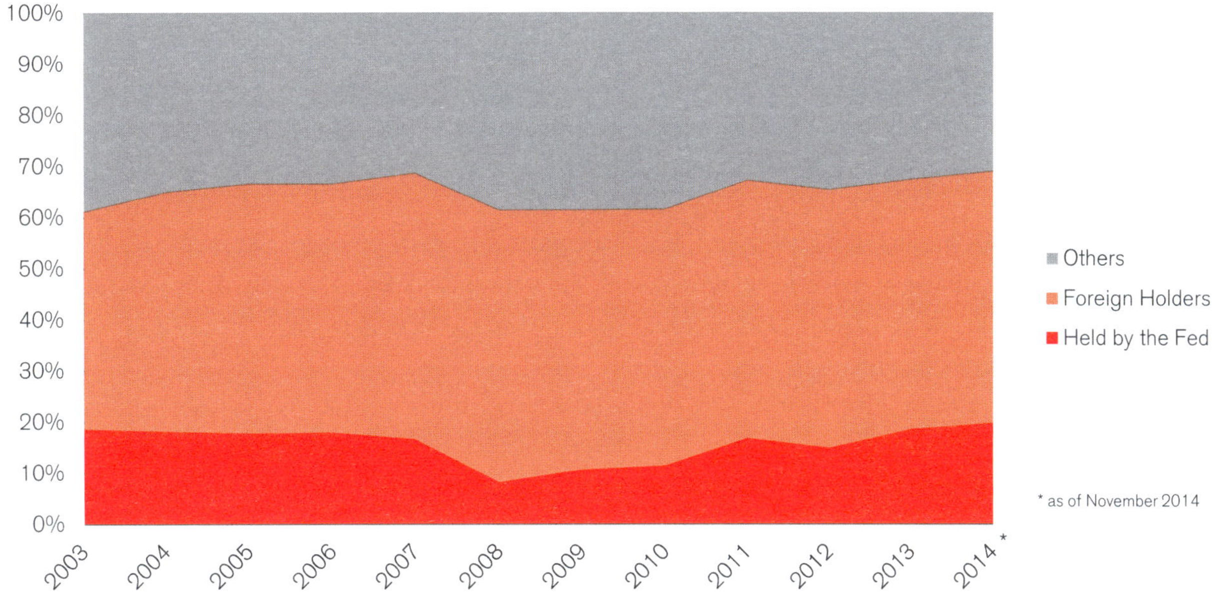

Source of underlying data: Federal Reserve Bank of St. Louis Economic Research; U.S. Department of the Treasury. Compiled by Duff & Phelps LLC.

At the end of November 2014, the relative share of U.S. Treasuries held by the Fed and foreign investors was 20% and 49% respectively, for a combined 69%. This combined level is actually similar to that observed at the end of 2007, prior to the onset of the Financial Crisis. However, as indicated above, the dollar amount of U.S. Treasuries has tripled after 2007, meaning that the Fed and foreign investors have absorbed over two-thirds of the available stock in the post-crisis period. Interestingly, a look at the composition of foreign investors reveals that since 2006 over two-thirds are actually foreign official institutions (i.e. central banks and central governments of foreign countries).[3.11, 3.12] Thus, a great majority of U.S. Treasuries are currently being held by either foreign government arms or central banks around the world (including the Fed).

A team of researchers has recently studied the impact that this massive amount of U.S. Treasury purchases by foreign investors and the Fed have had on long-term real rates. Specifically, using data through November 2012, the authors estimated that by 2008 foreign purchases of U.S. Treasuries had cumulatively reduced 10-year real yields by around 80 basis points. The subsequent Fed purchases through the various QE program implemented in the 2008–2012 period was estimated to incrementally depress 10-year real yields by around 140 basis points. Combining the impact of Fed and foreign investor purchases of U.S. Treasuries, real 10-year yields were depressed by 2.2% at the end of 2012, according to these authors' estimates.[3.13]

3.11 Source: Treasury International Capital (TIC) System's Portfolio Holdings of U.S. and Foreign Securities – A. Major Foreign Holders of U.S. Treasury Securities retrieved from http://www.treasury.gov/resource-center/data-chart-center/tic/Pages/ticsec2.aspx, February 5, 2015.

3.12 For a description of foreign official institutions, visit "TIC Country Codes and Partial List of Foreign Official Institutions" at: http://www.treasury.gov/resource-center/data-chart-center/tic/Pages/foihome.aspx

3.13 Kaminska, Iryna and Zinna, Gabriele, "Official Demand for U.S. Debt: Implications for U.S. Real Interest Rates". IMF Working Paper No. 14/66 (April 2014).

Now that the Fed has just concluded its third round of QE measures (QE3 was completed in October 2014) and signaled that an increase in the target federal funds rate may be on the horizon, the salient question may be what happens to rates as one of the largest purchasers in the market (the Fed) discontinues its QE operations. All other things held the same, rates would be expected to rise. But again, that is not happened thus far. In fact, the yield on 10-year U.S. Treasury bonds has dropped from 2.4% at the end of October to 2.2% at the end of December 2014. Likewise, the 20-year yield dropped from 2.8% to 2.5% over the same period. Why is that?

First of all, the size of the Fed's balance sheet is still considered enormous by historical standards and the Fed has expressed the intent to keep its holdings for a long time. For example, at its October 2014 meeting when announcing the conclusion of the QE3 program, the FOMC stated:[3.14]

> *"The Committee is maintaining its existing policy of reinvesting principal payments from its holdings of agency debt and agency mortgage-backed securities in agency mortgage-backed securities and of rolling over maturing Treasury securities at auction. This policy, by keeping the Committee's holdings of longer-term securities at sizable levels, should help maintain accommodative financial conditions."*

Translation: the Fed is keeping the size of its balance sheet constant for the foreseeable future, because it still wants to keep interest rates low.

A report released in November 2014 by Standard & Poor's (S&P) appears to concur with our interpretation:[3.15]

> *"Since QE works via a stock effect, as long as a central bank is maintaining a certain stock of QE, it is still "doing" QE. If a central bank has reached the maximum point of expanding its balance sheet, it is a little perverse to describe it as having "ended QE." Rather, what it will have ended are the asset purchases required to get it to the point of having done the maximum amount of QE it has decided to put in place."*

Secondly, there is another phenomenon helping push interest rates lower. Purchases of U.S. Treasury securities by foreign investors continue to grow at a fast pace. For example, net purchases at the end of November 2014 increased by $396 billion relative to a year earlier. This compares to the net purchases of $179 billion at the end of November 2013 over the prior year.[3.16] A Wall Street Journal analyst has recently summarized the puzzle of declining interest rates in 2014 as follows:[3.17]

> *"The overseas buying helps to unravel a mystery that has vexed commentators in 2014: How can bond prices keep rising and yields falling alongside gathering U.S. growth?"*

3.14 Press Release of FOMC's Monetary Policy Statement, October 29, 2014. For details visit: http://www.federalreserve.gov/monetarypolicy/fomccalendars.htm

3.15 S&P *Ratings Direct* report entitled "Economic Research: The Fed Is Continuing, Not 'Ending,' Quantitative Easing", November 4, 2014.

3.16 Source: Treasury International Capital (TIC) System's Portfolio Holdings of U.S. and Foreign Securities – A. Major Foreign Holders of U.S. Treasury Securities retrieved from http://www.treasury.gov/resource-center/data-chart-center/tic/Pages/ticsec2.aspx, February 5, 2015.

3.17 Zeng, M. (2014, December 15). Foreign Investors Pile Into Bonds. *The Wall Street Journal.* Retrieved from: http://www.wsj.com/articles/foreign-investors-pile-into-bonds-1418690550

In very simple terms, there are a couple of drivers that appear to be behind this continued demand by foreign investors: (i) a global flight to quality; and (ii) expectations that the Fed will be raising U.S. interest rates in 2015.

Global investors had enough reasons to seek safe haven investments during 2014. In general, political conflicts have risen in 2014 in various regions of the world, escalating further towards the end of the year. Major examples include (i) the Ukrainian government collapse, and ensuing fighting with pro-Russian separatists, leading to Russia's annexation of Crimea and invasion of eastern Ukraine; (ii) the emergence of the Islamic State of Iraq and Syria (ISIS), taking control of significant territory in Iraq and Syria through brutal methods; and (iii) the Ebola virus outbreak which started in West Africa and quickly created global epidemic fears.

In addition, concerns about a slowing global economy and deflationary pressures have also led global investors to seek safe haven investments, such as government bonds issued by the U.S., Germany, and Switzerland, to name a few. Recent tumbling oil prices have reinforced investor anxiety over stagnant growth in the Eurozone and Japan, as well as a deceleration in China and several other emerging-market countries.

On one hand, the sharp decline in oil prices has put additional pressure in an already very low inflation environment, considered by many as bordering on deflation territory. For perspective, the price of light sweet crude oil declined from $98/barrel at the end of 2013 to $53/barrel at the end of 2014, a 46% decline in a single year.[3.18] The potential benefit of lower oil prices to oil-importing nations has not (yet, at least) been felt on economic growth. Worryingly, should major economic regions such as the Eurozone enter into a deflationary path, one could use Japan's "lost decades" as a parallel to what might happen in the future.

Deflation risks and economic stagnation are precisely what led central banks in Japan and Eurozone to recently boost their respective monetary easing policies. In October 2014, Japan's central bank surprised the world by announcing a second program self-dubbed as "quantitative and qualitative easing" (QQE). Besides other measures, QQE2 proposed to increase the monetary base at a rate of JPY 80 trillion per year, compared with the previous rate of JPY 60 to 70 trillion.[3.19] In November, after the announcement of a second consecutive quarter of economic contraction, Japan's prime minister Shinzo Abe also proclaimed snap parliamentary elections, explicitly seeking endorsement to continue with the government's expansionary economic policies (also known as "Abenomics"). Since Abe's party managed to keep its two-third majority in the December 2014 elections, the current policies are expected to continue.

Elsewhere in the Eurozone, lackluster growth trends, coupled with deflation fears, induced the European Central Bank (ECB) to cut its benchmark rate to a new record low of 0.15% in early June, while also

[3.18] Source: S&P *Capital IQ* database.

[3.19] For a background on this and other QE programs implemented by the Bank of Japan consider reading this Standard & Poor's *Ratings Direct* report entitled "The Bank of Japan's 'Surprise' Move Should Not Have Been A Surprise", November 7, 2014.

announcing an unprecedented measure to charge negative interest rates on deposits held at the central bank.[3.20] The Eurozone economy was almost stagnant in the second quarter of 2014, with Germany actually contracting (partly due to the Ukraine-Russia conflict). The loss in economic momentum, coupled with early third-quarter indicators falling short of expectations, prompted the ECB to again decrease its benchmark rate to 0.05% in September, with rates on deposits held at the ECB cut further into negative territory. The ECB also confirmed the start of an asset-backed securities purchase program and unveiled a new euro-denominated covered bond purchase program, both expected to have a sizeable impact on the ECB's balance sheet. The ECB expects these asset purchase programs to last for at least two years. In December 2014, the ECB also announced a second longer-term refinancing operation and hinted at a new QE program to buy Eurozone government bonds. Through the end of December, government bond yields across Europe continued to fall to historic lows, amid mounting speculation of a larger scale sovereign debt purchase program, which was fuelled by statements made by ECB officials. For instance, German government securities with maturities up to 5 years all displayed negative yields as of December 31, 2014, while the 10-year Bund yield was only 0.5%.

The current economic conditions in the Eurozone and Japan are in stark contrast with the recent performance of the U.S. economy. The robust economic expansion in both the second and third quarters has led investors to believe the U.S. economy has finally gained some growth momentum. That, coupled with solid jobs gains, has made the Fed more confident that a rise in short-term interest rates may be in order. In fact, a majority of global investors appear to be expecting an increase in the federal funds rate sometime in 2015. The divergence in economic growth and monetary policies across the U.S. versus other major economic regions is actually contributing to the recent decline in U.S. Treasury yields. Ultimately, U.S. government bonds continue to offer more-attractive yields than bonds issued by other safe-haven countries, and a stronger dollar enables foreign investors to pick up extra returns on U.S. investments.

So, are artificially repressed U.S. Treasury yields sustainable? Sustainability implies that something can go on forever, but Stein's Law tells us that "If something cannot go on forever, it will stop".[3.21] A possible corollary of Stein's Law is that *if* the accommodative monetary policy (including the massive QE programs) by the Fed since the Financial Crisis "cannot go on forever", then the Fed may really not have much of a choice in whether to "stop" or not. Put simply, things that are destined to stop will stop by their own accord, one way or another. Whether it will be a "graceful dismount" is yet to be seen.

3.20 For a list of ECB's monetary policy decisions, visit: https://www.ecb.europa.eu/press/govcdec/mopo/2015/html/index.en.html

3.21 Professor Herbert Stein was a member and later chairman of the Council of Economic Advisers under Presidents Nixon and Ford. Source: Michael M. Weinstein, "Herbert Stein, Nixon Adviser And Economist, Is Dead at 83", *New York Times*, September 09, 1999.

In the short-term, there are probably still enough significant factors that will keep interest rates at artificial low levels. However, in the medium-term, borrowing any major setback in the global economy, investors seem to be expecting U.S. interest rates to start rising, albeit slowly, during 2015. We compiled consensus forecasts from reputable sources published close to year-end 2014. Exhibit 3.5 displays the average of consensus forecasts for 10-year U.S. Treasury bond yields from a variety of surveys through 2020.[3.22, 3.23] We then added a maturity premium to the 10-year yield, to arrive at an implied forecast for the 20-year government bond yield.[3.24]

Exhibit 3.5: Average forecasted 10-year U.S. Treasury Bond Yield and Implied 20-year U.S. Risk-free Rate (in percentage terms) December 2014

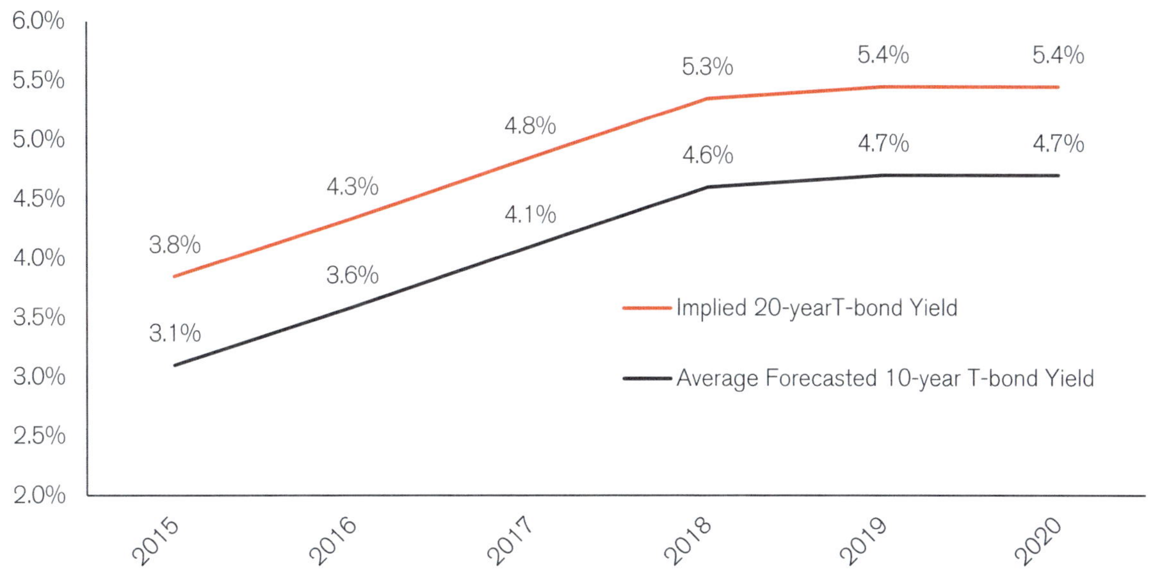

Sources of underlying data: Survey of Professional Forecasters; Livingston Survey; U.S. Consensus Forecast; *Blue Chip Economic Indicators*; and *Blue Chip Financial Forecasts*; S&P *Capital IQ* database. Compiled by Duff & Phelps LLC.

3.22 Sources: "Survey of Professional Forecasters: Fourth Quarter 2014", Federal Reserve Bank of Philadelphia (November17, 2014); "The Livingston Survey: December 2014", Federal Reserve Bank of Philadelphia (December 12, 2014); "US Consensus Forecast ", Consensus Economics Inc. (December 8, 2014); *Blue Chip Economic Indicators* (December 10, 2014); *Blue Chip Financial Forecasts* (December 1, 2014); S&P *Capital IQ*™ database.

3.23 Not all surveys provided consensus forecasts through 2020. At a minimum, all five sources included forecasts for 2015.

3.24 A maturity premium of approximately 70 basis points was added to the 10-year yield. This was based on the average yield spread between the 20- and the 10-year U.S. Treasury constant maturity bonds from December 2008 through December 2014. Had more recent data been used, when the yield spread has declined to a range of 30 to 40 basis points, would not materially change our main conclusion. While the magnitude of the maturity premium can be debated, using even the most recent 30 to 40 bps average yield spread would imply that as of December 2014 market participants expected the 20-year yield to reach close to 4.0% by 2016 (3.6% + approximately 0.4%).

Methods of Risk-free Rate Normalization

Normalization of risk-free rates can be accomplished in a number of ways, including (i) simple averaging, or (ii) various "build-up" methods.

The first normalization method entails calculating averages of yields to maturity on long-term government securities over various periods. This method's implied assumption is that government bond yields revert to the mean. In Exhibit 3.6, the solid red line is the spot yield on a 20-year U.S. government bond (December 2007–December 2014), and the dashed black line is the average monthly yield of the 20-year U.S. government bond over the previous 10 years, ending December 2014 (3.9%). Current government bond spot yields are lower than even the monthly average over the last 10 years. Taking the average over the last 10 years is a simple way of "normalizing" the risk-free rate. An issue with using historical averages, though, is selecting an appropriate comparison period that can be used as a reasonable proxy for the future.

Exhibit 3.6: Spot and Average Yields on 20-year U.S. Government
January 2008–December 2014

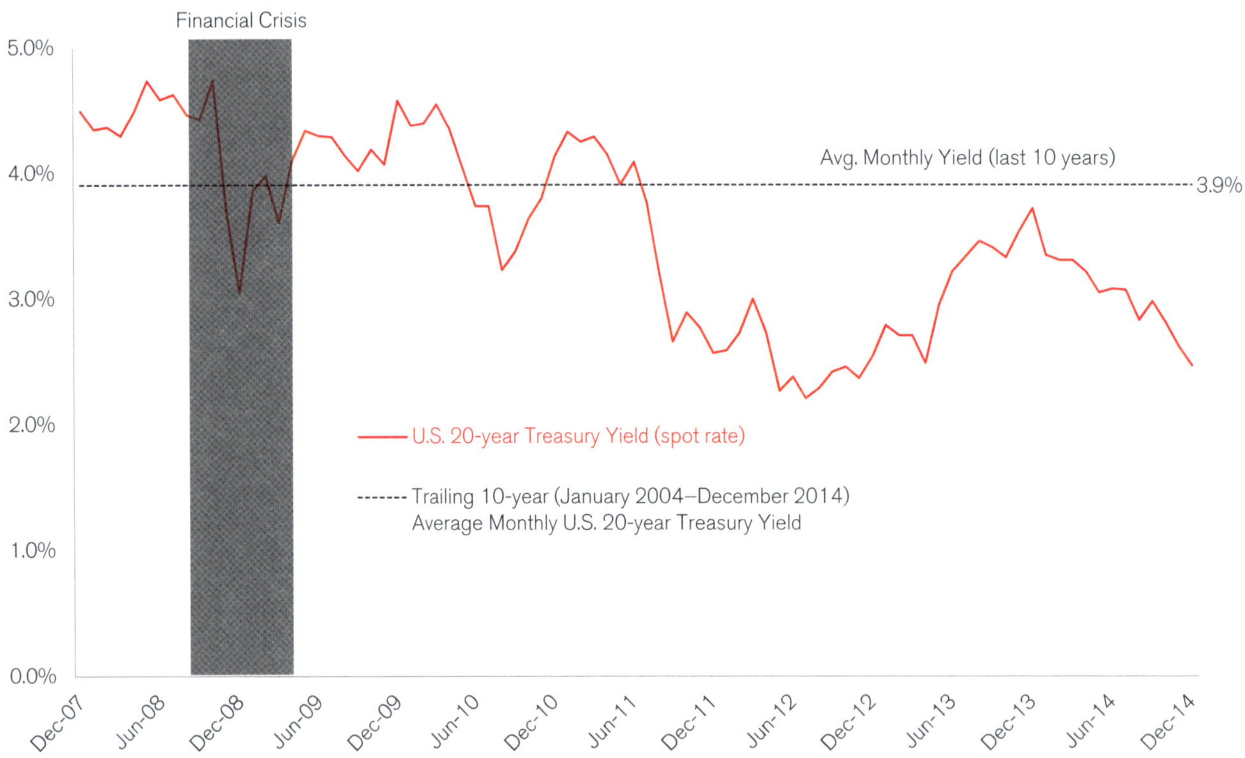

Source of underlying data: 20-year U.S. government bond series. Board of Governors of the Federal Reserve System website at: http:// www.federalreserve.gov/releases/h15/data.htm

The second normalization method entails using a simple build-up method, where the components of the risk-free rate are estimated and then added together. Conceptually, the risk-free rate can be (loosely) illustrated as the return on the following two components:[3.25]

Risk-free rate = Real Rate + Expected Inflation

Some academic studies have suggested the long-term *"real"* risk-free rate to be somewhere in the range of 1.3% to 2.0% based on the study of inflation swap rates and/or yields on long-term U.S. Treasury Inflation Protected Securities (TIPS).[3.26, 3.27, 3.28, 3.29]

The second component, *expected inflation*, can also be estimated in a number of ways. Monetary policymakers and academics have been monitoring several measures of market expectations of future inflation. One method of estimating long-term inflation is to take the difference between the yield on a 20-year U.S. government bond yield and the yield of a 20-year U.S. TIPS. This is also known as the "breakeven inflation".[3.30] This calculation is shown in Exhibit 3.7 over the time period July 2004–December 2014. As of December 31, 2014, the average monthly breakeven long-term inflation estimate over the time period July 2004–December 2014 using this method was 2.4% (4.0% government bond yield – 1.6% TIPS).

3.25 This is a simplified version of the "Fisher equation", named after Irving Fisher. Fisher's *"The Theory of Interest"* was first published by Macmillan (New York), in 1930.

3.26 TIPS are marketable securities whose principal is adjusted relative to changes in the Consumer Price Index (CPI).

3.27 Joseph Haubrich, George Pennacchi, and Peter Ritchken "Inflation Expectations, Real Rates, and Risk Premia: Evidence from Inflation Swaps," *Review of Financial Studies* Vol. 25 (5) (2012): 1588-1629.

3.28 Andrew Ang and Geert Bekaert "The Term Structure of Real Rates and Expected Inflation," *The Journal of Finance*, Vol. LXIII (2) (April 2008).

3.29 Olesya V Grishchenko and Jing-zhi Huang "Inflation Risk Premium: Evidence From the TIPS Market," *The Journal of Fixed Income*, Vol. 22 (4) (2013): 5-30.

3.30 Breakeven inflation is based on the differential between nominal and TIPS yields with equivalent maturity. However, several studies have documented that the breakeven inflation has not been a good predictor for inflation expectations. The differential between nominal and real rates is not only complicated by a liquidity premium, but also by the potential presence of the inflation risk premium, with both of these premiums varying through time.

Exhibit 3.7: Breakeven Long-Term Inflation Estimate (20 year Government Bond Yield – 20 year TIPS Yield)
July 2004 – December 2014

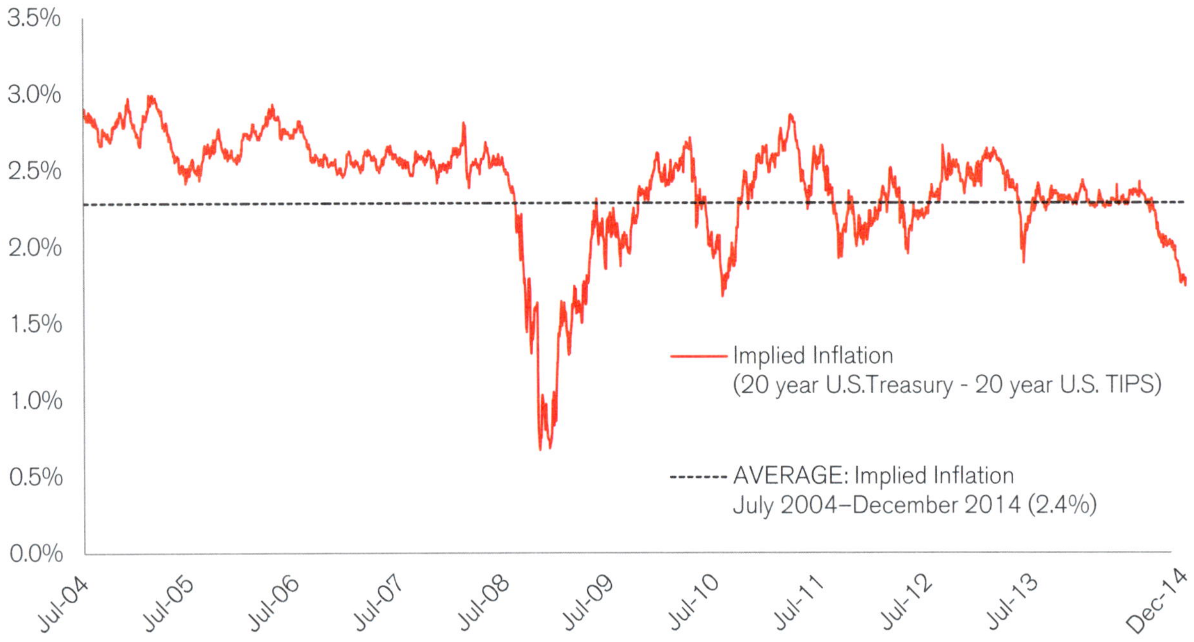

Source of underlying data: 20-year U.S. government bond series and 20-year TIPS series, Board of Governors of the Federal Reserve System website at: http://www.federalreserve.gov/releases/h15/data.htm. Calculated by Duff & Phelps LLC.

Additionally, in the U.S., there are a number of well-established surveys providing consensus estimates for expected inflation. One academic study has examined various methods for forecasting inflation over the period 1952–2004 and found that surveys significantly outperform other forecasting methods.[3.31] Exhibit 3.8. outlines some of the most prominent surveys in this area. Altogether, the year-end 2014 estimates of longer-term inflation range from 1.8% to 2.8%.

[3.31] Ang, A., G. Bekaert, and M. Wei. "Do macro variables, asset markets, or surveys forecast inflation better?" *Journal of Monetary Economics.* 54, 1163-1212.

Exhibit 3.8: Long-term Expected Inflation Estimates
Year-end 2014 (approx.)

Source	Estimate (%)
Livingston Survey (Federal Reserve Bank of Philadelphia)	2.3
Survey of Professional Forecasters (Federal Reserve Bank of Philadelphia)	2.2
Cleveland Federal Reserve	1.8
Blue Chip Financial Forecasts	2.3
University of Michigan Survey Next 5 Years Inflation Expectations	2.8
Range of Expected Inflation Forecasts	1.8% to 2.8%

Sources of underlying data: "The Livingston Survey: December 2014," Federal Reserve Bank of Philadelphia (December 12, 2014); "Survey of Professional Forecasters: Fourth Quarter 2014," Federal Reserve Bank of Philadelphia (November 17, 2014); *Blue Chip Financial Forecasts* 33 (12) (December 1, 2014); Federal Reserve Bank of Cleveland (estimates as of December 2014); Bloomberg.

Adding the estimated ranges for the "real" risk-free rate and longer-term inflation together produces an estimated normalized risk-free rate range of 3.1% to 4.8%, with a midpoint of 4.0% (difference due to rounding).

Range of Estimated Long-term Real Rate	1.3% to 2.0%
Range of Estimated Expected Inflation Forecasts	1.8% to 2.8%
Range of Estimated Long-term Normalized Risk-free Rate	3.1% to 4.8%
Midpoint	4.0%

Spot Yield or Normalized Yield?

Should the valuation analyst use the current market yield on risk-free U.S. government bonds ("spot" yield equal to 2.4% at December 31, 2014) or use a "normalized" risk-free yield when estimating the cost of equity capital?

As stated earlier, in most circumstances we would prefer to use the "spot" yield on U.S. government bonds available in the market as a proxy for the U.S. risk-free rate. However, during times of flight to quality and/or high levels of central bank intervention, those lower observed yields imply a lower cost of capital (all other factors held the same) – just the opposite of what one would expect in times of relative economy-wide distress – so a "normalization" adjustment may be considered appropriate. By "normalization" we mean estimating a rate that more likely reflects the sustainable average return of long-term risk-free rates. *If spot yield-to-maturity were used at these times, without any other adjustments, one would arrive at an overall discount rate that is likely inappropriately low vis-à-vis the risks currently facing investors.* Exhibit 3.9 shows the potential problems of simply using the spot yield-to-maturity on 20-year U.S. government bonds in conjunction with unadjusted U.S. historical equity risk premia. Data is displayed for year-end 2007 through year-end 2014. For example, in December 2008, at the height of the Financial Crisis (when risks were arguably at all-time highs), using the 1926–2008 historical ERP of 6.5% together with the spot 20-year yield of 3.0% would result in a base cost of equity capital of 9.5%. In contrast, the base cost of equity would be 11.6% (4.5% plus 7.1%) at year-end 2007, implying that risks were actually higher at the end of 2007 than at the end of 2008. From both a theoretical and practical standpoint, the reality is that investors likely perceived risks to be much higher in December 2008, relative to the December 2007. This demonstrates that a mechanical application of the data may result in nonsensical results.[3.32]

Exhibit 3.9: Spot 20-year U.S. Treasury Yield in Conjunction with Unadjusted "Historical" Equity Risk Premium

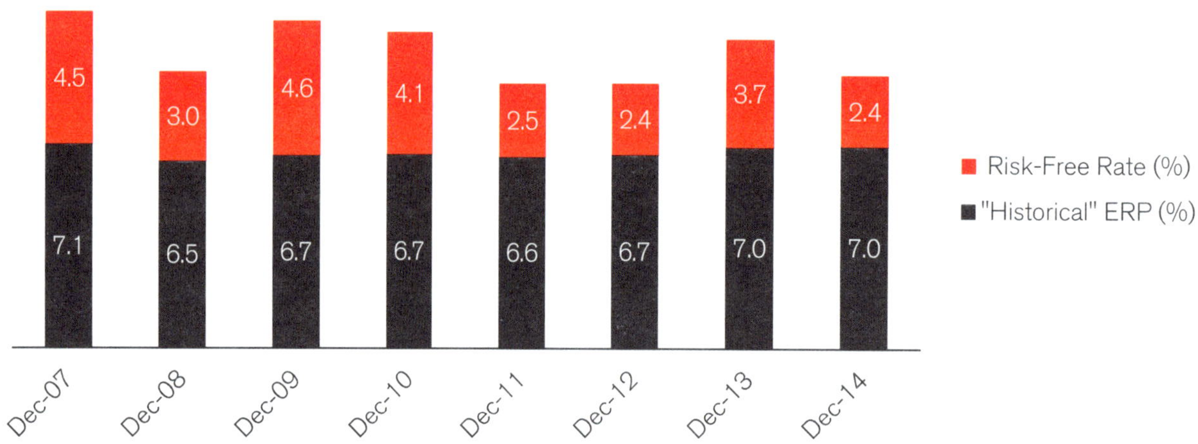

Source of underlying data: Morningstar *Direct* database. Used with permission. Risk-free rate data series used: Long-term Gov't Bonds (IA SBBI US LT Govt YLD USD). All rights reserved. Calculations performed by Duff & Phelps LLC.

Adjustments to the ERP or to the risk-free rate are, in principle, a response to the same underlying concerns and should result in broadly similar costs of capital. Adjusting the risk-free rate in conjunction with the ERP is only one of the alternatives available when estimating the cost of equity capital.

For example, one could use a spot yield for the risk-free rate, but *increase* the ERP or other adjustment to account for higher (systematic) risk. If the valuation analyst chooses to use the spot yield to estimate the cost of capital during periods when those yields are less than "normal," the valuation analyst must use an estimated ERP that is *matched* to (or implied by) those *below-normal* yields. However we note that the most commonly used data sources for ERP estimates are long-term series measured when interest rates were largely not subject to such market intervention. Using those data series with an abnormally low spot yield creates a mismatch.

[3.32] More detailed information on historical ERPs can be found later in this chapter.

Alternatively, if the valuation analyst chooses to use a normalized risk-free rate in estimating the cost of capital, the valuation analyst must again use an estimated ERP that is *matched* to those *normalized* yields. Normalizing the risk-free rate is likely a more direct (and more easily implemented) analysis than adjusting the ERP due to a *temporary* reduction in the yields on risk-free securities, while *longer-term* trends may be more appropriately reflected in the ERP.

We examined interest rates for the months since the Financial Crisis began. We also estimated a "normalized" yield each month using trailing averages and a build-up model. In the examples in this book, we are using data as of December 2014. We have chosen to use 4.0% as the normalized yield on U.S. 20-year government bonds as of December 31, 2014 as a proxy for a normalized risk-free rate of return.

Exhibit 3.15 (at the end of this chapter) displays the month by month spot yields on 20-year U.S. government bonds and the matching "normalized" yields (as suggested by Duff & Phelps) for months in which the normalized yields are greater than the corresponding spot yields. The months in which we believe a valuation analyst should consider using a normalized risk-free rate (or at least consider whether adjustments are warranted) are highlighted in bold and the "normalized" yields are shown in these months.

Equity Risk Premium[3.33]

The ERP (often interchangeably referred to as the *market risk premium*) is defined as the extra return (over the expected yield on risk-free securities) that investors expect to receive from an investment in the market portfolio of common stocks, represented by a broad-based market index (e.g., S&P 500 Index or the NYSE Index).

In a recent paper, the authors conclude that "The ERP is almost certainly the most important variable in finance."[3.34]

The ERP (or notational RP_m) is defined as:

Formula 3.1

$$RP_m = R_m - R_f$$

[3.33] Excerpted in part from Pratt and Grabowski, op.cit.: Chapters 8 and 8A and updated through December 31, 2013.

[3.34] Richard C. Grinold, Kenneth K. Kroner, and Laurence B. Siegel, "A Supply Model of the Equity Premium," in *Rethinking the Equity Risk Premium*, ed. P. Brett Hammond, Jr., Martin L. Leibowitz, and Lawrence B. Siegel (The Research Foundation of CFA Institute, 2011): 53.

where:

RP_m = Equity risk premium

R_m = Expected return on a diversified portfolio of equity securities, most often measured as the S&P 500 Index or the NYSE Index (for the U.S. market)

R_f = Expected risk-free rate

ERP is a forward-looking concept. It is an expectation as of the valuation date for which no market quotes are directly observable. ERP is a function of expected returns on a diversified portfolio of equities minus an expected yield on a risk-free security to which it is compared over a specified time period.

The ERP can be thought of in terms of an *unconditional* ERP (i.e., the long-term average through the business cycle) and a *conditional* ERP based on current levels of the stock market and economy relative to the long-term average.[3.35]

In this chapter, we are addressing returns of publicly traded stocks relative to an expected yield on a risk-free security. The ERP in conjunction with the risk-free rate, either normalized or actual, also establishes a beginning benchmark for estimating the appropriate discount rates for securities of closely held businesses.

Estimating the Equity Risk Premium

There is no single universally accepted methodology for estimating the ERP. A wide variety of premiums are used in practice and recommended by academics and financial advisors. These differences are often due to differences in how ERP is estimated.

Generally, we can categorize approaches for estimating the ERP as either an *ex post* approach or an *ex ante* approach.

For example, some valuation analysts define expected returns on common stocks in terms of averages of realized (historical) single-period returns while others define expected returns on common stocks in terms of realized multi-year compound returns. These are *ex post* approaches.

Some valuation analysts estimate the ERP using the returns on the diversified portfolio implied by expected (future) stock prices or expected dividends. These are *ex ante* approaches.

From an investment return perspective, the ERP is typically defined as the expected average annual compound return on a diversified portfolio of equity securities, most often measured as the S&P 500 Index or the NYSE Index for the U.S. market, minus the expected return on a risk-free security.[3.36]

3.35 Robert D. Arnott, "Historical Results," *Equity Risk Premium Forum, AIMR* (November 8, 2001): 27.

3.36 For example, see Peng Chen, "Will Bonds Outperform Stocks over the Long Run? Not Likely," in *Rethinking the Equity Risk Premium*, ed. P. Brett Hammond, Jr., Martin L. Leibowitz, and Lawrence B. Siegel (The Research Foundation of CFA Institute, 2011): 128.

If one is using *historical* risk premiums (sometimes called a "long-term historical ERP") as an estimator of *future* risk premiums (an *ex post* approach), the geometric average of realized returns is the estimator one should use in compounding future returns to estimate future wealth. But if one is using historical risk premiums as the estimator of the ERP for use in cost of capital models intended for discounting expected cash flows, the most widely used statistic is the arithmetic average of realized risk premiums.

Even if one is simply looking forward at prospective returns for the S&P 500 and the implied ERP (an *ex ante* approach), the arithmetic average equivalent of the implied ERP is a better statistic to use in cost of capital models intended for discounting expected cash flows.

Historical return and risk premium data is most often expressed in terms of one-year returns. In the *Valuation Handbook*, we have attempted to convert varying indications of the ERP such that they are measured in a consistent framework (e.g., a statistical estimator of the ERP in excess of 20-year U.S. government bonds).

Ex Post Approaches

While a valuation analyst can observe premiums realized over time by referring to historical data (i.e., realized risk premium approach or *ex post* approach), such realized premium data do not represent the ERP expected in those prior periods, nor do they represent the current ERP estimate. Rather, to the extent that realized premiums on the average equate to expected premiums in prior periods, such samples *may be* representative of current expectations. But to the extent that prior events that were not expected to occur caused realized returns to differ from prior expectations, such samples need to be adjusted to remove the effects of these nonrecurring events. One needs to understand which events might be considered nonrecurring and then adjust the data for them in order to improve the predictive power of the sample.

Further, *ex post* realized returns on stocks and realized risk premiums will be affected by differences between expected inflation at the time of an ERP estimate was made and the realized inflation subsequent to the date of the estimate. This difference will cause *ex post* stock returns and *ex post* risk premiums to differ from ERP estimates made in prior periods.

Ex Ante Approaches

Valuation analysts can derive forward-looking estimates for the ERP from forward-looking data at the time of the analysis (*ex ante* approach).[3.37] We can generally categorize four types of forward-looking data used in estimating the expected returns on a diversified portfolio of equities and, in turn, the ERP:

i. Data on the underlying expectations of growth in overall corporate earnings and dividends.

ii. Data aggregated from projections of analysts following the companies comprising the broad portfolio as to their expectations of dividends and future stock prices.

[3.37] See, for example, the discussion in Eugene F. Fama and Kenneth R. French, "The Equity Premium," *Journal of Finance* (April 2002): 637–659.

iii. Data on observations of risk premiums evidenced in the level of the S&P 500, corporate bond spreads (e.g., differences in yields on corporate bonds rated Baa and Aaa), or prices for credit default swaps.

iv. Surveys of expectations of respondents.

The goal of both the *ex post* and *ex ante* approaches is to estimate the *expected* ERP as of the valuation date.

Any estimate of the ERP must be made in relation to a risk-free security. That is, the ERP is measured as the difference between the expected return on a well-diversified portfolio of large company common stocks and the rate of return expected on a risk-free security.

In valuing going-concern businesses and long-term investments made by businesses, valuation analysts generally use long-term U.S. government bonds as the risk-free security and use an estimate of ERP developed relative to long-term U.S. government bonds. This convention both represents a realistic, simplifying assumption and is consistent with the theory of the CAPM.[3.38]

Most business investments have long durations and suffer from a reinvestment risk just as long-term government bonds do. As such, the use of long-term U.S. government bonds and an ERP estimated relative to such bonds more closely matches the investment horizon and risks confronting business managers in capital budgeting decisions, as well as in valuation issues.

Therefore, in the remainder of this chapter, we have translated all estimates of ERP to estimates relative to 20-year U.S. government bonds rates.

Unconditional ERP

We will first examine the *unconditional ERP* (i.e., long-term average) using realized risk premium data (the *ex post* approach). While academics and valuation analysts agree that ERP is a forward-looking concept, some valuation analysts, including taxing authorities and regulatory bodies, use historical data to estimate the ERP under the assumption that historical data are a valid proxy for current investor expectations. They like the appearance of accuracy, and we do emphasize the word *appearance*.

In the realized risk premium approach, the estimate of the ERP is the risk premium (realized return on stocks in excess of the risk-free rate) that investors have, on the average, realized over some historical holding period. The underlying theory is that the past provides a reasonable indicator of how the market will behave in the future, and also that investors' expectations are influenced by the historical performance of the market.

3.38 Eugene F. Fama, "Risk-Adjusted Discount Rates and Capital Budgeting Under Uncertainty," *Journal of Financial Economics* 5(1) (1977): 3– 24. This is true for both the original CAPM of Sharpe-Lintner-Mossin and the extension of the textbook CAPM, the intertemporal CAPM of Merton.

A more direct justification for use of the realized risk premium approach is the contention that, for whatever reason, securities in the past have been priced in such a way as to earn the returns observed. By using an estimated cost of equity capital incorporating the average of realized risk premiums, you may to some extent replicate this level of pricing.

The long-term average of realized risk premiums is calculated from varying rates of returns on common stocks over fluctuating risk-free rates. They are generally reported annually. A common practice adds the same long-term average realized risk premium (an *ex post* estimate of the ERP) to the market interest rate of the risk-free security throughout the following year regardless of the level of the rate on that security as of the valuation date.

This common practice implicitly either assumes that during upcoming periods the difference between the expected return on common stocks and U.S. government bonds is constant. Alternatively, this common practice implicitly assumes that any decrease or increase in the ERP as of the valuation date is short-term and that the ERP is mean reverting to the long-term average of realized risk premiums rather quickly.

Let us look at an example of the consequences of this common practice. If a valuation analyst were using the long-term average of realized risk premiums from 1926–2007 of 7.1% as the ERP estimate during 2008, that 7.1% ERP would have been added to the risk-free rate at any valuation date during 2008 regardless of the level of the risk-free rate during that year and regardless of any changes in risks in the economy.

For example, the yield on 20-year U.S. government bonds was 4.8% on October 31, 2008. But due to the increase in economic risks as the Financial Crisis unfolded, the yield had fallen due to the flight to quality to 3.7% as of November 30, 2008. Following common practice, the 7.1% would have been added to this lower yield even though risk had increased.[3.39]

The average realized risk premium is sensitive to the period chosen for the average. While the selection of 1926 as a starting point corresponds to the initial publishing of the forerunner to the current S&P 500 (the S&P Composite Index of 90 stocks), the choice of that date was otherwise arbitrary. Regarding the historical time period over which realized risk premiums should be calculated, one can look at the choice of period in two ways:

1. Reasons to focus on recent history:

   - The recent past may be most relevant to an investor.

   - Return patterns may change over time.

   - The longer period includes "unusual events" which may not be representation of today's economy.

[3.39] *2013 Ibbotson® SBBI® Valuation Yearbook* (Chicago: Morningstar, 2013): 57–61.

2. Reasons to focus on long-term history:

   - Long-term historical returns have shown surprising stability.
   - Short-term observations may lead to illogical forecasts.
   - Every period has dramatic historical events and we do not know what major events lie ahead.
   - Law of large numbers: More observations lead to a more accurate estimate.

Differences in one's approach to estimating the ERP hinge even more on the measure of expected return on equity securities.

In applying the realized risk premium approach, the valuation analyst selects the number of years of historical return data to include in the average. One school of thought holds that the future is best estimated using a very long horizon of past returns. Another school of thought holds that the future is best measured by the (relatively) recent past. These differences in opinion result in disagreement as to the number of years to include in the historical average.

Realized Historical Stock and Bond Returns

The highest-quality data are available for periods beginning in 1926 from the Center of Research in Security Prices (CRSP) at the University of Chicago. The *Valuation Handbook* contains summaries of returns on U.S. stocks and bonds derived from those data. The reported returns include the effects from the reinvestment of dividends.

Returns on common stocks have been assembled by various sources (and with various degrees of quality) for earlier periods. Reasonably good stock market return data are available back to 1872, and less reliable data are available back to the end of the eighteenth century. In the earliest period, the market consisted almost entirely of bank stocks, and by the mid-nineteenth century, the market was dominated by railroad stocks.[3.40] Data for government bond yield data have also been assembled for these periods. Exhibit 3.10 presents the realized average annual risk premiums for stocks assembled from various sources for alternative periods through 2014.

We measure the realized risk premium by comparing the stock market returns during the period to the income return on long-term U.S. government bonds (or total returns for the years before 1926).

Exhibit 3.10 displays the arithmetic average of realized risk premiums, the standard errors of estimate and the geometric average of the realized risk premiums.

[3.40] See Pratt and Grabowski, op.cit.: 143.

Exhibit 3.10: Realized Equity Risk Premiums: Stock Market Returns Minus U.S. Government Bonds Through 2014

Length (Yrs.)	Period Dates	Arithmetic Average (%)	Standard Deviation (%)	Standard Error (%)	Geometric Average (%)
20	1995-2014	6.84	19.59	4.38	4.72
30	1985-2014	6.79	17.22	3.14	5.01
40	1975-2014	6.60	16.55	2.62	4.93
50	1965-2014	4.63	16.95	2.40	3.02
89	1926-2014	7.00	20.17	2.14	4.83
115	1900-2014	6.69	19.79	1.85	4.61
143	1872-2014	5.92	18.80	1.57	4.07
217	1798-2014	5.13	17.99	1.22	3.45

Sources of underlying data: Data compiled from R. Ibbotson and G. Brinson, *Global Investing* (New York: McGraw-Hill, 1993); W. Schwert, "Indexes of U.S. Stock Prices from 1802 to 1987, " *Journal of Business* Vol. 63 (July 1990): 399–426; S. Homer and R. Sylla, *A History of Interest Rates*, 3rd ed. (Piscataway, NJ: Rutgers University Press, 1991); and CRSP and Morningstar *Direct* database. Calculations by Duff & Phelps LLC. Used with permission.

While some may question the relevance of averages including early periods for estimating today's ERP, what is striking is that the largest arithmetic average of one-year returns is the 89 years from 1926 to 2014.

Why use the income return on long-term government bonds? The income return in each period represented the expected yield on the bonds at the time of the investment. Investors make a decision to invest in the stock market today by comparing the expected return from that particular investment to the rate of return today on a benchmark security (in this case, the long-term U.S. government bond). While the investors did not know the stock market return when they invested at the beginning of each year, they did know the rate of interest promised on long-term U.S. government bonds when they were first issued. To try to match the expectations at the beginning of each year, we measure historical stock market returns on an expectation that history will repeat itself over the expected return on bonds in each year.

The realized risk premiums vary year to year, and the estimate of the *true* ERP resulting from this sampling is subject to some degree of error. We display the standard errors of estimate in Exhibit 3.10. The standard error of estimate allows you to measure the likely accuracy of using the realized risk premium as the estimate of the *true* ERP assuming that the observations are drawn from a distribution of returns that is still relevant. This statistic indicates the estimated range within which the *true* ERP falls (i.e., assuming normality, the true ERP can be expected to fall within two standard errors with a 95% level of confidence).

In choosing the years one includes in the estimate, the valuation analyst is looking for a period in which the realized returns best represent what might be expected in future periods. One might consider eliminating from the sample periods influenced by abnormal circumstances. Or one might consider a sample period with risk characteristics more comparable to the risk characteristics confronting investors today.

World War II Interest Rate Bias

Some observers have suggested that the period including the 1940s and the immediate post-World War II boom years may have exhibited unusually high average realized return premiums due to the Fed's intervention in interest rates.[3.41]

We consider the years 1942 through 1951 particularly problematic as they reflected a period of government-imposed stability in U.S. government bond interest rates. During World War II, the U.S. Treasury (Treasury) decreed that interest rates had to be kept at artificially low levels in order to reduce government financing costs. This led to the Fed's April 1942 public commitment to maintain interest rates at prescribed levels on U.S. government debt, both long term and short term.[3.42]

With regard to short-term interest rates, the Fed agreed to make a market in 3-month T-bills at a yield of 3/8 percent. With regard to longer-term securities, the Fed agreed to support interest rate ceilings; for example, it agreed to support 25-year U.S. government bond prices at a level consistent with a 2.5% interest rate ceiling.

After World War II, the Fed continued maintaining an interest rate ceiling due to the Treasury's pressure and, to a lesser extent, a fear of returning to the high unemployment levels of the Great Depression. The Treasury and the Fed ended the pegging of interest rates on T-bills in July 1947. But interest rate controls on long-term rates continued until postwar inflationary pressures caused the Treasury and the Fed to reach an accord announced March 4, 1951, freeing the Fed of its obligation of pegging interest rates.[3.43] Including this period in calculating realized returns is analogous to valuing airline stocks today by looking at prices of airline stocks when domestic airline fares were regulated.

To better understand the impact of the interest rate controls on the ERP, we examined the arithmetic average of realized risk premiums (based on one-year returns) for the period 1926–2014 and the arithmetic average of realized risk premiums (based on one-year returns) for the period 1926–2014 *excluding 1942 through 1951*. Exhibit 3.11 displays these results.

Exhibit 3.11: Realized Risk Premiums Including and Excluding the Years 1942–1951

Period Dates	Realized Risk Premiums (arithmetic average) (%)	Standard Deviations (%)
1926–2014	7.00	20.17
1926–2014 (excluding 1942–1951)	5.89	20.68

Source of underlying data: Morningstar *Direct* database. Copyright © 2014 Morningstar, Inc. All rights reserved. Calculations by Duff & Phelps LLC.

3.41 Jeremy Siegel, *Stocks for the Long Run* (New York: McGraw-Hill, 1994): 20.

3.42 Mark Toma, "Interest Rate Controls: The United States in the 1940's," *The Journal of Economic History* 52(3) (September 1992): 633-634.

3.43 Jerry W. Markham, *A Financial History of the United States*, vol. 1 (Armonk, NY: M.E. Sharpe, 2002): 299–300.

Eliminating the years 1942 through 1951 from the sample reduced the realized risk premium from the 7.00% to 5.89% for 1926–2014. One can interpret the realized risk premium data reported in the *SBBI Yearbook* as being biased high by as much as 1.11% (7.00% - 5.89%). We will call this the "WWII Interest Rate Bias." We use 1.11% as the adjustment below to indicate the extent of the possible bias created by this period in the indicated ERP estimates we display.

We are not questioning the accuracy of the realized risk premiums reported using the SBBI data. Rather, we believe that if one were using the realized return data as a basis for forecasting ERP, demonstrated bias should be removed where possible. Removing the data from 1942–1951 from the sample allows the valuation analyst to make the data more representative of what might be expected in future years. We believe that valuation analysts should consider the WWII Interest Rate Bias when estimating ERP using realized risk premium data.[3.44]

"Market" rates subject to control are really not market rates reflective of real interest rates plus the markets expectations of inflation. This was true during the 1942–1951 period and is true as we are writing this book due to the actions of the Fed through quantitative easing.

The summarized data in Exhibit 3.11 represent the arithmetic and geometric averages of realized risk premiums for one-year returns. That is, the dollars invested (including reinvested dividends) are reallocated to available investments annually, and the return is calculated for each year. The arithmetic average is the mean of the annual returns. The geometric average is the single compound return that equates the initial investment with the ending investment, assuming annual reallocation of investment dollars and reinvestment of dividends.

For example, assume the following series of stock prices (assuming no dividends):

Period	Stock Price ($)	Period Return (%)
1	10	n/a
2	20	100
3	10	-50

The arithmetic average of periodic returns equals (100%+ -50%)/2 = 25%, and the geometric average equals $[(1+r_1)(1+r_2)]^{1/2} - 1 = [(1+1.00 \times 1 - 0.5)]^{1/2} - 1 = 0\%$.

Realized risk premiums measured using the geometric (compound) averages are always less than those using the arithmetic average. The geometric mean is the lower boundary of the arithmetic mean, and the two are equal in the unique situation that every observation is identical. Further, the more variable the period returns, the greater the difference between the arithmetic and geometric averages of those returns. This is simply the result of the mathematics of a series that has experienced deviations.

3.44 Some disagree with our conclusion. See for example, Kevin Piccolo, "The Dangers of Normalization: An Interest-Rate Perspective," *The Value Examiner* (March/April 2012): 23-32.

The choice between using the geometric and arithmetic average is a matter of disagreement among academics and valuation analysts. Using the arithmetic average for discounting net cash flow receives the most support in the literature.[3.45] Some authors recommend a geometric average.[3.46]

Comparing Investor Expectations to Realized Risk Premiums

Much has been written comparing the realized risk premiums as reported in sources – such as past editions of the *SBBI Valuation Yearbooks* – and the ERP that must have been expected by investors, given the underlying economics of publicly traded companies (e.g., expected growth in earnings or expected growth in dividends) and the underlying economics of the economy (e.g., expected growth in gross domestic product (GDP)). Such studies conclude that investors could not have expected as large an ERP as the risk premiums actually realized.[3.47]

Ibbotson and Chen report on a study in which they estimated forward-looking long-term sustainable equity returns and expected ERPs since 1926. They first analyzed realized equity returns by decomposing returns into factors including inflation, earnings, dividends, price-to-earnings ratios, dividend payout ratios, book values, returns on equity, and GDP per capita (the fundamental building blocks of equity returns being "supplied" by companies).

They forecasted the ERP through supply-side models built from historical data by removing the price-to-earnings ratio inflation (a top-down approach for estimating the market's re-pricing due to the underlying economic changes in aggregate). Those authors determined that the long-term ERP that could have been expected, given the underlying economics, was less than the realized premium.[3.48]

We updated the "supply side" ERP over the1926–2014 for the *2015 Handbook*. The supply-side ERP estimate is 4.19% (on a geometric basis), and 6.21% (on an arithmetic basis). In comparison, the realized (historical) 1926–2014 ERP was 4.83% (on a geometric basis), and 7.00% (on an arithmetic basis).

We are using the methodology consistent with that used in the discontinued *SBBI Valuation Yearbook*. We used a normalized three-year average price-to-earnings ratios in the most recent period, instead of single year's price-to-earnings ratios in their calculation of the change in price-to-earnings ratios. That is, we examined the compound annual growth in price-to-earnings ratios from 1926 to the current year where the current year's price-to-earnings ratio is calculated using a three-year average of earnings.

3.45 See, for example, Paul Kaplan, "Why the Expected Rate of Return Is an Arithmetic Mean," *Business Valuation Review* (September 1995); *2012 Ibbotson® SBBI® Valuation Yearbook*: 56–57; Mark Kritzman, "What Practitioners Need to Know about Future Value, " *Financial Analysts Journal* (May/June 1994): 12–15; Zvi Bodie, Alex Kane, and Alan J. Marcus, *Investments* (Chicago: Irwin Professional Publishing, 1989): 720–723; Elroy Dimson, Paul Marsh and Mike Staunton, *Credit Suisse Global Investment Returns Sourcebook 2013* (London: Credit Suisse/London Business School, 2013).

3.46 See, for example, Aswath Damodaran, *Investment Valuation: Tools and Techniques for Determining the Value of Any Asset*, 3rd ed. (Hoboken, NJ: John Wiley & Sons, 2012): 162–163; Aswath Damodaran, "Equity Risk Premiums: Determinants, Estimation and Implications – the 2014 Edition," (March 2014): 26-27, available at http://ssrn.com/abstract=2409198

3.47 Several of those studies are summarized in Pratt and Grabowski, op.cit., Chapter 8A, "Deriving ERP Estimates": 147-153.

3.48 Roger G. Ibbotson and Peng Chen, "Long-Run Stock Market Returns: Participating in the Real Economy, " *Financial Analysts Journal* (January–February 2003): 88–98; see also Charles P. Jones and Jack W. Wilson, "Using the Supply Side Approach to Understand and Estimate Stock Returns," Working paper, June 6, 2006.

Using the three-year average allows the adjustment to smooth out the volatility of extraordinary events and allows earnings to better reflect a normalized trend.

In order to keep the measurement of the three-year average earnings consistent with the price of the S&P 500 index at the time that the supply side adjustment is calculated (e.g., the price of the S&P 500 at December 31, 2014, for the supply-side long-term ERP estimate as of the end of 2014), we used the three-year average based on the prior-year's earnings, the current year's earnings estimated at year end and the forecast earnings in the following year.

For example, the adjustment is based on the S&P 500 price at December 31, 2014, divided by the average of the earnings for the S&P 500 companies in 2013, which are known, 2014, which are estimated, and 2015, which are forecasted.[3.49] Obviously since the actual 2014 will not be known until 2015 and the forecast 2015 earnings will not be known until 2016, the adjustment as of the end of 2014 will change in the *Valuation Handbooks* to be published as of the end of 2015 and 2016.[3.50] The choice in constructing the three-year average is an exercise in judgment.[3.51]

We then adjusted the realized risk premiums from 1926 to the current year by removing this observed growth in price-to-earnings ratios, which had occurred primarily in the past 25 years.

William Goetzmann and Roger Ibbotson, commenting on the supply side approach of estimating expected risk premiums, note:

> *"These forecasts tend to give somewhat lower forecasts than historical risk premiums, primarily because part of the total returns of the stock market have come from price-earnings ratio expansion. This expansion is not predicted to continue indefinitely, and should logically be removed from the expected risk premium."* [3.52]

Chen estimated the ERP as of early 2011 relying on the supply side model exclusively.[3.53] To the authors of this book, this certainly indicates his preference of the supply side estimate to the straight historical average estimate.

3.49 The estimated top-down earnings estimate for the S&P 500 for the calendar year (in the analysis herein, 2015) *following* the most recently completed calendar year (in the analyses herein, 2014) used in the supply side ERP estimate is provided by Standard and Poor's at http://us.spindices.com/indices/equity/sp-500. For the *2015 Valuation Handbook*, the 2015 estimate was *not* available from S&P in time to include in the supply side ERP estimate herein, and so this estimate is based on the *average* of various analysts' top-down earnings estimates for the S&P 500 in 2015.

3.50 The geometric average supply-side ERP of 4.19% (see Exhibit 3.12) was converted into an (estimated) arithmetic average using the standard deviation of the annual returns of the S&P 500 total returns index, as measured over the period 1926–2014 (20.07%), which resulted in a supply-side arithmetic average ERP of 6.21%. The extra return was due to the price-to-earnings multiple increasing was 0.61% per annum in the calculation of the supply side ERP is based on the three-year averaging convention. The increase (using 1-year periods) through 2014 was 0.69% per annum.

3.51 Magdalena Mroczek, "Unraveling the Supply-Side Equity Risk Premium," *The Value Examiner* (January/February 2012): 19-24.

3.52 William N.Goetzmann and Roger G.Ibbotson, "History and the Equity Risk Premium," Chapter 12 in *Handbook of the Equity Risk Premium*, ed. Rajnish Mehra (Amsterdam: Elsevier, 2008): 522–523

3.53 Peng Chen, "Will Bonds Outperform Stocks over the Long Run? Not Likely," in *Rethinking the Equity Risk Premium*, ed. P. Brett Hammond, Jr., Martin L. Leibowitz, and Lawrence B. Siegel (The Research Foundation of CFA Institute, 2011): 117-129.

Since this adjustment for the growth in price-to-earnings ratios reflects primarily changes observed during the past 25 years and the supply-side analysis as we have implemented it makes no other adjustments to the realized returns, one might interpret that a forward estimate of the long-term ERP derived from data in this *2015 Valuation Handbook* should be 6.21% (supply-side model on an arithmetic average basis) minus the 1.11% WWII Interest Rate Bias discussed earlier, or 5.10% for one-year holding period returns.

Unconditional ERP Estimates

The following summarizes the long-term unconditional ERP estimates as of 2014:

Exhibit 3.12: Long-term Realized Risk Premiums Measured Relative to Long-term U.S. Government Bonds

Adjusted Realized Risk Premium	Period	Arithmetic Average (%)	Geometric Average (%)
Long-term "Historical" ERP	1926–2014	7.00	4.83
Long-term "Supply-side" ERP	1926–2014	6.21	4.19
"Supply-side" minus WWII Interest Rate Bias ERP	1926–2014	5.10	n/a

Source of underlying data: Morningstar *Direct* database. Calculations by Duff & Phelps LLC.

The analyses summarized in Exhibit 3.12 are estimates of ERP measured relative to U.S. government bonds and that, with the exception of periods of governmental intervention in U.S. government long-term bonds (i.e., the period resulting in the WWII Interest Rate Bias (1942–1951) as discussed above), the returns on bonds generally reflected a market based pricing of yields, not impacted by actions by the Fed to suppress yields on long-term U.S. government bonds.

If one concludes that the appropriate ERP to estimate a cost of equity capital estimate in early 2015 is the supply-side model (arithmetic average basis) minus the 1.11% WWII Interest Rate Bias, one should most appropriately add that ERP to a normalized yield on 20-year U.S. government bonds that reflects current inflation expectations.

We express the unconditional ERP in terms over an arithmetic average equivalent, which is appropriate for estimating single-period discount rates for discounting net cash flows to present value (e.g., the build-up method, the CAPM, etc.)

Conditional ERP

Prior to September 2008 and the Financial Crisis, it was quite common for analysts to be content to make an ERP estimate once each year. Even if the ERP changed month to month, the magnitude of the change was not very great. But beginning in September 2008, the stock market and the economy started to tumble into crisis and valuation analysts began to question their ERP estimates: (i) should one be adjusting their ERP more often than annually and (ii) if the answer to this question was "yes," then how should one estimate the ERP? Clearly, simply using a long-term average of realized risk premiums was not going to work during the Financial Crisis. This became very obvious at the end of December 2008.

If one simply added an estimate of the ERP taken from sources commonly used before the Financial Crisis to the spot yield on 20-year U.S. government bonds at month-end December 2008, one would have arrived at an estimate of the cost of equity capital that was too low.

As of December 2007, for example, the yield on 20-year U.S. government bonds equaled 4.5%, and the realized risk premium reported based on the average realized risk premiums for 1926–2007 was 7.1%. But at December 2008, the yield on 20-year U.S. government bonds was 3.0%, and the realized risk premium reported based on the average realized risk premiums for 1926–2008 was 6.5%.

So just at the time that the risk in the economy *increased* to arguably the highest point, the base cost of equity capital using realized risk premiums *decreased* from 11.6% (4.5% plus 7.1%) to 9.5% (3.0% plus 6.5%).[3.54]

Research has shown that ERP varies through business cycles.[3.55] We use the term *conditional ERP* to mean the ERP that reflects current market conditions. Those market conditions reflect both the risk of investments as viewed through the collective eyes of the marginal investors (those investors moving money into and out of investments at a particular date; i.e., those investors setting prices) and the collective risk aversion as viewed though those same marginal investors. For example, the ERP should be greater when uncertainty is greater and smaller when uncertainty is smaller.[3.56]

When the economy is near or in recession (as reflected in relatively low returns on stocks and greater economic uncertainty), the *conditional* ERP is likely at the higher end of the range (e.g., at December 31, 2008). When the economy improves (with expectations of improvements reflected in recent increasing stock returns), the *conditional* ERP likely moves toward the midpoint of the range. When the economy is near its peak (and reflected in relatively high stock returns and increased economic certainty), the *conditional* ERP is likely at the lower end of the range.

3.54 While some commentators proposed that analysts adjust their cost of capital estimates as of December 2008 by using a company-specific risk premium, the authors of this book believe that mischaracterizes the observed risks in the markets. Rather, risk-free interest rates declined dramatically due to primarily a flight-to-quality and the expected ERP increased. Neither of these events were company-specific risk issues. However, if the inclusion of increased market risk were done properly, the result should be the same.

3.55 See for example, Robert D. Arnott, "Equity Risk Premium Myths," and Antti Ilmanen, "Time Variation in the Equity Risk Premium," in *Rethinking the Equity Risk Premium*, ed. P. Brett Hammond, Jr., Martin L. Leibowitz, and Lawrence B. Siegel (The Research Foundation of CFA Institute, 2011).

3.56 See Martin Lettau, S. C. Ludvigson, and J. A. Wachter, "The Declining Equity Risk Premium: What Role Does Macroeconomic Risk Play?," *Review of Financial Studies* 21 (2008): 1675–1687. The authors linked changes in the ERP to changes in the volatility of economic variables such as employment, consumption, and growth in Gross Domestic Product.

Duff & Phelps Recommended ERP

In estimating the conditional ERP, valuation analysts cannot simply use the long-term historical ERP, whether as reported or adjusted as we discussed above. A better alternative would be to examine approaches that are sensitive to the current economic conditions.

Duff & Phelps employs a multi-faceted analysis to estimate the conditional ERP that takes into account a broad range of economic information and multiple ERP estimation methodologies to arrive at its recommendation.[3.57]

First, a reasonable range of normal or unconditional ERP is established.

Second, based on current economic conditions, Duff & Phelps estimates where in the range the true ERP likely lies (top, bottom, or middle) by examining the current state of the economy (both by examining the level of stock price indices as a forward indicator and examining economic forecasts), as well as the implied equity volatility and corporate spreads as indicators of perceived risk.

For example, since December 31, 2013, while the evidence is somewhat mixed, we see indications that equity risk in financial markets has stayed relatively constant, when estimated against a normalized risk-free rate of 4.0%. Exhibit 3.13 summarizes the primary economic and financial market indicators we analyzed at December 31, 2014 and how they have moved since December 31, 2013, with the corresponding relative impact on ERP indications:

Exhibit 3.13: Economic and Financial Market Indicators Considered in Duff & Phelps' ERP Recommendation

Factor	Change	Effect on ERP
U.S. Equity Markets	↑	↓
Implied Equity Volatility	↑	↑
Corporate Spreads	↑	↑
GDP Growth and GDP Growth Forecasts	↑	↓
Unemployment Environment	↓	↓
Consumer and Business Sentiment	↑	↓
Sovereign Credit Ratings	↔	↔

[3.57] For details on the Duff & Phelps recommended ERP over time, go to www.DuffandPhelps.com/CostofCapital

Finally, we examine other indicators that may provide a more quantitative view of where we are within the range of reasonable long-term estimates for the U.S. ERP.

Duff & Phelps currently uses several models as corroborating evidence:

- **Damodaran Implied ERP Model** – Professor Aswath Damodaran calculates implied ERP estimates for the S&P 500 and publishes his estimates on his website. Damodaran estimates an implied ERP by first solving for the discount rate that equates the current S&P 500 index level with his estimates of cash distributions (dividends and stock buybacks) in future years. He then subtracts the current yield on 10-year U.S. government bonds. Duff & Phelps then converts his estimate to an arithmetic average equivalent measured against the 20-year U.S. government bond rate.

  Damodaran has recently added new capabilities to his implied equity risk premium calculator. He now allows the user to select a variety of base cash flow yields, as a well as several expected growth rate choices for the following five years in the forecast. Each option for cash flow yields is independent of the growth rate assumptions, which means that the user can select up to 35 different combinations to estimate an implied ERP. Exhibit 3.14 shows the current options that a user can select to arrive at an implied ERP indication:

Exhibit 3.14: Professor Damodaran's Implied Equity Risk Premium Calculator
Cash Flow Yield (Dividends + Buybacks) and Growth Rate Options

S&P 500 Cash Flow Yield (Dividends + Buybacks)	S&P Earnings Growth Rates for Years 1 through 5 in the Projections
Trailing 12 months Dividend + Buyback Yield	Historical Growth Rate for the last 10 years
Average Dividend + Buyback Yield for the last 10 years	Bottom-up Forecasted Growth Rate for next 5 years
Average Dividend + Buyback Yield for the last 5 years	Top-Down Forecasted Growth Rate for next 5 years
Average Payout for the last 10 years	Fundamental Growth Rate (based on Current ROE)
Average Payout using S&P 500 Normalized Earnings	Fundamental Growth Rate (based on 10-Year Avg. ROE)
Dividends and Buybacks, Net of Stock Issuance	

Note: ROE = Return on Equity

Source of underlying data: Downloadable dataset entitled "Spreadsheet to compute ERP". To obtain a copy, visit: http://people.stern.nyu.edu/adamodar/

Based on one of Damodaran's estimates of the returns on the S&P 500 – as published on the home page of this website – as of the beginning of 2015 (using as the long-term growth rate the 10-year U.S. government bond rate), his implied ERP (converted to its arithmetic equivalent) was approximately 6.92% measured against an abnormally low 20-year U.S. government bond yield (2.47%).[3.58] The equivalent normalized implied ERP estimate was 5.39% measured against a normalized 20-year U.S. government bond yield (4.0%).[3.59] Testing the various available options outlined in Exhibit 3.14, we obtained a range of indications for a normalized arithmetic-average implied ERP estimate between 3.48% and 6.25% (once again, measured against a normalized 20-year U.S. government bond yield of 4.0%).

- **Default Spread Model (DSM)** – The Default Spread Model is based on the premise that the long term average ERP (the unconditional ERP) is constant and deviations from that average over an economic cycle can be measured by reference to deviations from the long term average of the default spread (Baa - Aaa).[3.60]

  At the end of both December 2014, the conditional ERP calculated using the DSM model was 5.0%. This model notably removes the risk-free rate itself as an input in the estimation of ERP. However, the ERP estimate resulting from the DSM is still interpreted as an estimate of the relative return of stocks in excess of risk-free securities.

- **Hassett Implied ERP (Hassett)** – Stephen Hassett has developed a model for estimating the implied ERP, as well as the estimated S&P 500 index level, based on the current yield on long-term U.S. government bonds and a risk premium factor (RPF).[3.61] The RPF is the empirically derived relationship between the risk-free rate, S&P 500 earnings, real interest rates, and real GDP growth to the S&P 500 index over time. The RPF appears to change only infrequently. The model can be used monthly to estimate the S&P 500 and the conditional ERP based on the current level of interest rates.[3.62]

3.58 Implied rate of return on the S&P 500 = 9.39% as of January 1, 2015, minus 2.47% actual rate on 20-year U.S. government bonds plus an adjustment to equate the geometric average ERP to its arithmetic equivalent. The result reflects conversion of the implied ERP to an arithmetic average equivalent.

3.59 Implied rate of return on the S&P 500 = 9.39% as of January1, 2015 minus 4.00% normalized rate on 20-year U.S. government bonds plus an adjustment to equate the geometric average ERP to its arithmetic equivalent. The result reflects conversion of the implied ERP to an arithmetic average equivalent.

3.60 The Default Spread Model presented herein is based on Jagannathan, Ravi, and Wang, Zhenyu," The Conditional CAPM and the Cross-Section of Expected Returns," *The Journal of Finance*, Volume 51, Issue 1, March 1996: 3-53. See also Elton, Edwin J. and Gruber, Martin J., Agrawal, Deepak, and Mann, Christopher "Is There a Risk Premium in Corporate bonds?", Working Paper, http://pages.stern.nyu.edu/~eelton/working_papers/corp%20bonds/Is%20there%20a%20risk%20premium%20in%20corporate%20bonds.pdf. Duff & Phelps uses (as did Jagannathan, Ravi, and Wang) the spread of high-grade corporates against lesser grade corporates. Corporate bond series used in analysis herein: Barclays US Corp Baa Long Yld USD (Yield) and Barclays US Corp Aaa Long Yld USD (Yield); Source: Morningstar *Direct*.

3.61 Stephen D. Hassett, "The RPF Model for Calculating the Equity Risk Premium and Explaining the Value of the S&P with Two Variables," *Journal of Applied Corporate Finance* 22, 2 (Spring 2010): 118–130.

3.62 For a more detailed description of Hassett's Risk Premium Factor model see Pratt and Grabowski, op.cit., Chapter 8A, "Deriving ERP Estimates": 167-168"

> Hassett's analysis uses the spot 10-year risk-free rate for the period from January 2008 through July 2011; thereafter, his analysis uses a normalized yield on U.S. Treasuries of 4.5% (2.0% real risk-free rate plus 2.5% inflation).[3.63] As of December 2014, using a normalized 4.5% risk-free rate, the S&P 500 index appeared to be slightly overvalued based on the Hassset model's predictions. Alternatively, based on the S&P 500 index level at the end of December 2014, the implied risk-free rate commensurate with the index closing price was 4.24%, which is approximate to the Duff & Phelps normalized risk-free rate.

While these additional models may be useful in suggesting the direction of changes in the conditional ERP, they are, like *all* methods of estimating the ERP, imperfect. Both the Damodaran Implied ERP Model, the Default Spread Model, and the Hassett model utilize assumptions that are subjective in nature. For example, the Damodaran Implied ERP Model assumes a long-term growth rate for dividends and buybacks that is largely a matter of judgment. Likewise, in the default spread model, the changes in spread are applied to a "benchmark" ERP estimate; the choice of that benchmark ERP is largely a matter of judgment.

Again, the inherent "imperfection" of any single ERP estimation model is precisely why Duff & Phelps takes into account a *broad* range of economic information and *multiple* ERP estimation methodologies to arrive at our conditional ERP recommendation.

After considering all of the evidence, Duff & Phelps recommends a conditional ERP as of early 2014 equal to 5.0% used in conjunction with a normalized risk-free rate of 4.0%.

Concluding on an ERP

What is a reasonable estimate of the *unconditional* or long-term average ERP?

Based on the data summarized above, we have the following evidence:

Historical Long-term ERP (1926–2014)	7.00%
Supply-side Long-term ERP (1926–2014)	6.21%
Supply-side Long-term ERP adjusted for WWII Interest Rate Bias	5.10%

Some valuation analysts expressed dismay over the necessity of considering a forward ERP since that would require changing their current cookbook practice of relying exclusively on the post-1925 historical arithmetic average of one-year realized risk premiums as their estimate of the ERP.

3.63 "S&P 500 Ends 2014 In Fair Value Range With Growth Likely In 2015" by Steve Hassett, Retrieved from: http://seekingalpha.com/article/2798645-s-and-p-500-ends-2014-in-fair-value-range-with-growth-likely-in-2015?ifp=0

But valuation is a forward-looking concept, not an exercise in mechanical application of formulas. Correct valuation methodology requires applying value drivers reflected in today's market pricing. We need to mimic the market. In our experience, you often cannot match current market pricing for equities using the post-1925 historical arithmetic average of one-year realized premiums as the basis for developing discount rates. The entire valuation process is based on applying reasoned judgment to the evidence derived from economic, financial, and other information and arriving at a well-reasoned opinion of value. Estimating the ERP is no different.

For example, recent court case decisions have supported and adopted the Ibbotson and Chen (updated in the *SBBI Valuation Yearbook*) supply-side ERP estimate; as a result, it would be an error to blindly assume that the post-1925 average of realized risk premiums is to be used as an ERP estimate by default.

Valuation analysts are advised to be familiar with the various choices regarding the ERP including the supply-side long-term ERP. This includes an understanding of the methodology and data in forward-looking models based on analysts' estimates, estimates based solely on historical data, "supply-side" ERP models and surveys. All of these methods can be informative. But *each* model has weaknesses that may disqualify it from being utilized as "the" single model.

For the *conditional* ERP as of December 31, 2014, we conclude 5.0%, matched with a normalized yield on 20-year U.S. government bonds equal to 4.0%, implying a 9.0% base cost of equity capital in the United States (see Exhibit 3.15).

We express these ERP estimates in terms over an arithmetic average equivalent which is appropriate for estimating single period discount rates for discounting net cash flows to present value (e.g., the build-up method and the CAPM).

Exhibit 3.15: Duff & Phelps Recommended U.S. ERP and Corresponding Risk-Free Rates January 2008–Present

	Duff & Phelps Recommended ERP	**Risk-Free Rate**
Year-end 2014 Guidance December 31, 2014	5.0%	4.0% Normalized 20-year Treasury yield *
Year-end 2013 Guidance December 31, 2013	5.0%	4.0% Normalized 20-year Treasury yield *
January 1, 2013 – February 27, 2013	5.5%	4.0% Normalized 20-year Treasury yield *
Year-end 2012 Guidance December 31, 2012	5.5%	4.0% Normalized 20-year Treasury yield *
Change in ERP Guidance January 15, 2012 – February 27, 2013	5.5%	4.0% Normalized 20-year Treasury yield *
Change in ERP Guidance September 30, 2011 – January 14, 2012	6.0%	4.0% Normalized 20-year Treasury yield *
July 1 2011 – September 29, 2011	5.5%	4.0% Normalized 20-year Treasury yield *
June 1, 2011 – June 30, 2011	5.5%	Spot 20-year Treasury Yield
May 1, 2011 – May 31, 2011	5.5%	4.0% Normalized 20-year Treasury yield *
December 1, 2010 – April 30, 2011	5.5%	Spot 20-year Treasury Yield
June 1, 2010 – November 30, 2010	5.5%	4.0% Normalized 20-year Treasury yield *
Change in ERP Guidance December 1, 2009 – May 31, 2010	5.5%	Spot 20-year Treasury Yield
June 1, 2009 – November 30, 2009	6.0%	Spot 20-year Treasury Yield
November 1, 2008 – May 31, 2009	6.0%	4.5% Normalized 20-year Treasury yield *
Change in ERP Guidance October 27, 2008 – October 31, 2008	6.0%	Spot 20-year Treasury Yield
January 1, 2008 – October 26, 2008	5.0%	Spot 20-year Treasury Yield

* Normalized in this context means that in months where the risk-free rate is deemed to be abnormally low, a proxy for a longer-term sustainable risk-free rate is used.

Chapter 4
Basic Building Blocks of the Cost of Equity Capital – Size Premium

Size as a Predictor of Equity Returns

The size effect is based on the empirical observation that companies of smaller size are associated with greater risk and, therefore, have greater cost of capital. The "size" of a company is one of the most important risk elements to consider when developing cost of equity capital estimates for use in valuing a business simply because size has been shown to be a *predictor* of equity returns. In other words, there is a significant (negative) relationship between size and historical equity returns – as size *decreases*, returns tend to *increase*, and vice versa.[4.1]

Traditionally, researchers have used market value of equity (market capitalization, or simply "market cap") as a measure of size in conducting historical rate of return studies. However, as we discuss later in this chapter, market cap is not the only measure of size that can be used to predict return, nor is it necessarily the best measure of size to use.

The creation of the Center for Research in Security Prices (CRSP) databases at the University of Chicago in the early 1960s was a big advancement in the research of security prices. The CRSP database includes U.S. equity total returns (capital appreciation plus dividends) going back to 1926.

Possibly the most notable reason that the establishment of the CRSP databases was so important was that it enabled researchers to look at stocks with different characteristics and analyze how their returns differed. One of the first characteristics that researchers analyzed was large-market-capitalization (large-cap) companies versus small-market-capitalization (small-cap) companies.

For example, a 1981 study by Rolf Banz examined the returns of New York Stock Exchange (NYSE) small-cap companies compared to the returns of NYSE large-cap companies over the period 1926–1975.[4.2] What Banz found was that the returns of small-cap companies were *greater* than the returns for large-cap companies. Banz's 1981 study is often cited as the first comprehensive study of the size effect.

4.1 This chapter is excerpted in part from Shannon P. Pratt and Roger J. Grabowski, *Cost of Capital: Applications and Examples* 5th ed. (Hoboken, NJ: John Wiley & Sons, 2014)

4.2 Rolf W. Banz, "The Relationship between Return and Market Value of Common Stocks," *Journal of Financial Economics* (March 1981): 3–18. This paper is often cited as the first comprehensive study of the size effect.

Possible Explanations for the Greater Returns of Smaller Companies

Some valuation analysts erroneously treat small firms as equivalent to scaled-down large firms. Valuation analysts know that small firms have risk characteristics that differ from those of large firms. For example, large firms may have greater ability to enter the market of the small firm and take market share. Large companies likely have more resources to "weather the storm" in economic downturns. Large firms can generally spend more on R&D, advertising, and typically even have greater ability to hire the "best and brightest". Larger firms may have greater access to capital, broader management depth, and less dependency on just a few customers. A larger number of analysts typically follow large firms relative to small firms, so there is probably more information available about large firms. Small firms have fewer resources to fend off competition and redirect themselves after changes in the market occur.[4.3]

Any one of these differences (not an all-encompassing list) would tend to *increase* investors' required rate of return to induce them to invest in small companies rather than investing in large companies.

The size effect is not without controversy, nor is this controversy something new. Traditionally, small companies are believed to have greater required rates of return than large companies because small companies are inherently riskier. It is not clear, however, whether this is due to size itself, or to other factors closely related to or correlated with size (e.g., liquidity).[4.4] The qualification that Banz noted in his 1981 article remains pertinent today:

> *"It is not known whether size* [as measured by market capitalization] *per se is responsible for the effect or whether size is just a proxy for one or more true unknown factors correlated with size."*

In this chapter, we first present empirical evidence for the size effect, followed by a discussion of common criticisms of the size effect.

The Size Effect: Empirical Evidence

Summary statistics over the period 1926–2014 period for CRSP NYSE/NYSE MKT/NASDAQ[4.5] deciles 1–10 are shown in Exhibit 4.1. As size (in this case, as measured by market cap) *decreases*, return tends to *increase*. For example, the annual arithmetic mean return of decile 1 (the largest-cap companies) was 11.15% over the 1926–2014 period, while the annual arithmetic mean return of decile 10 (the smallest-cap companies) was 20.62%. Note that this increased return comes at a price: risk (as measured by standard deviation) increases from 19.10% for decile 1 to 42.79% for decile 10. The relationship between risk and return is a fundamental principle of finance and for estimating the cost of capital.

4.3 M. S. Long and J. Zhang, "Growth Options, Unwritten Call Discounts and Valuing Small Firms," EFA 2004 Maastricht Meetings Paper no. 4057, March 2004. Available at http://www.ssrn.com/abstract=556203

4.4 Even after controlling for size, research suggests that liquidity is still a systematic factor and a predictor of returns. See Roger G. Ibbotson, Zhiwu Chen, and Wendy Y. Hu, "Liquidity as an Investment Style," Yale Working Paper, updated April 2012. Available at www.zebracapm.com

4.5 On October 1, 2008, NYSE Euronext acquired the American Stock Exchange (AMEX). The "NYSE MKT" is the former American Stock Exchange, or AMEX. The CRSP standard market-cap-based NYSE/AMEX/NASDAQ indices are now called the NYSE/NYSE MKT/NASDAQ indices.

Exhibit 4.1: Summary Statistics of Annual Returns (CRSP NYSE/NYSE MKT/NASDAQ Deciles) 1926–2014

Decile	Geometric Mean (%)	Arithmetic Mean (%)	Standard Deviation (%)
1-Largest	9.37	11.15	19.10
2	10.66	12.96	21.66
3	11.13	13.71	23.55
4	11.00	14.01	25.78
5	11.67	14.84	26.37
6	11.52	15.01	27.31
7	11.65	15.53	29.25
8	11.70	16.35	33.27
9	11.64	17.13	37.45
10-Smallest	13.55	20.62	42.79

Source of underlying data: CRSP U.S. Stock Database and CRSP U.S. Indices Database © 2015 Center for Research in Security Prices (CRSP®), University of Chicago Booth School of Business. CRSP NYSE/NYSE MKT/NASDAQ deciles 1–10. Used with permission. All rights reserved. Calculations performed by Duff & Phelps LLC.

The Size Effect Over Longer Periods

Exhibit 4.2 illustrates the size effect. As size (measured by market cap in this case) *decreases*, return tends to *increase*. For example, an investment of $1 in CRSP decile 1 (comprised of the largest companies) at the end of 1925 would have grown to $2,899 by the end of 2014, and an investment in CRSP decile 6 (comprised of medium-sized companies) would have grown to $16,372. However, an investment of $1 in CRSP decile 10 (comprised of the smallest companies) would have grown to $81,406 over the same period.

Exhibit 4.2: Terminal Index Values of CRSP NYSE/NYSE MKT/NASDAQ Deciles 1–10
Index (Year-end 1925 = $1)
January 1926–December 2014

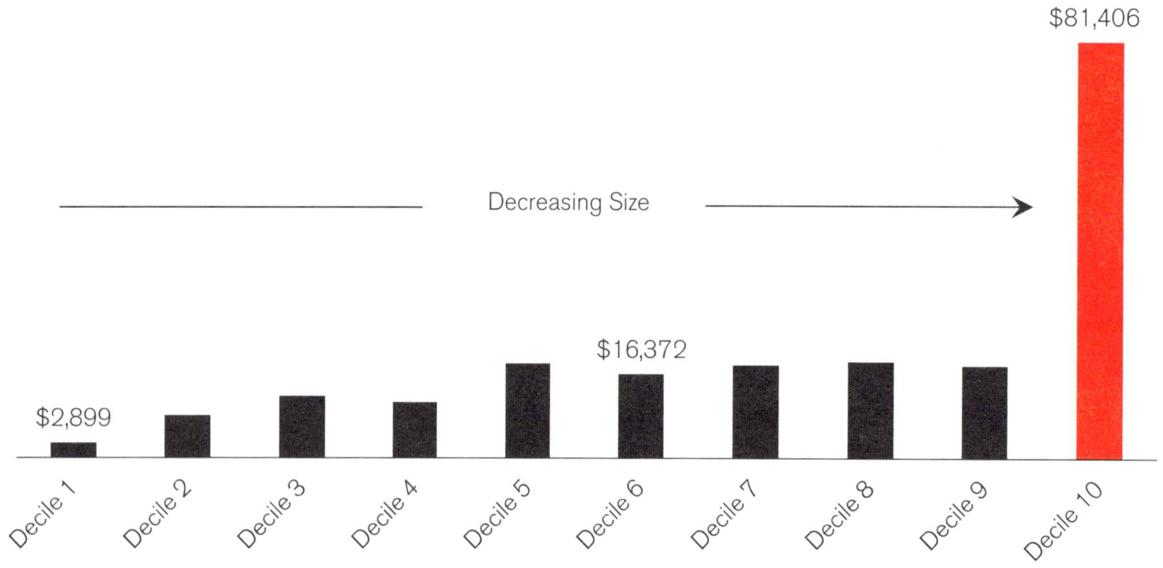

Source of underlying data: CRSP U.S. Stock Database and CRSP U.S. Indices Database © 2015 Center for Research in Security Prices (CRSP®), University of Chicago Booth School of Business. CRSP NYSE/NYSE MKT/NASDAQ deciles 1–10. Used with permission. All rights reserved. Calculations performed by Duff & Phelps LLC.

Exhibit 4.2 illustrates two other important concepts. The first is that the size effect is not "linear" – the size effect is clearly concentrated in the smallest-cap companies.[4.6]

The second is that over longer periods of time the size effect is *not* just evident for the smallest companies, but is evident for all but the largest groups of companies, including companies with a market capitalization in excess of several billions of dollars.

To illustrate this, decile 1 (large-cap companies) is compared to a portfolio comprised of equal parts of deciles 6–9 in Exhibit 4.3. An investment of $1 in a portfolio comprised of deciles 6–9 at the end of 1925 would have grown to $19,310 by the end of 2014 (remember – decile 10, which is comprised of the smallest-cap companies, is *excluded* from this analysis). Even with decile 10 *excluded*, the portfolio made up of deciles 6–9 outperformed large-cap companies over the 1926–2014 period.

[4.6] Some researchers have suggested that the size effect is concentrated in even smaller firms than discussed here. Horowitz, Loughran, and Savin found that if "...firms less than $5 million in value are excluded from the sample universe...", the size effect becomes insignificant, at least as measured over the 1963–1997 time period. Joel L. Horowitz, Tim Loughran, and N.E. Savin, "The disappearing size effect", *Research in Economics* (2000), 83-100.

Exhibit 4.3: Terminal Index Values of CRSP NYSE/NYSE MKT/NASDAQ Deciles 1 and a Portfolio Comprised of Deciles 6–9
Index (Year-end 1925 = $1)
January 1926–December 2014

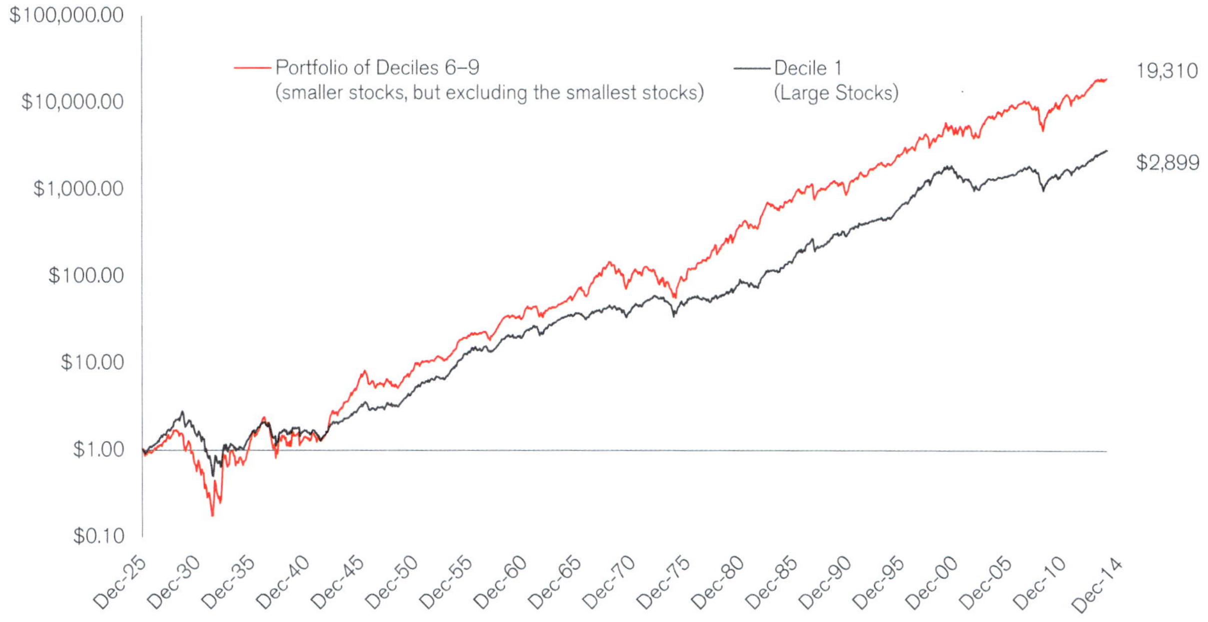

Source of underlying data: CRSP U.S. Stock Database and CRSP U.S. Indices Database © 2015 Center for Research in Security Prices (CRSP®), University of Chicago Booth School of Business. CRSP NYSE/NYSE MKT/NASDAQ deciles 1 and decile 6-9. Used with permission. Calculations performed by Duff & Phelps LLC.

Small-cap companies do not always outperform large-cap companies. As a matter of fact, small-cap companies' shorter-term behavior relative to large-cap companies can be quite erratic, so analyzing small-cap companies' performance relative to large-cap companies' performance over varying holding periods may be instructive in revealing longer-term trends.

In Exhibit 4.4, the percentage of periods in which small-cap companies outperformed large-cap companies is analyzed over 1-, 5-, 10-, 20- and 30-year holding periods. As the holding period is increased, small-cap companies tend to outperform large-cap companies in a greater number of periods. In other words, the *longer* small-cap companies are given to "race" against large-cap companies, the greater the chance that small-cap companies outpace their larger counterparts. For example, small-cap companies outperformed large-cap companies 80.8% of the time over all 20-year holding periods from January 1926 through December 2014. In contrast, large-cap companies outperformed small-cap companies only 19.2% over the same holding and time period.

Exhibit 4.4: Percentage of Periods that Small-cap Companies Outperform Large-cap Companies over 1-, 5-, 10-, 20-, and 30-year Holding Periods

Holding Period	1-year	5-years	10-years	20-years	30-years
Small-cap Companies Outperform (%)	53.8	58.7	70.9	80.8	90.4
Large-cap Companies Outperform (%)	46.2	41.3	29.1	19.2	9.6

Source of underlying data: CRSP U.S. Stock Database and CRSP U.S. Indices Database © 2015 Center for Research in Security Prices (CRSP®), University of Chicago Booth School of Business. Small-cap companies are represented by CRSP NYSE/NYSE MKT/NASDAQ decile 10; Large-cap companies are represented by CRSP NYSE/NYSE MKT/NASDAQ decile 1. The number of 1-, 5-, 10-, 20- and 30-year holding periods over the January 1926–December 2014 time horizon is 1057, 1009, 949, 829, and 709, respectively. Used with permission. All rights reserved. Calculations performed by Duff & Phelps LLC.

The Size Effect Tends to Stabilize Over Time

It may be instructive to examine the tendencies of small-cap stocks' performance versus large-cap stocks' performance over time periods with *fixed* starting dates and *variable* ending dates. This will help to see what happens as more time periods are added (and thus the importance of "unusual" time periods is diminished).

In Exhibit 4.5, the average difference in annual returns for small-cap companies minus large-cap companies was calculated for periods with fixed starting dates of 1926 (the first year data is available from CRSP), 1963 (the Risk Premium Report exhibits are calculated over the time period 1963–2014), and 1982 (the year following publication of Banz's 1981 article).[4.7]

On the far left side of Exhibit 4.5 for the series "Fixed Beginning Date Starting 1926", the first data point is the average difference in annual return for small-cap companies minus large-cap companies in 1926, the second data point (moving to the right) is the average difference in annual return for small-cap companies minus large-cap companies over the period 1926–1927, and then 1926–1928, etc., until the final data point on the far right is the average difference in annual return for small-cap companies minus large-cap companies over the period 1926–2014.

The same analysis is displayed for "Fixed Beginning Date Starting 1963", with the leftmost data point being the average difference in annual return for small-cap companies minus large-cap companies in 1963, and then (again, moving to the right) the average difference in annual return for small-cap companies minus large-cap companies over the periods 1963–1964, 1963–1965, etc., until the final data point on the far right is the average difference in annual return for small-cap companies minus large -cap companies over the period 1963–2014.

And finally, the same analysis for "Fixed Beginning Date 1982" is shown, with the leftmost data point being the average difference in annual return for small-cap companies minus large-cap companies in 1982, and the rightmost data point being the average difference in annual return for small-cap companies minus large-cap companies over the period 1982–2014.

[4.7] Banz, Rolf W. "The Relationship between Return and Market Value of Common Stocks." *Journal of Financial Economics* (March 1981): 3–18. Banz's 1981 article demonstrated that smaller-cap stocks exhibited significantly greater performance over larger-cap stocks over the period from 1926 to 1975.

Exhibit 4.5 suggests that while the size effect measured over shorter time periods may be quite erratic (and even negative at times), there seems to be an overall tendency toward stability as time periods are added and the longer the period over which it is measured (regardless of the start date). Further, this stability seems to be reached in "positive territory" (the rightmost points in Exhibit 4.5), suggesting a positive size effect over time.

Exhibit 4.5: CRSP Decile 10 minus Decile 1, Average Difference in Annual Returns
Fixed beginning date, variable ending dates
1926–2014, 1963–2014, 1982–2014

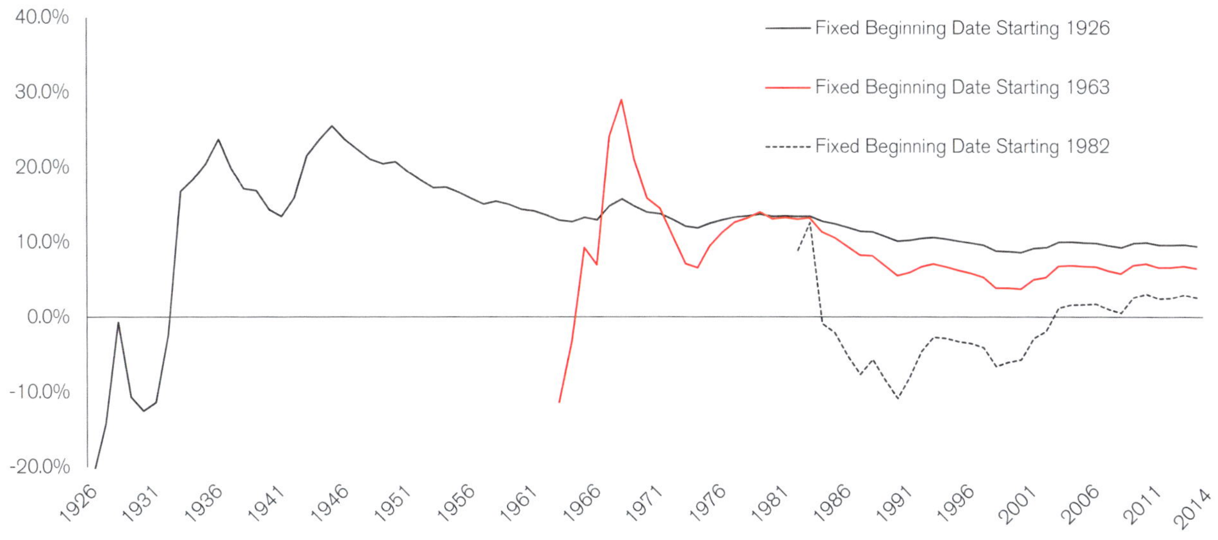

Source of underlying data: CRSP U.S. Stock Database and CRSP U.S. Indices Database © 2015 Center for Research in Security Prices (CRSP®), University of Chicago Booth School of Business. Small-cap companies are represented by CRSP NYSE/NYSE MKT/NASDAQ decile 10; Large-cap companies are represented by CRSP NYSE/NYSE MKT/NASDAQ decile 1. Used with permission. All rights reserved. Calculations performed by Duff & Phelps LLC.

The Size Effect Changes Over Time

The variability of the size effect is illustrated in Exhibit 4.6. In Exhibit 4.6, the size premium for CRSP decile 10 (comprised of the smallest companies) is calculated as of each year-end from 1962–2014 using the same methodology and data set as is currently used in the *Valuation Handbook* in the CRSP Deciles Size Premia study (and the same methodology and data set used previously in the former *SBBI Valuation Yearbook*).

For example, a hypothetical *Valuation Handbook* published in 1969 would have used data available from 1926–1968 to calculate CRSP decile 10's size premium, and this would have resulted in a size premium of approximately 9.2%. In a hypothetical *2000 Valuation Handbook*, using data from 1926–1999, the size premium for CRSP decile 10 would have been approximately 4.5%.

Exhibit 4.6: CRSP Decile 10 Size Premium
Year-end 1962 to Year-end 2014

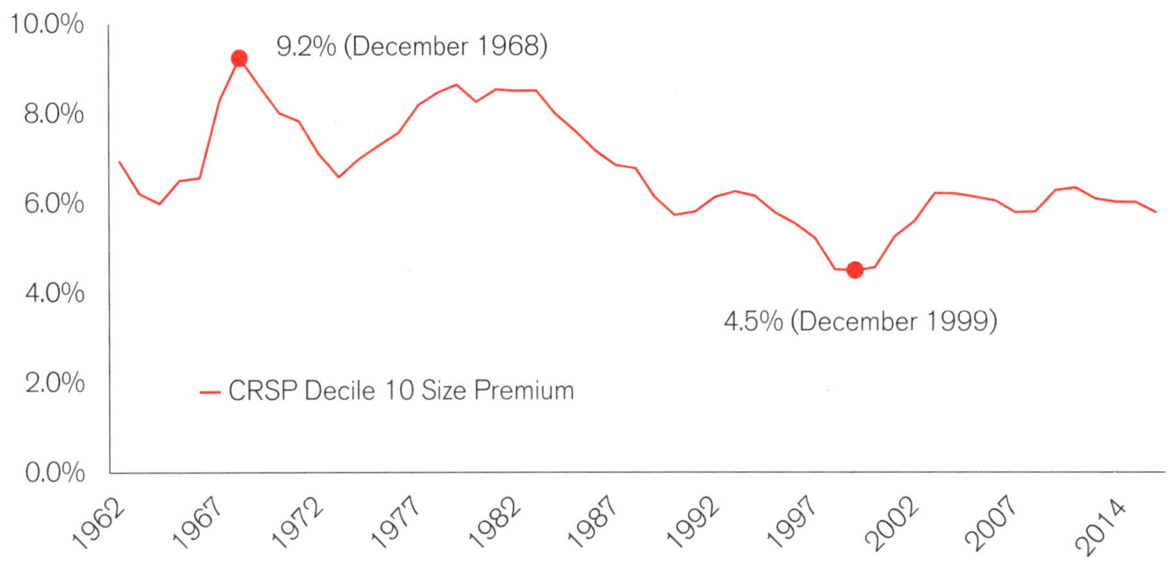

Sources of underlying data: (i) CRSP U.S. Stock Database and CRSP U.S. Indices Database © 2015 Center for Research in Security Prices (CRSP®), University of Chicago Booth School of Business; Small-cap companies are represented by CRSP NYSE/NYSE MKT/NASDAQ decile 10. (ii) Morningstar *Direct* database. The betas used as in input in calculating size premia were calculated using excess total returns over 30-day U.S. Treasury Bills. The market benchmark used in beta calculations is the S&P 500 total return index. Used with permission. All rights reserved. All calculations performed by Duff & Phelps LLC.

These examples provide evidence that the size effect is *cyclical*. That cyclicality is part of the risk of small companies; if small size companies *always* performed better than large companies, small size companies would be *less* risky than large-cap companies, not riskier. This is true even though the expected returns are higher for small-cap companies in the long-term. By analogy, bond returns occasionally outperform stock returns. For example, over the 10-year period ending December 2011, long-term U.S. government bonds returned 135.3% and the S&P 500 Index return 33.4%, yet few would contend that over time the expected return on bonds is greater than the expected return on stocks.[4.8]

Criticisms of the Size Effect

The size effect is *not* without controversy, though, and various commentators question its validity. In fact, some commentators contend that the historical data are so flawed that valuation analysts can dismiss all research results that support the size effect. For example, is the size effect merely the result of not measuring beta correctly? Are there market anomalies that simply cause the size effect to appear? Is size just a proxy for one or more factors correlated with size, suggesting that valuation analysts should use those factors directly rather than size to measure risk? Is the size effect hidden because of unexpected events?

4.8 Source of underlying data: Morningstar *Direct* database. Calculations performed by Duff & Phelps LLC.

Is the Size Effect the Result of Incorrectly Measuring Betas?

Some commentators have held that the size effect is in part a function of underestimating betas for troubled firms (which tend to populate the smaller deciles where size is measured by market cap). Including troubled companies could cause the size premium to be overestimated in the CRSP 10th decile and the sub-deciles 10a (and its upper and lower halves 10w and 10x) and 10b (and its upper and lower halves 10y and 10z), which are populated with the smallest companies as measured by market cap.

The most commonly used size premia is derived based on an ordinary least squares regression (OLS) beta. We examine two alternative methods of calculating the beta in order to compute a size premia, sum betas and annual betas.

Effects of the Size Premia when Using OLS Betas, Annual Betas, and Sum Betas

First, we calculated sum betas. Smaller companies generally trade more infrequently and exhibit more of a lagged price reaction (relative to the market) than do larger companies. One of the ways of capturing this lag movement is called "sum" beta. Sum betas are designed to compensate for the more infrequent trading of smaller company stocks.

Second, we calculated betas based on *annual* return data (rather than *monthly* data).

Both of these methods appear to correct for the low beta estimates of smaller companies. The sum beta estimates are greater for smaller companies than OLS betas, which are derived using non-lagged market benchmark data. The annual betas are also greater for smaller companies than the betas derived using monthly return data. The net result of the *greater* sum betas (or greater annual betas) is *smaller* size premia.

In Exhibit 4.7, OLS betas, sum betas, and annual betas are calculated for the CRSP standard deciles, decile 10 sub-deciles, and size groupings. In Exhibit 4.7, annual betas tend to be greater than OLS betas, and sum betas tend to be larger than both OLS and annual betas. The OLS betas and sum betas for the portfolios comprised of larger companies are approximately the same.

For example, the OLS beta for decile 1 (comprised of the largest companies) is 0.92, and the sum beta for decile 1 is 0.92. Alternatively, the OLS beta for decile 10 (comprised of the smallest companies) is 1.40, while the sum beta for decile 10 is 1.69. All things held the same, the *larger* sum beta of decile 10 implies a *smaller* size premia (3.74%) than implied for its OLS beta counterpart (5.78%)

Sum betas and annual betas tend to be larger for smaller companies than when using OLS betas. As a result, they tend to be less plagued by the overestimation problem due to incorrectly measuring beta.

Exhibit 4.7: OLS Betas, Sum Betas, and Annual Betas, and their Respective Implied Size Premia
As of December 31, 2014

Decile	OLS Beta	Size Premium (%)	Annual Beta	Size Premium (%)	Sum Beta	Size Premium (%)
1-Largest	0.92	-0.36	0.94	-0.52	0.92	-0.35
2	1.04	0.63	1.04	0.60	1.06	0.47
3	1.11	0.91	1.10	0.97	1.14	0.68
4	1.13	1.06	1.17	0.73	1.19	0.57
5	1.17	1.60	1.19	1.43	1.25	1.04
6	1.17	1.74	1.21	1.51	1.28	0.99
7	1.25	1.71	1.29	1.43	1.39	0.73
8	1.30	2.15	1.36	1.73	1.48	0.91
9	1.34	2.69	1.47	1.77	1.54	1.26
10-Smallest	1.40	5.78	1.59	4.41	1.69	3.74
Breakdown of 10th Decile						
10a	1.41	4.22	1.51	3.49	1.67	2.40
10w	1.38	3.18	1.40	3.04	1.58	1.84
10x	1.45	5.54	1.66	4.03	1.80	3.07
10b	1.37	8.94	1.74	6.37	1.71	6.57
10y	1.43	7.51	1.80	4.88	1.75	5.23
10z	1.29	11.98	1.60	9.81	1.64	9.51
Size Grouping						
Mid-Cap (3–5)	1.12	1.07	1.14	0.97	1.17	0.71
Low-Cap (6–8)	1.22	1.80	1.26	1.51	1.36	0.88
Micro-Cap (9–10)	1.35	3.74	1.51	2.61	1.59	2.09

Sources of underlying data: (i) CRSP U.S. Stock Database and CRSP U.S. Indices Database © 2015 Center for Research in Security Prices (CRSP®), University of Chicago Booth School of Business. (ii) Morningstar *Direct* database. Used with permission. All rights reserved. Calculations performed by Duff & Phelps LLC.

OLS and Sum betas are estimated from monthly return data in excess of the 30-day U.S. Treasury bill total return, January 1926–December 2014. Annual betas are estimated from annualized return data in excess of the 30-day U.S. Treasury bill total return, 1926–2014.

Historical risk-free rate represented by the 89-year arithmetic mean income return component of 20-year U.S. government bonds (5.07%).

Calculated in the context of the CAPM by multiplying the historical equity risk premium by beta. The historical equity risk premia in this example is estimated as the arithmetic annual mean return of the S&P 500 Index (12.07%) minus the arithmetic annual mean income return component of 20-year U.S. government bonds (5.07%) from 1926–2014.

A problem with annual betas is that oftentimes there are simply not enough annual periods to calculate a statistically significant beta (e.g., 5 periods of *annual* return data is likely not enough periods to estimate a meaningful beta). So in many cases, the choice distills down to a choice between OLS and sum beta.

In applying the capital asset pricing model (CAPM) (particularly for smaller businesses), we are looking for the most *accurate* estimate, and not the most *expedient* one. If you use an OLS beta for a small company by multiplying the OLS beta times the equity risk premium (ERP) estimate and adding an OLS-based size premium, you may not arrive at as accurate an estimate of the cost of equity capital as by multiplying a sum beta times the ERP estimate and adding a sum-beta-based size premium. You should be using the most accurate estimate of beta and the most accurate measure of the appropriate size premium. Having said that, whatever type of beta you ultimately choose to employ, you should match the source of the size premium (OLS or sum beta) with the type of beta estimate you have chosen for your subject company.

For example, for internal consistency, one should use a size premium derived using an OLS beta when the subject company beta is an OLS beta, and one should use a size premium derived using sum betas when the subject company beta is a sum beta (Exhibit 4.8).

Exhibit 4.8: Potential Impact on Cost of Equity Capital; Matching (or Mismatching) the Type of Beta Used in the CAPM Equation to the Type of Beta Used to Develop the Size Premium

		Beta Used in CAPM Equation	
Beta Used to Develop Size Premia		OLS Beta	Sum Beta
	OLS Beta	A – even –	B Higher COE
	Sum Beta	C Lower COE	D – even –

The resulting cost of equity capital resulting in the "matched" cases (Case A and Case D) do not necessarily have to equal (and likely will not), but they will tend to be within a reasonable range of each other. Using Cases B and C may lead to an incorrect estimate of cost equity capital. To be clear, we recommend using sum betas for the development of size premia, and to also use sum beta within the CAPM, (particularly if dealing with smaller companies), because sum betas tend to better explain the returns of smaller companies. However, in cases in which you do use OLS betas in CAPM, you should use an OLS beta derived size premium.

Data Issues

Critics of the size effect point out various issues with the data used, resulting in anomalies that people mistakenly have observed as the size effect. These data issues may include seasonality, bid/ask bounce bias, and delisting bias, among others.[4.9] In the following sections, we discuss the different compositions of portfolios in the CRSP Deciles Size Premia data set and the Risk Premium Report data set.

4.9 For a complete discussion of these issues, please refer to Pratt and Grabowski, op.cit.: Chapter 15A, "Other Data Issues Regarding the Size Effect."

Composition of the Smallest CRSP Deciles

We divided the CRSP 10th decile into subdeciles 10a and 10b (10a is the top half of the 10th decile, and 10b is the bottom half of the 10th decile) and further divided subdecile 10a into 10w and 10x, and subdecile 10b into 10y and 10z. This is the same breakdown of CRSP decile 10 that was previously presented in the former *SBBI Valuation Yearbook*.

As of December 31, 2014, the reported size premium for the smallest 5% of companies by market capitalization as represented by CRSP sub-decile 10b is 8.94%, and the size premium for the next smallest 5% of companies (as represented by CRSP sub-decile 10a) is 4.22%, a difference of 4.72%.

What kind of companies populate subdeciles 10b and its top and bottom halves, 10y and 10z? The CRSP Deciles Size Premia include all companies with no exclusion of speculative (e.g., start-up) or distressed companies whose market capitalization may be small because they are speculative or distressed. The inclusion of speculative or distressed companies in the database is one basis for criticism of the size effect. Exhibit 4.9 and Exhibit 4.10 display information about the types of companies that are included in decile 10y and decile 10z, respectively.[4.10]

[4.10] Exhibits 4.9 and 4.10 are as of September 2014 rather than December 2014 in order to mimic how the CRSP standard market-cap based portfolios are formed. The CRSP deciles portfolio compositions are reset quarterly (March, June, September, December), and then portfolio returns are calculated for these portfolio compositions over the *subsequent* quarter. As of December 2014, the most recent "reset" is September 2014.

Exhibit 4.9: Breakdown of Decile 10y Companies: Market Value of Equity between $116.330 and $190.529 million
September 30, 2014

Decile 10y	Market Value of Equity (in $millions)	Book Value of Equity (in $millions)	5-Year Average Net Income (in $millions)	Market Value of Invested Capital (in $millions)
95th Percentile	$184.296	$221.487	$12.990	$916.880
75th Percentile	169.295	143.466	5.544	269.470
50th Percentile	153.444	96.448	(1.655)	182.308
25th Percentile	133.020	45.969	(11.593)	158.543
5th Percentile	118.016	0.068	(51.481)	127.988

Decile 10y	Total Assets (in $millions)	5-Year Average EBITDA (in $millions)	Sales (in $millions)	Return on Book Equity (%)
95th Percentile	$1,546.505	$104.785	$848.898	22.0
75th Percentile	735.121	18.682	226.825	7.4
50th Percentile	190.485	5.474	72.727	0.0
25th Percentile	91.142	(4.248)	32.717	-24.0
5th Percentile	28.590	(22.671)	2.145	-114.8

Decile 10y	OLS Beta	Sum Beta
95th Percentile	2.42	2.82
75th Percentile	1.61	1.91
50th Percentile	1.09	1.27
25th Percentile	0.58	0.69
5th Percentile	0.18	0.15

Sources of underlying data: (i) CRSP U.S. Stock Database and CRSP U.S. Indices Database © 2015 Center for Research in Security Prices (CRSP®), University of Chicago Booth School of Business. (ii) S&P *Capital IQ*. Used with permission. All rights reserved. Calculations performed by Duff & Phelps LLC.

Exhibit 4.10: Breakdown of Decile 10z Companies: Market Value of Equity between $3.037 and $115.920 million
September 30, 2014

Decile 10z	Market Value of Equity (in $millions)	Book Value of Equity (in $millions)	5-Year Average Net Income (in $millions)	Market Value of Invested Capital (in $millions)
95th Percentile	$108.541	$131.007	$7.312	$216.725
75th Percentile	79.397	61.706	1.967	105.942
50th Percentile	53.003	31.117	(1.065)	72.103
25th Percentile	30.784	12.874	(7.526)	39.479
5th Percentile	11.522	0.190	(27.375)	15.437

Decile 10z	Total Assets (in $millions)	5-Year Average EBITDA (in $millions)	Sales (in $millions)	Return on Book Equity (%)
95th Percentile	$842.234	$22.161	$254.919	17.7
75th Percentile	241.047	4.704	59.578	6.0
50th Percentile	58.550	0.040	26.037	-2.1
25th Percentile	25.166	(4.601)	10.007	-40.4
5th Percentile	9.600	(18.053)	0.210	-189.7

Decile 10z	OLS Beta	Sum Beta
95th Percentile	2.39	3.05
75th Percentile	1.35	1.77
50th Percentile	0.76	1.04
25th Percentile	0.36	0.51
5th Percentile	0.16	0.26

Sources of underlying data: (i) CRSP U.S. Stock Database and CRSP U.S. Indices Database © 2015 Center for Research in Security Prices (CRSP®), University of Chicago Booth School of Business. (ii) S&P *Capital IQ*. Used with permission. All rights reserved. Calculations performed by Duff & Phelps LLC.

From these data we can conclude:

- Betas used for calculating the size premium for subdecile 10y and subdecile 10z (using the OLS method of calculating betas) generally *understate* the beta, and therefore *overstate* the size premium. Note the small betas for companies in the 25th and 5th percentiles.

- Subdecile 10y and subdecile 10z are populated by many large (but highly leveraged) companies with small market capitalizations that probably do not match the characteristics of financially healthy but small companies (see "Total Assets," 95th percentile measures).

Stocks of the *troubled* companies included in the data probably are trading like call options (unlimited upside, limited downside). Even if you were to use the sum beta method, the beta estimates would likely be underestimated and the size premium overstated (see "Return on Book Equity," 25th percentile and 5th percentile).

Before using the size premium data for 10b or its top and bottom halves, 10y and 10z, the valuation analyst likely should determine if the mix of companies that comprise the subdeciles are indeed comparable to the subject company.

Composition of the Smallest Risk Premium Report Studies Portfolio

The Risk Premium Report studies use a different methodology from the CRSP Deciles Size Premia studies. The Risk Premium Report studies screen out speculative start-ups, distressed (i.e., bankrupt) companies, and other high-financial-risk companies. These studies measure beta using the sum beta method. This methodology was chosen to counter the criticism of the size effect by some that the size premium is a function of the high rates of return for speculative companies and distressed companies in the data set.

The Risk Premium Report studies use the sum beta method to measure the size premium because it finds that betas of small companies in the data set (even after removing speculative, distressed, and other high-financial-risk companies) are underestimated if one uses the OLS method of estimating betas. Even after eliminating speculative, distressed, and other high-financial-risk companies and using the sum beta in measuring size, we still observe the size effect for a more recent period (since 1963).

The Risk Premium Report exhibits include a total of eight size measures, including six that are not based on market capitalization. Exhibit 4.11 shows the breakdown of companies in the Risk Premium Report exhibits in portfolio 25 (portfolio 25 is comprised of the smallest companies) for each of the eight size measures.

If the subject company is not highly levered, the companies in portfolio 25 may be more comparable to a small subject company, and therefore the size premium data for portfolio 25 may be more appropriate to use when dealing with very small companies.

Exhibit 4.11: Size Measure of Companies That Comprise Portfolio 25 of the *Risk Premium Report* December 31, 2014

Portfolio 25	Market Value of Equity (in $millions)	Book Value of Equity (in $millions)	5-Year Average Net Income (in $millions)	Market Value of Invested Capital (in $millions)
Largest Company	$318.619	$143.022	$7.750	$379.058
95th Percentile	298.690	134.828	7.382	342.159
75th Percentile	207.255	99.825	5.171	247.426
50th Percentile	113.183	57.788	3.075	140.260
25th Percentile	45.795	28.908	1.516	56.001
5th Percentile	16.233	11.422	0.330	21.432
Smallest Company	4.592	3.625	0.076	4.592

Portfolio 25	Total Assets (in $millions)	5-Year Average EBITDA (in $millions)	Sales (in $millions)	Number of Employees
Largest Company	$294.996	$34.459	$280.014	654
95th Percentile	281.796	32.277	254.774	591
75th Percentile	202.581	23.682	186.680	459
50th Percentile	119.066	12.374	106.294	253
25th Percentile	49.298	5.698	53.353	127
5th Percentile	16.063	1.595	17.048	10
Smallest Company	4.690	0.276	3.096	4

Sources of underlying data: (i) CRSP U.S. Stock Database and CRSP U.S. Indices Database © 2015 Center for Research in Security Prices (CRSP®), University of Chicago Booth School of Business. (ii) S&P *Research Insight*. Used with permission. All rights reserved. Calculations performed by Duff & Phelps LLC.

Financial services companies (i.e., SIC code 6; those companies in finance, insurance, or real estate) are *excluded* from Risk Premium Report portfolios, primarily because some of the financial data used in the Risk Premium Report is difficult to apply to companies in the financial sector (e.g., "sales" at commercial banks). In addition, financial services companies tend to support a much higher ratio of debt-to-equity than do other industries, and so including them with nonfinancial firms may be an apples-to-oranges comparison that could lead to improperly skewed results. Moreover, companies in the financial services sector were poorly represented during the early years of the Standard & Poor's *Compustat* database.

Because companies in SIC code 6 are excluded from the set of companies used to perform the analyses presented in the Risk Premium Report, the data should not be used by an analyst estimating the cost of equity capital for a financial services company or other company in SIC code 6.

We also publish accounting-based fundamental risk information about the companies that comprise the 25 size-ranked portfolios for *each* of the eight size measures analyzed in the Risk Premium Report exhibits. This information includes:

- Five-year average operating income margin
- Coefficient of variation in operating income margin
- Coefficient of variation in return on book equity

The first statistic measures profitability, and the latter two statistics measure volatility of earnings.

This information provides the analyst with two important capabilities:

1. Additional tools to determine if the mix of companies that comprise the Risk Premium Report's portfolios are indeed comparable to the subject company.

2. The opportunity to gauge whether an increase (or decrease) adjustment to a risk premium or size premium (and thus cost of equity capital) is indicated, based on the company-specific differences of the subject company's fundamental risk and the average fundamental risk of companies that make up the portfolios from which the risk premia are derived. (for more information, see the section entitled "Comparative Risk Study" in Chapter 10).

Has the Size Effect Disappeared in More Recent Periods?

Some research has suggested that in more recent years the size effect is greatly diminished, or has disappeared altogether. The point in time usually identified as the year after which the size effect is diminished is 1981. The primary reason for this is that in 1981 Banz examined the returns of NYSE small-cap companies compared to the returns of NYSE large-cap companies over the period 1926–1975, and found that there was a negative relationship between size as measured by market capitalization and return (i.e., as market capitalization *decreases*, returns *increase*). In effect, Banz is said to have "let the cat out of the bag" that small-cap companies offered greater returns, and that attracted more investment in small-cap companies. Prices were bid up, thus ultimately reducing the overall returns.

Hou and van Dijk posited that the apparent disappearance of the size effect after the early 1980s was due to cash flow shocks. Realized returns for small companies were generally less than expected because of negative cash flow shocks, and realized returns for large companies were generally greater than expected because of positive cash flow shocks.[4.11]

[4.11] Kewei Hou and Mathijs A. van Dijk, "Resurrecting the size effect: Firm size, profitability shocks, and expected stock returns", Ohio State University Fisher College of Business working paper, July 2012. Copy available at http://papers.ssrn.com/sol3/papers.cfm?abstract_id=1536804

What caused the cash flow shocks? The number of newly public firms in the United States increased dramatically in the 1980s and 1990s compared with prior periods, and the profitability and survival rate of the newly public firms was generally less than the profitability and survival rates for firms that went public in previous years. After adjusting realized returns for the cash flow shocks, the result was that returns of small firms on a pro forma basis exceeded the returns of large firms by approximately 10% per annum, consistent with the size premium in prior periods.

A more direct reason often cited for a diminished size effect in more recent years was possibly most succinctly stated by Horowitz, Loughran, and Savin, who suggested that "it is quite possible that as investors became aware of the size effect, small firm prices increased (thus lowering subsequent returns)."[4.12] This conjecture may be supported by the sheer number of small-cap companies that have come into existence since Banz's 1981 article that demonstrated that smaller-cap companies exhibited significantly greater performance over the period from 1926 to 1975.[4.13]

We performed analyses to investigate which of two hypothetical investors would have ended up with more money in their pocket over various holding periods within the full range of monthly CRSP decile data (January 1926–December 2014): the first investor invests only in small-cap companies, and the second investor only invests in large-cap companies.

To do this, we first calculated the terminal index value of $1.00 invested for every possible combination of monthly beginning dates and end dates for CRSP decile 1 (the largest-cap companies) and CRSP decile 10 (the smallest-cap companies) over the January 1926–December 2014 period.[4.14] The total number of monthly begin dates and end dates combinations between January 1926 and December 2014 is 570,846.

We then subtracted the terminal index value of large-cap companies from the terminal index value of small-cap companies for *each* of the 570,768 beginning date/end date combinations. If the terminal index value of small-cap companies was greater than the terminal index value of large-cap companies, this would indicate small-cap companies returned a higher return over that period for the investor.

Example: $1.00 invested in large-cap companies from January 1926 would have grown to $2,899.23 by the end of December 2014. Alternatively, $1.00 invested in small-cap companies from January 1926 would have grown to $81,406.44 by the end of December 2014. Investing in small-cap companies would have resulted in $78,507.21 ($81,406.44– $2,899.23) *more* money in one's pocket than investing in large-cap companies over this period.

These calculations were performed for *every* possible monthly beginning date and end date combination between January 1926 and December 2014.

4.12 Joel L. Horowitz, Tim Loughran, and N.E. Savin, "The disappearing size effect", *Research in Economics* (2000), page 98.

4.13 Banz, Rolf W. "The Relationship between Return and Market Value of Common Stocks." *Journal of Financial Economics* (March 1981): 3–18. Professor Banz's 1981 article is often cited as the first comprehensive study of the size effect.

4.14 The terminal index value in all cases presented here is the amount that $1 invested on the begin date would have grown to (or decreased to) as of the end date.

The result of this analysis was that small-cap companies outperformed large-cap companies in 480,423 of the cases (84%), and large-cap companies outperformed small-cap companies in 90,423 cases of the (16%).

In Exhibit 4.12, an abbreviated summary of these results is shown, where the holding periods are limited to *exactly* 1 month, 5-years, 10-years, 20-years, and 30-years, instead of all 570,768 possible start- and end-date combinations. Start dates covering the entire January 1926–December 2014 period are examined, as well as three more recent start date windows: January 1982–December 2014, January 1990–December 2014, and January 2000–December 2014. All three of the more recent start date windows are *after* Banz wrote his 1981 article that identified the size effect, and so they are labeled as "Post Banz." Also, in Exhibit 4.12 the number of periods examined is shown first, followed by the outperformance percentage of the total periods in parentheses.

In the top row of Exhibit 4.12 (in which the holding period is restricted to a *single* month), large-cap companies outperformed small-cap companies in the majority of cases (53%) over the entire 1926–2014 start date window, and also in the 1982–2014 and 1990–2014 "Post Banz" start date windows. In the 2000–2014 start date window, however, small-cap companies outperform, although barely (54%). As the holding period is increased from 1 month to 60 months (and longer), and as the time that small-cap companies and large-cap companies are given to "race" against each other was lengthened, small-cap companies again tend to outperform. For example, over the entire range of start dates (1926–2014), there are a total of 709 (641 + 68) holding periods that are *exactly* 360 months (30 years) long, with small-cap companies outperforming large-cap companies in 641 (90%) of them (bottom row, left column).

Exhibit 4.12: Small-cap Companies' Performance minus Large-cap Companies' Performance Over Periods of *Exactly* 1, 60, 120, 240, and 360 Months

Holding Period	All Dates 1926–2014	Post Banz 1982–2014	Post Banz 1990–2014	Post Banz 2000–2014
Exactly 1 month				
Small Stocks Outperform	506 (47%)	183 (46%)	149 (50%)	98 (54%)
Large Stocks Outperform	562 (53%)	213 (54%)	151 (50%)	82 (46%)
Exactly 60 months (5 years)				
Small Stocks Outperform	592 (59%)	178 (53%)	173 (72%)	109 (90%)
Large Stocks Outperform	417 (41%)	159 (47%)	68 (28%)	12 (10%)
Exactly 120 months (10 years)				
Small Stocks Outperform	673 (71%)	160 (58%)	160 (88%)	61 (100%)
Large Stocks Outperform	276 (29%)	117 (42%)	21 (12%)	0 (0%)
Exactly 240 months (20 years)				
Small Stocks Outperform	670 (81%)	119 (76%)	61 (100%)	–
Large Stocks Outperform	159 (19%)	38 (24%)	0 (0%)	–
Exactly 360 months (30 years)				
Small Stocks Outperform	641 (90%)	24 (65%)	–	–
Large Stocks Outperform	68 (10%)	13 (35%)	–	–

Source of underlying data: CRSP U.S. Stock Database and CRSP U.S. Indices Database © 2015 Center for Research in Security Prices (CRSP®), University of Chicago Booth School of Business. Large-cap companies and small-cap companies are represented by CRSP NYSE/NYSE MKT/NASDAQ decile 1 and 10, respectively. Used with permission. All rights reserved. Calculations performed by Duff & Phelps LLC.

These analyses suggest:

- The size effect is *cyclical.* Sometimes small-cap companies outperform large-cap companies, and sometimes large-cap companies outperform small-cap companies.

- The *longer* the holding period over which small-cap companies and large-cap companies are given to "race" against each other, the *more likely* it is that small-cap companies will outperform large-cap companies. This implies that over the longer-term (which is the default period over which most business valuations are done), the size effect is indeed a significant factor that should likely be accounted for in the development of cost of capital estimates.

- The 1980s were *not kind* to small capitalization stocks. During this period, the size effect likely was on a cyclical low, or even significantly negative.

Relationship of Size and Liquidity

Liquidity affects the cost of capital. For this purpose, *liquidity* refers to the speed at which a large quantity of a security can be traded with a minimal impact on the price and at the lowest cost. Banz's 1981 musing as to whether "...size per se is responsible for the effect or whether size is just a proxy for one or more true unknown factors correlated with size" may have been cannily prescient. Research on returns as related to "size" is abundant, but over time a growing body of work investigating the impact of "liquidity" on returns has emerged.

Capital market theory also assumes liquidity of investments. Many of the observations about risk and return are drawn from information for liquid investments. Investors desire liquidity and require greater returns for illiquidity. But the degree of liquidity is one of the risk factors for all investments. Any discussion of a liquidity premium, therefore, would be incomplete without accounting for underlying stock risks before considering relative liquidity.

Stocks of small companies generally do not have the same level of liquidity as large-company stocks. This is likely a function of the mix of shareholders and underlying risk characteristics. Many institutional investors do not own stocks in small companies because they have too much money to invest. Were they to invest as little as 1% of their available funds in a small company, they would be likely to control the company. Institutional investors generally want liquidity to move into and out of positions in a single firm. Therefore, one does not see the breadth of investors investing in small-company stocks.

Further, small companies are followed by only a small window of analysts, if at all. This makes it more difficult for investors to evaluate small firms.

Is the size premium simply the result of differences in liquidity? If one is valuing a small business, that business, if it were publicly traded, would likely never have the same breadth of shareholders as a large publicly traded company, and whatever impact the relative illiquidity of small companies has on the cost of capital will carry over to any small business.

Some analysts have suggested that the size effect should be set aside because various studies have ignored transaction costs in measuring rates of return. The analysts point out that small stocks often have higher transaction costs than large stocks. In addition, the historical size premium can be greatly reduced if one makes certain assumptions about transaction costs and holding periods. However, in applying the income approach to valuation, analysts typically use projected net cash flows that do not make any adjustment for an investor's hypothetical transaction costs. It may be that small stocks are priced in a way that increases the rates of return so as to reward investors for the costs of executing a transaction. If so, it would be a distortion to express the discount rate on a net-of-transaction-cost basis while the net cash flow projections are on a before-transaction-cost basis.

Academic studies support the hypotheses that illiquidity is a factor in pricing and returns of stocks and that returns of small firms are more sensitive to market liquidity. But the illiquidity factor does not capture the size effect completely. Moreover, any reasonable adjustment for transaction costs should recognize that investors can mitigate these costs on an annual basis by holding their stocks for a longer period. In fact, investors in small companies tend to have longer holding periods than investors in large companies.

First, let's examine some of the research.

As early as 1986, Amihud and Mendelson, demonstrated that "...market-observed average returns are an increasing function of the spread..." (i.e., less liquid stocks, as measured by a larger bid-ask spread, outperform more liquid stocks), and further concluded that the "...higher yields required on higher-spread stocks give firms an incentive to increase the liquidity of their securities, thus reducing their opportunity cost of capital".[4.15]

Ibbotson, Chen, Kim, and Hu suggest that while the typical measures of liquidity employed in the literature are each "...highly correlated with company size", they demonstrate that liquidity, as measured by annual stock turnover, "...is an economically significant investment style that is just as strong, but distinct from traditional investment styles such as size, value/growth, and momentum".[4.16] The authors go on to say that "...there is an incremental return from investing in less liquid stocks even after adjusting for the market, size, value/growth, and momentum factors", and conclude that "...equity liquidity is the missing equity style."

Ibbotson, Chen, and Hu identify two main sources of the greater returns of less liquid stocks. The first is that "investors like liquidity and dislike illiquidity", and "...a premium has to be paid for any characteristic that investors demand, and a discount must be given for any characteristic investors seek to avoid". Thus, "...the investor in less liquid stocks gets lower valuations, effectively buying stocks at a discount."

As we discussed in Chapter 2, one can think of risk in terms of popularity. For example, illiquidity is typically considered a risk, and less liquid stocks are considered less popular. One can classify less liquid stocks as less popular than brand name stocks that are in the news, having more analyst coverage and greater trading volume. Similarly, the size premium can be thought of as a risk measure that encompasses both illiquidity risk and underlying business risk; small capitalization stocks are typically less popular.

Ibbotson and Idzorek have concluded that share turnover is a better measure of popularity than other liquidity measures.[4.17] For example, a large company with lesser share turnover might be considered very liquid by some measures but because of its low share turnover might be considered relatively unpopular. Data displayed in Exhibit 4.13 demonstrate their observation that stocks with lesser turnover (those that are less popular) realize greater returns than those stocks with greater turnover that are considered more popular (and realize lesser returns).

4.15 Amihud, Yakov and Haim Mendelson, 1986, "Asset Pricing and the Bid-Ask Spread," *Journal of Financial Economics* 17, 223-249.

4.16 See Roger G. Ibbotson, Zhiwu Chen, Daniel Y.-J. Kim, and Wendy Y. Hu, "Liquidity as an Investment Style", *Financial Analysts Journal* Vol 69(3): 30-44. Copy available at www.zebracapm.com

4.17 Ibbotson and Idzorek, op.cit. :72.

Exhibit 4.13: Quartiles of Popularity as Measured by Share Turnover in U.S. Equity Markets 1972–2014

	Less popular (1)		More popular (2)	
	Q1	Q2	Q3	Q4
Annualized Return	15.36%	14.17%	12.61%	8.20%
Standard Deviation	20.06%	20.46%	22.55%	28.07%

(1) Quartile with lowest turnover, (2) Quartile with greatest turnover

Source of underlying data: Roger Ibbotson and Daniel Y.-Kim 2014 "Risk and Return within the Stock Market: 2015 Update," Working paper, available at research.zebracapital.com

Abbott investigated the relative importance of the size and liquidity risk factors.[4.18] The author used a multi-factor model including a trading cost measure and a liquidity premium factor[4.19] to assess the absolute contribution for each factor individually, as well as in combination with other factors, to form an estimate of the combined contribution of the factors considered in the estimate of the cost of equity capital.

As expected, Abbott found significant negative relationships between the size of the companies as measured by market value and his trading cost measure; stocks of larger firms can be traded at a lower cost. He found a similar relationship between liquidity and cost of trading. As stocks become more liquid, trading costs and price impact both decline, as suggested by theory.

The Risk Premium Report results demonstrate that size and fundamental risk of small companies are correlated (displayed in the "C" exhibits presented in Appendix 4 and discussed in Chapter 10). This leads in to consider that size may, in part at best, be a coincident indicator of fundamental company risk.

That same relationship may be creating the liquidity effect. That is, the underlying risks of small companies being greater than those of larger companies may cause investors to shy away from small companies, valuing their liquidity. Thus, reduced liquidity may also be a coincident indicator of fundamental risk.

In measuring the appropriate size premium when estimating the cost of equity capital for a division or reporting unit of a large public company or a closely held business, one need not separate the portion of the size premium that may be attributable to an illiquidity factor. One is estimating the cost of capital as if the market were pricing the risks of the subject business based on the average risk of other companies of comparable size including any portion of the risks due to illiquidity.

4.18 Ashok Bhardwaj Abbott (2015). Available from the author.

4.19 A measure of an individual stock's liquidity, with higher levels signifying that the current order flow in the market can absorb larger volumes of trading without affecting prices.

Key Things to Remember about the Size Premium

- The size effect is based on the empirical observation that companies of smaller size are associated with greater risk and, therefore, have greater costs of capital. In other words, there is a significant (negative) relationship between the size and historical equity returns – as size *decreases*, returns tend to *increase*, and vice versa.

- Traditionally, small companies are believed to have greater required rates of return than large companies because small companies are inherently riskier. It is not clear, however, whether this is due to size itself, or to another factor closely related to size.

- The size effect is not evident just for the smallest companies; it is evident for all but the largest groups of companies, including companies with a market capitalization in excess of several billions of dollars. However, the size effect is greatest with the smallest companies.

- Small-cap companies tend to outperform large-cap companies over longer periods. The longer the period over which small-cap companies and large-cap companies are give to "race" against each other, the more likely it is that small-cap companies will outperform large-cap companies. The size effect tends to stabilize over time.

- Use sum betas for the development of size premia, and use sum beta within the CAPM (particularly if dealing with very small companies), because sum betas tend to better explain the returns of smaller companies. However, in cases in which you do use OLS betas in CAPM, you should use an OLS-beta derived size premium.

- Risk Premium Report portfolios do not include start-up and high-financial-risk companies. The returns on these companies could be expected to be high because of their risk, not because of their size.

- Despite many criticisms of the size effect, it continues to be observed in data sources. Further, observation of the size effect is consistent with a modification of the pure CAPM. Studies have shown the limitations of beta as a sole measure of risk. The size premium is an empirically derived correction to the pure CAPM.

- While the 1980s were *not* kind to small-cap companies (the size effect likely was on a cyclical low, or even negative), the evidence suggests that after the 1980s, the size effect may again be entering a cyclical period of strength.

- If the valuation analyst is estimating the cost of equity capital of a closely held subject company on an "as if publicly" basis, the valuation assumption is that the subject company would have liquidity (if it was public) to approximately the average of comparable size public companies. The size premium published in the *Valuation Handbook* are appropriate to use in developing the cost of equity capital without separating the size effect from the liquidity effect.

- The size effect is not without controversy, nor is this controversy something new. Traditionally, small companies are believed to have greater required rates of return than large companies because small companies are inherently riskier. It is not clear, however, whether this is due to size itself, or to other factors closely related to or correlated with size (e.g., liquidity).

- One can think of risk in terms of popularity. Characteristics of investments that investors *desire* are "popular", while characteristics of investments that investors do *not* desire are not popular. All other things being equal, assets with popular characteristics will be priced higher and have lower returns than assets with unpopular characteristics, which will be priced lower and have higher returns. Popularity can include all sorts of other characteristics that do not fit well into the risk and return paradigm.

Chapter 5
Basic Building Blocks of the Cost of Equity Capital – Betas and Industry Risk Premia

In this chapter we first discuss beta, which is an important input needed when estimating cost of equity capital under the capital asset pricing model (CAPM), and then discuss industry risk premia (RP_i), which are a special type of beta modified for use within the build-up model.

Beta

Beta is a measure of the systematic risk of a stock; the tendency of a stock's price to correlate with changes in the market. The "market" is typically represented by a broad-based equity index that includes a wide range of industries, and arguably behaves like the market as a whole.

The market's beta is 1.0 by definition. A company with a beta equal to 1.0 has the same risk as the market (it theoretically moves up and down with the market *in tandem*), a company with a beta greater than 1.0 is riskier than the market (it theoretically moves up and down to a *greater* degree than the market), and a company with a beta less than 1.0 is less risky than the market (it theoretically moves up and down to a *lesser* degree than the market).

Betas for equity capital are used as a modifier to the equity risk premium (ERP) in the context of CAPM. Beta is the sole risk factor of the pure CAPM, the form of the CAPM most often shown in textbooks. The combination of equity beta for the subject business multiplied by the ERP equals the estimated risk premium for the subject business.[5.1]

Equity betas increase with the risk of the business. For example, the beta of an entity with greater business (operating) risk will tend to be greater than the beta of an entity with lesser business risk. Similarly, the beta of a entity with more debt in the capital structure will tend to be greater than the beta of an entity with lesser financial risk.

Beta estimates are generally derived from returns data of publicly traded securities. If one is valuing a closely held business or a nonpublic division or reporting unit, for example, one likely will be using the beta estimate of publicly traded securities as a proxy for the nonpublic business.

Published and calculated beta estimates for public stocks typically reflect the capital structure in place during the look-back period. In other words, individual leverage decisions by each publicly-traded company will impact its published (equity) beta. The beta estimates are typically made using realized returns for the subject business's stock and an index that represents the stock market as a whole. For example, many analysts use the S&P 500 Index as a proxy for the U.S. market. In the *2015 Valuation Handbook* the proxy for the market is the S&P 500 Index, unless otherwise stated.

5.1 This portion of the chapter is excerpted in part from Pratt and Grabowski, op.cit.: Chapter 11, "Beta: Differing Definitions and Estimates."

Other broad-based indices can be used as well, such as the Wilshire 5000, or the Morningstar U.S. Market Index (among others). As a matter of fact, as long as the index is broad-based and is representative of the market as a whole, it is arguably suitable for use as a market benchmark, and generally similar betas will be produced.

In Exhibit 5.1 the ordinary least squares (OLS) betas for the 60-month period ending December 2014 are calculated for 10 publically-traded U.S. companies, using three different broad-based U.S. equities indices. The OLS beta estimates are similar, regardless of the broad-based equities index chosen.

Exhibit 5.1: Company Betas Using Different Market Benchmarks

Company	S&P 500 Index	Wilshire 5000 Index	Morningstar U.S. Market Index
Apple Inc.	0.92	0.87	0.87
AT&T, Inc.	0.44	0.41	0.40
Caterpillar Inc.	1.68	1.67	1.67
The Coca-Cola Company	0.49	0.45	0.45
Exxon Mobil Corporation	0.88	0.84	0.84
Johnson & Johnson	0.54	0.51	0.51
Monsanto Company	1.37	1.32	1.32
The Procter & Gamble Company	0.39	0.36	0.36
Wal-Mart Stores Inc.	0.46	0.42	0.42
Wells Fargo & Company	1.09	1.06	1.05

Source of underlying data: (i) Standard and Poor's *Capital IQ* database (ii) Morningstar's *Direct* database. Used with permission. Betas calculated over the time period January 2010–December 2014 using excess total returns over 30-day U.S. Treasury Bills. Calculations performed by Duff & Phelps LLC.

The reason that the results are similar is because the correlation of the three market benchmark indices is very high. In Exhibit 5.2 a simple cross-correlation matrix is shown. The three broad-based market indices selected for this example are highly correlated over the January 2010–December 2014 time period that these betas were calculated (and highly correlated over longer time periods as well).

Exhibit 5.2: Correlation Matrix of the S&P 500 Index, the Wilshire 5000 Index, and the Morningstar U.S. Market Index
January 2010–December 2014

	S&P 500 Index	Wilshire 5000 Index	Morningstar U.S. Market Index
S&P 500 Index	1.000	–	–
Wilshire 5000 Index	0.998	1.000	–
Morningstar U.S. Market Index	0.998	1.000	1.000

Source of underlying data: Morningstar's *Direct* database. Used with permission. Calculations performed by Duff & Phelps LLC.

These betas sometimes are referred to as levered betas, since these beta estimates reflect the actual leverage in a company's capital structure. The adjustment for leverage differences is called unlevering and levering beta estimates.[5.2]

Estimation of Equity Beta

Beta, like cost of capital itself, is a forward-looking concept. It is intended to be a measure of the *expected* future relationship between the return on an individual security (or portfolio of securities) and the return on the market. In the CAPM, beta should be the expected beta.

The market, as measured by a broad-based equities index, is ultimately a proxy for the broader economy. In this context, beta is theoretically the expected sensitivity of the individual security to changes in the overall economy. The sensitivity of individual security returns is the sensitivity of the company to cash flow risks and discount rate risk. It represents the sensitivity of changing expectation about expected cash flows of the business relative to changing expectations about expected cash flows of the economy as a whole (i.e., the market) changing expectations for the ERP.[5.3]

Valuation analysts typically use beta estimates derived from regressions over look-back periods or other techniques to develop the expected beta for use in the CAPM. Newer estimation techniques, which we discuss later, use implied volatility derived from options to estimate expected betas.

There are two general ways for estimating betas:

1. A direct beta estimate (sometimes called a top-down estimate) for a public company comes from regressing excess returns of the public company's stock on the excess returns of a market portfolio over a look-back period.

2. A *proxy* beta can be estimated by:

    i. Identifying the businesses in which the subject entity operates.

    ii. Identifying guideline public companies and estimating their levered betas.

    iii. Unlevering the guideline public company beta estimates to get estimates of unlevered (asset) betas.

    iv. Taking an average, often a weighted average, of these unlevered betas, where the weights are based on the relative values (or operating income) of the businesses in which the subject entity operates.

    v. Levering the beta estimate using an appropriate debt-to-equity ratio for the subject entity.

5.2 For a comprehensive discussion of unlevering and levering beta estimates, see Pratt and Grabowski, op.cit.: Chapter 12, "Unlevering and Levering Equity Betas."

5.3 John Y. Campbell and Jianping Mei, "Where Do Betas Come From? Asset Price Dynamics and the Sources of Systematic Risk," *Review of Financial Studies* 6(3) (1993): 567–592.

You need to use a proxy beta when the subject business is a division, reporting unit, or closely held business.

The most widely used techniques for estimating beta generally use historical data over a sample or look-back period and assume that the future will be sufficiently similar to this past period to justify extrapolation of betas calculated using historical data.

For a publicly traded stock, you can estimate beta via regression (ordinary least squares (OLS) regression), regressing the excess returns on the individual security ($R_i - R_f$) against the excess returns on the market ($R_m - R_f$) during the look-back period. Formula 5.1 shows the regression formula.

Formula 5.1

$$(R_i - R_f) = \alpha + \beta \times (R_m - R_f) + \varepsilon$$

where:

R_i = Historical return for publicly traded stock, *i*

R_f = Risk-free rate

α = Regression constant

β = Estimated beta based on historical data over the look-back period

R_m = Historical return on market portfolio, *m*

ε = Regression error term

The resulting slope of the best-fit line is the beta estimate. In Exhibit 5.3 a "scatterplot" graph of Starbucks Corporation's excess returns and the S&P 500 excess returns are shown over the 60-month period January 2010–December 2014. The dashed trend line is defined by the equation *y=mx+b*, where "*b*" is the y-intercept, and "*m*" is the slope. The slope of the dashed trend line (0.8352) is the beta of Starbucks Corporation for the 60-month period ending December 31, 2014.

Exhibit 5.3: Starbucks Corp. Excess Returns versus S&P 500 Index Excess Returns Scatterplot
January 2010–December 2014

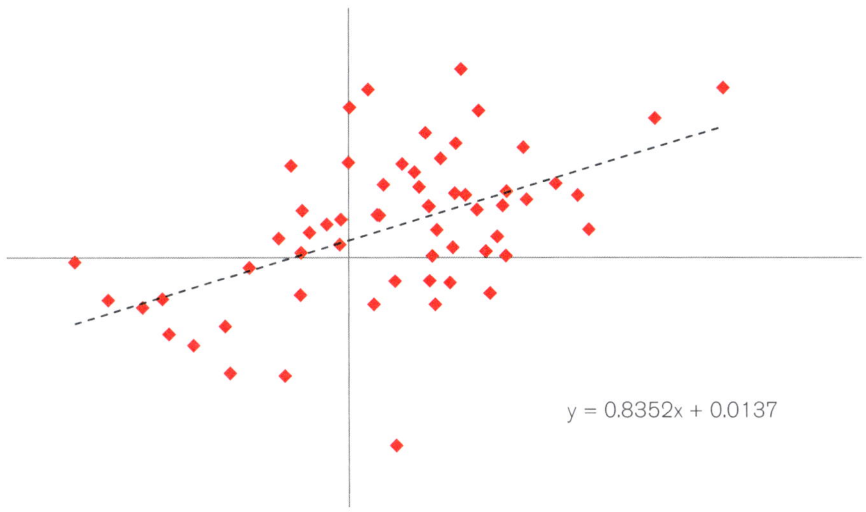

Source of underlying data: (i) Standard and Poor's *Capital IQ* database (ii) Morningstar *Direct* database. Used with permission. All rights reserved. Betas calculated over the time period January 2010–December 2014 using excess total returns over 30-day U.S. Treasury Bills. Calculations performed by Duff & Phelps LLC.

We use excess returns in all of our beta computations.[5.4] Some valuation analysts and other financial data services calculate betas using total returns for the subject security and for the market returns instead of excess returns. Other valuation analysts calculate returns for the subject security and for the market simply using changes in price and ignoring dividend returns.

Comparisons of beta estimates using excess returns or total returns show that, as a practical matter, it generally makes little difference in the aggregate. However, if one uses only changes in price and ignores dividend return, it may make a difference, at least for a stock whose returns are predominantly comprised of dividends.

Because beta is an expected sensitivity, any estimation using historical methods is subject to error. The analyst can gauge the quality of the beta by examining various statistics resulting from the regression used to estimate the beta. Two important statistics are:

- ***t*-statistic:** Indicates if the beta estimate is statistically different from zero, and is an indication of how useful the regression results are in estimating the relationship between the returns of the stock and the returns of the market. For example, a regression to calculate a beta using 60 months of data has 59 degrees of freedom, and needs to have a t-statistic of ± 1.67 (two-tailed test) for the beta to be "statistically different than 0" at a 90% confidence level.[5.5]

5.4 *SBBI* beta calculations used excess returns. For example, see *2013 SBBI Valuation Yearbook*: 72.

5.5 t-stat critical values *change* depending on the degrees of freedom and the confidence level. In the case of beta estimates using simple regression techniques, the degrees of freedom will be the number of periods minus 1. t-stat tables are available in almost any statistics book, and can also be looked up using Microsoft *Excel*'s TINV function (TINV assumes a two-tailed test, which is the proper test in this case).

- **Standard error of estimate:** Standard deviation of the estimate of the beta made by the sample used in the regression. This gives an indication of how close the estimated beta is to the "true" beta. For example, if Company ABC has a beta of 1.5 with standard error of 0.2, there is an approximate 68% probability that Company ABC's "true" beta falls between 1.3 (1.5 – 0.2) and 1.7 (1.5 + 0.2), and an approximate 95.5% chance that the company's "true" beta falls between 1.1 (1.5 – 0.4) and 1.9 (1.5 + 0.4).

In Exhibit 5.4, high standard error beta estimates are compared to low standard error beta estimates. Microsoft Corporation and Mannkind Corporation's beta estimates have an average standard error of 0.05 and 0.22, respectively, over the 60-month period January 2010–December 2014. The stability of Microsoft's beta (lower standard error) compared to the instability of Mannkind's beta (higher standard error) is apparent. Betas can (and do) change over time, but lack of stability may indicate that the beta is not of high statistical quality.

The concept that examining the beta estimate's standard error "gives an indication of how close the estimated beta is to the 'true' beta" can be illustrated by simple inspection of Exhibit 5.4 and asking the following questions: First, how confident would you be of claiming that Microsoft's "true" beta is around 1.0? Second, would you be *more* confident or *less* confident about making a similar claim about where Mannkind's "true" beta probably falls? The likely answer for many valuation analysts would be that Microsoft's estimated beta's *stability* over the 60-month period gives them more confidence in it than they might have in Mannkind's estimated betas, which are relatively unstable over the 60-month period.

Exhibit 5.4: 60-month Rolling Betas
High Standard Error Beta Estimate versus Low Standard Error Beta Estimates
January 2010–December 2014

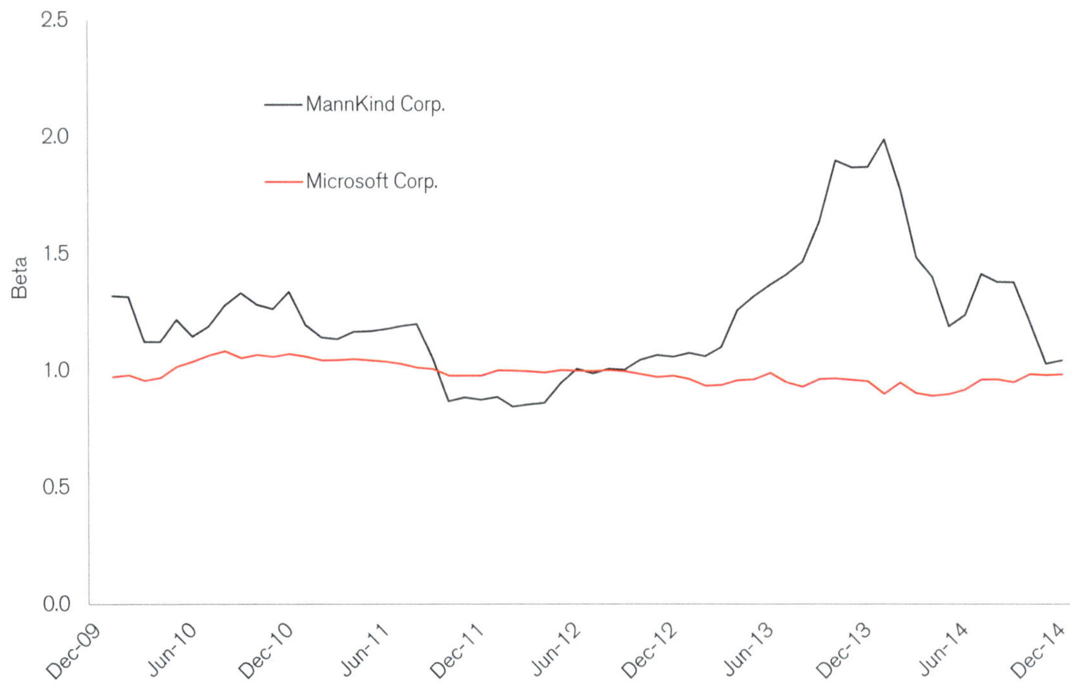

Source of underlying data: (i) Standard and Poor's *Capital IQ* database (ii) Morningstar *Direct* database. Used with permission. All rights reserved. Calculations performed by Duff & Phelps LLC.

Also, the analyst must be cautious of beta estimates using smaller public companies where there is no active market, as their betas tend to be underestimated using OLS beta estimates and by reference sources. The sum beta method of estimating betas helps correct for the tendency for OLS methods to underestimate betas. We discuss the use of the sum beta method of estimating beta later in this chapter. Further, the *greater* the sample of beta estimates drawn from guideline public companies of similar size as the subject business you use as the basis for the beta estimate of the subject business, generally the *better* the accuracy because the standard error of estimate is reduced.

Differences in Estimation of Equity Betas

Note that significant differences can exist among beta estimates for the same stock published by different financial reporting services. One of the implications of this is that a valuation analyst should try to use betas for guideline companies used in a valuation from the *same source*. While we recommend that valuation analysts calculate their own beta estimates, if you are *not* calculating beta yourself, and if the betas for all of the selected guideline companies are not available from a single source, the best solution probably may be to use the source providing betas for the *greatest* number of guideline companies, and not use betas from other sources for the others. This helps to avoid "an apples-and-oranges" mixture of betas calculated using different methodologies.

Differences in the beta measurement derive primarily from choices within four variables:

1. The length of the time period over which the historical returns are measured (i.e., the length of the look-back period)
2. The periodicity (frequency) of return measurement within that time period (e.g., weekly versus monthly, etc.)
3. The risk-free rate above which the excess returns are measured
4. The choice of which index to use as a market proxy

The length of time period over which the historical returns are measured can have significant impact on the beta estimate. If a fundamental change in the business environment in which an individual company (or even an industry) operates occurs, the valuation analyst should consider whether using historical data from *before* the change should be included in the overall analysis.

A simple example of this concept is provided in Exhibit 5.5. In Exhibit 5.5, a rolling 60-month beta is shown for the Financials sector over the time period January 2005–December 2014, which includes the Financial Crisis. Clearly something fundamentally changed in the Financials sector post-crisis. The question the valuation analyst should consider is whether the information embedded in the pre-crisis returns is still pertinent. If not, then the valuation analyst should consider shortening the look-back period over which the beta is calculated to exclude the pre-crisis returns information.

Exhibit 5.5: 60-month Rolling Beta of Financial Sector
January 2005–December 2014

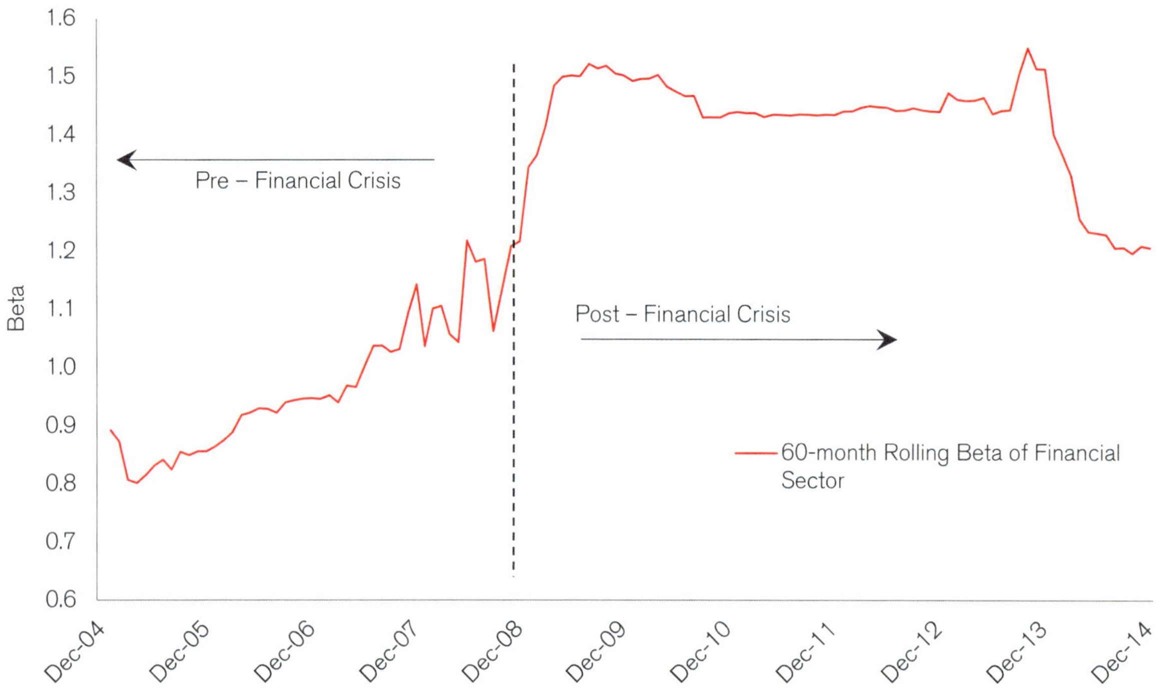

Source of underlying data: (i) Standard and Poor's *Capital IQ* database (ii) Morningstar's *Direct* database. The financials sector is represented by the S&P Composite 1500 Financials Index. The S&P Composite 1500 Financial Index® are comprised of members of the GICS® financial sector. Used with permission. All rights reserved. Calculations by Duff & Phelps LLC.

The overall goal is to look for the best beta estimate, reflecting the expected risk of the guideline companies, and ideally derived using the *same* data sets, methodologies, and time periods.

Tendency Toward Market or Industry Average

One technique used by Bloomberg and *Value Line* for adjusting historical betas weights the historical beta estimate by approximately two-thirds, and the market beta of 1.0 by approximately one-third. This adjustment is sometimes referred to as the "Blume" adjustment, or the "one third/two thirds" adjustment.[5.6] This is a *mechanical* "one size fits all" adjustment that has the net effect of adjusting historical betas that are *less* than 1.0 *upward*, and adjusting historical betas that are *greater* than 1.0 *downward*. The adjustment is said to create a "forward" (or prospective) estimated beta because this adjustment is based on the assumption that betas tend to move toward the market's beta (1.0) over time. It does not indicate that any adjustment to the data used in calculating the historical beta estimate was made.

5.6 Blume, M.E., "On the Assessment of Risk", *Journal of Finance*, vol. 26, 1971, pp.1–10. This adjustment is sometimes referred to as the "Blume" adjustment, or the "one third, two thirds" adjustment. The equation for this adjustment is $Beta_{adjusted} = 0.371 + 0.635Beta_{historical}$.

Another technique for adjusting beta estimates is a rather sophisticated technique called *Vasicek shrinkage*.[5.7] The general idea is that betas with the highest statistical standard errors are the least reliable estimates and are, therefore, adjusted toward the market, peer group, or industry average *more* than are betas with lower standard errors.[5.8] The Vasicek shrinkage technique is not a "one size fits all" technique like the Blume adjustment, and also offers the flexibility to adjusting to the market, peer group, or industry average.

Whether betas tend to move toward market averages or industry averages over time is an issue open to debate, although it seems more intuitive that companies in say, the pharmaceuticals industry will become more like the average *pharmaceutical* company over time, rather than look more like the average company in *any* industry. In 2010's *Global GT LP and Global GT LTD v. Golden Telecom, Inc.*, the Delaware Court of Chancery wrote that "... the historic beta is considered to have a fair amount of predictive power, and to be a reliable proxy for unobservable forward-looking betas ...there is support for the notion that more extreme betas tend to revert to the *industry mean* (emphasis added) over time." Furthermore, the Court noted that "... no reliable literature or evidence was presented to show that the beta of a telecom company like Golden, which operates in a risky market, will revert to 1.0."[5.9]

Lag effect

For all but the largest companies, the prices of individual stocks tend to react in part to movements in the overall market with a lag. The smaller the company, generally the greater the lag in the price reaction. This does not necessarily imply that the market itself is wholly inefficient, although the market for some stocks *is* more efficient than for other stocks. Large companies tend to be followed by more analysts and are owned by more institutional investors than are small-cap companies. Therefore, large-cap companies tend to react more quickly to changes in the economy or changes in the business (e.g., introduction of a new product, signing of a new major contract) nearly instantaneously, while smaller companies' stocks tend to react at a slower rate.

Because of the lag in all but the largest companies' sensitivity to movements in the overall market, traditional OLS betas tend to understate systematic risk. A *sum beta* consists of a multiple regression of a stock's current month's excess returns over the 30-day T-bill rate on the market's *current* month's excess returns and on the market's *previous* month's excess returns, and then a summing of the resulting coefficients. This helps to capture more fully the lagged effect of co-movement in a company's returns with returns on the market (market or systematic risk). Exhibit 5.6 includes a sampling of OLS and sum betas for companies across the size spectrum as of December 2014.

5.7 The formula was first suggested by Oldrich A. Vasicek, "A Note on Using Cross-Sectional Information in Bayesian Estimation of Security Betas," *Journal of Finance* (1973).

5.8 This was the adjustment used in the *Ibbotson Beta Book,* where this adjusted beta was labeled *Ibbotson Beta*. The Ibbotson *Beta Book* and the individual beta "tear" sheets previously available on the Morningstar website are no longer published.

5.9 *Global GT LP v. Golden Telecom, Inc.*, 993 A.2d 497 (Del. Ch. 2010); aff'd, 11 A.3d 214 (Del 2010).

Exhibit 5.6: Comparison of OLS Betas and Sum Betas for Companies of Varying Size
Market Capitalization as of December 2014

Company	Market Capitalization (in $millions)	OLS BETA	Sum Beta	Difference
The Coca-Cola Company	184,928.371	0.49	0.50	0.01
MasterCard Incorporated	99,329.995	0.92	0.99	0.06
DIRECTV	43,543.923	0.91	1.02	0.11
The Toro Company	3,557.982	0.95	1.12	0.17
Steven Madden, Ltd.	2,044.345	1.51	1.67	0.16
Overstock.com Inc.	583.135	0.80	1.07	0.27
Monster Worldwide, Inc.	409.842	2.51	2.90	0.39
Datalink Corporation	297.152	0.75	1.03	0.28

Source of underlying data: (i) Standard and Poor's *Capital IQ* database (ii) Morningstar *Direct* database. Used with permission. All rights reserved. Betas are estimated from monthly return data in excess of the 30-day U.S. Treasury bill total return, January 2010–December 2014. The S&P 500 Index was used as the market benchmark. Calculations performed by Duff & Phelps LLC.

In Exhibit 5.6, the *larger* the company, the *smaller* the difference between the OLS beta and the sum beta, and the *smaller* the company, the *greater* the difference between the OLS beta and the sum beta.[5.10] The research suggests that this understatement of systematic risk by the traditional beta measurements accounts in part, but certainly not totally, for the fact that small-cap companies achieve excess returns over their apparent CAPM-required returns (where the market equity risk premium is adjusted for beta).

The formula for the sum beta is:

Formula 5.2

$$\left(R_n - R_{f,n}\right) = \alpha + \beta_n \times \left(R_{m,n} - R_{f,n}\right) + \beta_{n-1} \times \left(R_{m,n-1} - R_{f,n-1}\right) + \varepsilon$$

$$SumBeta = \beta_n + \beta_{n-1}$$

[5.10] Exceptions to this pattern can be found, of course, but this is the general trend in the overall population of companies.

where:

R_n	= Return on individual security in current month
$R_{f,n}$	= Risk-free rate in current month
α	= Regression constant
β_n	= Estimated market coefficient based on sensitivity to excess returns on market portfolio in current month
R_m	= Historical return on market portfolio
$(R_{m,n} - R_{f,n})$	= Excess return on the market portfolio in the current month
β_{n-1}	= Estimated lagged market coefficient based on sensitivity to excess returns on market-portfolio last month
$(R_{m,n-1} - R_{f,n-1})$	= Excess return on market portfolio last month
ε	= Regression error term

Sum betas for individual stocks can be calculated using a spreadsheet such as Microsoft *Excel* and historical return data, which is available from several sources (e.g., Standard & Poor's *Capital IQ*.) Some analysts prefer to calculate their own sum betas for a peer group of public companies (which they use as a proxy for the beta of their subject private business in the context of CAPM) and thus make a smaller adjustment for the size effect. The theory is that the sum beta helps correct for the larger size effect that is principally due to a misspecification of beta when using traditional OLS betas for smaller companies. It should be noted that sum beta estimates may at times be statistically "noisy". When estimating a proxy beta using any look back method, valuation analysts should always be cautious when dealing with a small number of guideline companies.

Full-Information Beta

Ideally, one would like to have a sampling of betas from many "pure play" guideline public companies when estimating a proxy beta. "Pure play" companies are companies with say, at least 75% of revenue from a single Standard Industrial Classification (SIC) code. In some industries the *largest* participants may be conglomerates for which participation in the given industry is a *small* part of their overall revenues. In a strictly pure-play analysis, these companies would be *excluded*, even though they may be the dominant participant in the industry. The full-information beta approach enables the *inclusion* of these companies' participation in the industry in the beta calculation.[5.11]

The full-information beta methodology is based on the premise that a business can be thought of as a portfolio of assets. The full-information methodology is designed to capture the impact that the individual segments have upon the overall business beta. After identifying all companies having segment sales in an industry, the analyst calculates a beta estimate of those companies. The analyst then runs a multiple regression with betas as the dependent variables (applying a weight to each beta based on its relative market capitalization to the industry market capitalization) and sales of the segments of each of the companies in the industry as the independent variable. That is, one is measuring the relative impact on

[5.11] Paul D. Kaplan, and James D. Peterson. "Full-Information Industry Betas", *Financial Management*, Summer 1998.

the betas of companies in an industry based on the relative contributed (as measured typically by sales) each company has within the industry.

Applying market capitalization weights in the process tends to reduce the beta estimates because large capitalization companies on the average have lower betas than smaller companies. Measuring the impact on betas using segment sales data may present a problem in that the market weigh profits, not sales. This procedure may over-weight the relative importance of business segments having high sales and low profits.

Industry Risk Premia

Industry risk premia (RP_i) in the *2015 Valuation Handbook* are full-information betas that have been adjusted so that they can be added as a simple "up or down" adjustment in the build-up method.[5.12] The need for an industry risk adjustment within the context of the build-up method can be demonstrated simply by comparing the modified CAPM formula to the build-up formula.

The modified CAPM formula is:

Formula 5.3

$$k_e = R_f + \beta \times (RP_m) + RP_s$$

And the build-up formula is:

Formula 5.4

$$k_e = R_f + RP_m + RP_s + RP_i$$

where:

$k_{e,i}$ = Expected rate of return on security *i*

R_f = Risk-free rate of return

β = Beta

RP_m = Equity risk premium (market risk)

RP_s = Size premium

RP_i = Industry risk premium

5.12 Industry Risk Premia were previously published in Table 3-5, "Industry Premia Estimates" in the *Morningstar/Ibbotson SBBI Valuation Yearbook*. In the *2015 Valuation Handbook* these premia are still called "industry risk premia", but the nomenclature used within equations for this term is changed from "*IRP*" to "RP_i"

There are several common elements in the two equations. Both equations include a risk-free rate (R_f), an equity risk premium or market premium (RP_m), a size premium (RP_s), and (if the analyst deems it necessary) an additional adjustment for company-specific risk (RP_c). But, while the CAPM equation *includes* a beta (β), the build-up equation does *not*. This is where the industry risk premium comes in – the industry risk premium (RP_i) introduces a measure of beta risk into the build-up equation so that it more closely approximates the CAPM.

The *2015 Valuation Handbook* provides industry risk premia (RP_i) in Exhibit 5.7 at the end of this chapter. The industries for which industry risk premia are calculated are based on Standard Industrial Classification (SIC) codes. Each company's contribution to the adjustment shown is based on a full-information beta with each company's contribution to the full-information beta based on the segment sales reported in the company's 10-K for that SIC code.[5.13]

The analyst can download the list of companies included in the full-information beta calculation for each industry (and thus the industry risk premium), and can inspect the 10-Ks filed with the Securities and Exchange Commission for the companies included.[5.14] The descriptions of the companies included in the 10-K filings may provide the analyst with additional support for the similarities of the subject company to the companies (and business segments of companies) included in the full-information beta calculations. The segment information in the 10-K will also show the proportionate contribution to earnings, which may be very different than the proportionate contribution to revenue. While we use revenues because they are always positive numbers, in theory one should rely on segment profitability because stock returns are a function of profit, not revenue, and use of revenue segmenting may result in overweighting the low-profit segment.

The formula used to calculate industry risk premium (RP_i) is as follows:

Formula 5.5

$$RP_i = (FIB \times RP_m) - RP_m$$

where:

RP_i = Industry risk premium

FIB = Full-information beta for the industry

RP_m = ERP estimate used to calculate RP_i

5.13 Consistent with past *SBBI Valuation Yearbooks*.

5.14 To view the full list of companies, download the Industry Risk Premia Company List Report at www.DuffandPhelps.com/CostofCapital

Exhibit 5.7 displays the following data:

- SIC code
- SIC code description
- The number of companies included in the full-information beta calculation for each industry
- Full-information beta for each SIC code as of December 2014
- Three industry risk premiums calculated, using different ERP estimates:[5.15]

  Long-term, "historical" (i.e., realized) ERP: As of the end of 2014, the long-horizon historical equity risk premium was 7.00%.[5.16]

  Long-term "supply-side" ERP: As of the end of 2014, the long-horizon supply-side equity risk premium was 6.21%.[5.17]

  Duff & Phelps Recommended ERP: As of the end of 2014, the Duff & Phelps recommended ERP is 5.0% (developed in conjunction with a "normalized" long-term risk-free rate of 4.0%).

The industry risk premia previously published in Table 3-5 of the *SBBI Valuation Yearbook* were full-information betas converted to industry risk premia using the long-term "historical" ERP in Formula 5.5. Exhibit 5.7 provides industry risk premia calculated using the long-term "historical" ERP in the first column of industry risk premia (these industry risk premia are equivalent to the ones previously published in Table 3-5 of *SBBI Valuation Yearbook*).

In recognition that valuation analysts may use different ERP estimates, we have pre-calculated industry risk premia using two additional ERP estimates (the long-term "supply-side" ERP and the Duff & Phelps Recommended ERP).

For example, if you select SIC 281(Industrial Inorganic Chemicals), the full-information beta equals 1.24. Using the three ERP estimates, the following displays the calculation of the pre-calculated industry risk premia:

5.15 The industry risk premia *previously* published in Table 3-5 of the Morningstar/Ibbotson *SBBI Valuation Yearbook* were full-information betas converted to industry risk premia using only the "historical" long-term equity risk premium.

5.16 Calculated as the average annual return of the S&P 500 total return index minus the average annual return of the SBBI long-term (20-year) government bond income return series over the 1926–2014 time period. The long-horizon historical equity risk premium was previously published on the "back page" of the Morningstar/Ibbotson *SBBI Valuation Yearbook* (discontinued).

5.17 The supply-side equity risk premium was also previously published on the "back page" of the Morningstar/Ibbotson *SBBI Valuation Yearbook* (discontinued).

Using the long-term "historical" ERP:

$$RP_i = (FIB \times RP_m) - RP_m$$
$$1.67\% = (1.24 \times 7.00\%) - 7.00\% \text{ (difference due to rounding)}$$

Using the long-term "supply-side" ERP:

$$RP_i = (FIB \times RP_m) - RP_m$$
$$1.49\% = (1.24 \times 6.21\%) - 6.21\%$$

Using the Duff & Phelps Recommended ERP:

$$RP_i = (FIB \times RP_m) - RP_m$$
$$1.20\% = (1.24 \times 5.00\%) - 5.00\%$$

If you have concluded on a different ERP than is shown, a custom industry risk premium can be calculated in conjunction with Formula 5.5 . For example, if you have concluded that the future long-term ERP is 5.5%, then the custom industry risk premium for a full-information beta of 1.24 is:

$$RP_i = (FIB \times RP_m) - RP_m$$
$$1.32\% = (1.24 \times 5.50\%) - 5.50\%$$

Alternatively, if you have calculated your own custom peer group beta you can use Formula 5.5 to calculate a custom industry risk premium. For example, say you have calculated a peer group beta of 0.87, and that you are using the supply-side ERP, then the custom industry risk premium would be calculated as:

$$RP_i = (Peer\,Group\,Beta \times RP_m) - RP_m$$
$$-0.81\% = (0.87 \times 6.21\%) - 6.21\%$$

The industry risk premia (RP_i) can then be added to the build-up method as a simple up-or-down adjustment for "beta" risk:

$$k_e = R_f + RP_m + RP_s + RP_i$$

NOTE: *Industry risk premia are a measure of "beta" risk. Industry risk premium should not be used within the context of the CAPM or any other method of cost of capital estimation that already has a beta, because by doing so you will be double-counting beta risk.*

Full-Information Beta Methodology

The methodology used to calculate the full information betas (and thus the industry risk premia) in Exhibit 5.7 was nearly identical with how they were calculated in the former SBBI.[5.18] For example, the same database and data was used (Standard and Poor's *Research Insight*). The 3,870 U.S. companies included in the analysis had to have revenues of at least $100,000 in the most recent fiscal year, and have a market cap of at least $10,000 in the most recent month. The companies had to have an OLS beta greater than 0.0 and less than 5.0, and any resulting full information betas that were less than 0.0 or greater than or equal to 3.0 were eliminated.

However, there are also differences with the *2015 Handbook's* methodology for calculating industry risk premia compared to the former *SBBI Valuation Yearbook*'s methodology.

For example, instead of requiring that each company had to have "36 months of [return] data in the previous 60 months", we required "36 months of *contiguous* return data, *ending December 31, 2014*". The goal of our more stringent criteria was to *lessen* the threshold for excluding companies that had "spotty" data, and thus *increase* the data quality of the overall set.

A second difference was in the minimum number of companies participating in an industry (by SIC code) required in order to be included in the full-information beta regression analysis. We required a minimum of 10 participants in each industry; the former *SBBI* required 5 participants. The goal of this more stringent requirement was to eliminate SICs that have few participant companies, and are prone to high volatility from period to period.

5.18 The full-information betas published in the *2015 Valuation Handbook* (and in the former *SBBI Valuation Yearbook*) are based on an article by Paul D. Kaplan and James D. Peterson: "Full-Information Industry Betas", *Financial Management*, Summer 1998.

Exhibit 5.7: Industry Risk Premium (RP_i)
Through Year-end 2014

				Industry Risk Premia (%) using:		
SIC Code	Short Description	Number of Companies*	Full-Information Beta (FIB)	Long-term Historical ERP (7.00%)	Long-term Supply-Side ERP (6.21%)	Duff & Phelps Recommended ERP (5.00%)†
	Agriculture, Forestry, And Fishing					
01	Agricultural Production Crops	13	1.62	4.31	3.82	3.08
	Mining					
10	Metal Mining	19	1.20	1.38	1.23	0.99
12	Coal Mining	19	1.24	1.68	1.49	1.20
122	Bituminous Coal and Lignite Mining	19	1.38	2.68	2.38	1.92
13	Oil and Gas Extraction	197	1.18	1.27	1.13	0.91
131	Crude Petroleum and Natural Gas	163	1.17	1.17	1.04	0.84
138	Oil and Gas Field Services	47	1.36	2.55	2.26	1.82
1381	Drilling Oil and Gas Wells	18	1.60	4.19	3.72	3.00
1389	Oil and Gas Field Services, Not Elsewhere Classified	23	1.14	0.99	0.88	0.71
	Construction					
15	Building Construction General Contractors and Operative Builders	21	1.65	4.54	4.03	3.24
153	Operative Builders	15	1.64	4.47	3.96	3.19
16	Heavy Construction Other Than Building Construction Contractors	26	1.51	3.58	3.18	2.56
162	Heavy Construction, Except Highway and Street	21	1.50	3.53	3.13	2.52
1623	Water, Sewer, Pipeline, and Communications and Power Line	13	1.33	2.28	2.03	1.63
17	Construction Special Trade Contractors	23	1.02	0.15	0.13	0.11
173	Electrical Work	10	0.91	-0.64	-0.56	-0.45
	Manufacturing					
20	Food and Kindred Products	89	0.51	-3.41	-3.03	-2.44
203	Canned, Frozen, and Preserved Fruits, Vegetables, and Food Specialties	12	0.56	-3.11	-2.76	-2.22
204	Grain Mill Products	12	0.57	-3.01	-2.67	-2.15
208	Beverages	28	0.49	-3.58	-3.18	-2.56
2086	Bottled and Canned Soft Drinks and Carbonated Waters	16	0.46	-3.80	-3.37	-2.72
209	Miscellaneous Food Preparations and Kindred	17	0.46	-3.81	-3.38	-2.72
22	Textile Mill Products	11	1.52	3.64	3.23	2.60
23	Apparel, Other Finished Products Made from Fabrics and Similar Materials	28	1.16	1.12	0.99	0.80
25	Furniture and Fixtures	25	1.68	4.79	4.25	3.42
251	Household Furniture	13	1.56	3.90	3.46	2.78
26	Paper and Allied Products	34	0.51	-3.46	-3.07	-2.47
262	Paper Mills	11	0.83	-1.22	-1.08	-0.87
267	Converted Paper and Paperboard Products	15	0.33	-4.70	-4.17	-3.36
27	Printing, Publishing, and Allied Industries	32	1.57	3.95	3.51	2.83
28	Chemicals and Allied Products	362	0.82	-1.29	-1.14	-0.92
281	Industrial Inorganic Chemicals	35	1.24	1.67	1.49	1.20
2819	Industrial Inorganic Chemicals, Not Elsewhere Classified	20	1.64	4.48	3.98	3.20
282	Plastics Materials and Synthetic Resins, Synthetic	22	1.86	6.05	5.36	4.32
2821	Plastics Materials, Synthetic Resins, and Nonvulcanizable Elastomers	18	1.55	3.85	3.41	2.75
283	Drugs	246	0.70	-2.12	-1.88	-1.52
2834	Pharmaceutical Preparations	111	0.64	-2.54	-2.25	-1.81
2835	In Vitro and In Vivo Diagnostic Substances	33	0.82	-1.27	-1.13	-0.91
2836	Biological Products, Except Diagnostic Substances	101	0.83	-1.19	-1.06	-0.85
284	Soap, Detergents, and Cleaning Preparations; Perfumes, Cosmetics, and Other Toilet Preparations	20	0.58	-2.97	-2.63	-2.12
2844	Perfumes, Cosmetics, and Other Toilet Preparations	12	0.49	-3.60	-3.19	-2.57
286	Industrial Organic Chemicals	30	1.63	4.41	3.92	3.16
2869	Industrial Organic Chemicals, Not Elsewhere Classified	22	1.52	3.66	3.25	2.62
287	Agricultural Chemicals	15	1.39	2.70	2.39	1.93
289	Miscellaneous Chemical Products	19	1.61	4.27	3.79	3.05

* To view the full list of companies, download the Industry Risk Premia Company List Report at www.DuffandPhelps.com/CostofCapital

† The Duff & Phelps recommended ERP as of December 31, 2014 (5.0%) was developed *in relation* to a 4.0% "normalized" risk-free rate. The Duff & Phelps recommended ERP should be used with the risk-free rate that it was developed *in relation* to, per the schedule provided in Exhibit 3.15.

Exhibit 5.7: Industry Risk Premium (RP_i)
Through Year-end 2014

SIC Code	Short Description	Number of Companies*	Full-Information Beta (FIB)	Industry Risk Premia (%) using: Long-term Historical ERP (7.00%)	Long-term Supply-Side ERP (6.21%)	Duff & Phelps Recommended ERP (5.00%)†
	Manufacturing (continued)					
2899	Chemicals and Chemical Preparations, Not Elsewhere Classified	10	1.38	2.63	2.33	1.88
29	Petroleum Refining and Related Industries	28	1.39	2.75	2.44	1.97
291	Petroleum Refining	18	1.39	2.70	2.39	1.93
30	Rubber and Miscellaneous Plastics Products	45	1.08	0.55	0.49	0.39
308	Miscellaneous Plastics Products	32	1.66	4.61	4.09	3.29
3089	Plastics Products, Not Elsewhere Classified	22	1.49	3.41	3.02	2.44
31	Leather and Leather Products	11	1.09	0.62	0.55	0.44
32	Stone, Clay, Glass, and Concrete Products	31	2.02	7.11	6.31	5.08
327	Concrete, Gypsum, and Plaster Products	11	1.81	5.66	5.02	4.05
329	Abrasive, Asbestos, and Miscellaneous	14	1.83	5.78	5.13	4.13
33	Primary Metal Industries	59	1.69	4.80	4.26	3.43
331	Steel Works, Blast Furnaces, and Rolling and Finishing Mills	24	1.63	4.39	3.90	3.14
3312	Steel Works, Blast Furnaces (Including Coke Ovens), and Rolling Mills	13	1.62	4.37	3.88	3.12
335	Rolling, Drawing, and Extruding Of Nonferrous	20	1.65	4.55	4.03	3.25
34	Fabricated Metal Products, Except Machinery, and Transportation Equipment	81	1.46	3.18	2.83	2.28
342	Cutlery, Handtools, and General Hardware	16	1.33	2.29	2.03	1.64
344	Fabricated Structural Metal Products	29	1.68	4.74	4.21	3.39
3443	Fabricated Plate Work (Boiler Shops)	13	1.52	3.66	3.25	2.62
349	Miscellaneous Fabricated Metal Products	17	1.60	4.23	3.75	3.02
35	Industrial and Commercial Machinery and Computer Equipment	218	1.40	2.81	2.49	2.01
351	Engines and Turbines	17	1.78	5.47	4.85	3.91
352	Farm and Garden Machinery and Equipment	11	1.23	1.59	1.41	1.13
3523	Farm Machinery and Equipment	11	1.20	1.39	1.24	0.99
353	Construction, Mining, and Materials Handling	36	1.89	6.22	5.52	4.44
3531	Construction Machinery and Equipment	10	2.24	8.70	7.72	6.22
3533	Oil and Gas Field Machinery and Equipment	17	1.88	6.18	5.49	4.42
354	Metalworking Machinery and Equipment	12	1.47	3.32	2.94	2.37
355	Special Industry Machinery, Except Metalworking	30	1.63	4.42	3.92	3.16
3559	Special Industry Machinery, Not Elsewhere Classified	23	1.49	3.41	3.02	2.44
356	General Industrial Machinery and Equipment	39	1.46	3.20	2.84	2.29
3561	Pumps and Pumping Equipment	10	1.60	4.22	3.74	3.01
3569	General Industrial Machinery and Equipment, Not Elsewhere	11	1.66	4.63	4.11	3.31
357	Computer and Office Equipment	65	1.06	0.43	0.38	0.30
3572	Computer Storage Devices	11	1.28	1.96	1.74	1.40
3577	Computer Peripheral Equipment, Not Elsewhere Classified	16	2.14	7.96	7.06	5.69
358	Refrigeration and Service Industry Machinery	22	1.08	0.58	0.52	0.42
3585	Air-Conditioning and Warm Air Heating Equipment and Commercial and Industrial Refrigeration Equipment	15	1.17	1.19	1.06	0.85
36	Electronic and Other Electrical Equipment and Components, Except Computer Equipment	309	1.33	2.31	2.05	1.65
361	Electric Transmission and Distribution Equipment	14	1.49	3.46	3.07	2.47
362	Electrical Industrial Apparatus	31	1.65	4.54	4.03	3.25
3621	Motors and Generators	15	1.68	4.75	4.22	3.40
3629	Electrical Industrial Apparatus, Not Elsewhere Classified	11	2.13	7.93	7.03	5.66
363	Household Appliances	10	1.04	0.31	0.27	0.22
364	Electric Lighting and Wiring Equipment	15	1.37	2.59	2.30	1.85
365	Household Audio and Video Equipment, and Audio	10	1.77	5.39	4.78	3.85
366	Communications Equipment	68	1.33	2.29	2.03	1.64

* To view the full list of companies, download the Industry Risk Premia Company List Report at www.DuffandPhelps.com/CostofCapital

† The Duff & Phelps recommended ERP as of December 31, 2014 (5.0%) was developed *in relation* to a 4.0% "normalized" risk-free rate. The Duff & Phelps recommended ERP should be used with the risk-free rate that it was developed *in relation* to, per the schedule provided in Exhibit 3.15.

Exhibit 5.7: Industry Risk Premium (RP_i)
Through Year-end 2014

SIC Code	Short Description	Number of Companies*	Full-Information Beta (FIB)	Industry Risk Premia (%) using: Long-term Historical ERP (7.00%)	Long-term Supply-Side ERP (6.21%)	Duff & Phelps Recommended ERP (5.00%)†
	Manufacturing (continued)					
3661	Telephone and Telegraph Apparatus	22	1.49	3.42	3.03	2.44
3663	Radio and Television Broadcasting and Communications Equipment	33	1.12	0.87	0.77	0.62
3669	Communications Equipment, Not Elsewhere Classified	13	1.67	4.67	4.14	3.34
367	Electronic Components and Accessories	153	1.32	2.27	2.01	1.62
3672	Printed Circuit Boards	18	1.66	4.60	4.08	3.29
3674	Semiconductors and Related Devices	95	1.27	1.91	1.70	1.37
3679	Electronic Components, Not Elsewhere Classified	29	1.69	4.85	4.30	3.47
369	Miscellaneous Electrical Machinery, Equipment, and Supplies	27	1.62	4.32	3.83	3.09
37	Transportation Equipment	112	1.21	1.47	1.30	1.05
371	Motor Vehicles and Motor Vehicle Equipment	61	1.52	3.62	3.21	2.59
3711	Motor Vehicles and Passenger Car Bodies	10	1.19	1.34	1.19	0.95
3714	Motor Vehicle Parts and Accessories	47	1.66	4.59	4.07	3.28
372	Aircraft and Parts	33	0.89	-0.78	-0.69	-0.56
3728	Aircraft Parts and Auxiliary Equipment, Not Elsewhere Classified	19	1.06	0.43	0.38	0.31
38	Measuring, Analyzing, and Controlling Instruments; Photographic, Medical and Optical Goods; Watches and Clocks	240	0.96	-0.25	-0.22	-0.18
381	Search, Detection, Navigation, Guidance, Aeronautical, and Nautical Systems, Instruments, and Equipment	16	0.72	-1.96	-1.73	-1.40
382	Laboratory Apparatus and Analytical, Optical, Measuring, and Controlling Instruments	90	1.23	1.59	1.41	1.14
3823	Industrial Instruments for Measurement, Display, and Control of Process Variables; and Related Products	15	1.17	1.20	1.07	0.86
3825	Instruments for Measuring and Testing of Electricity and Electrical Signals	19	1.74	5.15	4.57	3.68
3826	Laboratory Analytical Instruments	21	1.01	0.05	0.04	0.04
3829	Measuring and Controlling Devices, Not Elsewhere Classified	21	1.51	3.53	3.14	2.53
384	Surgical, Medical, and Dental Instruments and Supplies	135	0.87	-0.90	-0.80	-0.64
3841	Surgical and Medical Instruments and Apparatus	43	0.88	-0.84	-0.74	-0.60
3842	Orthopedic, Prosthetic, and Surgical Appliances and Supplies	35	0.68	-2.21	-1.96	-1.58
3845	Electromedical and Electrotherapeutic Apparatus	62	1.10	0.68	0.60	0.49
39	Miscellaneous Manufacturing Industries	34	0.84	-1.12	-0.99	-0.80
394	Dolls, Toys, Games and Sporting and Athletic	15	0.84	-1.14	-1.01	-0.81
399	Miscellaneous Manufacturing Industries	16	1.08	0.53	0.47	0.38
3999	Manufacturing Industries, Not Elsewhere Classified	11	1.09	0.66	0.58	0.47
	Transportation, Communications, Electric, Gas, and Sanitary Services					
40	Railroad Transportation	12	1.03	0.24	0.22	0.17
4011	Railroads, Line-Haul Operating	10	0.99	-0.10	-0.09	-0.07
42	Motor Freight Transportation and Warehousing	29	1.02	0.12	0.11	0.09
421	Trucking and Courier Services, Except Air	27	1.01	0.08	0.08	0.06
4213	Trucking, Except Local	21	1.30	2.09	1.86	1.50
44	Water Transportation	16	0.57	-3.04	-2.70	-2.17
45	Transportation By Air	21	1.35	2.44	2.16	1.74
451	Air Transportation, Scheduled, and Air Courier	14	1.35	2.46	2.18	1.76
4512	Air Transportation, Scheduled	11	1.34	2.41	2.14	1.72
46	Pipelines, Except Natural Gas	20	0.61	-2.72	-2.41	-1.94
4612	Crude Petroleum Pipelines	11	0.04	-6.75	-5.99	-4.82
4613	Refined Petroleum Pipelines	10	0.74	-1.79	-1.59	-1.28
47	Transportation Services	31	0.94	-0.39	-0.34	-0.28
473	Arrangement Of Transportation Of Freight and Cargo	24	1.13	0.92	0.82	0.66
48	Communications	102	0.75	-1.74	-1.55	-1.25

* To view the full list of companies, download the Industry Risk Premia Company List Report at www.DuffandPhelps.com/CostofCapital

† The Duff & Phelps recommended ERP as of December 31, 2014 (5.0%) was developed *in relation* to a 4.0% "normalized" risk-free rate. The Duff & Phelps recommended ERP should be used with the risk-free rate that it was developed *in relation* to, per the schedule provided in Exhibit 3.15.

Exhibit 5.7: Industry Risk Premium (RP_i)
Through Year-end 2014

SIC Code	Short Description	Number of Companies*	Full-Information Beta (FIB)	Industry Risk Premia (%) using: Long-term Historical ERP (7.00%)	Long-term Supply-Side ERP (6.21%)	Duff & Phelps Recommended ERP (5.00%)†
	Transportation, Communications, Electric, Gas, and Sanitary Services (continued)					
481	Telephone Communications	32	0.51	-3.40	-3.02	-2.43
4812	Radiotelephone Communications	14	0.29	-4.97	-4.41	-3.56
4813	Telephone Communications, Except Radiotelephone	26	0.79	-1.44	-1.28	-1.03
483	Radio and Television Broadcasting Stations	32	1.43	3.00	2.66	2.14
4832	Radio Broadcasting Stations	12	1.56	3.92	3.48	2.80
4833	Television Broadcasting Stations	24	1.44	3.05	2.70	2.18
484	Cable and Other Pay Television Services	20	1.03	0.18	0.16	0.13
489	Communications Services, Not Elsewhere	30	1.11	0.77	0.69	0.55
49	Electric, Gas, and Sanitary Services	139	0.39	-4.24	-3.76	-3.03
491	Electric Services	58	0.33	-4.67	-4.14	-3.34
492	Gas Production and Distribution	64	0.55	-3.16	-2.80	-2.26
4922	Natural Gas Transmission	35	0.52	-3.38	-2.99	-2.41
4923	Natural Gas Transmission and Distribution	15	0.75	-1.74	-1.54	-1.24
4924	Natural Gas Distribution	33	0.45	-3.86	-3.43	-2.76
494	Water Supply	13	0.42	-4.03	-3.57	-2.88
495	Sanitary Services	19	0.56	-3.11	-2.76	-2.22
	Wholesale Trade					
50	Wholesale Trade-durable Goods	104	1.22	1.56	1.38	1.12
501	Motor Vehicles and Motor Vehicle Parts and Supplies	12	0.91	-0.64	-0.57	-0.46
504	Professional and Commercial Equipment and Supplies	25	0.98	-0.14	-0.12	-0.10
5045	Computers and Computer Peripheral Equipment and Software	14	1.35	2.44	2.17	1.74
505	Metals and Minerals, Except Petroleum	12	1.61	4.25	3.77	3.04
506	Electrical Goods	20	1.75	5.28	4.69	3.77
5065	Electronic Parts and Equipment, Not Elsewhere Classified	12	1.46	3.21	2.85	2.30
508	Machinery, Equipment, and Supplies	22	1.04	0.27	0.24	0.20
51	Wholesale Trade-non-durable Goods	90	0.77	-1.58	-1.40	-1.13
512	Drugs, Drug Proprietaries, and Druggists' Sundries	14	0.71	-2.00	-1.77	-1.43
514	Groceries and Related Products	16	0.03	-6.76	-6.00	-4.83
517	Petroleum and Petroleum Products	35	0.96	-0.27	-0.24	-0.19
5171	Petroleum Bulk stations and Terminals	18	0.78	-1.57	-1.39	-1.12
5172	Petroleum and Petroleum Products Wholesalers, Except Bulk Stations and Terminals	20	1.53	3.71	3.29	2.65
	Retail Trade					
53	General Merchandise Stores	19	0.54	-3.19	-2.83	-2.28
533	Variety Stores	11	0.49	-3.55	-3.15	-2.54
54	Food Stores	18	0.87	-0.88	-0.78	-0.63
541	Grocery Stores	12	0.86	-0.96	-0.85	-0.68
55	Automotive Dealers and Gasoline Service Stations	24	0.98	-0.12	-0.11	-0.09
56	Apparel and Accessory Stores	50	1.21	1.44	1.27	1.03
562	Women's Clothing Stores	14	1.70	4.87	4.32	3.48
565	Family Clothing Stores	14	0.90	-0.70	-0.62	-0.50
566	Shoe Stores	11	1.19	1.32	1.17	0.94
57	Home Furniture, Furnishings, and Equipment Stores	18	0.75	-1.75	-1.55	-1.25
58	Eating and Drinking Places	46	0.63	-2.58	-2.29	-1.85
59	Miscellaneous Retail	83	1.15	1.02	0.90	0.73
591	Drug Stores and Proprietary Stores	14	1.13	0.93	0.83	0.67
594	Miscellaneous Shopping Goods Stores	15	1.69	4.82	4.28	3.44
596	Nonstore Retailers	34	1.19	1.36	1.21	0.97
5961	Catalog and Mail-Order Houses	32	1.22	1.53	1.36	1.10

* To view the full list of companies, download the Industry Risk Premia Company List Report at www.DuffandPhelps.com/CostofCapital

† The Duff & Phelps recommended ERP as of December 31, 2014 (5.0%) was developed *in relation* to a 4.0% "normalized" risk-free rate. The Duff & Phelps recommended ERP should be used with the risk-free rate that it was developed *in relation* to, per the schedule provided in Exhibit 3.15.

Exhibit 5.7: Industry Risk Premium (RP_i)
Through Year-end 2014

SIC Code	Short Description	Number of Companies*	Full-Information Beta (FIB)	Industry Risk Premia (%) using: Long-term Historical ERP (7.00%)	Long-term Supply-Side ERP (6.21%)	Duff & Phelps Recommended ERP (5.00%)†
	Retail Trade (continued)					
599	Retail Stores, Not Elsewhere Classified	11	0.85	-1.03	-0.92	-0.74
5999	Miscellaneous Retail Stores, Not Elsewhere Classified	10	0.84	-1.11	-0.98	-0.79
	Finance, Insurance, and Real Estate					
60	Depository Institutions	505	1.24	1.67	1.48	1.20
602	Commercial Banks	363	1.32	2.25	2.00	1.61
603	Savings Institutions	130	0.91	-0.62	-0.55	-0.45
6035	Savings Institutions, Federally Chartered	97	0.93	-0.47	-0.42	-0.34
6036	Savings Institutions, Not Federally Chartered	33	0.88	-0.85	-0.76	-0.61
609	Functions Related To Depository Banking	12	0.89	-0.74	-0.66	-0.53
61	Non-depository Credit Institutions	83	1.35	2.43	2.16	1.74
614	Personal Credit Institutions	22	1.11	0.79	0.70	0.57
615	Business Credit Institutions	30	1.33	2.33	2.06	1.66
6153	Short-Term Business Credit Institutions, Except Agricultural	16	1.50	3.52	3.12	2.52
6159	Miscellaneous business Credit Institutions	15	0.87	-0.92	-0.81	-0.66
616	Mortgage Bankers and Brokers	24	1.36	2.53	2.25	1.81
6162	Mortgage Bankers and Loan Correspondents	21	1.31	2.19	1.95	1.57
62	Security and Commodity Brokers, Dealers, Exchanges, and Services	87	1.59	4.14	3.67	2.96
621	Security Brokers, Dealers, and Flotation	30	1.80	5.57	4.95	3.98
628	Services Allied With The Exchange Of Securities	60	1.60	4.19	3.72	3.00
6282	Investment Advice	55	1.59	4.11	3.65	2.94
63	Insurance Carriers	105	1.13	0.94	0.84	0.67
631	Life Insurance	42	1.82	5.76	5.11	4.11
632	Accident and Health Insurance and Medical	27	0.67	-2.34	-2.07	-1.67
6321	Accident and Health Insurance	14	0.30	-4.87	-4.32	-3.48
6324	Hospital and Medical Service Plans	14	0.63	-2.58	-2.29	-1.84
633	Fire, Marine, and Casualty Insurance	56	0.86	-0.99	-0.88	-0.71
635	Surety Insurance	14	1.84	5.86	5.20	4.19
64	Insurance Agents, Brokers, and Service	20	0.82	-1.29	-1.14	-0.92
65	Real Estate	75	1.66	4.63	4.11	3.31
651	Real Estate Operators (except Developers) and Lessors	38	0.74	-1.83	-1.62	-1.31
6512	Operators of Nonresidential Buildings	21	0.71	-2.04	-1.81	-1.46
653	Real Estate Agents and Managers	13	1.35	2.42	2.14	1.73
655	Land Subdividers and Developers	23	1.65	4.52	4.01	3.23
6552	Land Subdividers and Developers, Except Cemeteries	22	1.62	4.36	3.86	3.11
67	Holding and Other Investment Offices	301	0.92	-0.54	-0.47	-0.38
679	Miscellaneous Investing	300	0.93	-0.52	-0.46	-0.37
6792	Oil Royalty Traders	15	0.81	-1.31	-1.16	-0.94
6794	Patent Owners and Lessors	54	1.23	1.63	1.45	1.17
6798	Real Estate Investment Trusts	162	0.91	-0.65	-0.57	-0.46
6799	Investors, Not Elsewhere Classified	31	1.09	0.66	0.59	0.47
	Services					
70	Hotels, Rooming Houses, Camps, and Other Lodging Places	19	1.53	3.68	3.26	2.63
72	Personal Services	11	1.08	0.56	0.50	0.40
73	Business Services	462	1.16	1.10	0.98	0.79
731	Advertising	14	1.73	5.13	4.55	3.66
735	Miscellaneous Equipment Rental and Leasing	23	1.35	2.48	2.20	1.77
7359	Equipment Rental and Leasing, Not Elsewhere Classified	20	0.98	-0.14	-0.12	-0.10
736	Personnel Supply Services	25	1.84	5.87	5.21	4.20
7361	Employment Agencies	15	1.45	3.15	2.80	2.25

* To view the full list of companies, download the Industry Risk Premia Company List Report at www.DuffandPhelps.com/CostofCapital

† The Duff & Phelps recommended ERP as of December 31, 2014 (5.0%) was developed *in relation* to a 4.0% "normalized" risk-free rate. The Duff & Phelps recommended ERP should be used with the risk-free rate that it was developed *in relation* to, per the schedule provided in Exhibit 3.15.

Exhibit 5.7: Industry Risk Premium (RP_i)
Through Year-end 2014

SIC Code	Short Description	Number of Companies*	Full-Information Beta (FIB)	Industry Risk Premia (%) using: Long-term Historical ERP (7.00%)	Long-term Supply-Side ERP (6.21%)	Duff & Phelps Recommended ERP (5.00%)†
	Services (continued)					
737	Computer Programming, Data Processing, and Other Computer Related Services	356	1.12	0.87	0.77	0.62
7372	Prepackaged Software	141	1.15	1.03	0.91	0.74
7373	Computer Integrated Systems Design	58	1.16	1.10	0.98	0.79
7374	Computer Processing and Data Preparation and Processing Services	37	0.94	-0.45	-0.40	-0.32
7375	Information Retrieval Services	104	1.19	1.35	1.19	0.96
7379	Computer Related Services, Not Elsewhere Classified	38	0.75	-1.77	-1.57	-1.27
738	Miscellaneous Business Services	42	1.22	1.54	1.37	1.10
7389	Business Services, Not Elsewhere Classified	34	1.17	1.22	1.08	0.87
75	Automotive Repair, Services, and Parking	10	2.04	7.24	6.43	5.18
76	Miscellaneous Repair Services	11	1.16	1.10	0.98	0.79
78	Motion Pictures	19	1.38	2.67	2.37	1.91
781	Motion Picture Production and Allied Services	11	0.96	-0.25	-0.22	-0.18
7812	Motion Picture and Video Tape Production	10	0.96	-0.31	-0.27	-0.22
79	Amusement and Recreation Services	46	1.63	4.41	3.91	3.15
799	Miscellaneous Amusement and Recreation	33	1.54	3.79	3.37	2.71
7999	Amusement and Recreation Services, Not Elsewhere Classified	17	1.57	3.97	3.52	2.84
80	Health Services	65	1.27	1.86	1.65	1.33
805	Nursing and Personal Care Facilities	10	1.79	5.50	4.88	3.93
806	Hospitals	13	1.51	3.54	3.14	2.53
807	Medical and Dental Laboratories	17	0.77	-1.61	-1.43	-1.15
809	Miscellaneous Health and Allied Services, Not	18	0.86	-0.98	-0.87	-0.70
8099	Health and Allied Services, Not Elsewhere Classified	11	1.44	3.11	2.76	2.22
82	Educational Services	23	1.48	3.34	2.97	2.39
822	Colleges, Universities, and Professional Schools	15	1.43	3.00	2.66	2.14
87	Engineering, Accounting, Research, Management, and Related Services	100	0.97	-0.24	-0.22	-0.17
871	Engineering, Architectural, and Surveying	23	1.30	2.11	1.87	1.51
8711	Engineering Services	23	1.50	3.52	3.12	2.51
872	Accounting, Auditing, and Bookkeeping Services	11	0.89	-0.75	-0.66	-0.53
873	Research, Development, and Testing Services	34	1.03	0.23	0.20	0.16
8731	Commercial Physical and Biological Research	22	1.14	0.99	0.88	0.71
874	Management and Public Relations Services	39	0.91	-0.66	-0.58	-0.47
8742	Management Consulting Services	27	0.96	-0.31	-0.28	-0.22

* To view the full list of companies, download the Industry Risk Premia Company List Report at www.DuffandPhelps.com/CostofCapital

† The Duff & Phelps recommended ERP as of December 31, 2014 (5.0%) was developed *in relation* to a 4.0% "normalized" risk-free rate. The Duff & Phelps recommended ERP should be used with the risk-free rate that it was developed *in relation* to, per the schedule provided in Exhibit 3.15.

Debt Betas

The risk of debt capital can be measured by the beta of the debt capital (β_d). In cases where the debt capital is publicly traded, the β_d can be measured in a manner identical to measuring the beta of equity. For publicly traded debt, a regression of returns provides an estimate of β_d.

The general formula for estimating the beta for debt (e.g., traded bonds) is:[5.19]

Formula 5.6

$$R_d = \alpha + \beta_d \times \left(R_m - R_f\left(1-t\right)\right) + \varepsilon$$

where:

R_d	=	Rate of return on subject debt (e.g., bond) capital
α	=	Regression constant
β_d	=	Estimated beta for debt capital based on historical data
R_m	=	Historical rate of return on the "market"
t	=	Income tax rate
ε	=	Regression error term

That estimate indicates how the market views the riskiness of the debt as the rate of return on the stock market changes (i.e., as riskiness of equity changes).

The risk implied by debt beta is a function of the amount of debt in the capital structure; the variability of earnings before interest, taxes, depreciation, and amortization (EBITDA); the level and variability of EBITDA/sales; and so on. These are fundamental risks that the interest (and principal) will or can be paid when due.

Betas of debt generally correlate with credit ratings. While there is no data source that we know of that publishes debt betas for individual debt issuances at this time, the Exhibit 5.8 displays debt betas by credit rating as of year-end 2014. An analyst needs to estimate an approximate credit rating (synthetic credit rating) for the business debt that is not rated by Moody's, Standard & Poor's, or Fitch (discussed in Chapter 1 in in the section entitled "Estimating the Cost of Debt Capital"). The observed betas by debt rating can be used in conjunction with the equity beta unlevering and levering formulas which require debt beta estimates.

In Exhibit 5.9, the 60-month rolling average debt beta of Barclays U.S. credit grade indices (investment grade and non-investment grade) are plotted over the time horizon December 2006–December 2014. Intuitively, the debt betas of non-investment grade credit ratings are consistently larger (implying greater systematic risk) than debt betas of investment grade credit ratings.

5.19 Simon Benninga, *Financial Modeling* 2nd ed. (Cambridge, MA: MIT Press, 2000): 414.

Exhibit 5.8: Quarterly Debt Betas
March 2013–December 2014, Quarterly

Moody's Ratings	2013				2014			
	Mar	Jun	Sep	Dec	Mar	Jun	Sep	Dec
Aaa	0.00	0.00	-0.11	-0.07	-0.34	-0.33	-0.35	-0.37
Aa	0.10	0.09	0.04	0.04	-0.07	-0.10	-0.13	-0.13
A	0.20	0.20	0.13	0.05	-0.03	-0.07	-0.10	-0.11
Baa	0.27	0.28	0.24	0.12	0.11	0.07	0.03	0.03
Ba	0.49	0.51	0.47	0.28	0.40	0.32	0.29	0.30
B	0.62	0.60	0.55	0.43	0.63	0.50	0.47	0.50
Caa	0.94	0.95	0.89	0.69	0.84	0.75	0.72	0.75
Ca–D	1.35	1.33	1.24	1.13	1.12	0.88	0.79	0.79

Source of Underlying data: Corporate bond series used in analysis herein: Barclays US Corp Aaa Long TR USD, Barclays US Corp Aa Long TR USD, Barclays US Corp A Long TR USD, Barclays US Corp Baa Long TR USD , Barclays US Corp Ba Long TR USD, Barclays US Corp B Long TR USD, Barclays US Corp Caa Long TR USD, Barclays US HY Ca to D TR USD. Source: Morningstar *Direct*. Calculations by Duff & Phelps LLC.

Exhibit 5.9: 60-month Rolling Average Debt Beta of Aaa–Baa and Debt Beta of Ba–D
December 2006–December 2014

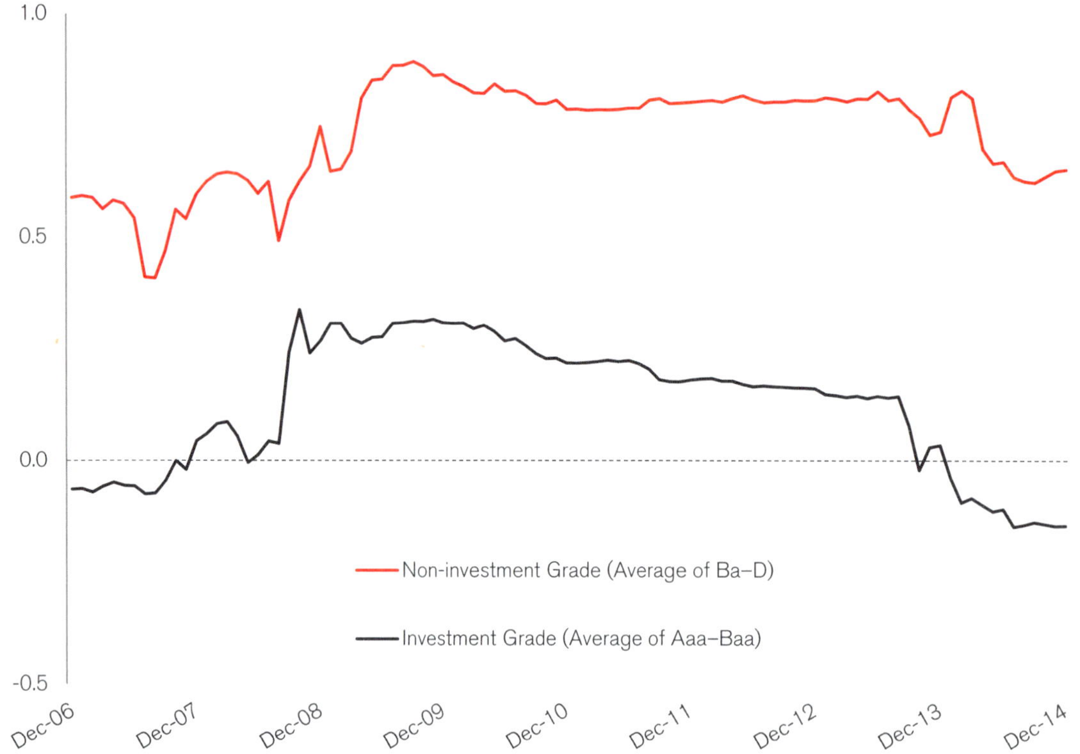

Source of Underlying data: Corporate bond series used in analysis herein: (i) Investment grade: Barclays US Corp Aaa Long TR USD, Barclays US Corp Aa Long TR USD, Barclays US Corp A Long TR USD, Barclays US Corp Baa Long TR USD , (ii) Non-investment grade: Barclays US Corp Ba Long TR USD, Barclays US Corp B Long TR USD, Barclays US Corp Caa Long TR USD, Barclays US HY Ca to D TR USD. Source: Morningstar *Direct*. Calculations by Duff & Phelps LLC.

Unlevering and Levering Equity Betas

Published and calculated betas for publicly traded stocks typically reflect the capital structure of each respective company at market values. These betas are sometimes referred to as *levered betas,* that is, betas reflecting the leverage in the company's capital structure.

Levered betas incorporate two risk factors that bear on systematic risk: business (or operating) risk and financial (or capital structure) risk. Removing the effect of financial leverage (i.e., unlevering the beta) leaves the effect of business risk only. The unlevered beta is often called an asset beta. Asset beta is the beta that would be expected were the company financed only with equity capital. When a firm's beta estimate is measured based on observed historical total returns (as most beta estimates are), its measurement necessarily includes volatility related to the company's financial risk. In particular, the equity of companies with higher levels of debt is riskier than the equity of companies with less leverage (all else being equal).

If the leverage of the division, reporting unit, or closely held company subject to valuation differs significantly from the leverage of the guideline public companies selected for analysis, or if the debt levels of the guideline public companies differ significantly from one another, it typically is desirable to remove the effect that leverage has on the betas before using them as a proxy to estimate the beta of the subject company.

Various authors have proposed alternative methodologies for unlevering and levering betas. These methodologies are generally functions of the risk of realizing the tax savings resulting from the tax deductions resulting from the interest expense of the debt component of the capital structure.

For example, if the guideline public company is losing money, has tax-loss carry- forwards from prior periods, or is marginally profitable, the tax savings from current interest payments will not be recognized in the current period; in essence, the cost of debt is greater by the loss or deferral of the income tax savings. This risk is captured both in the levered equity beta observed in the market and by the observed debt beta.

The debt beta captures the sensitivity recognized by the market to the risk of the debt as business conditions improve or deteriorate. The greater the debt beta, the more the market recognizes that the debt is sharing risk with the equity. If there were no assumed risk sharing, then the observed debt beta would be zero.

In Chapter 10 in the section entitled "Overview of the Methodology and Assumptions Used to Unlever Risk Premia" we discuss how we unlever the reported risk premiums. That formula incorporates a debt beta.

Key Things to Remember about Betas and the Industry Risk Premia

- An equity beta is a measure of the sensitivity of the movement in returns on a particular stock to movements in returns on some measure of the market. As such, beta scales market or systematic risk. In cost of capital estimation, beta is used as a modifier to the general equity risk premium in using the CAPM.

- There are many variations on the way betas are estimated by different sources of published betas and by valuation analysts. Thus, a beta for a stock estimated by one source may be very different from a beta estimated for the same stock by another source.

- Betas are an important element in estimating the cost of equity capital. The process of estimating beta requires considerable diligence, effort, and judgment on the part of the analyst.

- Industry risk premiums are used to have the build-up method more closely approximate the CAPM.

- Industry risk premiums are valid only to the extent that the subject company's risk characteristics are similar to the weighted average of the companies that make up the industry for the SIC code.

- Industry risk premia in the *2015 Valuation Handbook* are full-information betas that have been adjusted so that they can be added as a simple "up or down" adjustment in the build-up method. Industry risk premium should not be used within the context of the CAPM or any other method of cost of capital estimation that already has a beta, because by doing so you will be double-counting beta risk.

Chapter 6
Basic Building Blocks of the Cost of Equity Capital – Company-specific Risk Premia

Introduction

In this chapter we turn our attention to the last of the basic building blocks of the cost of equity capital, the company-specific risk premium (C-SRP). Identifying and quantifying a C-SRP is one of the most controversial and elusive areas of business valuation.[6.1] It is an adjustment common to both the build-up methods and CAPM.

The term company-specific risk is used to describe a variety of adjustments to the cost of equity capital. In a purely theoretical sense, the models used to estimate cost of capital generally assume that risks that can be "diversified away" are not compensable; this risk is properly called "unsystematic risk". Having said that, part of the problem that has been created in practice is that the intended meaning of the term "company-specific risk" can vary from person to person. For example, is a "company-specific" risk adjustment necessary in a hypothetical case in which the guideline public companies and the subject company are identical in every way? Many analysts would contend that the answer to this question is "no" – although this answer probably has very little to do with the theoretical definition of company-specific risk. What is probably intended is that no further adjustment may be necessary because the peer group in this hypothetical case (being identical to the subject) acts as a perfect proxy.

Different adjustments to the cost of equity capital are made in practice under the heading C-SRP. Among the adjustments labeled C-SRP are:

- **Adjustments for differences in risk:** Adjustments to cost of equity capital estimates derived from a sample of guideline public companies to account for differences in risk between a subject company that is not public (e.g., a closely held business, a division, or a reporting unit) and the guideline public companies.

- **Adjustments for Risk in Net Cash Flows and Biased Projections:** Adjustments to cost of equity capital estimates to account for risk in the net cash flows and biased projections provided for use in the valuation process.

- **Adjustments for Other Risk Factors:** For example, adjustments to cost of equity capital estimates to account for risks accepted by investors that may not hold diversified portfolios of investments.

[6.1] This chapter is excerpted in part from Shannon P. Pratt and Roger J. Grabowski, *Cost of Capital: Applications and Examples* 5th ed. (Hoboken, NJ: John Wiley & Sons, 2014)

This inconsistent use of the term C-SRP has led to considerable confusion in addition to its subjective nature. Former Chancellor Strine of the Delaware Court of Chancery stated the court's perspective on this issue:

> *Much more heretical to CAPM, however, the build-up method typically incorporates heavy dollops of what is called "company-specific risk," the very sort of unsystematic risk that the CAPM believes is not rewarded by the capital markets and should not be considered in calculating a cost of capital. The calculation of a company-specific risk is highly subjective and often is justified as a way of taking into account competitive and other factors that endanger the subject company's ability to achieve its projected cash flows. In other words, it is often a back-door method of reducing estimated cash flows rather than adjusting them directly. . . .*[6.2]

Others add a note of caution to an indiscriminant use of a C-SRP. They point out that many of the characteristics that are often cited as reasons for the addition of a company-specific risk adjustment are "the very attributes that generally define small companies", and therefore adding a company-specific risk may be double counting risks already embodied in the size premium adjustment.[6.3]

Adjustments for Differences in Risk

Let us begin by addressing C-SRP in the context of an adjustment to cost of equity capital estimates derived from a sample of guideline public companies to account for differences in risk between a subject company that is not public and the guideline public companies. Many analysts are able to express qualitative reasons for C-SRPs, but rarely provide data relating those qualitative factors to actual measurements in expected return. This lack of empirical support adds to the skepticism about the use of company-specific risk factors.

To help focus the discussion, let us assume that we are estimating the cost of equity capital by using the modified version of the CAPM. Many of the same issues surface if one were using a build-up method including an industry risk premium, which is a special type of beta modified for use within the build-up model.

Beta Suffers from Measurement Error

When an analyst is estimating the cost of equity capital for a public company, the analyst can directly observe the market's pricing of risk specific for the subject company. Every change in the public company's stock price signals the market's assessment of the company's risk relative to its expected returns given the current economic environment.

The beta estimate for the public company derived from a look-back method is an estimate of that specific company's measure of market risk (i.e., a company-specific risk factor). The public company is generally

6.2 *Delaware Open MRI Radiology Associates, P.A. v. Howard B. Kessler et al.* (Court of Chancery of State of Delaware, Cons C.A. No. 275-N).

6.3 Ted Israel, "The Generous Helping of Company-Specific Risk that May Already be Included in Your Size Premia", *Business Valuation Update*, Vol. 17, No. 6, June 2011.

its own best guideline public company; the market is confronted with pricing that company's own characteristics.

Some analysts may jump to the conclusion that this beta estimate captures the entirety of the market's pricing of risk. But, beta estimates suffer from measurement error.

For example, while beta is a forward-looking risk concept, the most commonly employed method for estimating beta uses regression analysis of *prior* period excess returns. During that prior period (look-back period, typically 60 months), some of the observed excess returns of the subject company stock are explained by the market risk expected by and priced by the market.

But some of the excess returns of the subject company stock resulted from unexpected events that the market could never have anticipated at the beginning of the look-back period, so they could never have been included in the pricing of risk by the market at the beginning of the look-back period, nor likely ever can be expected to be repeated in the future.

Therefore, in estimating the beta using a regression of excess returns over a look-back period, one can only estimate expected *future* beta with error. Valuation analysts are accustomed to adjusting subject company historical financial statements for nonrecurring events that are unrepresentative of the expected future financial results, but it is quite another thing to separate the relationship between expected returns that are likely to continue and be priced by the market from observations during the look-back period that one would consider nonrecurring.

One may find that estimating betas using observed returns over a look-back period at times provides an illogical estimate of beta. For example, for new public companies, there may not be enough data over the look-back period to produce a meaningful estimate of beta. Or, the subject company may have experienced a significant change during the look-back period that fundamentally changes the company (for example, a merger during the look-back period, or a downward assessment by the market in the future prospects of the business leading to a downward repricing of the company's stock price during the look-back period), and thus changes the way the market views the risk of the company. In such circumstances, if one needs to estimate a beta for a publicly traded company or provide a double check to the result provided by a regression, a commonly used method is to compare the beta estimate for the subject company to the median of the beta estimates of a sampling of guideline public companies (bottom-up approach). But the risks of the subject public company often do not match those of the median of the guideline public companies and may not even really match the risks of any of the guideline public companies used to develop the median.

Proxy Beta Estimates

When an analyst is estimating the cost of capital for a division or reporting unit of a public company or a closely held company, no direct observations of returns are available. This means that there are two major tasks confronting the analyst:

1. Develop a proxy beta estimate by matching the subject company's business risk characteristics to guideline public companies to understand how the market might price the market risk of the subject business if it in fact were public (i.e., what would be its beta estimate were it public).

2. Estimating additional risk factors priced by the market.

Let us address the task of matching business risk characteristics to develop a beta or proxy beta estimate. In the ideal situation, the analyst could identify "pure play" public companies (companies whose revenues are predominantly derived from a single business line such that their business risks would mirror those of the subject company). The beta estimates would likely fall into a tight range, and a measure of central tendency would likely be a good proxy beta estimate.

But finding pure play companies with the mix of business risks that *exactly* match those of the subject business can be difficult, if not impossible. Often the matching is done in terms of the SIC codes of the guideline public companies, but their actual mix of businesses can be quite different. Accordingly, the valuation analyst then must assess whether factors affecting a company's competitive position in the industry or its unique characteristics would cause investors to view that company's risk *differently* than the average risk characteristics of the guideline public companies to which it is being compared.

Alternatively, if there were sufficient pure play guideline public companies that had nearly the same risk characteristics as the subject company such that the market pricing of those risk characteristics could be observed, there would be no need to adjust for market risks that differ from those of the pure play guideline public companies.

However, there are often insufficient or even no pure play guideline public companies with risk characteristics matching those of the subject company. In those cases the analyst must look to how the market prices various risk characteristics to develop an estimate of the market risk. That is, if a sample of guideline public companies provides a poor or even meaningless estimate of the market risk that the subject company would experience were it public, it is appropriate to add or subtract a C-SRP to mimic the hypothetical pricing of the subject company's market risk.

The proper estimation of beta should help the valuation analysts better match the risk and return as priced by the market as observed in the guideline public companies with the appropriate risk and return for the subject division, reporting unit, or closely held business.[6.4]

6.4 See Pratt and Grabowsk, op.cit.: Chapter 11, "Beta: Differing Definitions and Estimates," and Chapter 12, "Unlevering and Levering Equity Betas."

Even for a company whose stock is publicly traded, one may need to develop a "proxy" beta by relying on inputs derived from a sampling of guideline public companies, because the beta estimate derived from the publicly traded stock itself may result in an unreliable estimate of the cost of equity capital.

Beta alone is not the only risk factor priced by the market (i.e., beta is not the only systematic risk factor).[6.5] So even having a direct estimate of beta stills leaves the analyst with the task of estimating other risk factors that are priced by the market.

Adjustments for Risk in Net Cash Flows and Biased Projections

Another commonly cited reason for a C-SRP is that the projections provided do not adequately capture the range of possible outcomes or there is bias, management or otherwise, reflected in the projections. According to the generally held theory surrounding using the CAPM, for example, as the basis for estimating the cost of capital, bad outcomes should be reflected in the various possible cash flows, with the expected cash flows reflecting both the more likely scenarios but also scenarios that will have a negative impact on net cash flows.

For example, assume that the subject business is an agribusiness operation, located in South Texas, which "dry farms" (relying only on rainfall) its tillable acres to grow cotton and milo crops. The pure play guideline public companies raise many more crop types; their holdings are geographically dispersed around the United States and Mexico, and, generally, they both dry farm and irrigate their crops, depending on the crops.

The underlying variability of the net cash flows of the South Texas agribusiness operation is much greater than that of the guideline public companies, year after year. Adding downside scenarios for negative events would serve to lower the mean of the distribution and better approximate the expected cash flows. Some would argue that there is greater inherent variability in the net cash flows that can be addressed through a variety of scenarios. While it may be appropriate to adjust for this greater risk by including a C-SRP in the cost of capital, a discussion of this issue is beyond the scope of this text.

The analyst must show how the distribution of possible net cash flows may differ in order to justify adding a C-SRP in estimating the cost of capital. The following discussion on bias in projections provides some guidance in this regard.

6.5 See Pratt and Grabowski, op.cit.: Chapter 13, "Criticism of CAPM and Beta versus Other Risk Measures."

Bias in Projections

Adding a company-specific risk premium to the discount rate is a commonly applied method to account for the overly optimistic forecasts.[6.6]

In the context of the modified CAPM we get the following:

$$k_e = R_f + \beta \times (RP_m) + RP_s \pm RP_c$$

where:

k_e	=	Cost of equity capital
R_f	=	Risk-free rate
β	=	Beta
RP_m	=	Equity risk premium (also referred as ERP)
RP_s	=	Size premium
RP_c	=	Company-specific risk premium (C-SRP) due to biased cash flow estimates

This commonly applied method of adjusting the discount rate does have a conceptual basis in cases where the range of possible cash flows included in the estimate of the expected cash flows omits a scenario that results in a permanent downside impact on the range of cash flows.

One of the first tasks is to test the forecasts to determine if forecasts prepared in prior periods have consistently been biased. Even in circumstances where the forecasts have been prepared in the normal course of business, it is not unusual for the forecast to be aspirational, rather than expectational. That is, they represent management's belief as to what can be accomplished if they succeed in carrying out their business plan. Businesspeople by their nature are optimists. Rarely are the projections tempered for possible downside outcomes.[6.7] One common method to assess for aspirational bias is to compare a series of historical forecasts to the actual subsequent performance and derive a "batting average" of sorts to consider in adjusting the current projections.

Expected cash flows should account for downside scenarios, of course, but sometimes the forecasts prepared by management and used in a valuation can be somewhat rosy in that they may reflect successful outcomes only, rather than reflecting the range of possible outcomes (both good and bad) that should be included in estimated expected cash flows.

Forecasts may also be biased high because they do not take into account the possibility that cash flows will in fact stop because of a possible downside risk that simply causes the business to stop operating

6.6 On the other hand, projections prepared in conjunction with some litigation disputes are often biased downward.

6.7 Richard Ruback, "Downsides and DCF: Valuing Biased Cash Flow Forecasts," *Journal of Applied Corporate Finance* 23(2) (Spring 2011): 8 –17.

(e.g., loss of the contract with the sole customer of the business). If such risks exist, it is common to simply increase the discount rate to account for the risk (i.e., add a C-SRP).

The risks to a company's cash flow may also *change* (in addition to ceasing operations) over time. For example, a parts supplier to an automobile manufacturer may have a contract to supply parts for an existing model of automobile (the contract likely specifies pricing but does not guarantee quantity). The risks to the cash flows during the current life of that model are significantly less than the risks to the cash flows after the current model life ends. As planning for a replacement model moves ahead before the current model life ends, the parts supplier will need to bid against other parts suppliers for that new model. This may indicate that the discount rate should change (be increased) after the current model life ends. There is a risk that net cash flows will be reduced if the parts supplier is unsuccessful in gaining a contract on a subsequent model. Possible net cash flows will likely not end if the parts supplier is not awarded a subsequent contract, as there will be replacement parts to be supplied, but the risks to the net cash flows have increased significantly.

Some Possible Courses of Action

It is often difficult for the analyst to obtain from management a distribution of possible outcomes, though the analyst should investigate the impacts on possible net cash flow outcomes if various events may take place. For example, what would be the impact on net cash flow if the subject company's largest customer reduced its purchases by, say, 25%? Or what would be the impact on net cash flows if competition caused the subject company to reduce its pricing by 10%? In this way, even if the analyst chooses to adjust the discount rate for the biased cash flow estimates rather than adjust the distribution of net cash flows, the analyst can test the impact of the addition to the cost of capital by hypothesizing a reasonable distribution of net cash flows. The key is to gain an understanding of the business risks through the interviews with management and through careful analysis of the income statements. Assessing risks initiates the valuation process and continues throughout.

Furthermore, developing a probability analysis of possible net cash flows with one of the outcomes predicting net cash flows equal to zero can assist the analyst in understanding the relative magnitude of his or her subjective assessment of the risk represented by the addition of a C-SRP. We recommend that an analyst closely examine the probability of a zero net cash flow scenario in the distribution of possible net cash flows as a check on any C-SRP added to the discount rate to account for the chance that the subject company may be forced to shut down because of a company-specific risk factor.[6.8]

Adjustments for Other Risk Factors

The cost of equity capital under pure CAPM is based on a company's systematic (or market) risk as measured by beta and not on any other risk factors. Investors are much less diversified than expected, even after consideration of the efforts of investment advisors urging them to diversify. Further, many do not hold the market portfolio as predicted by the pure CAPM. Based on these findings, it is reasonable to

[6.8] See also Atuna Saha and Burton G. Malkiel, "Valuation of Cash Flows with Time-Varying Cessation Risk," *Journal of Business Valuation and Economic Loss Analysis* 7(1) (2012): Article 3.

assume that investor rates of return expectations are influenced by risk factors beyond beta. The market has been found to price other risk factors beyond beta.

One such risk factor, firm size, is priced by the market as a risk factor (or as a proxy for other risk factors). While the pure CAPM would classify the size premium as unsystematic, we have found the size premium to be systematic. There is a predictable pattern of how the market prices this risk. Another company-specific risk issue is distress.[6.9]

Matching Fundamental Risk and Return

Valuation analysts typically have quantified the relationship between risk and expected return only by measuring risk in terms of beta and size. While company size is a risk factor in and of itself, Grabowski and King, original co-authors of what is now the Risk Premium Report's Risk Study, were interested in understanding whether the stock market recognized risk as measured by fundamental or accounting information.

The measures of company risk derived from accounting information may also be called fundamental or accounting measures of company risk to distinguish them from a stock–market–based measure of equity risk such as beta. The Risk Premium Report Risk Study uses three alternative measures of company risk, the first of which is a measure of profitability; the latter two are measures of earnings variability):

1. Operating margin (the lower the operating margin, the greater the risk)
2. Coefficient of variation in operating margin (the greater the coefficient of variation in operating margin, the greater the risk)
3. Coefficient of variation in return on equity (the greater the coefficient of variation in return on equity, the greater the risk)

Exhibit 6.1: Operating Margin (i.e. "profitability") and Variability of Earnings versus Risk

6.9 See Pratt and Grabowski, op.cit.: Chapter 17, "Distressed Businesses."

The Risk Premium Report's Risk Study documents the relationship between equity returns and the three fundamental risk measures. Exhibit 6.2 displays the observed relationships for the three risk measures and the risk premiums. By each measure of risk covered in the Risk Study, the result is a clear relationship between risk and historical equity returns. The portfolios of companies with higher risk have yielded higher rates of return. How to use the Risk Study is discussed in detail in Chapter 10.

In the first graph (upper left), one sees that as the average operating profit margin decreases (more risk), the returns increase. In the second graph (upper right), one sees that as the variability in the operating income increases (more risk), the returns increase. In the third graph (bottom), one sees that as the variability in the return on equity (ROE) increases (more risk), the returns increase.

Exhibit 6.2: Risk Premium Report-Risk Study

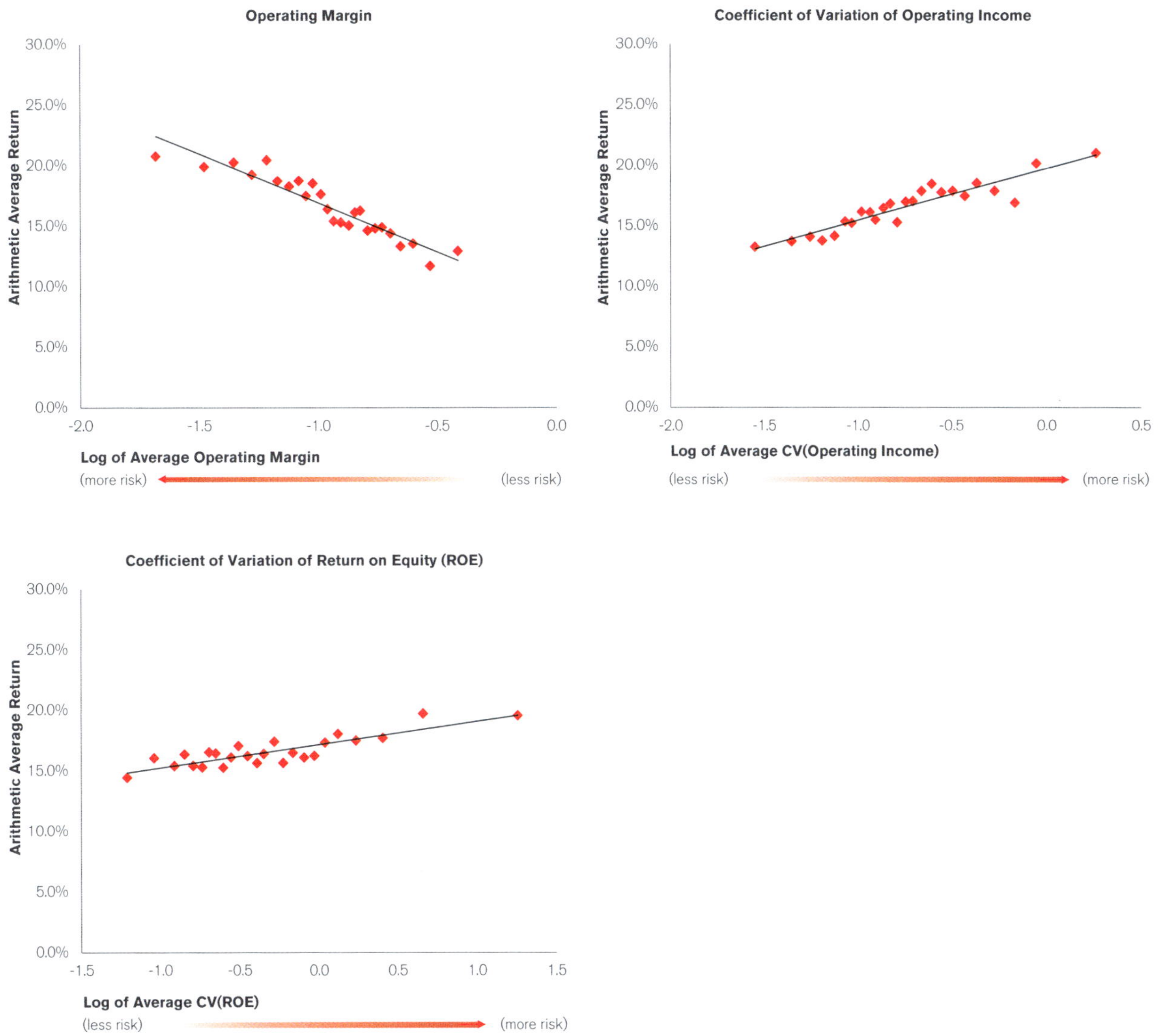

Source of underlying data: Derived from data from the Center for Research in Security Prices. © CRSP®, Center for Research in Security Prices, University of Chicago Booth School of Business. Used with permission. All rights reserved. Calculations by Duff & Phelps LLC.

A variety of academic studies have examined the relationship between financial statement data and various aspects of business risk.[6.10] Research has shown that measures of earnings volatility can be useful in explaining credit ratings, predicting bankruptcy, and explaining the CAPM beta.

Cost to Cure

One way to account for company-specific risk is to estimate the *cost to cure* that risk. For example, if a company-specific risk is reliant on a key salesperson for a large amount of sales, then the cost of buying life insurance sufficient to reimburse the company for the possible loss of that person due to death is one measure of the cost to cure that risk. Another company-specific risk that may be accounted for by estimating the cost to cure is potential environmental cleanup costs. One can estimate the probability-weighted costs of remediation, given the possibility that a cleanup will be required and the possible timing of a required cleanup.

Applying an adjustment for company-specific risk using the cost to cure is completely consistent with capital market theories, as these are adjustments to the expected cash flows.

Key Things to Remember about Company-specific Risk Premia

- Quantifying company-specific risk is one of the most controversial and elusive areas of business valuation.

- Valuation analysts who have written on company-specific risk reinforce the fact that the courts disapprove of unsubstantiated company-specific risk premiums. Those authors advise valuation professionals that courts do not find the company-specific risk premium to be reliable, and therefore caution them to avoid utilizing *unsubstantiated* premiums when offering expert testimony.

- Many of the characteristics that are often cited as reasons for the addition of a company-specific risk adjustment are the very attributes that generally define small companies, and therefore adding a company-specific risk may be double counting risks already embodied in the size premium adjustment. Thus the company-specific risk premium should be used judiciously.

- The company-specific risk premium is an adjustment that can be made by the valuation analyst to the data contained in the *Valuation Handbook.*

[6.10] A survey of the academic research can be found in Gerald White, Ashwinpaul Sondi, and Haim Fried, *The Analysis and Use of Financial Statements*, 3rd ed. (Hoboken, NJ: John Wiley & Sons, 2003): Chapter 18.

Chapter 7
The CRSP Deciles Size Premia Studies and the Risk Premium Report Studies – A Comparison

The CRSP Deciles Size Premia Study had been published in the Morningstar/Ibbotson *SBBI Valuation Yearbook* since 1999; the Risk Premium Report's Size Study was first published in 1996.

Both studies are now published in the *2015 Valuation Handbook – Guide to Cost of Capital.*

The CRSP Deciles Size Premia Study and the Risk Premium Report's Size Study examine the relationship between size and return, and both find that size and return are negatively correlated (as size *decreases*, return tend to *increase*, and vice versa).

However, there are significant differences between the two data sets used in the studies that the valuation analysts should be aware of. In this chapter, we first provide a brief history of both studies, and then discuss the two studies' similarities and differences.

History of the CRSP Deciles Size Premia Studies[7.1]

In 1976, Professor Roger Ibbotson co-published a seminal study analyzing the long-term returns of the principal asset classes in the United States economy. His findings documented the relationship between risk and return and quantified the ability to reduce risk through diversification. The study of long-term returns on asset classes also led to the development of such relevant cost of capital concepts as the equity risk premium and the size premium. The original 1976 study was extended into the *Ibbotson®Stocks, Bonds, Bills, and Inflation® (SBBI®) Classic Yearbook* which has been revised and updated annually for more than 25 years.[7.2] The source of return data used was the Center for Research in Security Prices (CRSP) at the University of Chicago.

A separate version of the *SBBI Classic* publication was developed based upon a series of workshops Ibbotson Associates held on the cost of capital. This publication was called the *Ibbotson SBBI Valuation Yearbook*, and was published from 1999–2013. In late 2013, Morningstar (which acquired Ibbotson Associates in 2006) announced that it will no longer publish the *Ibbotson SBBI Valuation Yearbook* and other valuation publications and products.

The size premia and industry risk premia data previously published in the *Ibbotson SBBI Valuation Yearbook* are now published in the *2015 Valuation Handbook.*

7.1 This section excerpted from the former *2013 SBBI Valuation Yearbook*, Introduction, page 1 (Morningstar, Chicago, 2013). The *SBBI Valuation Yearbook* is discontinued.

7.2 Morningstar continues to publish the *SBBI Classic Yearbook*. The *SBBI Classic Yearbook* is an analysis of the relative performance of various asset classes in the U.S., and does not provide extensive valuation data or methodology.

History of the Risk Premium Report Studies

In 1990, Roger Grabowski began closely studying the relationship between company size and stock returns.[7.3] Grabowski's early research focused on size as measured by market capitalization, but quickly advanced to two additional areas of inquiry: whether stock returns were predicted by (i) measures of size other than market capitalization, and also whether stock returns were predicted by (ii) fundamental risk measures based on accounting data. To investigate these questions, in 1992 Grabowski, working with a colleague, contracted with CRSP to build a database that combined stock prices, number of shares, and dividend data from the CRSP database with accounting and other fundamental accounting data from the Standard & Poor's *Compustat* database.

What they found was that as size *decreases*, or risk *increases* (as measured by fundamental accounting data), returns tend to *increase* (and vice versa). Thereafter, they published a series of articles reporting their findings, culminating with a seminal 1996 article and a subsequent article in 1999 which together serve as the foundation of the Risk Premium Report Size and Risk Studies.[7.4, 7.5]

Data Sources

The methodologies and data used to form the CRSP Decile portfolios are similar to the methodologies and data used to form the Risk Premium Report portfolios. However, there are significant differences, including:

- Financial service companies are *not* excluded from the CRSP Decile portfolios.
- The CRSP Deciles do *not* exclude "high-financial-risk" companies from the portfolios used to create its size premia.
- The CRSP Deciles portfolios are rebalanced quarterly, rather than annually.
- The CRSP Deciles portfolios' returns are market-cap-weighted, rather than equal-weighted.

CRSP Deciles Size Premia[7.6]

The data sources and methodologies used in the former *Ibbotson SBBI Valuation Yearbook* are the *same* as those used for the CRSP Deciles Size Premia in the *2015 Valuation Handbook*. The portfolios used in the CRSP Deciles Size Premia are created by CRSP.

7.3 Roger Grabowski, FASA, is a managing director in the Duff & Phelps Chicago office and part of the firm's Valuation Advisory Service practice. He is also co-author with Dr. Shannon Pratt of *Cost of Capital: Applications and Examples*, 5th Edition (John Wiley & Sons, 2014).

7.4 Roger J. Grabowski and David King, "New Evidence on Size Effects and Equity Returns", *Business Valuation Review* (September 1996, revised March 2000), & Roger J. Grabowski and David King, "New Evidence on Equity Returns and Company Risk", *Business Valuation Review* (September 1999, revised March 2000). The research began when King and Roger Grabowski were at Price Waterhouse, predecessor firm to PricewaterhouseCoopers.

7.5 The *Risk Premium Report* studies were published as the *Standard & Poor's Corporate Value Consulting Risk Premium Report* for reports from 2002 to 2004 and as the *PricewaterhouseCoopers Risk Premium Reports* and *Price Waterhouse Risk Premium Reports* for years before 2002.

7.6 This section excerpted from the former *2013 SBBI Valuation Yearbook*, page 85 (Morningstar, Chicago, 2013). The *SBBI Valuation Yearbook* is discontinued.

CRSP has refined the methodology of creating size-based portfolios and has applied this methodology to the entire universe of NYSE/NYSE MKT/NASDAQ-listed securities going back to 1926. The New York Stock Exchange universe excludes:

- Closed-end mutual funds
- Preferred stocks
- Real estate investment trusts
- Foreign stocks
- American Depository Receipts
- Unit investment trusts
- Americus Trusts

All companies on the NYSE are ranked by the combined market capitalization of their eligible equity securities. The companies are then split into 10 equally populated groups, or deciles. Eligible companies traded on the NYSE MKT (the former AMEX) and the Nasdaq National Market (NASDAQ) are then assigned to the appropriate deciles according to their capitalization in relation to the NYSE breakpoints.

The portfolios are rebalanced quarterly, using closing prices for the last trading day of March, June, September, and December. Securities added during the quarter are assigned to the appropriate portfolio when two consecutive month-end prices are available. If the final NYSE price of a security that becomes delisted is a month-end price, then that month's return is included in the quarterly return of the security's portfolio. When a month-end NYSE price is missing, the month-end value of the security is derived from merger terms, quotations on regional exchanges, and other sources. If a month-end value still is not determined, the last available daily price is used. Base security returns are monthly holding period returns. All distributions are added to the month-end prices, and appropriate price adjustments are made to account for stock splits and dividends. The return on a portfolio for one month is calculated as the weighted average of the returns for its individual stocks. Annual portfolio returns are calculated by compounding the monthly portfolio returns.[7.7]

Risk Premium Report Portfolios

The universe of companies used to perform the analyses presented in the Risk Premium Report is comprised of those companies that are found in *both* the CRSP and Standard and Poor's *Compustat* database. The following types of firms are then excluded:

7.7 According to CRSP document "Stock & Index RELEASE NOTES, December 2014 Annual UPDATE" (available at: http://crsp.chicagobooth.edu/files/images/release_notes/mdaz_201412_annual.pdf), CRSP reviewed the "shares outstanding" history from 1925–1946 of the CRSP standard market-cap-weighted portfolios as part of a larger pre-1946 shares review project. This review of the database caused small changes in the average annual returns over the 1926–2013 period (as of last year's December 2013 release date) when compared to the average annual returns over the 1926–2013 period (as of this year's December 2014 release date). These changes were not material: the largest/smallest change was 0.11%/-0.11; the average/median change was 0.002%/-0.004%).

- American depository receipts (ADRs)
- Non-operating holding companies
- Financial service companies (SIC code 6)
- Unseasoned companies
- High-financial-risk companies[7.8]

Financial service companies (those companies in finance, insurance, or real estate) are *excluded* because some of the financial data used is difficult to apply to companies in the financial sector (e.g., "sales" at a commercial bank). In addition, financial service companies tend to support a much higher ratio of debt to equity than do other industries, and so including them in with non-financial firms may be an "apples to oranges" comparison that could lead to improperly skewed results.

Valuation analysts should *not* use the Risk Premium's Size Study or Risk Study results to estimate cost of equity capital for a financial services company. Financial services companies include those companies in finance, insurance, or real estate (i.e. companies with an SIC Code that begins with "6").

The small-cap universe may consist of a disproportionate number of start-up companies and recent initial public offerings. These "unseasoned" companies may be inherently riskier than companies with a track record of viable performance. For this reason (for each year since 1963), the universe of companies is screened to exclude companies with any of the following characteristics:

- Companies lacking 5 years of publicly traded price history.
- Companies with sales below $1 million in any of the previous five fiscal years.
- Companies with a negative 5-year-average EBITDA (earnings before interest, taxes, depreciation and amortization) for the previous five fiscal years.
- Companies not listed on one of the major US stock exchanges (NYSE, NYSE MKT[7.9] or NASDAQ).

The Risk Premium Report portfolios exclude "high-financial-risk" companies from the portfolios used to create its premia, but provide further analysis of these companies *separately* in its High-Financial-Risk study. These companies have any of the following characteristics:

- Companies that Standard & Poor's has identified in the *Compustat* database as in bankruptcy or in liquidation.

7.8 This division of the universe of companies between seasoned and low financial risk companies and unseasoned a high financial risk companies is consistent with the valuation theory that matching risk characteristics provides more accurate valuation results. See for example Friedrich Sommer, Christian Rose and Arnt Wöhrmann, "Negative Value Indicators in Relative Valuation - An Empirical Perspective," *Journal of Business Valuation and Economic Loss Analysis* 2014 Vol. 9(1): 23–54

7.9 The "NYSE MKT" is the former American Stock Exchange, or AMEX.

- Companies with a "5-year average net income available to common equity" less than zero for the previous five years (either in absolute terms or as a percentage of the book value of common equity).

- Companies with "5-year-average operating income" (net sales minus cost of goods sold; selling, general and administrative expenses; and depreciation) less than zero for the previous five years (either in absolute terms or as a percentage of net sales).

- Companies with negative book value of equity at any one of the company's previous five fiscal year-ends.

- Companies with a debt-to-total capital ratio exceeding 80%, (debt is measured in book value terms, and total capital is measured as book value of debt plus market value of equity).

After these exclusions, the next step is to determine portfolio breakpoints for each of the eight size measures' 25 portfolios. Similar to the CRSP Decile portfolios, the upper and lower "boundaries" of each portfolio (i.e., breakpoints) for the Risk Premium Report portfolios are represented by the largest and smallest New York Stock Exchange (NYSE) company, respectively, in each of the 25 portfolios.

For example, to determine the breakpoints for the 25 portfolios ranked by "Total Assets", all of the companies in the base set that are traded on the NYSE are ranked from largest (in total assets) to smallest (in total assets), and then divided into 25 equally populated portfolios. Portfolio 1 made up of the largest companies and Portfolio 25 made up of the smallest companies.

Once portfolio breakpoints are determined, companies from the NYSE MKT (formerly the AMEX) universe and the NASDAQ universe are added to the appropriate portfolio, depending on their size with respect to the breakpoints (this is also very similar to what is done to form the CRSP Decile portfolios). Since NYSE MKT and NASDAQ companies are generally small relative to NYSE companies, their addition to the data set produces portfolios that are more heavily populated at the "small cap" end of the spectrum. The portfolios are rebalanced annually.

The equity returns for each of the 25 portfolios returns are calculated using an equal-weighted average of the companies in the portfolio, and these returns are then used to calculate the size premia and risk premia (and other useful information and statistics) for each.

Equal-weighted rather than market-cap-weighted returns are used in the formation of the Risk Premium Report portfolios because one could consider the former type of returns most relevant to the analyst applying the results of the Risk Premium Report in practice.

Specifically, the Risk Premium Report analysis of equal-weighted returns mimics the approach of the valuation analyst matching his or her subject company with a group of guideline firms based on a set of risk characteristics that includes size and financial risk. As the returns of each firm in the group of guideline firms are potentially equally informative about the effect of matching (risk) characteristics on the cost of equity, the equal-weighted realized returns of the peer group are likely more relevant to the analysis than are the market-cap-weighted returns. Using equal-weighted returns is also analogous to analysts using equal-weighted valuation multiples in the market approach to valuation.

Definitions of "Size"

Likely the most significant difference between the two studies is that the CRSP Deciles Size Premia measures "size" solely by market value of equity ("market capitalization", or simply "market cap"), while the Risk Premium Report measures size by market capitalization, plus seven additional measures of size:

i. Market capitalization

ii. Book value of equity

iii. 5-year average net income

iv. Market value of invested capital (MVIC)

v. Total assets

vi. 5-year average EBITDA

vii. Sales

viii. Number of employees

Time Period Examined

The CRSP Deciles Size Premia are calculated over the time horizon 1926–present year. The Risk Premium Report size and risk premia are calculated over the time horizon 1963–present year.[7.10]

Generally, advocates of using the longest period for which returns are available argue that long-term returns are stable and that using shorter horizons would exclude events that could potentially re-occur. Advocates of using a shorter time horizon argue that some previous events are unlikely to re-occur, or that the relationship between stocks and bonds has changed in more recent years.

Number of Portfolios

The CRSP Deciles Size Premia have 10 portfolios (i.e., deciles) for which size premia are calculated. Decile 1 is comprised of the largest companies, and decile 10 is comprised of the smallest companies. Decile 10 is further split into 10w, 10x, 10y, and 10z.

The Risk Premium Report Size and Risk Studies have 25 portfolios. Portfolio 1 is comprised of the largest companies, and portfolio 25 is comprised of the smallest companies.

[7.10] In the *2015 Valuation Handbook*, the *CRSP Decile* studies and *Risk Premium Report* studies examine the time periods 1926–2014 and 1963–2014, respectively.

Portfolio Overlap

The CRSP Deciles Size Premia portfolios and size groupings *overlap*. The Risk Premium Report portfolios do *not* overlap. "Overlap" occurs when a subject company can properly be placed in *multiple* portfolios or size groupings, and can lead to significantly different cost of equity estimates.

For example, say Company ABC has an estimated market cap of no more than $10 million. A valuation analyst using the CRSP Deciles Size Premia exhibits can properly place Company ABC into *four* different size groupings: Micro-Cap, Decile 10, portfolio 10b, and portfolio 10z. In the *2015 Valuation Handbook* these size grouping have size premia of 3.74%, 5.78%, 8.94%, and 11.98%, respectively. Choosing the appropriate size grouping is left to the valuation analyst.

A valuation analyst using the Risk Premium Report exhibits can properly place Company ABC into only a *single* market capitalization grouping. For example, Company ABC, with a market capitalization of $10 million, can be properly placed into portfolio 25 of Exhibit B-1 only, which has a smoothed size premium of 7.03%.

Some valuation analysts argue that size grouping "overlap" introduces a level of subjectivity that may lead to "goal-seeking" of cost equity capital estimates. For example, using the CRSP Deciles Size Premia cited in the previous example, the difference in Company ABC's cost of equity capital estimate could vary by as much as nearly 8.24%, depending on which size grouping the valuation professional decides to place the subject company into (Micro-Cap, Decile 10, portfolio 10b, or portfolio 10z).[7.11] Others argue that valuation analysts need this flexibility in order to "choose the size premium that is most statistically relevant for their application." [7.12]

Guideline Portfolio Method and Regression Equation Method

The CRSP Deciles Size Premia provide a *single* way to match their subject company's market capitalization with the appropriate size premium (which is, in essence, the "guideline portfolio" method).

The Risk Premium Report portfolios provide *two* ways to match the subject company's size (or risk) characteristics to the appropriate size (or risk) premium (the "guideline portfolio method" and the "regression equation method").

For more about matching the subject company's characteristics with the appropriate premium, please see Chapter 8, "CRSP Deciles Size Premia Examples" and Chapter 9 "Risk Premium Report Exhibit – General Information".

7.11 The 8.24% that the cost of equity capital estimate could vary is the "high" size premium estimate (11.98%) minus the "low" size premium estimate (3.74%).

7.12 Michael W. Barad, "Size Matters: How to Apply Size Premium Metrics When Size-Based Category Breakpoints Overlap", *The Value Examiner* (November/December 2009).

Risk Premia Over CAPM (Size Premia)

The CRSP Deciles Size Premia study and the Risk Premium Report's Size Study provide the traditional "risk premia over CAPM", commonly referred to as "size premia". Size premia represent the difference between historical (observed) excess return and the excess return predicted by the capital asset pricing model (CAPM). Size premia can be added to cost of capital estimation models as an adjustment for the additional risk of smaller companies relative to large companies.

Both the CRSP Deciles Size Premia and the Risk Premium Report are "beta-adjusted". A "beta-adjusted" size premia has been adjusted to remove the portion of excess return that is attributable to beta, leaving only the size effect's contribution to excess return. The size premia in both studies are calculated in essentially the same way – as the difference in historical portfolio excess returns (i.e., what *actually* happened), and the excess returns that CAPM would have *predicted*. Excess returns are defined here as portfolio returns over and above the risk-free asset's returns.

Exhibit 7.1 provides an overview of the CRSP deciles and size groupings in terms of relative size (by aggregate market capitalization) and number of companies as of December 31, 2014.

Decile 1 has 191 companies in it, and accounts for nearly two-thirds of aggregate market cap (64.25%). Decile 10 has 951 companies in it, and accounts for less than 1% of aggregate market cap (0.59%).

Exhibit 7.1: Aggregate Market Capitalization and Company Counts of the CRSP (NYSE/NYSE MKT/ NASDAQ) Deciles and Size Groupings
December 31, 2014

Decile	Historic Average Percentage of Total Capitalization	Recent Number of Companies	Recent Decile Market Capitalization (in $thousands)	Recent Percentage of Total Capitalization
1-Largest	63.06%	191	14,808,784,274	64.25%
2	13.96%	208	3,247,447,914	14.09%
3	7.57%	198	1,579,432,904	6.85%
4	4.74%	222	1,042,428,212	4.52%
5	3.26%	222	694,147,086	3.01%
6	2.42%	272	585,657,120	2.54%
7	1.79%	323	449,325,255	1.95%
8	1.33%	421	333,731,801	1.45%
9	1.04%	413	173,673,205	0.75%
10-Smallest	0.83%	951	135,401,288	0.59%
Mid-Cap 3-5	15.57%	642	3,316,008,202	14.39%
Low-Cap 6-8	5.54%	1,016	1,368,714,176	5.94%
Micro-Cap 9-10	1.87%	1,364	309,074,493	1.34%

Source of underlying data: Calculated (or derived) based on data from CRSP ©2015 Center for Research in Security Prices (CRSP®), The University of Chicago Booth School of Business (2015). Calculations by Duff & Phelps LLC.

In Exhibit 7.2, the largest company in each of the CRSP (NYSE/NYSE MKT/NASDAQ) deciles and size groupings (by market capitalization) as of September 30, 2014.

Exhibit 7.2: Largest Company (by market capitalization) in CRSP (NYSE/NYSE MKT/NASDAQ) Deciles and Size Groupings
September 30, 2014

Decile	Company Name	Recent Market Capitalization (in $thousands)
1-Largest	Apple Inc.	591,015,721
2	Cummins Inc.	24,272,837
3	Murphy Oil Corp.	10,105,622
4	Alaska Airgroup Inc.	5,844,592
5	Great Plains Energy Inc.	3,724,186
6	Wolverine World Wide Inc.	2,542,913
7	Wesco Aircraft Holdings Inc.	1,686,860
8	First Bancorp P R	1,010,634
9	G P Strategies Corp.	548,839
10-Smallest	M V Oil Trust	300,725

Source of underlying data: CRSP databases ©2015 Center for Research in Security Prices (CRSP®), The University of Chicago Booth School of Business (2015).

In the following sections we provide an example of (i) calculating a CRSP Deciles Size Premia and (ii) a Risk Premium Report, using example data from each of the two data sets.

Size Premium Calculation: CRSP Deciles Size Premia

In the *2015 Valuation Handbook*, the CRSP Deciles Size Premia are calculated over the years 1926–2014. The following statistics are calculated over this time period:

- The "historical" average annual long-term equity risk premium is 7.00%
- The average annual risk-free rate is 5.07%
- CRSP portfolio 10b average annual return equals 23.62%
- CRSP portfolio 10b OLS beta equals 1.37

The beta-adjusted size premium for CRSP portfolio 10b is calculated as follows:

10b Size Premium = actual excess return – excess return predicted by CAPM

Looking at Exhibit 7.3, the *actual* excess return of portfolio 10b is 18.54% (23.62% - 5.07%) (difference due to rounding), and the excess return that CAPM *predicted* is 9.60% (1.37 x 7.00%) (difference due to rounding). The size premium for CRSP portfolio 10b is therefore 8.94%, which is "what actually happened" (18.54%) minus "what CAPM predicted" (9.60%). This is what is meant when we say that the beta of smaller companies doesn't explain all of their returns. In this simple example, beta fell 8.94% short of explaining what actually happened.

Exhibit 7.3: CRSP (NYSE/NYSE MKT/NASDAQ) Deciles; Returns in Excess of CAPM (i.e., beta-adjusted Size Premia)

Size Grouping		OLS Beta	Arithmetic Mean	Return in Excess of Risk-free Rate (actual)	Return in Excess of Risk-free Rate (as predicted by CAPM)	Size Premium
Mid-Cap (3–5)		1.12	14.00%	8.93%	7.86%	1.07%
Low-Cap (6–8)		1.22	15.44%	10.36%	8.56%	1.80%
Micro-Cap (9–10)		1.35	18.26%	13.18%	9.45%	3.74%
Breakdown of Deciles 1–10						
1-Largest		0.92	11.15%	6.08%	6.44%	-0.36%
2		1.04	12.96%	7.89%	7.26%	0.63%
3		1.11	13.71%	8.64%	7.73%	0.91%
4		1.13	14.01%	8.93%	7.88%	1.06%
5		1.17	14.84%	9.76%	8.16%	1.60%
6		1.17	15.01%	9.94%	8.21%	1.74%
7		1.25	15.53%	10.46%	8.75%	1.71%
8		1.30	16.35%	11.27%	9.12%	2.15%
9		1.34	17.13%	12.06%	9.36%	2.69%
10-Smallest		1.40	20.62%	15.54%	9.76%	5.78%
Breakdown of 10th Decile						
10a		1.41	19.14%	14.07%	9.85%	4.22%
	10w	1.38	17.93%	12.86%	9.68%	3.18%
	10x	1.45	20.73%	15.66%	10.12%	5.54%
10b		1.37	23.62%	18.54%	9.60%	8.94%
	10y	1.43	22.55%	17.48%	9.97%	7.51%
	10z	1.29	26.06%	20.99%	9.01%	11.98%

Source of underlying data: Calculated (or derived) based on data from CRSP ©2015 Center for Research in Security Prices (CRSP®), The University of Chicago Booth School of Business (2015). Calculations by Duff & Phelps LLC.

Size Premium Calculation: Risk Premium Report

In the *2015 Valuation Handbook*, the Risk Premium Report size studies are calculated over the years 1963–2014. The following statistics are calculated over this time period:

- The "historical" average annual long-term equity risk premium is 5.05%.

- The average annual risk-free rate is 6.61%.
- In Risk Premium Report Exhibit B-3 (25 portfolios sorted from largest companies to smallest companies by net income), portfolio 25 average annual return equals 21.43%
- In Risk Premium Report Exhibit B-3, portfolio 25 has a sum beta of 1.32

The beta-adjusted size premium for Risk Premium Report Exhibit B-3, portfolio 25, is calculated as follows:

Exhibit B-3, portfolio 25 Size Premium = actual excess return – excess return predicted by CAPM

The *actual* excess return of Exhibit B-3, portfolio 25 is 14.82% (21.43% - 6.61%), and the excess return that CAPM *predicted* is 6.67% (1.32 x 5.05%). The (un-smoothed; see next section) size premium for Exhibit B-3 portfolio 25 is therefore 8.15%, which is "what actually happened" (14.82%) minus "what CAPM predicted" (6.67%).

"Smoothed" Premia versus "Average" Premia

The CRSP Deciles Size Premia are not smoothed.

We recommend using the "smoothed" size premia (and risk premia) in the Risk Premium Report. Smoothing the premia essentially averages out the somewhat scattered nature of the raw average premia. The "smoothed" average risk premium is generally the more appropriate indicator for most of the portfolio groups. It should be noted, however, that at the largest-size and smallest-size ends of the range, the average historical risk premiums may tend to jump off of the smoothed line, particularly for the portfolios ranked by size measures that incorporate market capitalization (Exhibits A-1 and A-4).

OLS Beta versus Sum Beta

The CRSP Deciles Size Premia use ordinary least square (OLS) betas to calculate the size premia shown in Appendix 3 (the size premia in Appendix 3 are the *same* size premia previously published on the *SBBI Valuation Yearbook*'s "back page" ("Key Variables in Estimating the Cost of Capital"). Sum beta equivalents to these OLS size premia estimates are available in Chapter 4, "Basic Building Blocks of the Cost of Equity Capital – Size Premium".

The Risk Premium Report uses "sum" betas in all calculations. Sum betas have been shown to be better predictors of smaller companies' expected returns. To learn more about sum betas, see Chapter 5, "Basic Building Blocks of the Cost of Equity Capital – Betas and Industry Risk Premia".

Risk Premia Over the Risk Free Rate

The Risk Premium Report exhibits also provides a second type of premia, "risk premia over the risk-free rate". Risk premia over the risk-free rate are provided in the Size Study's A exhibits, and in the Risk-Study's D exhibits.

Risk premia over the risk-free rate in the Size Study's A exhibits and the Risk Study's D exhibits represent the overall difference between the historical (observed) return of equities over the risk-free rate, and are therefore a measure of risk in terms of the combined effect of *market* risk and *size* risk. These premia are simply added to the risk-free rate, within the context of the build-up method.

The CRSP Deciles Size Premia do not include "risk premia over the risk-free rate".

Unlevered Premia

The Risk Premium Report provides "levered" and "unlevered" size and risk premia. Unlevered premia are used to estimate cost of equity capital assuming a firm is financed 100% with equity and 0% debt.

The CRSP Deciles Size Premia do not include "unlevered" premia.

Risk Study

The Risk Premium Report includes the Risk Study in addition to the Size Study. The CRSP Deciles Size Premia include only a size study.

The Risk Study is an extension of the Size Study. The main difference between them is that while the Size Study analyzes the relationship between size and return, the Risk Study analyzes the relationship between fundamental risk measures (based on accounting data) and return. These are called "fundamental" measures of company risk to distinguish these risk measures from a stock market based measure of equity risk such as beta. As in the Size Study, 25 portfolios are created, but instead of being ranked by eight alternative measures of size as is done in the Size Study, the Risk Study portfolios are ranked by three fundamental risk measures:

- Five-year average operating income margin
- Coefficient of variation in operating income margin
- Coefficient of variation in return on book equity

The first statistic measures profitability and the other two statistics measure volatility of earnings. All have been shown to be predictors of equity returns. The Risk Study exhibits provide the valuation analyst with an additional method for estimating cost of equity capital.

Characteristics of Companies in Portfolios

The Risk Premium Report includes detailed information about the characteristics of the companies that comprise the portfolios used to create its premia, and provides the valuation analyst with a mechanism to further refine cost of equity estimates by gauging how "alike or different" the subject company is compared to the companies that make up the portfolios (see the section entitled "Comparative Risk Study" in Chapter 10).

The CRSP Deciles Size Premia provide some information about the characteristics of the companies that comprise the portfolios used to create the published size premia, but do not presently provide a mechanism for using this information to further refine cost of equity estimates.

Online Applications

The Risk Premium Report Study and CRSP Deciles Size Premia Study have online companion applications that automatically calculate levered and unlevered cost of equity estimates using both the build-up method and the CAPM, and then provides full summary output in both Microsoft *Word* and Microsoft *Excel* format.[7.13]

Exhibit 7.4 (next page) summarizes the similarities and differences between the Risk Premium Report Study and the CRSP Deciles Size Premia Study.

[7.13] Business Valuation Resources (BVR) and ValuSource have both developed online companion applications to the *2015 Valuation Handbook*. Both BVR's online version, the "*Risk Premium Toolkit*" (previously named the "*Risk Premium Calculator*"), and ValuSource's version, the "*Cost of Capital Analyzer*", are designed to help the valuation analyst use the *2015 Valuation Handbook's* data as efficiently as possible (both the CRSP Deciles Size Premia Studies and the Risk Premium Report Studies data are included). Both versions automatically calculate and properly apply the ERP Adjustment to all methods of cost of equity capital methods available when using the Risk Premium Report exhibits. The online "*Risk Premium Toolkit*" is available from BVR at www.BVResources.com/DuffPhelps or by calling 1 (503) 291-7963 extension 2. The "*Cost of Capital Analyzer*" is available from ValuSource at www.valusource.com/vhb or by calling 1 (800) 825-8763.

Exhibit 7.4: Risk Premium Report Study and the CRSP Deciles Size Premia Study Comparison Table

	CRSP Deciles Size Premia Study	**Risk Premium Report Study**
Time horizon over which data is analyzed	1926–present year	1963–present year
Size study included	Yes	Yes
Size measures used	Market Cap	Market Cap + 7 alternative size measures
Premia over CAPM (i.e., size premia)	Yes	Yes
"Risk premia over the risk-free rate"	No	Yes
Unlevered premia (in addition to levered premia)	No	Yes
Risk Study (in addition to Size Study)	No	Yes
Risk measures used	NA	Operating Margin, CV Operating Margin, CV ROE
Can be used to estimate COE using build-up method	Yes	Yes
Can be used to estimate COE using CAPM model	Yes	Yes
Number of portfolios	10 Deciles + 10w, 10x, 10y, 10z	25
Regression formulas available for estimating "exact" interpolated premia "in between" portfolios, or for estimating premia for very small companies	No	Yes
Portfolio overlap*	Yes	No
Exclusion of financial companies	No	Yes
Exclusion of high-financial-risk companies	No	Yes
Analysis of high-financial-risk companies	NA	Yes
Specific information about the companies that comprise the portfolios	Yes	Yes
Mechanism to further refine cost of equity estimates by gauging how "alike or different" the subject company is when compared to the companies that make up the portfolios	No	Yes
Optional online *Risk Premium Toolkit*** (BVR) or *Cost of Capital Analyzer* (ValuSource)	Yes	Yes

* Portfolio overlap refers to whether a subject company can be properly placed in multiple size groupings or portfolios.

** Previously named the "*Risk Premium Calculator*".

Chapter 8
CRSP Deciles Size Premia Examples

The *2015 Valuation Handbook's* "CRSP Deciles Size Premia" are the same size premia that were previously published in the *SBBI Valuation Yearbook*. The CRSP Deciles Size Premia can be used to estimate the cost of equity capital using the build-up method and the capital asset pricing model (CAPM). In this chapter, examples for using the data properly are provided. For more information about the theoretical basis of the build-up and CAPM models, see Chapter 2, "Methods for Estimating the Cost of Equity Capital".

A size premium is necessary for both the build-up method and the CAPM when using the CRSP Deciles Size Premia data set to estimate the cost of equity capital. Examination of market evidence shows that within the context of CAPM, beta does not fully explain the difference between small company returns and large company returns. In other words, the *actual* (historical) excess return smaller companies earn tends to be greater than the excess return *predicted* by the CAPM for these companies. This "premium over CAPM" is commonly known as a "beta-adjusted size premium" or simply "size premium".

The size premia in both data sets (CRSP Deciles Size Premia exhibits and Risk Premium Report exhibits) in the *2015 Valuation Handbook* are "beta-adjusted". In other words, the portion of excess return that is not attributable to beta is controlled for, or *removed*, leaving only the size effect's contribution to excess return. These premia are appropriate for use in the CAPM, and in build-up methods that *do not otherwise already have a measure of size risk.*

Industry risk premia (RP_i) in the *2015 Valuation Handbook* are full-information betas that have been adjusted so that they can be added as a simple "up or down" adjustment when the build-up method is employed to estimate the cost of equity capital. Adding both a size premium and an industry risk premium to the build-up method is *not* double-counting. The size premium is "beta-adjusted", and the industry risk premium is the beta risk. These two premia are designed to account for two *different* types of risk.

Build-up Example

The build-up method is an additive model commonly used for calculating the required rate of return on equity capital. As the name implies, successive "building blocks" are summed, each representing the additional risk inherent to investing in alternative assets. An example of this is the extra return (i.e. "premium"), that investors demand for investing in stocks versus investing in a riskless security.

The build-up equation for use with the CRSP Deciles Size Premia exhibits is as follows:[8.1]

$$k_{e,i} = R_f + RP_m + RP_s + RP_i$$

[8.1] The *2015 Valuation Handbook* provides data and methodology that can be used to estimate cost of equity capital *prior* to any additional "company-specific" risk premiums (RP_c) that may be deemed applicable by the individual valuation analyst.

where:

$k_{e,i}$ = Expected rate of return on security i (this is "cost of equity capital")

R_f = Risk-free rate as of the valuation date (typically a long-term U.S. government bond yield)

RP_m = General equity risk premium (i.e. "ERP") estimate for the "market"

RP_s = Risk premium for smaller size (i.e. "premium over CAPM", or "size premium")

RP_i = Industry risk premium

In the build-up method, we start with the risk-free rate (R_f), and then add the general equity risk premium or market premium (RP_m), a premium for small size (RP_s), and an industry risk premium (RP_i).[8.2]

All of the information to estimate cost of equity using the CRSP Deciles Size Premia data exhibits as of December 31, 2014 (the "data through" date of the *2015 Valuation Handbook*) can be found in the following two tables:

Appendix 3, "CRSP Deciles Size Premia: Key Variables"[8.3]

- R_f (risk-free rate)
- RP_m (equity risk premium)
- RP_s (size premium)

Exhibit 5.7, "Industry Risk Premia (RP_i)" (found in Chapter 5)[8.4]

- RP_i (industry risk premium)

Estimate the cost of equity capital for a company in SIC 36 (Electronic and Other Electrical Equipment and Components, Except Computer Equipment) with a market cap of $340 million using the build-up equation:

$$k_{e,i} = R_f + RP_m + RP_s + RP_i$$

8.2 The industry risk premium was referred to as "IRP" in equations in the former *SBBI Valuation Yearbook*. In the *2015 Valuation Handbook*, the industry risk premium is referred to as "RP_i" in equations. Other than that, the industry risk premia in the *2015 Valuation Handbook* are exactly the same concept as they were in the former *SBBI Valuation Yearbook* – an adjustment that inserts a measure of "beta" risk into the build-up equation to make it more comparable to the CAPM. For more information, see Chapter 5, "Basic Building Blocks of the Cost of Equity Capital – Betas and Industry Risk Premia".

8.3 Appendix 3, "CRSP Deciles Size Premia: Key Variables" includes all of the data previously published on the *SBBI Valuation Yearbook's* "back page", which was entitled "Key Variables in Estimating the Cost of Capital".

8.4 Exhibit 5.7, "Industry Risk Premia (RP_i)" is the equivalent of Table 3-5, "Industry Premia Estimates" in the former Morningstar/Ibbotson *SBBI Valuation Yearbook*.

Referring to Appendix 3, the risk-free rate (R_f) is the "Long-term (20-year) U.S. Treasury Coupon Bond Yield" (2.40%):

$$k_{e,i} = 2.40\% + RP_m + RP_s + RP_i$$

Referring again to Appendix 3, the equity risk premium (RP_m) is the "Long-horizon expected equity risk premium (historical)" (7.00%):

$$k_{e,i} = 2.40\% + 7.00\% + RP_s + RP_i$$

Referring again to Appendix 3, the size premium (RP_s) is the "Size Premium (Return in Excess of CAPM)". The estimated market cap of \$340 million places the company in the Micro-Cap category, which has a size premium of 3.74%. The company's market cap of \$340 million could also place it in Decile 9, which has a size premium of 2.69%. The choice of which size category the company more properly belongs in falls ultimately to the valuation analyst (and his or her intimate knowledge of the subject company). However, placing the company in the broader size category (Micro-Cap) is likely the more *conservative* estimate. The \$340 million market capitalization falls comfortably in the *middle* of the smallest and largest companies of the Micro-Cap size category (\$3.037 million and \$548.839 million, respectively), and \$340 million falls closer to the *bottom* of the Decile 9 size category's range of smallest and largest companies (\$300.752 million and \$548.839 million, respectively).

In this example we will use the more conservative size premium of the broader Micro-Cap category, 3.74%:

$$k_{e,i} = 2.40\% + 7.00\% + 3.74\% + RP_i$$

Finally, referring to Exhibit 5.7, the industry risk premium (RP_i) is the "Industry Risk Premia (%) calculated using" either (i) the "Long-term *Historical* ERP", (ii) the Long-term Supply-Side ERP, or (iii) the Duff & Phelps Recommended ERP. We selected the "Long-horizon expected equity risk premium (historical)" as our market premium in this example (7.00%), and so the appropriate industry risk premium to select is the industry risk premium calculated using the long-term *historical* ERP.[8.5] For SIC 36, this is 2.31%. The cost of equity capital estimate for this company using the build-up method is 15.45%:

$$15.45\% = 2.40\% + 7.00\% + 3.74\% + 2.31\%$$

Alternatively, if you have calculated your own *custom* peer group beta you can calculate a custom industry risk premium. For example, if you have calculated a custom peer group beta of 1.35, and you are using the "historical" ERP, then the custom industry risk premium (RP_i) is:[8.6]

8.5 Alternatively, had we selected the "Long-horizon expected equity risk premium (*supply-side*)" as our market premium from Appendix 3, the appropriate industry risk premium from Exhibit 5.7 would be the industry risk premium calculated using the long-term *supply-side* ERP.

8.6 See Formula 5.3 in Chapter 5, "Basic Building Blocks of the Cost of Equity Capital – Betas and Industry Risk Premia."

$$RP_i = (Peer\,Group\,Beta \times RP_m) - RP_m$$
$$2.45\% = (1.35 \times 7.00\%) - 7.00\%$$

NOTE: *Industry risk premia (RP_i) are a measure of "beta" risk. Industry risk premium should not be used within the context of the CAPM or any other method of cost of capital estimation that already has a beta, because by doing so you will be double-counting beta risk.*

CAPM Example

The capital asset pricing model (CAPM) is the most widely used method for estimating the cost of equity capital. For example, one survey found that while many firms use multiple methods of estimating the cost of equity capital, 75% of them use the CAPM.[8.7] Despite its criticisms, the CAPM has been one of the most widely used models for estimating the cost of equity capital for more than 30 years.

The CAPM equation for use with the CRSP Deciles Size Premia exhibits is as follows:[8.8]

$$k_{e,i} = R_f + \beta \times (RP_m) + RP_s$$

where:

$k_{e,i}$ = Expected rate of return on security i (this is "cost of equity capital")

R_f = Risk-free rate as of the valuation date (typically a long-term U.S. government bond yield)

β = A measure of market (i.e., systematic) risk of a stock; the sensitivity of changes in the returns (dividends plus price changes) of a stock relative to changes in the returns of a specific market benchmark or index.

RP_m = General equity risk premium (i.e. "ERP") estimate for the "market"

RP_s = Risk premium for smaller size (i.e. "premium over CAPM", or "size premium")

With CAPM, we start with the risk-free rate (R_f), and then add the equity risk premium (RP_m) multiplied by a beta (β), and then add a premium for size (RP_s).

All of the information to estimate cost of equity using the CRSP Deciles Size Premia exhibits as of December 31, 2014 (the "data through" date of the *2015 Valuation Handbook*) can be found in the following table (with the exception of beta):

8.7 John R. Graham and Campbell R. Harvey, "The Theory and Practice of Corporate Finance," *Journal of Financial Economics* (May 2001): 187–243.

8.8 The *2015 Valuation Handbook* provides data and methodology that can be used to estimate cost of equity capital *prior* to any additional "company-specific" risk premiums (RP_c) that may be deemed applicable by the individual valuation analyst.

Appendix 3, "CRSP Deciles Size Premia: Key Variables"[8.9]

- R_f (risk-free rate)
- RP_m (equity risk premium)
- RP_s (size premium)

Estimate the cost of equity capital for a company in SIC 36 (Electronic and Other Electrical Equipment and Components, Except Computer Equipment) with a market cap of $340 million using the CAPM equation:

$$k_{e,i} = R_f + \beta \times (RP_m) + RP_s$$

Referring to Appendix 3, the risk-free rate (R_f) is the "Long-term (20-year) U.S. Treasury Coupon Bond Yield" (2.40%):

$$k_{e,i} = 2.40\% + \beta \times (RP_m) + RP_s$$

Referring again to Appendix 3, the equity risk premium (RP_m) is the "Long-horizon expected equity risk premium (historical)" (7.00%):

$$k_{e,i} = 2.40\% + \beta \times (7.00\%) + RP_s$$

Referring again to Appendix 3, the size premium (RP_s) is the "Size Premium (Return in Excess of CAPM)". The estimated market cap of $340 million places the company in the Micro-Cap category, which has a size premium of 3.74%. The company's market cap of $340 million could also place it in Decile 9, which has a size premium of 2.69%. The choice of which size category the company more properly belongs in falls ultimately to the valuation analyst (and his or her intimate knowledge of the subject company). However, placing the company in the broader size category (Micro-Cap) is likely the more *conservative* estimate. The $340 million market capitalization falls comfortably in the *middle* of the smallest and largest companies of the Micro-Cap size category ($3.037 million and $548.839 million, respectively), and $340 million falls closer to the *bottom* of the Decile 9 size category's range of smallest and largest companies ($300.752 million and $548.839 million, respectively).

In this example we will use the more conservative size premium of the broader Micro-Cap category, 3.74%:

$$k_{e,i} = 2.40\% + \beta \times (7.00\%) + 3.74\%$$

8.9 Appendix 3, "CRSP Deciles Size Premia: Key Variables" includes all of the data previously published on the Morningstar/Ibbotson *SBBI Valuation Yearbook's* "back page", which was entitled "Key Variables in Estimating the Cost of Capital".

The only input not available from Appendix 3 is the beta (β). The analyst could use the "full-information" beta for SIC code 36 (1.33) from Exhibit 5.7, which would result in a cost of equity capital estimate of 15.45%:

$$15.45\% = 2.40\% + 1.33 \times (7.00\%) + 3.74\%$$

An excellent source of industry and peer group betas for use in the analyst's custom CAPM estimate of cost of equity capital is the *Valuation Handbook – Industry Cost of Capital*.[8.10, 8.11] For example, in the *2014 Valuation Handbook – Industry Cost of Capital*, the median "SIC Composite" adjusted peer group beta is 1.3.

In addition to industry and peer group betas (both levered and unlevered), the *Valuation Handbook – Industry Cost of Capital* provides eight (8) cost of equity capital estimates for each of the industries covered in the book (depending on data availability), cost of debt capital and weighted average cost of capital (WACC) estimates, plus capital structure, valuation multiples, industry betas, and more. The analyst can use this information to (i) benchmark, (ii) supplement, and (iii) strengthen his or her own custom cost of capital analysis.[8.12]

Alternatively, analysts can calculate their own *custom* peer group beta estimates using the guideline companies they have selected as the best proxies for their particular subject company, or select a group of published betas from another published source such as Bloomberg.

8.10 The *2014 Valuation Handbook – Industry Cost of Capital* (with data through March 2014) was published in October 2014 by Duff and Phelps. The 2015 version of the "industry" book is scheduled for release in late May 2015 (with data through March 2015), and will be published by John Wiley and Sons. The *Valuation Handbook – Industry Cost of Capital* provides the same type of rigorous industry-level analysis previously published in the green-cover Morningstar/ Ibbotson *Cost of Capital Yearbook* (discontinued in 2013). Like the previous Morningstar/Ibbotson *Cost of Capital Yearbook*, the *Valuation Handbook – Industry Cost of Capital* is published with data through March, and includes three intra-year quarterly updates (June, September, and December; updates are not sold separately, and only as a group). And, like the previous Morningstar/Ibbotson *Cost of Capital Yearbook*, the new *Valuation Handbook – Industry Cost of Capital* analyzes over 200 U.S. industries identified by their Standard Industrial Classification (SIC) code. To order copies of the *Valuation Handbook - Industry Cost of Capital* and its quarterly updates, please go to www.wiley.com/go/ValuationHandbooks

8.11 See Exhibit 1.4 herein for a sample industry analysis page from the *2014 Valuation Handbook – Industry Cost of Capital*.

8.12 A normal and prudent step in any analysis is to perform some benchmarking as a "reasonableness" test. The information in the *Valuation Handbook – Industry Cost of Capital* helps the analyst answer the question, "How does my own analysis of the subject company compare to the subject company's peers (i.e., the industry)?"

Key Things to Remember about the CRSP Deciles Size Premia

- When using the CRSP Deciles Size Premia exhibits, a size premium is added to both the build-up and CAPM estimates of cost of equity capital.

- The size premia in both data sets (CRSP Deciles Size Premia exhibits and Risk Premium Report exhibits) in the *2015 Valuation Handbook* are "beta-adjusted". In other words, the portion of excess return that is not attributable to beta is controlled for, or removed, leaving only the size effect's contribution to excess return.

- Size premia are appropriate for use in the capital asset pricing model (CAPM), and in build-up methods that *do not otherwise already have a measure of size risk.*

- Industry risk premia (RP_i) are a measure of "beta" risk. Industry risk premium should not be used within the context of the CAPM or any other method of cost of capital estimation that already has a beta, because by doing so you will be double-counting beta risk.

- The size premia in Appendix 3 use ordinary least square (OLS) betas to derive the size premia. Equivalent size premia calculated using sum betas are available in Exhibit 4.7 in Chapter 4.

- When using the CRSP Deciles Size Premia data set to select an ERP (long-term "historical ERP or long-term "supply-side" ERP), the corresponding risk-free rate should be the spot rate. The Duff & Phelps recommended ERP as of December 31, 2014 (5.0%) was developed *in relation* to a 4.0% "normalized" risk-free rate. The Duff & Phelps recommended ERP should be used with the risk-free rate that it was developed *in relation* to, per the schedule provided in Exhibit 3.15.

Chapter 9
Risk Premium Report Exhibits – General Information

In Chapter 9, general information about the Risk Premium Report exhibits is presented. In Chapter 10, detailed examples for estimating cost of equity capital using the Risk Premium Exhibits are provided.

Appropriate Use of the Risk Premium Report Exhibits

The risk premia and size premia reported in the Risk Premium Report exhibits can be used to develop cost of equity capital estimates using both the build-up method and the capital asset pricing model (CAPM). The Risk Premium Report exhibits are primarily designed to be used to develop cost of equity capital estimates for the large majority of companies that are fundamentally healthy, and for which a "going concern" assumption is appropriate. As such, high-financial-risk (i.e. "distressed") companies are excluded from the base dataset and analyzed separately in the Risk Premium Report exhibits' "High-Financial-Risk Study."

Because financial services companies are excluded from the base set of companies used to develop the analyses presented in the Risk Premium Report exhibits, these exhibits should *not* be used to estimate cost of equity capital for financial services companies. Financial services companies include those companies in finance, insurance, or real estate (i.e. companies with an SIC Code that begins with "6").

The data used in the Risk Premium Report exhibits is drawn from information on public companies. Therefore, the resulting cost of equity capital estimates using the data are "as if public".

The Risk Premium Report exhibits can be used to develop estimates of cost of equity capital for divisions, reporting units and closely held businesses without "guessing" at the value of the business before one begins the analysis. Rather, fundamental measures of firm size (e.g., sales, net income, EBITDA) and risk (e.g., operating margin) can be used to directly estimate cost of equity capital for non-public businesses.

How the Risk Premium Report Exhibits are Organized

The Risk Premium Report exhibits include the Size Study, the Risk Study, the High-Financial-Risk Study, and the Comparative Risk Study.

- **Size Study:** Comprised of Exhibits A-1 through A-8 (used in the build-up method) and Exhibits B-1 through B-8 (used in CAPM). Analyzes the relationship between equity returns and company size, using eight measures of company size:

    i. Market capitalization

    ii. Book value of equity

iii. 5-year average net income

iv. Market value of invested capital (MVIC)

v. Total assets

vi. 5-year average EBITDA

vii. Sales

viii. Number of employees

- **Risk Study:** Comprised of Exhibits D-1, D-2, and D-3 (fundamental measures of risk based on accounting data). Analyzes the relationship between equity returns and three accounting-based fundamental risk measures:

  i. Five-year average operating income margin

  ii. Coefficient of variation in operating income margin

  iii. Coefficient of variation in return on book equity

- **High-Financial-Risk Study:** Comprised of Exhibits H-A, H-B, and H-C. Exhibit H-A is the high-financial-risk equivalent to the A exhibits, Exhibit H-B is the high-financial-risk equivalent to the B exhibits, and Exhibit H-C is the high-financial-risk equivalent to the C exhibits. Analyzes the relationship between equity returns and high-financial-risk, as measured by the Altman z-Score.

- **Comparative Risk Study:** Comprised of the C exhibits, when used in conjunction with the D exhibits. The C Exhibits can help valuation analysts further refine their cost of equity capital estimates by comparing their subject company's fundamental risk factors to the fundamental risk factors of the companies that comprise the 25 Size Study portfolios.

Exhibit 9.1: The Size Study, Risk Study, High-Financial-Risk Study, Comparative Risk Study, and Corresponding Exhibits

Size Study	**Risk Study**
Exhibits A-1 through A-8	Exhibits D-1 through D-3
Exhibits B-1 through B-8	

High-Financial-Risk Study	**Comparative Risk Study**
Exhibits H-A, H-B, and H-C	Exhibits C-1 through C-8

Cost of Equity Capital Estimation Methods Available

Exhibit 9.2 provides a complete list of the methods available when using the Risk Premium Report exhibits to estimate cost of equity capital, their respective equations, and which data exhibit the inputs for each of the methods is found in.

Exhibit 9.2: All Available Cost of Equity Capital Estimation Methods in the Risk Premium Report

Study	Method	Cost of Equity Capital Formula	Data Exhibit	ERP Adjustment?
Size Study	Build-up 1	$k_e = R_f + RP_{m+s}$ $+ ERP\ Adjustment$	A Exhibits	Yes
Size Study	Build-up 1-unlevered	$k_e = R_f + RP_{m+s,\ unlevered}$ $+ ERP\ Adjustment$	C Exhibits	Yes
Size Study	CAPM	$k_e = R_f + (\beta{*}ERP) + RP_s$	B Exhibits	No
Size Study	Build-up 2	$k_e = R_f + ERP + RP_s + RP_i$	B Exhibits	No
Risk Study	Build-up 3	$k_e = R_f + RP_{m+c}$ $+ ERP\ Adjustment$	D Exhibits	Yes
Risk Study	Build-up 3-unlevered	$k_e = R_f + RP_{m+c,\ unlevered}$ $+ ERP\ Adjustment$	D Exhibits	Yes
High-Financial-Risk Study	Build-up 1-High-Financial-Risk	$k_e = R_f + RP_{m+s,\ high\text{-}financial\text{-}risk}$ $+ ERP\ Adjustment$	H-A Exhibits	Yes
High-Financial-Risk Study	CAPM-High-Financial-Risk	$k_e = R_f + (\beta{*}ERP) + RP_{s,\ high\text{-}financial\text{-}risk}$	H-B Exhibits	No

Exhibit 9.2 also identifies which of the estimation methods require an "ERP Adjustment". The ERP Adjustment is an important additional step that must be taken when using certain kinds of Risk Premium Report risk premia. The ERP adjustment is discussed in detail in the next section.

Proper Application of the Equity Risk Premium (ERP) Adjustment[9.1]

In this section, the following topics are discussed:

- The ERP Adjustment Defined
- When the ERP Adjustment is Necessary
- Calculating the ERP Adjustment

[9.1] Business Valuation Resources (BVR) and ValuSource have both developed online companion applications to the *2015 Valuation Handbook*. Both BVR's online version, the "*Risk Premium Toolkit*" (previously named the "*Risk Premium Calculator*"), and ValuSource's version, the "*Cost of Capital Analyzer*", are designed to help the valuation analyst use the *2015 Valuation Handbook's* data as efficiently as possible (both the CRSP Deciles Size Premia Studies and the Risk Premium Report Studies data are included). Both versions automatically calculate and properly apply the ERP Adjustment to all methods of cost of equity capital methods available when using the Risk Premium Report exhibits. The online "*Risk Premium Toolkit*" is available from BVR at www.BVResources.com/DuffPhelps or by calling 503-291-7963 extension 2. The "*Cost of Capital Analyzer*" is available from ValuSource at www.valusource.com/vhb or by calling 1 (800) 825-8763.

The ERP Adjustment Defined

The equity risk premium (ERP) Adjustment is needed to account for the difference between the forward-looking ERP as of the valuation date that the analyst has selected to use in his or her cost of equity capital calculations, and the historical (1963–present) ERP that was used as a *convention* in the calculations performed to create the Risk Premium Report exhibits.[9.2] In other words, if a user's estimate of the ERP on a forward-looking basis is materially different from the historical ERP as measured over the time horizon 1963–present, it is reasonable to assume that the *other* historical portfolio returns reported here would differ on a forward-looking basis by a similar amount. The ERP Adjustment accounts for this difference.

The historical 1963–present ERP is used as the convention to use in the calculations for two straightforward reasons.

First, it would be quite impractical to recalculate and publish the Risk Premium Report exhibits using *every* conceivable ERP that an valuation analyst might select. We know that there is a wide diversity in practice among academics and valuation analysts with regards to ERP estimates, and we also know that there is also a wide diversity of ERP estimates used by financial professionals in valuation engagements. So, a *single* ERP is selected as a convention to calculate all of the size and risk premia, and the individual analyst adjusts accordingly, relative to their selected ERP as of the valuation date.

Second, the1963–present time horizon corresponds to when the accounting and returns data are available from the CRSP and Compustat databases, and so selecting the same time horizon seemed a natural choice.

When the ERP Adjustment is Necessary

The general rules of whether the ERP Adjustment is necessary are:

- If you are using a "risk premium over the risk-free rate" (RP_{m+s}) from the A, C, D, H-A, or H-C Risk Premium Report exhibits, then the ERP Adjustment is *always* needed.

- If you using a Risk Premium Report "size premium" (RP_s), from Exhibits B-1 through B-8, or from the Exhibit H-B (Exhibit H-B is the "high-financial-risk" version of the "B" exhibits), then the ERP Adjustment is *never* needed, regardless of what ERP you select in your cost of equity capital estimates

This information is summarized in Exhibit 9.3.

9.2 All data in the *2015 Valuation Handbook's* Risk Premium Report exhibits is calculated over the time horizon 1963–2014 (52 years). All data in the *2015 Valuation Handbook's* CRSP Decile Size Premium exhibits is calculated over the time horizon 1926–2014 (89 years).

Exhibit 9.3: When the ERP Adjustment is Necessary

ERP Adjustment *Always* Necessary *(these premia are all "Risk Premia Over the Risk-free Rate")*	ERP Adjustment *Never* Necessary *(these premia are all "Size Premia")*
Exhibits A-1 through A-8	Exhibits B-1 through B-8
Exhibits C-1 through C-8	Exhibit H-B
Exhibits D-1 through D-3	
Exhibits H-A or H-C	

Note that in Exhibit 9.2, the "Build-up 1" method and the "CAPM" method are highlighted. These two methods are probably the most commonly used methods of estimating cost of equity capital using the Risk Premium Report exhibits. The first one (Build-up 1) uses a risk premium over the risk-free rate (from the A Exhibits) as an input, and the second one (CAPM) uses a size premium (from the B Exhibits) as an input. Thus, in many cases the question of whether the ERP Adjustment is necessary reduces to the following:

- If you are using Build-up 1, *apply* the ERP Adjustment to your cost of capital estimate.
- If you are using CAPM, do *not* apply the ERP Adjustment to your cost of capital estimate.

Why is the ERP Adjustment Necessary?

There are two types of premia in the Risk Premium Report exhibits. The first type of premia is "risk premia over the risk-free rate" (RP_{m+s}), which are a measure of risk in terms of the combined effect of *market* risk and *size* risk. Risk premia over the risk-free rate are simply added to a risk-free rate to estimate cost of equity capital when using the build-up method.

The second type of premia published in the Risk Premium Report exhibits is "risk premia over CAPM" (RP_s), which are commonly referred to as "beta adjusted size premia", or simply "size premia", and are a measure of *size* risk. Size premia can be added as an adjustment for the additional risk of smaller companies when using the CAPM.

The ERP adjustment is necessary when using risk premia over the risk-free rate because these premia measure risk in terms of the combined effect of *market* risk and *size*, the historical *market* risk premium used to calculate these premia is embedded in them. If the user selects an ERP for use in his or her cost of equity capital calculations that is *different* from the historical market risk premium that is *embedded* in these premia, it is reasonable to assume that the historical portfolio returns used in the exhibits would differ on a forward-looking basis by a similar differential, and an adjustment must therefore be made to account for this difference.

On the other hand, the Risk Premium Report's beta-adjusted size premia measure risk in terms of the effect of *size* risk only, and therefore do *not* have the historical 1963–present historical *market* risk premium embedded in them. Methods that utilize the Risk Premium Report's size premia (RP_s) therefore do not require an ERP adjustment in any case, regardless of the ERP that is selected for use in the cost of equity capital calculations.

What if the ERP Adjustment is not made to the models in Exhibit 9.2 that indicate that the adjustment is necessary? In cases where the ERP Adjustment is not applied as indicated in Exhibit 9.2, the net effect is that the historical 1963–2014 ERP used in the calculations to create the *2015 Valuation Handbook's* Risk Premium Report exhibits is *embedded* in the user's cost of equity capital estimate. This may (or may not) be the ERP that the user wishes to use as of his or her valuation date.

For example, the ERP used as a convention in the calculations to create the *2015 Valuation Handbook's* Risk Premium Report exhibits was the historical 1963–2014 market risk premium (5.1%). If the user estimates cost of equity capital using the "Build-up 1" method (which requires an ERP Adjustment) the ERP embedded in his or her estimate is 5.1% even though it is not "visible" in the equation. If in the same valuation engagement the user has estimated cost of equity capital using CAPM and selects say, the supply side ERP (6.2%) to use in the CAPM equation, then *two different ERPs* have effectively been used in the *same* engagement (5.1% in the case of the Build-up 1 estimate, and 6.2% in the case of the CAPM estimate). The way to bring them back into harmony is simply to always apply the ERP Adjustment as indicated in Exhibit 9.2.

Calculating the ERP Adjustment For Use with 2015 Valuation Handbook Data

The ERP Adjustment is calculated as the simple difference between the ERP the user has selected for use in his or her cost of equity capital estimates *minus* the historical 1963–present ERP. In the *2015 Valuation Handbook*, the historical ERP used as a convention in the calculations of the Risk Premium Report exhibits was 5.05% (5.1% rounded).[9.3] The ERP adjustment for Risk Premium Report data published in the *2015 Valuation Handbook* is therefore calculated as follows:

ERP Adjustment = ERP that User has selected – Historical ERP (1963–2014)

ERP Adjustment = ERP that User has selected – 5.1%

For example, if you selected the Duff & Phelps' recommended ERP of 5.0% to use in your year-end 2014 cost of capital estimates, then the ERP adjustment would be -0.1% (5.0% - 5.1%).[9.4] Alternatively, if you selected the *2015 Handbook's* supply-side ERP of 6.21% (6.2%, rounded), then the ERP Adjustment would be 1.1% (6.2% - 5.1%).[9.5]

9.3 Calculated as the average annual return difference between the total return of the S&P 500 Index and the income return of long-term U.S. government bonds. Source of underlying data: Morningstar *Direct* database.

9.4 As of December 31, 2014 the Duff & Phelps recommended ERP is 5.0%, developed relative to a *normalized* risk-free rate of 4.0%. Within the context of cost of equity capital estimation models, the Duff & Phelps recommended ERP should be used in conjunction with the risk-free rate it was developed in relation to (in this case, 4.0%). For more information, see Exhibit 3.15 in Chapter 3, "Basic Building Blocks of the Cost of Equity Capital – Risk-free Rate and Equity Risk Premium".

9.5 The supply side ERP is developed relative to a "spot" risk-free rate (as opposed to "normalized" risk-free rate). Within the context of cost of equity capital estimation models, the supply side should therefore be used in conjunction with the risk-free rate it was developed in relation to (in this case, the spot rate).

Calculating the ERP Adjustment in Prior Years

In Exhibit 9.4, additional information about the historical ERP used as a convention to calculate the premia in previous versions of the *Risk Premium Report* is included for completeness and convenience.[9.6]

Exhibit 9.4: Historical Market Risk Premiums Used in *Previous* Risk Premium Report Calculations
2011 Report – 2015 Report

Report Year	Period	Historical ERP (%)
2015 Risk Premium Report	1963-2014	5.1
2014 Risk Premium Report	1963-2013	4.9
2013 Risk Premium Report	1963-2012	4.5
2012 Risk Premium Report	1963-2011	4.3
2011 Risk Premium Report	1963-2010	4.4

"Smoothed" Premia versus Using "Average" Premia

The premia presented in the Risk Premium Report exhibits are "smoothed" across portfolios using regression analysis.[9.7] This regression analysis is also used as the basis for the "regression equation method" discussed in the next section. Smoothing the premia essentially averages out the somewhat scattered nature of the raw average premia. The "smoothed" average risk premium is generally the most appropriate indicator for most of the portfolio groups. It should be noted, however, that at the largest-size and smallest-size ends of the range, the average historical risk premiums may tend to jump off of the smoothed line, particularly for the portfolios ranked by size measures that incorporate market capitalization (Exhibits A-1 and A-4).

The "Guideline Portfolio Method" versus the "Regression Equation Method"

The Risk Premium Report exhibits provide two ways for valuation analysts to match their subject company's size characteristics with the appropriate smoothed premium to be used to estimate the cost of equity capital: the "guideline portfolio" method and the "regression equation" method.

The major difference between the guideline portfolio method and the regression equation method is illustrated in Exhibits 9.5a and 9.5b, which are abbreviated portions of Portfolio 24 and Portfolio 25 from Risk Premium Report Exhibit A-3.[9.8]

9.6 The *Risk Premium Report* was published annually from 1996–2013. Starting in 2014, the *Report's* data is published in the hardcover *Valuation Handbook*. The *Risk Premium Report* itself is no longer published as a stand-alone publication.

9.7 The "average" risk premia serve as the dependent variable in the regression (the thing being "predicted"); the base-10 log values of the average size (or risk) serve as the independent variable (the "predictor"). Because the size (or risk) measure is expressed in logarithms, this is equivalent to the change in size (or risk) premium given the percentage change in the size (or risk) of the companies from portfolio to portfolio.

9.8 Exhibit A-3 consists of 25 portfolios sorted from largest (Portfolio 1) to smallest (Portfolio 25) according to 5-year average net income (Portfolios 3 through 23 are not shown in Exhibits 9.5a and 9.5b).

Exhibit 9.5a represents the guideline portfolio method. In Exhibit 9.5a the average net income of Portfolio 24 is $11 million, and the average net income of Portfolio 25 is $3 million. If you are using the guideline portfolio method and Subject Company ABC's 5-year average net income is, say, $6 million, you would select Portfolio 25's published risk premium of 13.53%, because $6 million is closer to $3 million than it is to $11 million. Alternatively, if Subject Company XYZ's 5-year average net income is, say, $2 million, you would *again* select Portfolio 25's published risk premium of 13.53%, because $2 million is closest to Portfolio 25's average net income of $3 million.

The regression equation method, however, allows the valuation analyst to calculate a custom *interpolated* risk premia "in between" portfolios, and also to calculate custom *interpolated* smoothed risk premia for companies with size characteristics less than the average size in Portfolio 25.

Exhibit 9.5b represents the regression equation method. In Exhibit 9.5b, Subject Company ABC's net income of $6 million falls *in between* the average net income of Portfolio 24 ($11 million) and Portfolio 25 ($3 million), and the regression equation method enables the valuation analyst to calculate an exact interpolated smoothed risk premium of 12.90%, which is *in between* the published risk premia of Portfolio 24 (12.19%) and Portfolio 25 (13.53%).

In the second case, Subject Company XYZ's net income of $2 million is *smaller* than the average size of $3 million in Portfolio 25, and an exact interpolated smoothed risk premium of 14.16% is calculated, which is *higher* than the 13.53% risk premium of Portfolio 25.

These results are intuitive – as size decreases, risk premia (and thus cost of equity capital) tend to increase. In the next section, an example of how to calculate custom "interpolated" smoothed premium using the Risk Premium Report's regression equation method is provided.

Exhibit 9.5a: Guideline Portfolio Method

Portfolio Rank By Size	Average Net Inc. (in $millions)	*Smoothed Average Risk Premium*
1	8,922	*4.51%*
2	2,422	*6.01%*
///	///	///
24	11	*12.19%*
Subject Company ABC →	6 ↓	
25	3 →	*13.53%*
Subject Company XYZ →	2 ↑	

Exhibit 9.5b: Regression Equation Method

Portfolio Rank By Size	Average Net Inc. (in $millions)	*Smoothed Average Risk Premium*
1	8,922	*4.51%*
2	2,422	*6.01%*
///	///	///
24	11	*12.19%*
Subject Company ABC →	6 →	12.90%
25	3	*13.53%*
Subject Company XYZ →	2 →	14.16%

Example: Calculating an Interpolated Premium Using the Regression Equation Method

In almost all cases, the subject company's size will not exactly match the average size characteristics of the guideline portfolio (in the Risk Premium Report exhibits) or the decile (in the CRSP Deciles Size Premia exhibits). The Risk Premium Report exhibits provide both the "guideline portfolio method" and "regression equation method" for matching the subject company's size (and risk) characteristics to the appropriate size (or risk) premium. The regression equation method enables Risk Premium Report exhibits users to calculate an interpolated smoothed premium "in between" portfolios based upon the subject company' specific size characteristics.[9.9]

The regression equation method is outlined in this section first. Then, a discussion (and guidance) is provided on what to do when the size characteristics of subject company are *less* than the characteristics of the average size of the companies that comprise the Risk Premium Report exhibits' 25th portfolios.

In each of the Risk Premium Report exhibits, regression equations are provided. For example, the regression equation for Risk Premium Report Exhibit A-3 is:

*= 14.953% - 2.644% * LOG(Net Income)*

The 5-year average net income of the companies that comprise Exhibit A-3's Portfolio 24 is $11 million, and the 5-year average net income of the companies comprising Portfolio 25 is $3 million. If you were using the guideline portfolio method and the subject company had 5-year net income of say, $6 million, you would select Portfolio 25's risk premium of 13.53% when employing the build-up method because $6 million is closer to $3 million than it is to $11 million.

But the subject company's 5-year net income of $6 million is *in between* the average net income of Portfolios 24 and 25, and you may prefer to calculate a custom interpolated smoothed premium in *between* portfolios 24 and 25 rather than simply using the published 13.53% premium. This is easy to do using the "regression equation" method – just substitute the 5-year net income (in $ millions) of your subject company (in this case, "6") for "net income" into the regression equation listed on Exhibit A-3:[9.10]

*= 14.953% - 2.644% * LOG(6)*

*= 14.953% - 2.644% * 0.7782*

= 12.90%

Portfolio 24's published smoothed premium is 12.19%, Portfolio 25's published smoothed premium is 13.53%, and the calculated interpolated smoothed premium based on the subject company's 5-year net income of $6 million is in between these two premiums, at 12.90%. Each exhibit in the Risk

9.9 The CRSP Size Premia exhibits presently provide the "guideline portfolio" method, but have no mechanism in place for calculating custom size premia "in between" deciles.

9.10 In this equation, rather than using the traditional multiplication symbol "x," we put the equation into the Microsoft Excel format by using the character "*". Also, remember to enter the amount in "millions" (e.g., $6,000,000 should be entered as 6).

Premium Report will have a *different* regression equation. We recommend using as many of the size and risk measures as possible for best results.

Tips Regarding the Regression Equation Method

- The regression equations are *different* for each exhibit.
- Estimate cost of equity capital using as many of the eight A exhibits (A-1 through A-8) that are available for the subject company, and then calculate the average and median of all of these estimates. This principle is also true when using the B exhibits (B-1 through B-8) to estimate cost of equity capital using the CAPM.

Can the Regression Equation Method be Used If the Subject Company is Small?

The previous example was for a subject company whose size characteristics were *greater* than the average company in Portfolio 25 (comprised of the smallest companies). Can we apply the Risk Premium Report data for a subject company whose size characteristics are *less* than the average company included in Portfolio 25?

The short answer is "Yes". It may be appropriate to extrapolate the risk premium for companies whose size characteristics are less than the average characteristics of the companies comprising the bottom half of Portfolio 25 using the regression equation method. While extrapolating a statistical relationship far beyond the range of data used in analysis is generally not recommended, in cost of capital analyses (or any analysis for that matter), there is always the question of "compared to what?" Put simply, while it may not be ideal to extrapolate a statistical relationship beyond a certain range, one may be confronted with a situation in which no better measure is available.

Specifically, in cases where the size characteristic of the subject company is significantly *less* than that of the average company included in Portfolio 25 for any given size measure, the valuation analyst may report the individual, average and the median premia (and corresponding cost of equity capital estimates) using both the guideline portfolio method and the regression equation method (using all of the subject company size characteristics that are available). However, we recommend that the valuation analyst consider disclosing that the subject company's selected size metric is less than, for instance, the smallest of companies included in Portfolio 25 of a particular size measure. Once again, reporting all of the information in a transparent way is preferable to not reporting it at all, especially in cases where no better alternative is available.

For more information, see the section in Chapter 10 entitled "Calculating Custom Interpolated Premia for Smaller Companies".

Size Study or Risk Study?

Use both. Analysts can use the Size Study if it has been determined that the risks of the subject company are comparable to the average of the portfolio companies of comparable size (e.g., comparable operating margin). One can determine the relative risk characteristics by looking at Exhibits C-1 through C-8.

But, we do not know precisely how the market prices risk. The Risk Study provides returns based on risk measures regardless of size. One would likely expect that returns are greater for say, Portfolio 25, in the size measured portfolios rather than Portfolio 25 in the risk measured portfolio because sometimes a large company has risk measures more like a small company, and vice versa. How much higher/lower can these returns be? The D exhibits may help identify the magnitude of the return adjustment. Detailed examples on how to use the Risk Study can be found in Chapter 10.

Key Things to Remember About the Risk Premium Report Exhibits

- The Risk Premium Report exhibits include the Size Study, the Risk Study, the High-Financial-Risk Study, and the Comparative Risk Study.

- The risk premia and size premia reported in the Risk Premium Report exhibits can be used to develop cost of equity capital estimates using both the build-up method and the capital asset pricing model (CAPM).

- Because financial services companies are excluded from the base set of companies used to develop the analyses presented in the Risk Premium Report exhibits, these exhibits should *not* be used to estimate cost of equity for financial services companies.

- If you using a Risk Premium Report "size premium" (RP_s), then the ERP Adjustment is *never* needed, regardless of what ERP you select to use in your cost of equity capital estimates. If you are using a Risk Premium Report "risk premium over the risk-free rate" (RP_{m+s}), then the ERP Adjustment is *always* needed.

- The "smoothed" average risk premium is generally the most appropriate indicator for most of the portfolio groups. The valuation analyst can use either the smoothed average premium *published* for each guideline portfolio, or *calculate* a "custom' interpolated smoothed average premium using the regression equations associated with each exhibit.

- The Risk Premium Report exhibits provide two ways for valuation analysts to match their subject company's size characteristics with the appropriate smoothed premium to be used to estimate the cost of equity capital: the "guideline portfolio" method and the "regression equation" method. The regression equation method allows the valuation professional to calculate a custom *interpolated* risk premia "in between" portfolios, and also to calculate custom *interpolated* risk premia for companies with size characteristics less than the average size in Portfolio 25.

- It may be appropriate to extrapolate the risk premium for companies whose size characteristics are *less* than the average characteristics of the companies comprising the bottom half of Portfolio 25 using the regression equation method.

Chapter 10
Risk Premium Report Exhibits – Examples

In this chapter, we first discuss concepts that are specific to each of the four Risk Premium Report studies (Size Study, Risk Study, High-Financial-Risk Study, Comparative Risk Study), and then provide detailed examples for using the data in each to estimate the cost of equity capital.

Size Study

The size of a company is one of the most important risk elements to consider when developing cost of equity estimates for use in valuing a firm. Traditionally, researchers have used market value of equity (i.e., "market capitalization" or simply "market cap") as a measure of size in conducting historical rate of return research. For example, the Center for Research in Security Prices (CRSP) "deciles" are developed by sorting U.S. companies by market capitalization. Another example is the Fama-French "Small minus Big" (SMB) series, which is the difference in return of "small" stocks minus "big" (i.e., large) stocks, as defined by market capitalization.[10.1, 10.2]

Reasons for Using Additional Measures of Size

There are several reasons for using other measures of size in *addition* to the traditional measure of size, market value of equity.

First, financial literature indicates a bias may be introduced when ranking companies by market value of equity because a company's market value of equity may be affected by characteristics of the company other than size.[10.3] In other words, some companies might be small because they are risky (high discount rate), rather than risky because they are small (low market capitalization). One simple example could be a company with a large asset base, but a small market capitalization as a result of high leverage or depressed earnings. Another example could be a company with large sales or operating income, but a small market capitalization due to being highly leveraged.

Second, market capitalization may be an imperfect measure of the risk of a company's operations.

Third, using alternative measures of size may have the practical benefit of removing the need to first make a "guesstimate" of size in order to know which portfolio's premium to use (this issue is commonly referred to as the "circularity" issue). When you are valuing a closely held company, you are trying to determine market value of equity. If you need to make a guesstimate of the subject company' market

10.1 To learn more about the Center for Research in Security Prices (CRSP) at the University of Chicago Booth School of Business, visit www.CRSP.com

10.2 Eugene Fama is the Robert R. McCormick Distinguished Service Professor of Finance at the University of Chicago, and Ken French is the Roth Family Distinguished Professor of Finance at the Tuck School of Business at Dartmouth College. Fama and French are prolific researchers and authors who have contributed greatly to the field of modern finance. Fama and French's paper "The Cross-Section of Expected Stock Returns" was the winner of the 1992 Smith Breeden Prize for the best paper in the *Journal of Finance*. Fama is also chairman of the Center for Research in Security Prices (CRSP) at the University of Chicago Booth School Of Business

10.3 "A Critique of Size Related Anomalies," Jonathan Berk, *Review of Financial Studies*, vol. 8, no. 2 (1995)

value of equity first in order to know which size premium to use, the "circularity" problem is introduced. While market capitalization, at least for a closely held firm, is *not* generally available, other size measures, such as total assets or net income, *are* generally available.[10.4]

Finally, when doing analysis of any kind it is generally prudent to approach things from multiple directions if at all possible. This is good practice for several reasons, with the most important being that it has the potential of strengthening the conclusions of the analysis.

The Difference between the Size Study's A Exhibits and the B Exhibits

The results of the Size Study are presented in Exhibits A-1 through A-8 and Exhibits B-1 through B-8. The main difference between the A and B exhibits is how they are used. The A exhibits are used if you are using a "build-up" method to develop cost of equity capital estimates, and the B exhibits are used if you are using the capital asset pricing model (CAPM) to develop cost of equity capital estimates. This difference in usage is a function of the type of "risk premia" presented in each of the exhibits:

The A exhibits provide "risk premia over the risk-free rate" (RP_{m+s}) in terms of the combined effect of *market* risk and *size* risk for 25 portfolios ranked by eight alternative measures of size. These premia can be added to a risk-free rate (R_f) to estimate cost of equity capital in a build-up model.

The B exhibits provide "risk premia over CAPM" (i.e., size premia) (RP_s) in terms of size risk for 25 portfolios ranked by eight alternative measures of size. These premia are commonly known as beta-adjusted size premia, or simply size premia. These premia can be added as a size adjustment to a basic CAPM to estimate cost of equity capital.[10.5]

The Difference Between "Risk Premia Over the Risk-Free Rate" and "Risk Premia Over CAPM"

Risk Premium Over Risk-Free Rate (RP_{m+s})

"Risk premia over the risk-free rate" represent the difference between the historical (observed) total return of equities over the risk-free rate.[10.6] A long-run average historical risk premium is often used as an indicator of the expected risk premium of a typical equity investor. Total returns are based on dividend income plus capital appreciation and represent returns after corporate taxes (but before owner-level taxes). To estimate the historical risk premiums in the *2015 Valuation Handbook*, the average total return for each of the 25 size-ranked portfolios is calculated over the sample period, and then the average income return of long-term U.S. government bonds (using SBBI data) over the same period is subtracted.

10.4 For further discussion of the history of the size premium and criticisms of the size premium, see Chapters 14 and 15 in *Cost of Capital: Applications and Examples* 5th ed. by Shannon Pratt and Roger Grabowski, Wiley (April, 2014).

10.5 The basic CAPM formula is *Cost of Equity Capital = Risk-Free Rate + (Beta x ERP)*. A "modified CAPM" usually refers to the common modification to the CAPM formula that is used to incorporate an adjustment for size: *Cost of Equity Capital = Risk-Free Rate + (Beta x ERP) + Size Premium*. Please note that the modified CAPM as presented is after addition of a size premium and prior to the addition of any "company-specific" risk premiums that the individual valuation analyst may deem appropriate.

10.6 Risk premia over the risk-free rate and size premia are presented in the Risk Premium Report Exhibits. The CRSP Deciles Size Premia exhibits present size premia, but do not include risk premia over the risk-free rate.

For example, the average annual arithmetic return for portfolio 25 in Exhibit A-3 (size measure: 5-year average net income) over the time period 1963–2014 is 21.43%, and the average annual income return of long-term U.S. government bonds over the same period is 6.61%. This implies that the "risk premium over the risk-free rate" is 14.82% (21.43% - 6.61%) for this portfolio. This difference is a measure of risk in terms of the combined effect of *market* risk and *size* risk.

As of December 31, 2014, the average risk premium over the risk-free rate for portfolio 1 (comprised of the largest companies) for all *eight* of the size measures analyzed in the Size Study was 6.13%, and the average risk premium over the risk-free rate for portfolio 25 (comprised of the smallest companies) for all *eight* of the size measures was 14.30%, a difference of 8.17% (14.30% - 6.13%). There is a clear negative relationship between "size" and premium over long-term bonds (i.e. as size decreases, the return over the risk-free rate increases).

Because risk premia over the risk-free rate have an embedded measure of market (i.e. "beta") risk, these premia *are* appropriate for use in "build-up" methods that do *not* already include a measure of market risk, but are *not* appropriate for use in models (e.g. CAPM) that already have a measure of market risk.

Risk premia over the risk-free rate (RP_{m+s}) are presented in Exhibits A-1 through A-8. In the *2015 Valuation Handbook*, these risk premia are calculated over the period 1963 (the year that the *Compustat* database was inaugurated) through December 2014.

Both risk premia over the risk-free rate *and* size premia are presented in the Risk Premium Report Exhibits. The CRSP Deciles Size Premia exhibits present size premia, but do not include risk premia over the risk-free rate.

Size Premia (RP_s)

"Risk Premia over CAPM" represent the difference between historical (observed) excess return and the excess return predicted by CAPM. Years ago, the "small stock premium" was calculated as the simple difference in small company returns versus large company returns.[10.7] However, an examination of the betas of large stocks versus small stocks revealed that within the context of the capital asset pricing model (CAPM), beta (a measure of market risk) did not fully explain all of the difference between large company returns and small company returns. The observed (i.e., historical) excess return of portfolios comprised of smaller stocks tended to be greater than the excess return predicted by the CAPM. What followed from this observation is what is now commonly referred to as the "size premium". To learn more about the size effect, see Chapter 4.

Size premia are presented in the both the Risk Premium Report Exhibits and the CRSP Deciles Size Premia exhibits. The methodology employed to calculate the size premia in both data sets is very similar, and distills down to measuring the difference in historical excess returns (i.e. "what actually happened"),

[10.7] For example, in early versions of what would evolve into the *SBBI Classic Yearbook* (Morningstar, Chicago 2014) the "small stock premium" was calculated as the simple difference between a "small company stock" series and the Standard and Poor's (S&P) Composite Index (i.e., the S&P 500 Index).

and the excess returns that CAPM would have predicted. Detailed examples of the derivation of size premia for both data sets are provided in Chapter 7, "The CRSP Deciles Size Premia Studies and the Risk Premium Report Studies – A Comparison".

The "A" and "B" Exhibits: Summary of Data Presented

While the A and B exhibits present different types of risk premia, both the A and B exhibits' 25 portfolios are ranked by the same eight alternative measures of size, which are described in Exhibit 10.1.[10.8] Each of the exhibits A-1 through A-8 and B-1 through B-8 displays one line of data for each of the 25 size-ranked portfolios.

Exhibit 10.1: Eight Alternative Measures of Size

Exhibits A-1 and B-1 Market value of common equity (common stock price times number of common shares outstanding).	**Exhibit A-5 and B-5** Total Assets (as reported on the balance sheet).
Exhibit A-2 and B-2 Book value of common equity (does not add back the deferred tax balance)	**Exhibit A-6 and B-6** 5-year average earnings before interest, income taxes, depreciation and amortization (EBITDA) for the previous five fiscal years (operating income before depreciation plus non-operating income).
Exhibit A-3 and B-3 5-year average net income for previous five fiscal years (net income before extraordinary items).	**Exhibit A-7 and B-7** Sales (net).
Exhibit A-4 and B-4 Market value of invested capital (MVIC) (market value of common equity plus carrying value of preferred stock plus long-term debt (including current portion) and notes payable).	**Exhibit A-8 and B-8** Number of employees (number of employees, either at year-end or yearly average, including part-time and seasonal workers and employees of consolidated subsidiaries; excludes contract workers and unconsolidated subsidiaries).

The A and B exhibits include the statistics outlined in Exhibit 10.2 for each of the size measures outlined in Exhibit 10.1.

[10.8] For a detailed description of the Standard and Poor's *Compustat* data items used in the Risk Premium Report exhibits, please see Appendix A.

For comparative purposes, the average returns from the SBBI series for Large Companies (essentially the S&P 500 Index), Small Companies, and Long-Term Government Bond Income Returns for the period 1963 through the latest year are also reported in each exhibit.[10.9]

Exhibit 10.2: Statistics Reported for 25 size-ranked portfolios in the Size Study's A and B Exhibits

Exhibits A-1 through A-8	**Exhibits B-1 through B-8**
• The number of companies in each portfolio at the beginning of the latest year.	• Average of the sorting criteria (e.g., average number of employees) for the latest year used in determining the size of the companies (i.e., the size criteria when the latest year's portfolios are formed). For example, the market value in exhibit B-1 is the market value of equity at the beginning of the latest year. The other size criteria are based on what was known at the beginning of the latest year when the portfolios are formed.
• Beta calculated using the "sum beta" method applied to monthly returns for 1963 through the latest year (see Chapter 5 for a description of the "sum beta" method).	• Beta estimate calculated using the "sum beta" method applied to monthly returns for 1963 through the latest year (see Chapter 5 for a description of the "sum beta" method).
• Standard deviation of annual historical equity returns.	• Arithmetic average historical equity return since 1963.
• Geometric average historical equity return since 1963.	• Arithmetic average historical risk premium over long-term Treasuries (average return on equity in excess of long-term Treasury bonds) since 1963 (RP_{m+s}).
• Arithmetic average historical equity return since 1963.	• Indicated CAPM premium, calculated as the beta of the portfolio multiplied by the average historical market risk premium since 1963 (measured as the difference between SBBI Large Stock total returns and SBBI income returns on long-term Treasury bonds).
• Arithmetic average historical risk premium over long-term Treasuries (average return on equity in excess of long-term Treasury bonds) since 1963 (RP_{m+s}).	• Premium over CAPM, calculated by subtracting the "Indicated CAPM Premium" from the "Arithmetic Risk Premium" (RP_s).
• "Smoothed" average historical risk premium: the fitted premium from a regression with the average historical risk premium as dependent variable and the logarithm of the average sorting criteria as independent variable. (We present the coefficients and other statistics from this regression analysis in the top right hand corner of the exhibits) (RP_{m+s})	• "Smoothed" Premium over CAPM: the fitted premium from a regression with the historical "Premium over CAPM" as dependent variable and the logarithm of the average sorting criteria as independent variable (RP_s)
• Average carrying value of preferred stock plus long-term debt (including current portion) plus notes payable ("Debt") as a percent of MVIC since 1963.	

10.9 Source: Morningstar *Direct* database.

Calculating Custom Interpolated Premia for Smaller Companies

The Risk Premium Report exhibits provide two ways for valuation analysts to match their subject company's size characteristics with the appropriate smoothed premium: the "guideline portfolio" method and the "regression equation" method. The regression equation method allows the valuation analyst to calculate a custom *interpolated* risk premia "in between" portfolios, and also to calculate custom *interpolated* risk premia for companies with size characteristics smaller than the average size in Portfolio 25.

In order to assess the appropriateness of using the regression equations for small companies, Exhibit 10.3 is provided. Exhibit 10.3 can help the valuation analyst gauge the size characteristics of the subject company relative to the size characteristics of companies that comprise Portfolio 25 for each of the eight size measures, and provide support for the additional adjustment provided by the regression equations. .

Portfolio 25

The size characteristics for portfolio 25 for each of the eight size measures in both the Risk Premium Report exhibits A-1 through A-8 and B-1 through B-8 are shown in Exhibit 10.3. While the A and B exhibits present *different* types of risk premia, the A and B exhibits are:

- Comprised of the *same* set of companies, and

- Ranked by the *same* eight alternative measures of size.

This is done intentionally. It ensures that the "risk premia over the risk-free rate" that are published in the A exhibits and used in the build-up method are "apples to apples" when compared to the size premia that are published in the B exhibits and used in the CAPM.

Exhibit 10.3: Size Characteristics of the Companies that Comprise Portfolio 25, by Percentile

Portfolio 25	Market Value of Equity (in $millions)	Book Value of Equity (in $millions)	5-Year Average Net Income (in $millions)	Market Value of Invested Capital (in $millions)
Largest Company	$318.619	$143.022	$7.750	$379.058
95th Percentile	298.690	134.828	7.382	342.159
75th Percentile	207.255	99.825	5.171	247.426
50th Percentile	113.183	57.788	3.075	140.260
25th Percentile	45.795	28.908	1.516	56.001
5th Percentile	16.233	11.422	0.330	21.432
Smallest Company	4.592	3.625	0.076	4.592

Portfolio 25	Total Assets (in $millions)	5-Year Average EBITDA (in $millions)	Sales (in $millions)	Number of Employees
Largest Company	$294.996	$34.459	$280.014	654
95th Percentile	281.796	32.277	254.774	591
75th Percentile	202.581	23.682	186.680	459
50th Percentile	119.066	12.374	106.294	253
25th Percentile	49.298	5.698	53.353	127
5th Percentile	16.063	1.595	17.048	10
Smallest Company	4.690	0.276	3.096	4

The use of Exhibit 10.3 is straightforward. For example, the "95th Percentile" of size in Portfolio 25 for "5-year Average Net Income" is $7.382 million, which means that 95% of the companies in Portfolio 25 have average income that is less than $7.382 million (alternatively this means that 5% of the companies in Portfolio 25 have average income that is greater than $7.382 million). Or, looking to the 5th percentile, 5% of the companies in Portfolio 25 have average income that is less than $0.330 million (alternatively, this means that 95% of the companies in Portfolio 25 have average income that is greater than $0.330 million).

To provide even greater detail about the composition of the portfolios used to calculate the premia in the Risk Premium Report, starting with the 2013 Report, Exhibit 10.3 also includes the *smallest* and *largest* companies in the 25th portfolio of each of the eight size measures. For example, the largest company in Portfolio 25 for "5-year Average Net Income" is $7.750 million. Alternatively, the smallest company in Portfolio 25 for "5-year Average Net Income" is $0.076 million.

When using the Risk Premium Report exhibits to estimate cost of equity capital for a subject company in Portfolio 25, three cases are possible:

Case 1: *All* of the subject company's size characteristics are *greater* than the smallest companies in Portfolio 25 of each of the eight size measures reported in Exhibit 10.3.

In Case 1, the valuation professional can report the individual, average and median premia (and corresponding cost of equity capital estimates) using both the guideline portfolio method and calculated using the regression equation method (using all of the subject company size characteristics that are available).[10.10]

Case 2: *Some* of the subject company's size characteristics are *greater* than the smallest companies in Exhibit 10.3, and *some* of the subject company's size metrics are *less* than the smallest companies in Exhibit 10.3.

In Case 2, the valuation analyst may consider reporting the individual, average and median premia (and corresponding cost of equity capital estimates) using both the guideline portfolio method and calculated using the regression equation method (using all of the subject company size characteristics that are available) segregated in three different groupings:

- The premia calculated using subject company size characteristics that are *greater* than the smallest company;
- The premia calculated using subject company size characteristics that are *less* than the smallest company; and
- A combined grouping of all the premia calculated using subject company size characteristics (both those *greater* than, and *less* than, the smallest company).

In many cases, the difference between the three groupings' concluded cost of equity capital estimates will be small.

Case 3: *None* of the subject company's size characteristics are *greater* than the smallest companies as reported in Exhibit 10.3.

In Case 3, the valuation analyst may report the individual, average and median premia (and corresponding cost of equity capital estimates) using both the guideline portfolio method and calculated using the regression equation method (using all of the subject company size characteristics that are available). We recommend that the valuation analyst disclose that the subject company's size characteristics are less than the smallest companies included in Portfolio 25 for all size measures.

[10.10] The Risk Premium Report analyzes the relationship between return and eight different measures of size. It would *not* be unusual for fewer than the maximum number of eight size measures or fewer than the maximum number of three risk measures to be used when estimating cost of equity using the Risk Premium Report exhibits. When using the Risk Premium Report's "Size Study," the minimum number of size measures required is one. However, we recommend using as many size measures as possible for best results.

Overview of Methods Used to Estimate Cost of Equity Capital Using the Size Study

The Risk Premium Report's Size Study provides a total of four different ways to estimate the cost of equity capital. There are two methods of estimating cost of equity capital for a subject company, Build-up 1 and CAPM, plus one method for estimating *unlevered* cost of equity capital (assuming a firm is financed 100% with equity and 0% debt).[10.11]

A fourth method is provided we call "build-up 2".[10.12] The Size Study can be used in conjunction with the industry risk premia previously published in the *SBBI Valuation Edition Yearbook*, and now published in the *2015 Valuation Handbook* (see Exhibit 5.7). Build-up 2 incorporates a separate variable for the industry risk premium. To do this, a rudimentary adjustment is made to a full-information beta to calculate an industry risk premium that can be used within the context of Risk Premia Report data.

The cost of equity capital estimation methods provided by the Risk Premium Report's Size Study are summarized in Exhibit 10.4. An example of each (using the guideline portfolio method and the regression equation method) is provided in the following section.

Exhibit 10.4: Methods of Estimating Cost of Equity Capital Using the Risk Premium Report's Size Study

Study	Method	Cost of Equity Capital Formula
Size Study	Build-up 1	$k_e = R_f + RP_{m+s} + ERP\ Adjustment$
Size Study	Build-up 1-Unlevered	$k_e = R_f + RP_{m+s,\ unlevered} + ERP\ Adjustment$
Size Study	CAPM	$k_e = R_f + (\beta * ERP) + RP_s$
Size Study	Build-up 2	$k_e = R_f + ERP + RP_s + RP_i$

10.11 Unlevered risk premia over the risk-free rate are presented in Exhibits C-1 through C-8.

10.12 There are various "build-up" methods in the *2015 Valuation Handbook*. Giving them names like "Build-up" 1, "Build-up 2", etc., was necessary so as to differentiate them from one another.

Size Study Examples: Assumptions Used

Valuation Date

The *2015 Valuation Handbook* is calculated with "data through" December 31, 2014, and so for all examples of estimating the cost of equity capital using the Risk Premium Report exhibits, the *valuation date* is December 31, 2014.

ERP and Risk-free Rate

As of December 31, 2014, the Duff & Phelps recommended equity risk premium (ERP) was 5.0%, developed relative to a "normalized" long-term treasury yield of 4.0%. For all examples of estimating the cost of equity capital using the Risk Premium Report exhibits, the assumed ERP is therefore 5.0%, and the risk-free rate used is 4.0%. For more information about the Duff & Phelps recommended ERP and normalized risk-free rates, see Chapter 3, "Basic Building Blocks of the Cost of Equity Capital – Risk-free Rate and Equity Risk Premium".

The use of the Duff & Phelps recommended ERP and a 4.0% normalized risk-free rate in no way precludes valuation analysts from using different ERP estimates or different risk-free-rates. However, it is important to *match* the ERP with the risk-free rate it was developed in relation to. For the supply side ERP was developed in relation to long-term spot risk-free rates, not normalized rates. So if the supply-side ERP is selected, analysts should likely use "spot" rates rather than a "normalized" rates.[10.13]

Beta and Industry Risk Premium

For the CAPM examples (which require a beta), a beta of 1.2 is assumed. For the Build-up 2 examples, which requires an industry risk premium (RP_i), a "full-information" (FIB) beta of 1.2 is assumed, implying an RP_i (when using the assumed 5.0% ERP used in these examples) of 1.0% calculated as follows:

$$RP_i = (FIB \times RP_m) - RP_m$$

$$1.0\% = (1.20 \times 5.00\%) - 5.00\%$$

For a detailed discussion about betas and industry risk premia, see Chapter 5, "Basic Building Blocks of the Cost of Equity Capital – Betas and Industry Risk Premia".

10.13 Exhibit 3.15 summarizes the Duff & Phelps recommended ERP and corresponding risk-free rate *over time* (January 2008–present).

Hypothetical Subject Company Size Characteristics

There are up to eight alternative size measures that can be used with any of the four methods of estimating cost of equity capital provided by the *Size Study*. It would *not* be unusual for fewer than eight of these measures to be available for any given subject company. For example, market value of equity will probably not be available for a closely-held company, nor will market value of invested capital (in which market value of equity is embedded). In cases where fewer than eight size measures are available, it is generally acceptable to use the size measures that *are* available.

In each of the examples of using the Size Study to estimate cost of equity capital, the hypothetical subject company size measures summarized in Exhibit 10.5 will be used (total assets of $300 million, for instance, will be used in all examples).

Exhibit 10.5: Hypothetical Subject Company Size Characteristics
(Used in all Size Study examples)

		Appropriate Exhibit			
	Size Measure (in $millions, except for Number of Employees)	**Build-up 1**	**Build-up 1 -Unlevered**	**CAPM**	**Build-up 2**
Market Value of Equity	$120	A-1	C-1	B-1	B-1
Book Value of Equity	$100	A-2	C-2	B-2	B-2
5-year Average Net Income	$10	A-3	C-3	B-3	B-3
Market Value of Invested Capital	$180	A-4	C-4	B-4	B-4
Total Assets	$300	A-5	C-5	B-5	B-5
5-year Average EBITDA	$30	A-6	C-6	B-6	B-6
Sales	$250	A-7	C-7	B-7	B-7
Number of Employees	200	A-8	C-8	B-8	B-8

Exhibit 10.5 also includes the data exhibits in which the appropriate risk premia for each of the size measures can be found. For example, for use in the Build-up 1 method, risk premia over the risk-free rate (RP_{m+s}) for "Total Assets" are found in Exhibit A-5. For use in the CAPM method, the appropriate premia over CAPM ($RP_{s,}$ or "size premia) for "Total Assets" are found in Exhibit B-5.

Please note that for any given valuation engagement these inputs may be (and probably will be) different than the ones used in the examples.

Size Study Examples

Build-up 1

The Build-up 1 method is an additive model commonly used for calculating the required rate of return on equity capital. As the name implies, successive "building blocks" are summed, each representing the additional risk inherent to investing in alternative assets. The Size Study calculates average "risk premia over the risk-free rate" (RP_{m+s}) from 1963 through December 2014 for each of the 25 size-ranked portfolios. These RP_{m+s} premia are found in Exhibits A-1 through A-8, and can be added to a risk-free rate to estimate cost of equity capital (k_e) using the Build-up 1 method.

The build-up 1 equation is:

$$k_{e\ build\text{-}up\ 1} = R_f + RP_{m+s} + ERP\ Adjustment$$

Note that the "ERP Adjustment" is a necessary adjustment when using build-up 1. The equity risk premium adjustment is made to reconcile the historical data presented in the Risk Premium Report exhibits with the forward-looking ERP chosen by the individual analyst as of the valuation date. For a detailed discussion of the ERP Adjustment, see the section in Chapter 9 entitled, "Proper Application of the Equity Risk Premium (ERP) Adjustment".

The historical ERP from 1963–2014 (5.1%) was used as an input in performing the analysis in the 2014 Report, and is thus embedded in the RP_{m+s} premia. In these examples we have selected to use an ERP of 5.0%, and the ERP Adjustment is relatively small:

$$ERP\ Adjustment = User's\ ERP - Historical\ (1963-2014)\ ERP$$

$$ERP\ Adjustment = \text{-}0.1\% = 5.0\% - 5.1\%$$

This implies that on a forward-looking basis as of the valuation date, investors expected to earn -0.1% less than they realized on average over the period 1963–2014. It is reasonable to assume that the other historical portfolio returns reported here would differ on a forward-looking basis by a similar differential.

Examples of both the guideline portfolio method and the regression equation method follow, starting with the simpler guideline portfolio method. In general, the regression equation method is preferred because this method allows for interpolation between the individual guideline portfolios, although the guideline portfolio method is less complicated, and more direct.

Example 1a: Build-up 1 Method (using guideline portfolios)

To estimate the cost of equity capital (k_e) with the Build-up 1 method using "guideline portfolios", three pieces of information are needed:

- Risk-free rate (R_f)
- Risk premium over the risk-free rate (RP_{m+s})
- Equity risk premium Adjustment *(ERP Adjustment)*

We have assumed a risk-free rate of 4.0% for all examples, and the ERP Adjustment has been calculated as -0.1%, so the only missing input is the risk premium over the risk-free rate (RP_{m+s}).

$k_{e\ build\text{-}up\ 1} = 4.0\% + RP_{m+s} + -0.1\%$

Gathering the RP_{m+s} premia is straightforward. Match the various size measures of the subject company with the guideline portfolios composed of companies of similar size in Exhibits A-1 through A-8, and identify the corresponding *smoothed average risk premium.*

For example, according to Exhibit 10.5, our hypothetical subject company has a market value of equity of $120 million, and the appropriate data exhibit is Exhibit A-1 (25 portfolios sorted by market value of equity). An abbreviated version of Exhibit A-1 is shown in Exhibit 10.6. Of the 25 portfolios, the portfolio that has an average market value *closest* to the subject company's $120 million market value is Portfolio 25 ($132 million). The corresponding *smoothed average risk premium* is 13.92% (13.9%, rounded).

Exhibit 10.6: Companies Ranked by Market Value of Equity (Exhibit A-1)

Portfolio Rank by Size	Average Mkt. Value (in $millions)	Log of Average Mkt. Value	Number as of 2014	Beta (SumBeta) Since '63	Standard Deviation of Returns	Geometric Average Return	Arithmetic Average Return	Arithmetic Average Risk Premium	*Smoothed Average Risk Premium*	Average Debt/ MVIC
1	178,744	5.25	39	0.83	16.01%	10.90%	12.13%	5.52%	*3.22%*	14.12%
2	53,009	4.72	36	0.96	16.87%	9.77%	11.15%	4.54%	*5.02%*	19.00%
3	32,537	4.51	29	0.92	15.58%	10.43%	11.66%	5.04%	*5.75%*	20.61%
///										
24	412	2.62	88	1.24	24.96%	16.72%	19.45%	12.84%	*12.23%*	24.78%
25	132	2.12	267	1.28	29.92%	19.09%	22.92%	16.31%	***13.92%***	27.48%

This process is continued for each of the eight size characteristics that are available for the subject company. Looking again to Exhibit 10.5, our hypothetical subject company has a book value of equity of $100 million, and the appropriate data exhibit is Exhibit A-2 (25 portfolios ranked by book value of equity). An abbreviated version of Exhibit A-2 is shown in Exhibit 10.7. Of the 25 portfolios, the portfolio that has an average book value of equity value *closest* to the subject company's $100 million market value is Portfolio 25 ($65 million). The corresponding *smoothed average risk premium* is 12.49% (12.5%, rounded).

Exhibit 10.7: Companies Ranked by Book Value of Equity (Exhibit A-2)

Portfolio Rank by Size	Average Book Val. (in $millions)	Log of Average Book Val.	Number as of 2014	Beta (SumBeta) Since '63	Standard Deviation of Returns	Geometric Average Return	Arithmetic Average Return	Arithmetic Average Risk Premium	*Smoothed Average Risk Premium*	Average Debt/ MVIC
1	55,457	4.74	35	0.81	15.54%	10.97%	12.37%	5.76%	*5.04%*	23.36%
2	18,036	4.26	29	0.87	16.26%	10.94%	12.41%	5.80%	*6.27%*	27.49%
3	11,882	4.07	32	0.90	16.17%	11.97%	13.48%	6.87%	*6.73%*	28.44%
///										
24	185	2.27	108	1.27	24.72%	15.00%	18.14%	11.53%	*11.32%*	22.66%
25	65	1.81	251	1.26	25.67%	15.55%	18.89%	12.28%	***12.49%***	23.27%

After all of the available size measures for the subject company have been matched to the closest guideline portfolio in the appropriate exhibit and the corresponding *smoothed average risk premium* has been identified for each, the subject company's cost of equity capital can be estimated, as shown in Exhibit 10.8.

Exhibit 10.8: Build-up 1 Method Cost of Equity Capital Estimate (using guideline portfolios)

	Size Measure (in $millions, except for Number of Employees)	Appropriate Exhibit	Guideline Portfolio	Risk-Free Rate, R_f	Smoothed Premia Over Risk-Free Rate, RP_{m+s}	ERP Adjustment	Cost of Equity Capital k_e
Market Value of Equity	$120	A-1	25	4.0% +	13.9% +	-0.1% =	**17.8%**
Book Value of Equity	$100	A-2	25	4.0% +	12.5% +	-0.1% =	16.4%
5-year Average Net Income	$10	A-3	24	4.0% +	12.2% +	-0.1% =	16.1%
Market Value of Invested Capital	$180	A-4	25	4.0% +	13.8% +	-0.1% =	17.7%
Total Assets	$300	A-5	24	4.0% +	11.7% +	-0.1% =	15.6%
5-year Average EBITDA	$30	A-6	25	4.0% +	13.2% +	-0.1% =	17.1%
Sales	$250	A-7	24	4.0% +	11.4% +	-0.1% =	**15.3%**
Number of Employees	200	A-8	25	4.0% +	12.4% +	-0.1% =	16.3%
		Mean (average) values		4.0% +	12.6% +	-0.1% =	**16.5%**
		Median (typical) values		4.0% +	12.5% +	-0.1% =	**16.4%**

The cost of equity capital for the hypothetical subject company in this example has an estimated cost of capital ranging from 15.3% to 17.8%, with a mean (average) and median (typical) cost of equity capital of 16.5% and 16.4%, respectively.

Example 1b: Build-up 1 Method (using regression equations)

When the subject company size measures do not exactly match the respective average company size of the guideline portfolios, the data exhibits provide a straightforward way to interpolate an "exact" risk premium over the risk-free rate (RP_{m+s}) between guideline portfolios using the "regression equation" method.

The *only* difference between estimating cost of equity capital using the build-up 1 method using "guideline portfolios method" (as in the previous example) and using the "regression equation method" (this example) is how the risk premia over the risk-free rate (RP_{m+s}) are identified.

In the previous example, the *smoothed average risk premia* published in the Risk Premium Report exhibits for the appropriate guideline portfolios were used to estimate cost of equity capital. In this example, the regression equations found on each of the data exhibits will be used to calculate a "custom" interpolated *smoothed average risk premia*, based upon the specific size measures of the subject company.

This example utilizes the same long-term risk-free rate (4.0%) and the ERP Adjustment (-0.1%) established in the previous example, so the only missing input is the risk premium over the risk-free rate (RP_{m+s}). Again, according to Exhibit 10.5, our hypothetical subject company has a market value of equity of $120 million, and the appropriate data exhibit is Exhibit A-1 (25 portfolios sorted by market value of equity).

The regression equation provided in Exhibit A-1 (25 portfolios ranked by market value of equity), is:

Smoothed Risk Premium (RP_{m+s}) = *21.167% – 3.418% * Log (Market Value)*

To calculate an interpolated risk premium, substitute the subject company's $120 million market value into the regression equation as follows:[10.14]

Smoothed Risk Premium (RP_{m+s}) = *21.167% – 3.418% * Log (120)*

The interpolated smoothed risk premium for "market value of equity" is therefore 14.1%:

*14.1% = 21.167% – 3.418% * 2.079*

This process is continued for each of the eight size characteristics that are available for the subject company. Our hypothetical subject company has a book value of equity of $100 million, and the appropriate data exhibit is Exhibit A-2 (25 portfolios ranked by book value of equity).

The regression equation provided in Exhibit A-2 (25 portfolios ranked by book value of equity), is:

Smoothed Risk Premium (RP_{m+s}) = *17.084% – 2.540% * Log (Book Value)*

To calculate an interpolated smoothed risk premium, substitute the subject company's $100 million book value of equity into the regression equation as follows:

Smoothed Risk Premium (RP_{m+s}) = *17.084% – 2.540% * Log (100)*

10.14 Please note that the logarithmic relationship is base-10, and that the financial size data is in millions of dollars, such that the log of $120 million is log (120), not log (120,000,000). The formula to calculate a value's base-10 logarithm in Microsoft Excel is "=log (value)". The "*" used in the regression equation is the symbol used in Microsoft Excel to denote the multiplication symbol, "x". The "*" format is also used to denote multiplication in the regression equations in the data exhibits.

The interpolated smoothed risk premium for "book value of equity" is therefore 12.0%:

*12.0% = 17.084% – 2.540% * 2.000*

Exhibit 10.9 shows the calculations for each of the eight size measure's "custom" interpolated smoothed average risk premia over the risk-free rate (RP_{m+s}).

Exhibit 10.9: Build-up 1 Method Calculation of RP_{m+s} Premia (using regression equations)

	Size Measure (in $millions, except for Number of Employees)	Appropriate Exhibit	Appropriate Regression Equation		Smoothed Premia Over Risk-Free Rate RP_{m+s}
Market Value of Equity	$120	A-1	Smoothed Premium = 21.167% – 3.418% * Log(Market Value)	=	14.1%
Book Value of Equity	$100	A-2	Smoothed Premium = 17.084% – 2.540% * Log(Book Value)	=	12.0%
5-year Average Net Income	$10	A-3	Smoothed Premium = 14.953% – 2.644% * Log(Net Income)	=	12.3%
Market Value of Invested Capital	$180	A-4	Smoothed Premium = 21.024% – 3.282% * Log(MVIC)	=	13.6%
Total Assets	$300	A-5	Smoothed Premium = 18.743% – 2.699% * Log(Assets)	=	12.1%
5-year Average EBITDA	$30	A-6	Smoothed Premium = 16.366% – 2.685% * Log(EBITDA)	=	12.4%
Sales	$250	A-7	Smoothed Premium = 16.769% – 2.103% * Log(Sales)	=	11.7%
Number of Employees	200	A-8	Smoothed Premium = 17.329% – 2.010% * Log(Employees)	=	12.7%

After the "custom" interpolated *smoothed average risk premia* have been calculated for all of the available size measures for the subject, the subject company's cost of equity capital can be estimated, as shown in Exhibit 10.10.

Exhibit 10.10: Build-up 1 Method Cost of Equity Capital Estimate (using regression equations)

	Size Measure (in $millions, except for Number of Employees)	Appropriate Exhibit	Risk-Free Rate, R_f	Smoothed Premia Over Risk-Free Rate, RP_{m+s}	ERP Adjustment	Cost of Equity Capital k_e
Market Value of Equity	$120	A-1	4.0% +	14.1% +	-0.1% =	**18.0%**
Book Value of Equity	$100	A-2	4.0% +	12.0% +	-0.1% =	15.9%
5-year Average Net Income	$10	A-3	4.0% +	12.3% +	-0.1% =	16.2%
Market Value of Invested Capital	$180	A-4	4.0% +	13.6% +	-0.1% =	17.5%
Total Assets	$300	A-5	4.0% +	12.1% +	-0.1% =	16.0%
5-year Average EBITDA	$30	A-6	4.0% +	12.4% +	-0.1% =	16.3%
Sales	$250	A-7	4.0% +	11.7% +	-0.1% =	**15.6%**
Number of Employees	200	A-8	4.0% +	12.7% +	-0.1% =	16.6%
	Mean (average) values		4.0% +	12.6% +	-0.1% =	**16.5%**
	Median (typical) values		4.0% +	12.4% +	-0.1% =	**16.3%**

The cost of equity capital for the hypothetical subject company in this example has an estimated cost of capital ranging from 15.6% to 18.0%, with a mean (average) and median (typical) cost of equity capital of 16.5 and 16.3%, respectively.

Unlevered Cost of Equity Capital

Unlevered premia are used to estimate cost of equity capital assuming a firm is financed 100% with equity and 0% debt. Generally, as the percentage of leverage (debt) in a company's capital structure increases, the cost of equity capital increases.

The C exhibits provide *unlevered* "risk premia over the risk-free rate", and enable the valuation analyst to estimate an unlevered cost of equity estimate for the subject company. The C exhibits' unlevered premia are informative in that they generally indicate that the market views smaller companies' operations to be riskier than the operations of larger companies (i.e., unlevered risk premiums *increase* as size *decreases*).

The C exhibits also enable a second important capability. The C exhibits provide "comparative risk statistics" that enable the valuation analyst to gauge how "alike or different" the subject company is from the average company that comprises the portfolios in the A and B exhibits. This is an important capability that forms the basis of the Comparative Risk Study. The Comparative Risk Study helps the valuation analyst to potentially "fine tune" the risk premia over the risk-free rate and size premia in the A and B exhibits, respectively, and thus further refine his or her overall cost of equity capital estimate. Examples of using this capability to further refine cost of equity capital estimates are discussed later in this chapter under the section entitled "Comparative Risk Study".

In this section, we first discuss the Risk Premium Report's unlevering and levering methodology, and then provide examples of estimating unlevered cost of equity capital.

Overview of the Methodology and Assumptions Used to Unlever Risk Premia

The average (levered) risk premia presented in Exhibits A-1 through A-8 are unlevered as follows:[10.15]

$$RP_{m+s,\ unlevered} = RP_{m+s,\ levered} - ((W_d\ /\ W_e)\ x\ (\beta_u - \beta_d)\ x\ RP_m)$$

where:

$RP_{m+s,\ unlevered}$ = Unlevered realized risk premium over the risk-free rate

$RP_{m+s,\ levered}$ = Levered realized risk premium over the risk-free rate

β_u = Unlevered equity beta

β_d = Debt beta, assumed equal to 0.1

RP_m = Equity risk premium (ERP) estimate for the "market", represented by the average historical risk premium since 1963

W_d = Percent of debt capital in capital structure

W_e = Percent of equity capital in capital structure

The average debt to equity (W_d/W_e) ratio of the portfolio is based on the average debt to MVIC for the portfolio since 1963. A debt beta (β_d) of 0.1 is assumed, which is the average estimated debt beta for the companies included in portfolios 1 through 25 over the years 1963 through 2014 after excluding high-financial-risk companies.

A debt beta greater than zero indicates debt capital bears risk of variability of operating net cash flow because interest payments and principal repayments may not be made when owed, implying that tax deductions on the interest expense may not be realized in the period in which the interest is paid. Preferred capital is included with debt capital in measuring the effect of leverage on the risk of equity capital, which is consistent with recent research.

For a detailed discussion about debts betas, see Chapter 5, "Basic Building Blocks of the Cost of Equity Capital – Betas and Industry Risk Premia".

An example of unlevering the average risk premia from the A exhibits is demonstrated using the information found in Exhibit 10.11, 10.12, and 10.13 (these are abbreviated versions of Exhibits A-2, B-2, and C-2, respectively).

[10.15] Derived from R.S. Harris and J. J. Pringle, "Risk-Adjusted Discount Rates – Extensions from the Average Risk Case," *Journal of Financial Research* (Fall 1985) 237-244. Also see: Arzac, Enrique R., and Lawrence R. Glosten. "A Reconsideration of Tax Shield Valuation." *European Financial Management* (2005): 453-461. For a more complete discussion see chapter 12 in *Cost of Capital: Applications and Examples* 5th ed. by Shannon Pratt and Roger Grabowski, Wiley (April, 2014).

The average unlevered risk premium of Portfolio 25 in Exhibit C-2 (Figure 10.13) is 10.91%, calculated using the following information from Exhibits 10.11, 10.12, and 10.13:

- The arithmetic average risk premium of Portfolio 25 in Exhibit A-2 (see Exhibit 10.11) is 12.28%.
- The debt to market value of equity (W_d/W_e) of Portfolio 25 in Exhibit C-2 (see Exhibit 10.13) is 30.33%.
- The unlevered sum beta (β_u) of Portfolio 25 in Exhibit C-2 (see Exhibit 10.13) is 0.99.
- The debt beta (β_d) is an assumed 0.1, as discussed previously.

The market premium (RP_m) used to calculate the data in the 2015 Risk Premium Report exhibits is the historical ERP from 1963–2014, 5.05%.

Unlevering the average (levered) risk premium in Exhibit A-2 (12.28%), can be accomplished as follows (difference due to rounding):

$$RP_{m+s,unlevered} = RP_{m+s,levered} - ((Wd/We) \times (\beta u - \beta d) \times RPm)$$

$$10.91\% = 12.28\% - (30.33\% \times (0.99 - 0.1) \times 5.05\%)$$

Exhibit 10.11: Risk Premium Report Exhibit A-2 (abbreviated)
Companies Ranked by Book Value of Equity
Risk Premia Over the Risk-Free Rate (RP_{m+s})
1963–2014

Portfolio Rank by Size	Average Book Val. (in $millions)	Beta (SumBeta) Since '63	Arithmetic Average Risk Premium
1	55,457	0.81	5.76%
2	18,036	0.87	5.80%
///			
25	65	1.26	12.28%

Exhibit 10.12: Risk Premium Report Exhibit B-2 (abbreviated)
Companies Ranked by Book Value of Equity
Size Premia
1963–2014

Portfolio Rank by Size	Average Book Val. (in $millions)	Premium over CAPM
1	55,457	1.66%
2	18,036	1.42%
///		
25	65	5.92%

Exhibit 10.13: Risk Premium Report Exhibit C-2 (abbreviated)
Companies Ranked by Book Value of Equity
Comparative Risk Characteristics
1963–2014

Portfolio Rank by Size	Average Book Value (in $millions)	Average Debt to Market Value of Equity	Average Unlevered Risk Premium	Average Unlevered Beta
1	55,457	30.48%	4.92%	0.64
2	18,036	37.92%	4.74%	0.66
///				
25	65	30.33%	10.91%	0.99

Unlevered Risk Premia – Reconciliation of the A, B, and C Exhibits

Reconciliation of the levered and unlevered betas for use in CAPM (found in Exhibits B-2 and C-2, respectively) now reconcile with the levered and unlevered arithmetic average risk premia for the build-up (found in Exhibits A-2 and C-2, respectively), as demonstrated below using the values from the previous example and the premium over CAPM shown in Exhibit 10.13:

Levered risk premium = Levered beta x Historical market risk premium + Premium over CAPM (i.e. "size premum")

12.28% = 1.26 x 5.05% + 5.92%

Unlevered risk premium = Unlevered beta x Historical market risk premium + Premium over CAPM (i.e. "size premum")

10.91% = 0.99 x 5.05% + 5.92%

Levering

What if the debt-to-market-value-of-equity ratio (W_d / W_e) of the subject company is different than the average (W_d / W_e) of the companies making up Portfolio 25 (30.33% in this case)? It may be possible to adjust the (levered) risk premiums over the risk-free rate (RP_{m+s}) from Exhibits A-1 through A-8 for differences in financial leverage between the subject company and the given guideline portfolio. Again, the average (levered) risk premia presented in Exhibits A-1 through A-8 are unlevered as follows:

$$RP_{m+s,\ unlevered} = RP_{m+s,\ levered} - ((W_d/W_e) \times (\beta_u - \beta_d) \times RP_m)$$

The unlevered risk premia over the risk-free rate in the C exhibits, which assume a firm is financed 100% with equity and 0% debt, are calculated by unlevering the average risk premia in the A exhibits. In the example, the unlevered risk premium over the risk-free rate ($RP_{m+s,\ unlevered}$) for Portfolio 25 in Exhibit C-2 (10.91%) was calculated by unlevering the average risk premium over the risk-free rate (RP_{m+s}) for Portfolio 25 in Exhibit A-2 (12.28%). This calculation was performed assuming the 30.33% average debt-to-market-value-of-equity ratio (W_d/W_e) of the companies making up Portfolio 25. The percentage of debt in the capital structure went from 30.33% to 0%, and the unlevered risk premia is lower than the levered risk premium.

This formula can be rearranged to "lever":

$$RP_{m+s,\ levered} = RP_{m+s,\ unlevered} + ((W_d/W_e) \times (\beta_u - \beta_d) \times RP_m)$$

If the subject company has a W_d / W_e ratio that is less (say 20%) than the average W_d / W_e of the guideline portfolio (30.33%), the unlevered risk premium may be levered at the subject company's lower ratio:

11.81% = 10.91% + ((20%) x (0.99 – 0.1) x 5.05%)

The subject company has less debt relative to equity than the average company in the guideline portfolio (20% versus 30.33%), and the relevered risk premium is lower than the average levered risk premium of the guideline portfolio (11.81% versus 12.28%). Generally, as the percentage of leverage (debt) in a company's capital structure decreases, risk to equity investors decreases (and vice versa).

Estimating Cost of Equity Capital Using the "Build-up 1-Unlevered" Method

Estimating cost of equity capital with the "build-up 1-unlevered" method is identical to estimating cost of equity capital with the build-up 1 method, with one exception: instead of using the *levered* risk premia over the risk-free rate (RP_{m+s}) found in Exhibits A-1 through A-8, the *unlevered* risk premia over the risk-free rate ($RP_{m+s,\ unlevered}$) found in Exhibits C-1 through C-8 are used. These unlevered risk premia can then be added to a risk-free rate to estimate unlevered cost of equity capital ($k_{e,\ unlevered}$).

Because the unlevered risk premia presented in the C exhibits have an embedded measure of market (i.e. "*beta*") risk, they are not appropriate for use in models (e.g. CAPM) that already have a measure of market (beta) risk.

Examples of both the guideline portfolio method and the regression equation method follow, starting with the guideline portfolio method.

Example 2a: Build-up 1-Unlevered Method (using guideline portfolios)

The build-up 1-unlevered equation is:

$$k_{e\ build\text{-}up\ 1} = R_f + RP_{m+s,\ unlevered} + ERP\ Adjustment$$

Note that the "ERP Adjustment" is a necessary adjustment when using build-up 1-unlevered. For a detailed discussion of the ERP Adjustment, see the section in Chapter 9 entitled, "Proper Application of the Equity Risk Premium (ERP) Adjustment".

To estimate an unlevered cost of equity capital ($k_{e,\ unlevered}$) with the build-up 1-unlevered using the "guideline portfolio" method, three pieces of information are needed:

- Risk-free rate (R_f)
- Risk premium over the risk-free rate ($RP_{m+s,\ unlevered}$)
- Equity risk premium adjustment *(ERP Adjustment)*

We have assumed a risk-free rate of 4.0% for all examples, and the ERP Adjustment has been calculated as -0.1% in a previous example, so the only missing input is the risk premium over the risk-free rate ($RP_{m+s,\ unlevered}$):

$$k_{e\ build\text{-}up\ 1} = 4.0\% + RP_{m+s,\ unlevered} + -0.1\%$$

Gathering the $RP_{m+s,unlevered}$ premia is straightforward. Match the various size measures of the subject company with the guideline portfolios composed of companies of similar size in Exhibits C-1 through C-8, and identify the corresponding *smoothed average unlevered risk premium.*

For example, according to Exhibit 10.5, our hypothetical subject company has a market value of equity of $120 million, and the appropriate data exhibit is Exhibit C-1 (25 portfolios sorted by market value of equity). An abbreviated version of Exhibit C-1 is shown in Exhibit 10.14. Of the 25 portfolios, the portfolio that has an average market value *closest* to the subject company's $120 million market value is Portfolio 25 ($132 million). The corresponding *smoothed average unlevered risk premium* is 12.25% (12.3%, rounded).

Exhibit 10.14: Exhibit C-1 (abbreviated)
Companies Ranked by Market Value of Equity
Unlevered Risk Premia Over the Risk-Free Rate (RP_{m+s})
1963–2014

Portfolio Rank by Size	Average Mkt. Value (in $millions)	Log of Average Mkt. Value	Number of Firms	Arithmetic Average Risk Premium	Average Debt to MVIC	Average Debt to Market Value of Equity	Average Unlevered Risk Premium	***Smoothed Average Unlevered Risk Premium***
1	178,744	5.25	39	5.52%	14.12%	16.44%	4.99%	*2.56%*
2	53,009	4.72	36	4.54%	19.00%	23.45%	3.72%	*4.19%*
3	32,537	4.51	29	5.04%	20.61%	25.96%	4.19%	*4.85%*
←				///				→
24	412	2.62	88	12.84%	24.78%	32.95%	11.41%	*10.72%*
25	132	2.12	267	16.31%	27.48%	37.90%	14.67%	***12.25%***

This process is continued for each of the eight size characteristics that are available for the subject company. After all of the available size measures for the subject company have been matched to the closest guideline portfolio in the appropriate exhibit and the corresponding *smoothed average unlevered risk premium* has been identified for each, the subject company's cost of equity capital can be estimated, as shown in Exhibit 10.15.

Exhibit 10.15: Build-up 1-Unlevered Method Cost of Equity Capital Estimate (using guideline portfolios)

Size Measure (in $millions, except for Number of Employees)		Appropriate Exhibit	Guideline Portfolio	Risk-Free Rate, R_f	Smoothed Unlevered Premia Over Risk-Free Rate, $RP_{m+s,\ unlevered}$	ERP Adjustment	Cost of Equity Capital k_e
Market Value of Equity	$120	C-1	25	4.0% +	12.3% +	-0.1% =	**16.2%**
Book Value of Equity	$100	C-2	25	4.0% +	11.0% +	-0.1% =	14.9%
5-year Average Net Income	$10	C-3	24	4.0% +	10.7% +	-0.1% =	14.6%
Market Value of Invested Capital	$180	C-4	25	4.0% +	12.2% +	-0.1% =	16.1%
Total Assets	$300	C-5	24	4.0% +	10.4% +	-0.1% =	14.3%
5-year Average EBITDA	$30	C-6	25	4.0% +	11.8% +	-0.1% =	15.7%
Sales	$250	C-7	24	4.0% +	10.0% +	-0.1% =	**13.9%**
Number of Employees	200	C-8	25	4.0% +	11.0% +	-0.1% =	14.9%
		Mean (average) values		4.0% +	11.2% +	-0.1% =	**15.1%**
		Median (typical) values		4.0% +	11.0% +	-0.1% =	**14.9%**

The unlevered cost of equity capital for the hypothetical subject company in this example has an estimated unlevered cost of capital ranging from 13.9% to 16.2%, with a mean (average) and median (typical) cost of equity capital of 15.1% and 14.9%, respectively.

Note that the *unlevered* cost of equity capital estimates calculated in this example are *less* than the *levered* cost of equity capital estimates calculated in Examples 1a and 1b. Again, this is because the unlevered risk premia used to estimate unlevered cost of equity capital are developed assuming a firm is financed 100% with equity and 0% debt. Generally, as the percentage of leverage (debt) in a company's capital structure decreases, risk to equity investors decreases (and vice versa).

Example 2b: Build-up 1-Unlevered Method (using regression equations)

The *only* difference between estimating unlevered cost of equity capital ($k_{e,\ unlevered}$) using the build-up 1-unlevered method using "guideline portfolios" method (Example 2a) and using the "regression equation" method (this example) is how the unlevered risk premia over the risk-free rate ($RP_{m+s,\ unlevered}$) are identified.

This example utilizes the same long-term risk-free rate 4.0% and the ERP Adjustment (-0.1%) established in a previous example, so the only missing input is the unlevered risk premium over the risk-free rate ($RP_{m+s,unlevered}$). Again, according to Exhibit 10.5, our hypothetical subject company has a market value of equity of $120 million, and the appropriate data exhibit is Exhibit C-1 (25 portfolios sorted by market value of equity).

The regression equation provided in Exhibit C-1 is:

*Smoothed Unlevered Premium = 18.810% - 3.094% * Log(Market Value)*

To calculate an interpolated smoothed unlevered risk premium, simply substitute the subject company's $120 million market value into the regression equation as follows:

Smoothed Unlevered Premium ($RP_{m+s,\ unlevered}$) = *18.810% - 3.094% * Log(120)*

The interpolated smoothed unlevered risk premium over the risk-free rate for "market value of equity" is therefore 12.4%:

*12.4% = 18.810% - 3.094% * 2.079*

This process is continued for each of the eight size characteristics that are available for the subject company. Exhibit 10.16 shows the calculations for each of the eight size measure's "custom" interpolated smoothed average unlevered risk premia over the risk-free rate ($RP_{m+s,\ unlevered}$).

Exhibit 10.16: Calculation of $RP_{m+s,\ unlevered}$ Premia (using regression equations)

	Size Measure (in $millions, except for Number of Employees)	Appropriate Exhibit	Appropriate Regression Equation		Smoothed Unlevered Premia Over Risk-Free Rate, $RP_{m+s,\ unlevered}$
Market Value of Equity	$120	C-1	Smoothed Unlevered Premium = 18.810% – 3.094% * Log(Market Value)	=	12.4%
Book Value of Equity	$100	C-2	Smoothed Unlevered Premium = 15.386% – 2.397% * Log(Book Value)	=	10.6%
5-year Average Net Income	$10	C-3	Smoothed Unlevered Premium = 13.286% – 2.433% * Log(Net Income)	=	10.9%
Market Value of Invested Capital	$180	C-4	Smoothed Unlevered Premium = 19.000% – 3.073% * Log(MVIC)	=	12.1%
Total Assets	$300	C-5	Smoothed Unlevered Premium = 17.274% – 2.653% * Log(Assets)	=	10.7%
5-year Average EBITDA	$30	C-6	Smoothed Unlevered Premium = 14.699% – 2.532% * Log(EBITDA)	=	11.0%
Sales	$250	C-7	Smoothed Unlevered Premium = 15.105% – 2.001% * Log(Sales)	=	10.3%
Number of Employees	200	C-8	Smoothed Unlevered Premium = 15.689% – 1.924% * Log(Employees)	=	11.3%

After the custom interpolated *smoothed average unlevered risk premia* have been calculated for all of the available size measures for the subject company, the subject company's unlevered cost of equity capital can be estimated, as shown in Exhibit 10.17.

Exhibit 10.17: Build-up 1-Unlevered Method Cost of Equity Capital Estimate (using regression equations)

	Size Measure (in $millions, except for Number of Employees)	Appropriate Exhibit	Risk-Free Rate, R_f	Smoothed Unlevered Premia Over Risk-Free Rate, $RP_{m+s,\ unlevered}$	ERP Adjustment	Cost of Equity Capital k_e
Market Value of Equity	$120	C-1	4.0% +	12.4% +	-0.1% =	**16.3%**
Book Value of Equity	$100	C-2	4.0% +	10.6% +	-0.1% =	14.5%
5-year Average Net Income	$10	C-3	4.0% +	10.9% +	-0.1% =	14.8%
Market Value of Invested Capital	$180	C-4	4.0% +	12.1% +	-0.1% =	16.0%
Total Assets	$300	C-5	4.0% +	10.7% +	-0.1% =	14.6%
5-year Average EBITDA	$30	C-6	4.0% +	11.0% +	-0.1% =	14.9%
Sales	$250	C-7	4.0% +	10.3% +	-0.1% =	**14.2%**
Number of Employees	200	C-8	4.0% +	11.3% +	-0.1% =	15.2%
	Mean (average) values		4.0% +	11.2% +	-0.1% =	**15.1%**
	Median (typical) values		4.0% +	11.0% +	-0.1% =	**14.9%**

The unlevered cost of equity capital for the hypothetical subject company in this example has an estimated cost of capital ranging from 14.2% to 16.3%, with a mean (average) and median (typical) cost of equity capital of 15.1% and 14.9%, respectively.

Estimating Cost of Equity Capital Using the Capital Asset Pricing Model (CAPM)

The CAPM is the most widely used method for estimating the cost of equity capital. The Risk Premium Report Size Study calculates average "risk premia over CAPM" (i.e., beta adjusted size premia) for each of the 25 size-ranked portfolios. These size premia (RP_s) are found in Exhibits B-1 through B-8, and can be added to the CAPM as an adjustment for the higher expected returns of smaller companies.

The modified CAPM formula is:[10.16]

$$k_{e,\ CAPM} = R_f + (\beta \times ERP) + RP_s$$

Example 3a: CAPM (using guideline portfolios)

To estimate the cost of equity capital (k_e) with the CAPM method using "guideline portfolios", four pieces of information are needed:

- Risk-free rate (R_f)
- Beta (β)
- Equity risk premium (RP_m, otherwise known as ERP),
- Risk premium over CAPM (RP_s, otherwise known as a beta-adjusted "size premium")

[10.16] The basic CAPM formula is $k_{e,\ CAPM} = R_f + (\beta \times ERP)$. "Modified" CAPM usually refers to the CAPM "modified" to account for risk not captured in the basic CAPM (in this case, "size" risk).

We have assumed a risk-free rate of 4.0% and an ERP of 5.0% for all examples. A beta of 1.2 is assumed for the CAPM examples. The ERP Adjustment is *not* needed when estimating cost of equity capital using the Risk Premium Report exhibits' size premia.[10.17] The only missing input is the size premium (RP_s):

$$k_{e\ CAPM} = 4.0\% + (1.2 \times 5.0\%) + RP_s$$

Gathering the *size* premia (RP_s) is straightforward. Match the various size measures of the subject company with the guideline portfolios composed of companies of similar size in Exhibits B-1 through B-8, and identify the corresponding *smoothed average size premium*.

For example, according to Exhibit 10.5, our hypothetical subject company has a market value of equity of $120 million, and the appropriate data exhibit is Exhibit B-1 (25 portfolios sorted by market value of equity). An abbreviated version of Exhibit B-1 is shown in Exhibit 10.18. Of the 25 portfolios, the portfolio that has an average market value *closest* to the subject company's $120 million market value is Portfolio 25 ($132 million). The corresponding *smoothed average size premium* is 7.03% (7.0%, rounded).

Exhibit 10.18: Exhibit B-1 (abbreviated)
Companies Ranked by Market Value of Equity
Size Premia
Data for Year Ending December 31, 2014

Portfolio Rank by Size	Average Mkt. Value (in $millions)	Log of Average Mkt. Value	Beta (SumBeta) Since '63	Arithmetic Average Return	Arithmetic Average Risk Premium	Indicated CAPM Premium	Premium over CAPM	*Smoothed Premium over CAPM*
1	178,744	5.25	0.83	12.13%	5.52%	4.21%	1.31%	-1.07%
2	53,009	4.72	0.96	11.15%	4.54%	4.84%	-0.30%	0.29%
3	32,537	4.51	0.92	11.66%	5.04%	4.67%	0.38%	0.84%
///								
24	412	2.62	1.24	19.45%	12.84%	6.27%	6.57%	5.74%
25	132	2.12	1.28	22.92%	16.31%	6.47%	9.84%	**7.03%**

This process is continued for each of the eight size characteristics that are available for the subject company. After all of the available size measures for the subject company have been matched to the closest guideline portfolio in the appropriate exhibit and the corresponding *smoothed average size premium* has been identified for each, the subject company's cost of equity capital can be estimated, as shown in Exhibit 10.19.

[10.17] For a detailed discussion of the ERP Adjustment, see the section entitled "Proper Application of the Equity Risk Premium (ERP) Adjustment" in Chapter 9.

Exhibit 10.19: CAPM Cost of Equity Capital Estimate (using guideline portfolios)

Size Measure (in $millions, except for Number of Employees)		Appropriate Exhibit	Guideline Portfolio	Risk-Free Rate, R_f	Beta β	ERP	Smoothed Risk Premia over CAPM (size premium) RP_s	Cost of Equity Capital k_e
Market Value of Equity	$120	B-1	25	4.0% +	(1.2 x	5.0%) +	7.0% =	**17.0%**
Book Value of Equity	$100	B-2	25	4.0% +	(1.2 x	5.0%) +	5.6% =	15.6%
5-year Average Net Income	$10	B-3	24	4.0% +	(1.2 x	5.0%) +	5.6% =	15.6%
Market Value of Invested Capital	$180	B-4	25	4.0% +	(1.2 x	5.0%) +	6.8% =	16.8%
Total Assets	$300	B-5	24	4.0% +	(1.2 x	5.0%) +	5.2% =	15.2%
5-year Average EBITDA	$30	B-6	25	4.0% +	(1.2 x	5.0%) +	6.2% =	16.2%
Sales	$250	B-7	24	4.0% +	(1.2 x	5.0%) +	5.1% =	**15.1%**
Number of Employees	200	B-8	25	4.0% +	(1.2 x	5.0%) +	6.0% =	16.0%
		Mean (average) values		4.0% +	(1.2 x	5.0%) +	5.9% =	**15.9%**
		Median (typical) values		4.0% +	(1.2 x	5.0%) +	5.8% =	**15.8%**

The hypothetical subject company in this example has an estimated cost of capital ranging from 15.1% to 17.0%, with a mean (average) and median (typical) cost of equity capital of 15.9% and 15.8%, respectively.

Example 3b: CAPM (using regression equations)

The *only* difference between estimating cost of equity capital (k_e) using the CAPM method using "guideline portfolios" (Example 3a) and using "regression equations" is how the size premia (RP_s) are identified.

In the previous example, the smoothed size premia *published* in the Risk Premium Report exhibits for the appropriate guideline portfolios were used to estimate cost of equity capital. In this example, however, the regression equations found in each of the data exhibits will be used to calculate "custom" interpolated smoothed size premia, based upon the specific size measures of the subject company.

This example utilizes the same long-term risk-free rate of 4.0%, ERP of 5.0%, and beta of 1.2 used in a previous example, so the only missing input is the size premium (RP_s). Again, according to Exhibit 10.5, our hypothetical subject company has a market value of equity of $120 million, and the appropriate data exhibit is Exhibit B-1 (25 portfolios sorted by market value of equity).

The regression equation provided in Exhibit B-1 is:

*Smoothed Size Premium = 12.505% – 2.585% * Log (Market Value)*

To calculate an interpolated smoothed size premium for the subject company's $120 million market value, simply substitute the market value into the regression equation as follows:

Smoothed Size Premium (RP_s) *= 12.505% – 2.585% * Log (120)*

The interpolated smoothed size premium for "market value of equity" is therefore 7.1%:

*7.1% = 12.505% – 2.585% * 2.079*

This process is continued for each of the eight size characteristics that are available for the subject company. Exhibit 10.20 shows the calculations for each of the eight size measure's custom interpolated smoothed size premium (RP_s).

Exhibit 10.20: Calculation of Size Premia (RP_s) (using regression equations)

	Size Measure (in $millions, except for Number of Employees)	Appropriate Exhibit	Appropriate Regression Equation		Smoothed Risk Premia over CAPM (size premium) RP_s
Market Value of Equity	$120	B-1	Smoothed Premium = 12.505% – 2.585% * Log(Market Value)	=	7.1%
Book Value of Equity	$100	B-2	Smoothed Premium = 8.469% – 1.599% * Log(Book Value)	=	5.3%
5-year Average Net Income	$10	B-3	Smoothed Premium = 7.428% – 1.743% * Log(Net Income)	=	5.7%
Market Value of Invested Capital	$180	B-4	Smoothed Premium = 11.936% – 2.355% * Log(MVIC)	=	6.6%
Total Assets	$300	B-5	Smoothed Premium = 9.690% – 1.736% * Log(Assets)	=	5.4%
5-year Average EBITDA	$30	B-6	Smoothed Premium = 8.239% – 1.723% * Log(EBITDA)	=	5.7%
Sales	$250	B-7	Smoothed Premium = 8.662% – 1.405% * Log(Sales)	=	5.3%
Number of Employees	200	B-8	Smoothed Premium = 10.011% – 1.612% * Log(Employees)	=	6.3%

After the custom interpolated *smoothed size premia* have been calculated for all of the available size measures for the subject company, the subject company's cost of equity capital can be estimated, as shown in Exhibit 10.21.

Exhibit 10.21: CAPM Cost of Equity Capital Estimate (using regression equations)

	Size Measure (in $millions, except for Number of Employees)	Appropriate Exhibit	Risk-Free Rate, R_f	Beta β	ERP	Smoothed Risk Premia over CAPM (size premium) RP_s	Cost of Equity Capital k_e
Market Value of Equity	$120	B-1	4.0% +	(1.2 x	5.0%) +	7.1% =	**17.1%**
Book Value of Equity	$100	B-2	4.0% +	(1.2 x	5.0%) +	5.3% =	15.3%
5-year Average Net Income	$10	B-3	4.0% +	(1.2 x	5.0%) +	5.7% =	15.7%
Market Value of Invested Capital	$180	B-4	4.0% +	(1.2 x	5.0%) +	6.6% =	16.6%
Total Assets	$300	B-5	4.0% +	(1.2 x	5.0%) +	5.4% =	15.4%
5-year Average EBITDA	$30	B-6	4.0% +	(1.2 x	5.0%) +	5.7% =	15.7%
Sales	$250	B-7	4.0% +	(1.2 x	5.0%) +	5.3% =	**15.3%**
Number of Employees	200	B-8	4.0% +	(1.2 x	5.0%) +	6.3% =	16.3%
	Mean (average) values		4.0% +	(1.2 x	5.0%) +	5.9% =	**15.9%**
	Median (typical) values		4.0% +	(1.2 x	5.0%) +	5.7% =	**15.7%**

The cost of equity capital for the hypothetical subject company in this example has an estimated cost of capital ranging from 15.3% to 17.1%, with a mean (average) and median (typical) cost of equity capital of 15.9% and 15.7%, respectively.

Estimating Cost of Equity Capital Using the "Build-up 2" Method

The Risk Premium Report's Size Study can be used in conjunction with the industry risk premia previously published in the *SBBI Valuation Edition Yearbook*, and now published in the *2015 Valuation Handbook* in Exhibit 5.7.[10.18]

The "build-up 1" method presented previously in Examples 1a and 1b utilizes a risk premia over the risk-free rate that are a measure of risk in terms of the combined effect of *market* risk and *size* risk. Build-up 2, however, adds the equity risk premium and a *separate* beta-adjusted size premium to the risk-free rate, and *then* accounts for market (i.e., beta) risk by adding an industry risk premium. As such, build-up 2 is a hybrid of the CAPM method and Build-up 1 method, with beta risk taking the form of an industry risk premium (RP_i). [10.19]

Because Risk Premium Report size premia are "beta adjusted"[10.20], without the addition of an industry risk premium (RP_i), beta risk is not accounted for:

$$\underbrace{k_{e\ build\text{-}up\ 2} = R_f + ERP + RP_s}_{\text{No Beta Risk}} + \underbrace{RP_i}_{\text{Beta Risk}}$$

An industry risk premium is just a beta "scaled around zero" so that it becomes a simple up or down adjustment when used within the context of a build-up method. To create industry risk premia in the *2015 Valuation Handbook*, we transform what are known as "full-information" (industry) betas into industry risk premia using the formula (FIB x ERP) – ERP. The result is:

- A full-information beta = 1 (which matches the "market's" beta) will become an industry risk premium of "0" (*equal* in risk to the market);
- A full-information beta > 1 will become an industry risk premium *greater* than zero (*riskier* than the market), and
- A full-information beta < 1 will become an industry risk premium less than zero (*less* risky than the market).

10.18 A detailed discussion of betas and industry risk premia is in Chapter 5, "Basic Building Blocks of the Cost of Equity Capital – Betas and Industry Risk Premia".

10.19 The industry risk premia previously published in the *SBBI Valuation Yearbook's* Table 3-5 were denoted as "IRP" in equations. In the *2015 Valuation Handbook* industry risk premia are denoted as "RP_i" in equations. This change in nomenclature was done to match the nomenclature used in *Cost of Capital: Applications and Examples* 5th ed. (Hoboken, NJ: John Wiley & Sons, 2014).

10.20 All Risk Premium Report size premia *and* CRSP Deciles Size Premia published in the *2015 Valuation Handbook* are "beta-adjusted". A beta-adjusted size premium has been adjusted to remove that portion of excess return that is attributable to beta, leaving only the size effect's contribution to excess return.

Example 4a: Build-up 2 Method (using guideline portfolios)

To estimate the cost of equity capital (k_e) with the build-up 2 method using "guideline portfolios", four pieces of information are needed:

- Risk-free rate (R_f)
- Equity risk premium ($RP_{m,}$ otherwise known as ERP),
- Risk premium over CAPM ($RP_{s,}$ otherwise known as a beta-adjusted "size premium")
- Industry Risk Premium (RP_i)

We have assumed a risk-free rate of 4.0%, an ERP of 5.0%, and an industry risk premium of 1.0% for all Build-up 2 examples.[10.21] The only missing input is the size premium (RP_s):

$k_{e\ build\text{-}up\ 2} = 4.0\% + 5.0\% + RP_s + 1.0\%$

The ERP Adjustment is *not* needed when estimating cost of equity capital using the Risk Premium Report exhibits' size premia.[10.22]

Gathering the *size* premia (RP_s) is straightforward. Match the various size measures of the subject company with the guideline portfolios composed of companies of similar size in Exhibits B-1 through B-8, and identify the corresponding *smoothed average size premium.*

For example, according to Exhibit 10.5, our hypothetical subject company has a market value of equity of $120 million, and the appropriate data exhibit is Exhibit B-1 (25 portfolios sorted by market value of equity). An abbreviated version of Exhibit B-1 is shown in Exhibit 10.22. Of the 25 portfolios, the portfolio that has an average market value *closest* to the subject company's $120 million market value is Portfolio 25 ($132 million). The corresponding *smoothed average size premium* is 7.03% (7.0%, rounded).

10.21 The assumed industry risk premium of 1.0% is derived by a transformation of the assumed beta of 1.2 that was used for the CAPM examples, using the Duff & Phelps recommended ERP of 5.0%. 1.0% = (1.2 x 5.0%) – 5.0%

10.22 For a detailed discussion of the ERP Adjustment, see the section entitled "Proper Application of the Equity Risk Premium (ERP) Adjustment" in Chapter 9.

Exhibit 10.22: Exhibit B-1 (abbreviated)
Companies Ranked by Market Value of Equity
Size Premia
Data for Year Ending December 31, 2014

Portfolio Rank by Size	Average Mkt. Value (in $millions)	Log of Average Mkt. Value	Beta (SumBeta) Since '63	Arithmetic Average Return	Arithmetic Average Risk Premium	Indicated CAPM Premium	Premium over CAPM	*Smoothed Premium over CAPM*
1	178,744	5.25	0.83	12.13%	5.52%	4.21%	1.31%	-1.07%
2	53,009	4.72	0.96	11.15%	4.54%	4.84%	-0.30%	0.29%
3	32,537	4.51	0.92	11.66%	5.04%	4.67%	0.38%	0.84%
///								
24	412	2.62	1.24	19.45%	12.84%	6.27%	6.57%	5.74%
25	132	2.12	1.28	22.92%	16.31%	6.47%	9.84%	**7.03%**

This process is continued for each of the eight size characteristics that are available for the subject company. After all of the available size measures for the subject company have been matched to the closest guideline portfolio in the appropriate exhibit and the corresponding *smoothed average size premium* has been identified for each, the subject company's cost of equity capital can be estimated, as shown in Exhibit 10.23.

Exhibit 10.23: Build-up 2 Method Cost of Equity Capital Estimate (using guideline portfolios)

	Size Measure (in $millions, except for Number of Employees)	Appropriate Exhibit	Guideline Portfolio	Risk-Free Rate, R_f	ERP	Smoothed Risk Premia over CAPM (size premium) RP_s	Industry Risk Premia RP_i	Cost of Equity Capital k_e
Market Value of Equity	$120	B-1	25	4.0% +	5.0% +	7.0% +	1.0% =	**17.0%**
Book Value of Equity	$100	B-2	25	4.0% +	5.0% +	5.6% +	1.0% =	15.6%
5-year Average Net Income	$10	B-3	24	4.0% +	5.0% +	5.6% +	1.0% =	15.6%
Market Value of Invested Capital	$180	B-4	25	4.0% +	5.0% +	6.8% +	1.0% =	16.8%
Total Assets	$300	B-5	24	4.0% +	5.0% +	5.2% +	1.0% =	15.2%
5-year Average EBITDA	$30	B-6	25	4.0% +	5.0% +	6.2% +	1.0% =	16.2%
Sales	$250	B-7	24	4.0% +	5.0% +	5.1% +	1.0% =	**15.1%**
Number of Employees	200	B-8	25	4.0% +	5.0% +	6.0% +	1.0% =	16.0%
		Mean (average) values		4.0% +	5.0% +	5.9% +	1.0% =	**15.9%**
		Median (typical) values		4.0% +	5.0% +	5.8% +	1.0% =	**15.8%**

The hypothetical subject company in this example has an estimated cost of capital ranging from 15.1% to 17.0%, with a mean (average) and median (typical) cost of equity capital of 15.9% and 15.8%, respectively.

Example 4b: Build-up 2 Method (using regression equations)

The *only* difference between estimating cost of equity capital (k_e) using the Build-up 2 method using "guideline portfolios" and using "regression equations" is how the size premia (RP_s) are identified.

In the previous example, the smoothed size premia *published* in the Risk Premium Report exhibits for the appropriate guideline portfolios were used to estimate cost of equity capital. In this example, however, the regression equations found in each of the data exhibits will be used to calculate "custom" interpolated smoothed size premia, based upon the specific size measures of the subject company.

This example utilizes the same long-term risk-free rate of 4.0%, ERP of 5.0%, and IRP of 1.0% used in the previous example, so the only missing input is the size premium (RP_s). Again, according to Exhibit 10.5, our hypothetical subject company has a market value of equity of $120 million, and the appropriate data exhibit is Exhibit B-1 (25 portfolios sorted by market value of equity).

The regression equation provided in Exhibit B-1 is:

*Smoothed Size Premium = 12.505% – 2.585% * Log (Market Value)*

To calculate an interpolated smoothed size premium for the subject company's $120 million market value, simply substitute the market value into the regression equation as follows:

Smoothed Size Premium (RP_s) *= 12.505% – 2.585% * Log (120)*

The interpolated smoothed size premium for "market value of equity" is therefore 7.1%:

*7.1% = 12.505% – 2.585% * 2.079*

This process is continued for each of the eight size characteristics that are available for the subject company. Exhibit 10.24 shows the calculations for each of the eight size measure's "custom" interpolated smoothed size premium (RP_s).

Exhibit 10.24: Calculation of Size Premia (RP_s) (using regression equations)

	Size Measure (in $millions, except for Number of Employees)	Appropriate Exhibit	Appropriate Regression Equation		Smoothed Risk Premia over CAPM (size premium) RP_s
Market Value of Equity	$120	B-1	Smoothed Premium = 12.505% – 2.585% * Log(Market Value)	=	7.1%
Book Value of Equity	$100	B-2	Smoothed Premium = 8.469% – 1.599% * Log(Book Value)	=	5.3%
5-year Average Net Income	$10	B-3	Smoothed Premium = 7.428% – 1.743% * Log(Net Income)	=	5.7%
Market Value of Invested Capital	$180	B-4	Smoothed Premium = 11.936% – 2.355% * Log(MVIC)	=	6.6%
Total Assets	$300	B-5	Smoothed Premium = 9.690% – 1.736% * Log(Assets)	=	5.4%
5-year Average EBITDA	$30	B-6	Smoothed Premium = 8.239% – 1.723% * Log(EBITDA)	=	5.7%
Sales	$250	B-7	Smoothed Premium = 8.662% – 1.405% * Log(Sales)	=	5.3%
Number of Employees	200	B-8	Smoothed Premium = 10.011% – 1.612% * Log(Employees)	=	6.3%

After the "custom" interpolated *smoothed size premia* have been calculated for all of the available size measures for the subject company, the subject company's cost of equity capital can be estimated, as shown in Exhibit 10.25.

Exhibit 10.25: Build-up 2 Method Cost of Equity Capital Estimate (using regression equations)

	Size Measure (in $millions, except for Number of Employees)	Appropriate Exhibit	Risk-Free Rate, R_f	ERP	Smoothed Risk Premia Over CAPM (size premium), RP_s	Industry Risk Premia RP_i	Cost of Equity Capital k_e
Market Value of Equity	$120	B-1	4.0% +	5.0% +	7.1% +	1.0% =	**17.1%**
Book Value of Equity	$100	B-2	4.0% +	5.0% +	5.3% +	1.0% =	15.3%
5-year Average Net Income	$10	B-3	4.0% +	5.0% +	5.7% +	1.0% =	15.7%
Market Value of Invested Capital	$180	B-4	4.0% +	5.0% +	6.6% +	1.0% =	16.6%
Total Assets	$300	B-5	4.0% +	5.0% +	5.4% +	1.0% =	15.4%
5-year Average EBITDA	$30	B-6	4.0% +	5.0% +	5.7% +	1.0% =	15.7%
Sales	$250	B-7	4.0% +	5.0% +	5.3% +	1.0% =	**15.3%**
Number of Employees	200	B-8	4.0% +	5.0% +	6.3% +	1.0% =	16.3%
	Mean (average) values		4.0% +	5.0% +	5.9% +	1.0% =	**15.9%**
	Median (typical) values		4.0% +	5.0% +	5.7% +	1.0% =	**15.7%**

The cost of equity capital for the hypothetical subject company in this example has an estimated cost of capital ranging from 15.3% to 17.1%, with a mean (average) and median (typical) cost of equity capital of 15.9% and 15.7%, respectively.

Risk Study

The Risk Premium Report's Risk Study is an extension of the Size Study. The main difference between the Risk Study and the Size Study is that the Size Study analyzes the relationship between *size* and return, and the Risk Study analyzes the relationship between *fundamental risk measures* (based on accounting data) and return. These are called "fundamental" measures of company risk to distinguish these risk measures from a stock market based measure of equity risk such as beta. A variety of academic studies have examined the relationship between financial statement data and various aspects of business risk.[10.23] Research has shown that measures of earnings volatility can be useful in explaining credit ratings, predicting bankruptcy, and explaining the CAPM beta.

As in the Size Study, 25 portfolios are created, but instead of being ranked by eight alternative measures of size as is done in the Size Study, the Risk Study portfolios are ranked by three fundamental risk measures:

- Five-year average operating income margin
- Coefficient of variation in operating income margin
- Coefficient of variation in return on book equity[10.24]

The first statistic measures profitability and the other two statistics measure volatility of earnings. Companies with *lower* operating margins tend to be *riskier* (and vice versa). Companies with *greater* coefficient of variation of earnings (as measured by operating income margin and return on book equity) tend to be *riskier* (and vice versa).

Size and Risk

Traditionally, valuation analysts have used company size as a factor in determining discount rates for smaller companies. The historical data as presented in the Risk Premium Report studies and in the CRSP Deciles Size Premia studies, verify that small companies have, in fact, earned higher rates of return over long-run periods.

Some have pointed that researchers may be mixing a "size" effect with a "risk" effect when measuring company size by market value, but market value is not just a function of size; it is also a function of the discount rate.[10.25] In other words, some companies might be small because they are risky, rather than risky because they are small.

The Risk Study goes *beyond* size and investigates the relationship between equity returns and fundamental risk measures. Does the evidence support the claim that smaller companies inherently have greater risk? The Risk Study analyzes this question, and demonstrates that as company size decreases,

10.23 A survey of the academic research can be found in *The Analysis and Use of Financial Statements*, 3rd edition, White et al., Wiley (2003), chapter 18.

10.24 Coefficient of variation is defined here as the standard deviation divided by the mean.

10.25 "A Critique of Size Related Anomalies," Jonathan Berk, *Review of Financial Studies*, vol. 8, no. 2 (1995).

measures of risk calculated from financial statement data do, as a matter of fact, tend to increase. The data clearly shows that as fundamental risk increases in the form of lower profitability or greater variability of earnings, the return over the risk-free rate tends to increase.

Previously, it was demonstrated in the Risk Premium Report's Size Study that there is a clear inverse relationship between size and historical rates of return (as size *decreases*, returns tend to *increase*). In the Risk Premium Report's Risk Study, the data show a clear *direct* relationship between accounting-data-based fundamental risk measures and historical rates of return (as fundamental risk *increases*, returns tend to *increase*).

In Exhibit 10.26, the average annual return of the 25 portfolios of *each* of the three fundamental risk measures analyzed in the Risk Study is calculated over the time horizon 1963–2014, with risk increasing from left to right. For example, the portfolios comprised of companies with the *highest* operating margins and *least* coefficient of variation for operating income margin and return on book equity are on the left side of the graph; the portfolios comprised of companies with the *lowest* operating margins and *greatest* coefficient of variation for operating income margin and return on book equity are on the *right* side of the graph

In the Risk Premium Report exhibits, the average annual return of the portfolios made up of companies with the *lowest* risk as measured by each of the three fundamental risk measures was 13.5%, while the average annual return of the portfolios made up of companies with the *highest* risk was 20.4%, as shown in Exhibit 10.26.

Exhibit 10.26: Average Annual Return, Risk Study's Three Measures of Fundamental Risk 1963–2014

Reasons for Using Fundamental Measures of Risk in Addition to Measures of Size

First, certain measures of size (such as market value of equity) may be imperfect measures of the risk of a company's operations in some situations. For example, a company with a large and stable operating margin may have a small and unstable market value of equity if it is highly leveraged. In this case the risk of the underlying operations is low while the risk to equity is high. Second, while small size may indicate greater risk, some small companies may maintain near economic monopolies by holding a geographic niche or market niche such that their true riskiness is less than what would be indicated by their size.

Alternatively, while larger size (as measured by sales, for example) may indicate less risk, some companies may be riskier than the average of companies with similar sales. For example, assume the subject company was expecting to emerge from reorganization following bankruptcy. The risk premium appropriate for this company may be more accurately imputed from the pro-forma operating profit (after removing non-recurring expenses incurred during the bankruptcy) than from its size as measured by sales. In other words, the subject company may be riskier than companies with similar sales volumes.

Use of fundamental accounting measures of risk allows for direct assessment of the riskiness of the subject company. For example, if the appropriate risk premium for the subject company when measuring risk by one or more fundamental risk measures is different than the risk premium based on size measures, this difference may be an indication of the "company-specific" differences of the subject company's fundamental risk and the average fundamental risk of companies that make up the portfolios from which the risk premia are derived.[10.26]

The D Exhibits: Summary of Data Presented

Exhibits D-1, D-2, and D-3: The D exhibits provide risk premia over the risk-free rate in terms of the combined effect of market risk and company-specific risk, as represented by the differences in three alternative accounting-based measures of fundamental risk (RP_{m+c}).

Each of the exhibits D-1 through D-3 present 25 portfolios ranked by three fundamental risk factors (based on accounting data), as described in Exhibit 10.27.[10.27]

10.26 *Valuing a Business*, 4th ed., Pratt et al, McGraw-Hill (2000), p 181. Examples of risks that are typically referred to as "company-specific" risk can include concentration of customer base, key person dependence, key supplier dependence, or any number of other factors that are perceived as unique to the subject company.

10.27 For a detailed description of the Standard and Poor's *Compustat* data items used as inputs in the calculation of the data in the Risk Premium Report exhibits, please see Appendix A.

Exhibit 10.27: Three Measures of Fundamental Risk in the Risk Study's D Exhibits

---

Exhibit D-1

Operating Margin: The mean operating income for the prior five years divided by the mean sales for the prior five years. Operating income is defined as sales minus cost of goods sold plus selling, general, and administrative expenses plus depreciation. Note that this composite ratio is usually very close to a simple average of the annual ratios of operating income to sales, except in extreme cases generally involving companies with high growth rates.

Exhibit D-2

Coefficient of Variation of Operating Margin: The standard deviation of operating margin over the prior five years divided by the average operating margin for the same years. Note that for calculating this coefficient, average operating margin is a simple average of the annual ratios of operating income to sales rather than the composite ratio used in exhibit D-1.

Exhibit D-3

Coefficient of Variation of Return on Book Value of Equity: The standard deviation of return on book equity for the prior five years divided by the mean return on book equity for the same years. Return on book equity is defined as net income before extraordinary items minus preferred dividends divided by book value of common equity.

The D exhibits include the statistics outlined in Exhibit 10.28 for each of the risk measures outlined in Exhibit 10.27. For comparative purposes, the average returns from the SBBI series for large companies (essentially the S&P 500 Index), small companies, and long-term government bond income returns for the period 1963 through the latest year are also reported on each exhibit.[10.28]

Exhibit 10.28: Statistics Reported for 25 fundamental-risk-ranked portfolios in the Risk Study's D Exhibits

- The average of the sorting criteria for the latest year (e.g., the average operating margin for the latest five years before 2014). Note that the reported average risk statistics in exhibits D-1, D-2, and D-3 are *not* the same numbers as reported in exhibits C-1 through C-8. In exhibits C-1 through C-8, the reported statistics are calculated for portfolios of companies grouped according to size and are averages since 1963. In exhibits D-1, D-2, and D-3, the reported statistics are calculated for portfolios grouped according to risk, independent of the "size" of the companies, and are not averages since 1963
- Log (base-10) of the median of the sorting criteria.
- The number of companies in each portfolio as of 2014.
- Standard deviation of annual historical equity returns.
- Beta calculated using the "sum beta" method applied to monthly returns for 1963 through the latest year.
- Unlevered beta calculated using the "sum beta" method applied to monthly returns for 1963 through the latest year.
- Geometric average historical equity return since 1963.
- Arithmetic average historical equity return since 1963.
- Arithmetic average historical risk premium over long-term Treasuries (average return on equity in excess of long-term Treasury bonds) since 1963. (RP_{m+s+c})
- Average Debt as a percent of the MVIC since 1963.
- Smoothed average historical risk premium over long-term Treasuries (average return on equity in excess of long-term Treasury bonds) since 1963: the fitted premium from a regression with the historical "risk premium over long-term Treasuries" as dependent variable and the logarithm of the average sorting criteria as independent variable. (RP_{m+s+c})
- Unlevered arithmetic average historical risk premium over long-term Treasuries (average return on equity in excess of long-term Treasury bonds) since 1963. ($RP_{m+s+c,\ unlevered}$)

[10.28] Source: Morningstar *Direct* database.

Is Size Correlated with Market and Fundamental Risk Measures?

The *same* universe of companies used to create the A, B, and C exhibits is the *same* universe of companies used to create the D exhibits. However, the *composition* of any of the 25 portfolios in the D exhibits is *different* from the composition of the 25 portfolios in the A, B, C exhibits.

In the case of the A and B exhibits, the portfolios are sorted (largest to smallest) by each of eight alternative measures of *size*, and *then* the fundamental risk characteristics of each portfolio are calculated and reported in the C exhibits. In the case of the D exhibits, the *same* set of companies that are in the A, B, and C exhibits are sorted by each of the three *fundamental risk measures* (from highest to lowest) to form 25 risk-ranked portfolios, and then the average risk characteristics of each portfolio are calculated.

Why the composition of any one of the D exhibit's 25 portfolios is likely different than the composition of any one of the A, B, and C exhibits 25 portfolios can be illustrated with a simple example. Say you have 10 companies and you sort them by *size* (from largest to smallest). Then (using the *same* 10 companies), you sort them again by a *fundamental risk measure* like operating margin (from highest to lowest). Will the order necessarily be the same? Probably not.

Nonetheless, the Risk Premium Exhibits do suggest that size is correlated with market measures. For example, as size measures decrease in Exhibit 10.29 (from left to right), the beta (both levered and unlevered) of the portfolios increase (as expected).[10.29]

Exhibit 10.29: Average Levered and Unlevered Sum Beta (all eight size measures)

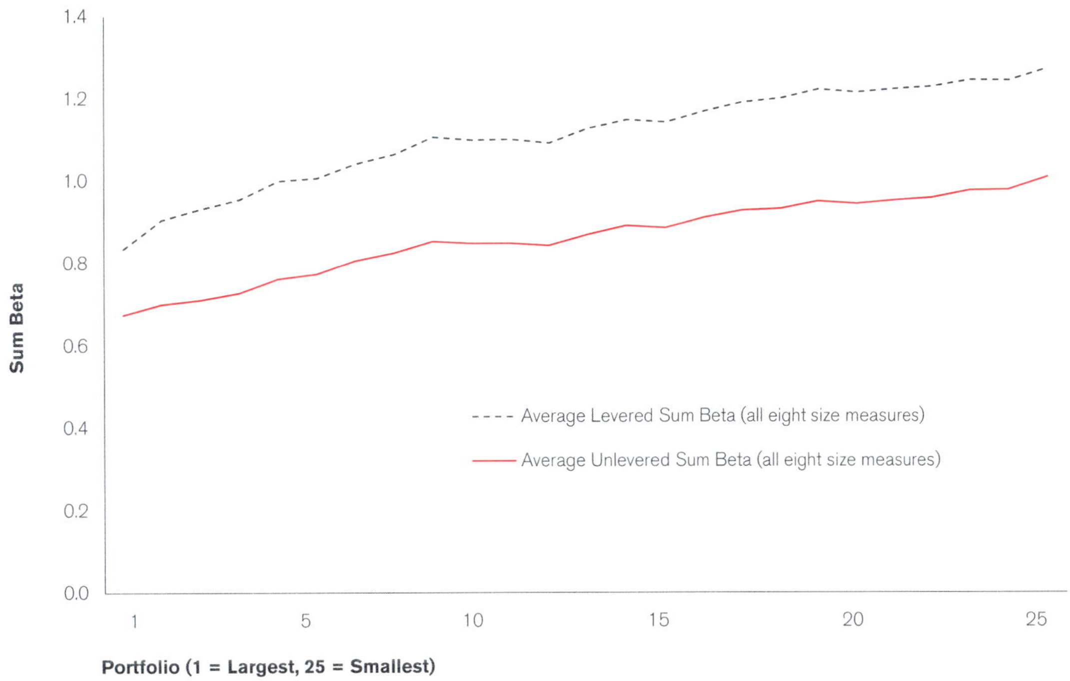

[10.29] In the research on "size" as reported in this report, we have determined that, in the context of the CAPM, the higher betas of the small companies explain some but not all of the higher average historical equity returns in these portfolios.

The data also suggests that this correlation extends to the three fundamental measures of risk. For example, in Exhibit 10.30, as size measures *decrease* (from left to right), operating margin of the portfolios *decreases* (indicating increased risk).

Exhibit 10.30: Average Operating Margin (all eight size measures)
1963–2014

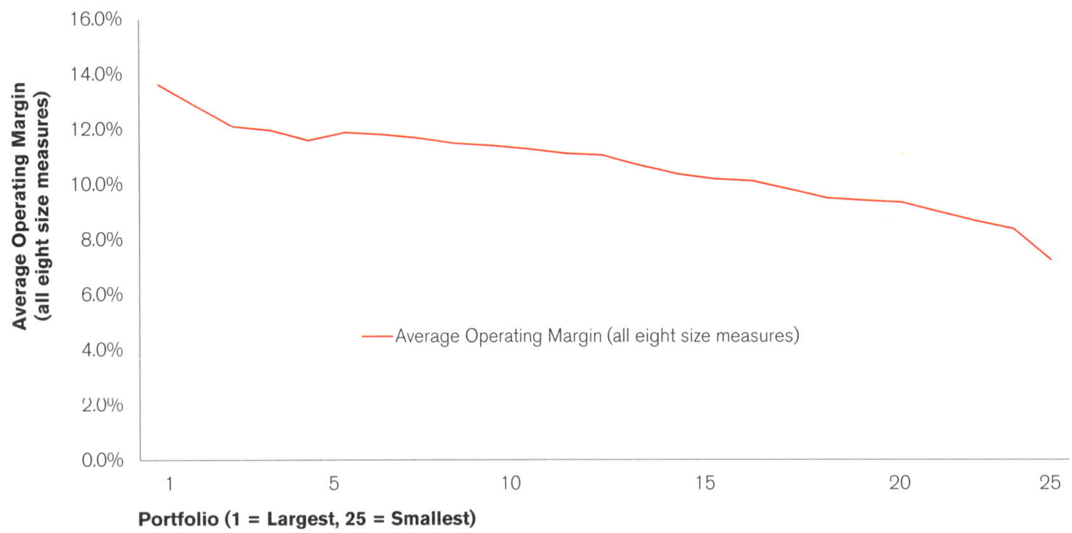

And in Exhibit 10.31, as size measures *decrease* (from left to right), average coefficient of operating margin and average coefficient of variation of ROE of the portfolios *increase* (indicating increased risk).

Exhibit 10.31: Average Coefficient of Operating Margin and Average Coefficient of Variation of ROE
All 8 Size Measures
1963–2014

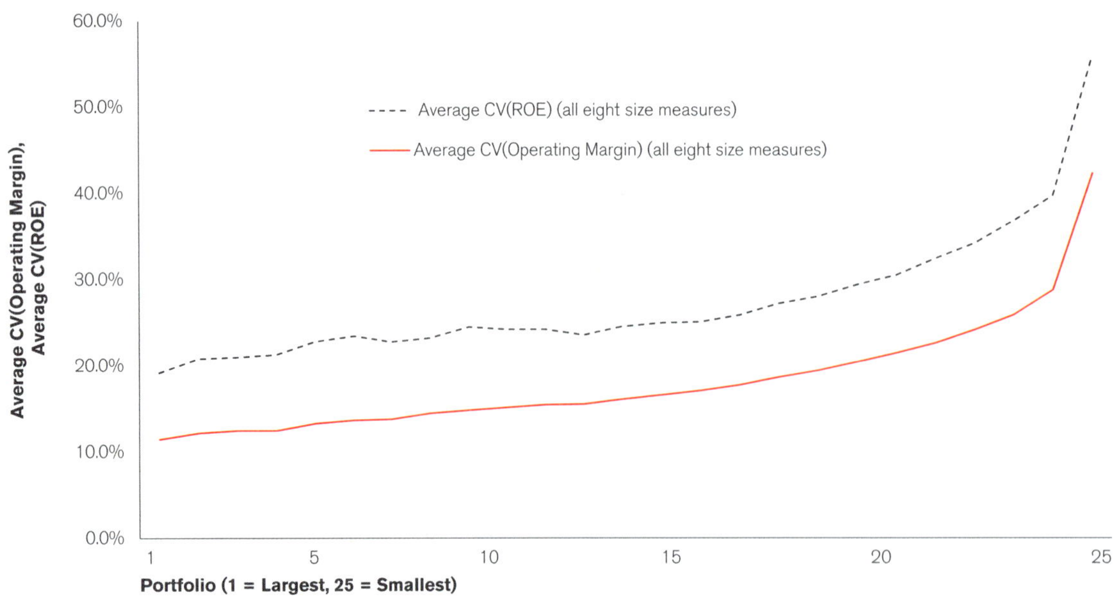

While the correlation between fundamental measures of risk and size demonstrated in Exhibits 10.30 and 10.31 implies that there may be an embedded "size effect" component in the Risk Study's RP_{m+c} premia, the magnitude of this embedded size effect is difficult to quantify. In any case, the size effect embedded in the Risk Study's RP_{m+c} premia are in all likelihood not equivalent to the size effect embedded in the Size Study's RP_{m+s} premia, which are a measure of risk in terms of the combined effect of *market* risk and *size* risk.

Overview of Methods Used to Estimate Cost of Equity Capital Using the Risk Study

The Risk Premium Report's Risk Study provides one method of estimating cost of equity capital for a subject company, build-up 3, and one method for estimating *unlevered* cost of equity capital (the cost of equity capital assuming a firm is financed 100% with equity and 0% debt), build-up 3-unlevered.

These two methods are summarized in Exhibit 10.32:

Exhibit 10.32:

Method	Cost of Equity Capital Formula
Build-up 3	$k_e = R_f + RP_{m+c} + ERP\ Adjustment$
Build-up 3-Unlevered	$k_e = R_f + RP_{m+c,\ unlevered} + ERP\ Adjustment$

Risk Study Examples: Assumptions Used

The Risk Study's D exhibits provide "risk premia over the risk-free rate" in terms of the combined effect of market risk and company-specific risk. As such, the same assumptions that were used in the Build-up 1 examples (which utilized "risk premia over the risk-free rate" from the A exhibits) can be used:

- Valuation Date: December 31, 2014[10.30]
- ERP: 5.0% [10.31]
- Risk-free Rate: 4.0% (normalized rate)
- ERP Adjustment: -0.1%[10.32]

10.30 The "data through" date of the *2015 Valuation Handbook* is December 31, 2014.

10.31 The Duff & Phelps recommended ERP as of December 31, 2014 is 5.0%, and is intended to be used in conjunction with a 4.0% normalized risk-free rate, as reported in Exhibit 3.15, "Duff & Phelps Recommended ERP and Corresponding Risk-Free Rate January 2008–Present". For detailed information about the ERP and risk-free rates, see Chapter 3, "Basic Building Blocks of the Cost of Equity Capital – Risk-free Rate and Equity Risk Premium".

10.32 The ERP adjustment is *never* necessary when using size premia, but is *always* necessary when using "risk premia over the risk-free rate", such as are found in the D exhibits. The ERP adjustment in this example is calculated as the difference between the ERP selected to use in these examples (5.0%) and the historical 1963–2014 ERP (5.1%) that was used as a convention to calculate the 2015 Risk Premium Report exhibits. For detailed information about the ERP Adjustment, see the section entitled "Proper Application of the Equity Risk Premium (ERP) Adjustment" in Chapter 9, "Risk Premium Report Exhibits – General Information".

Gathering Accounting Information to Calculate Fundamental Risk Measures

The first step in using the Risk Study to estimate cost of equity capital is to gather the accounting-based information for the subject company that is needed to calculate the three fundamental risk measures analyzed in the Risk Study.

To calculate "operating margin" and "coefficient of variation of operating margin", net sales and operating income are needed.

To calculate "coefficient of variation of ROE", book value and net income before extraordinary items are needed. The accounting information for the last 5 years needed to calculate the three fundamental risk measures for our hypothetical subject company is summarized in Exhibits 10.33 and 10.34.

Hypothetical Subject Company Fundamental Risk Characteristics

The three fundamental risk measures (five-year average operating income margin, coefficient of variation in operating margin, coefficient of variation in return on book equity) that will be used in the two Risk Study examples are calculated in Exhibits 10.33 and 10.34, and summarized in Exhibit 10.35.

It is important to note that the subject company information necessary to calculate all of these measures may not be available. In these cases, it is generally acceptable to use the fundamental risk measures that are available. It is recommended, however, that users calculate available risk measures for the subject company using *at least* the three most recent years of data, and the five most recent years of data for best results.

Exhibit 10.33: Subject Company Operating Margin and Coefficient of Variation of Operating Margin (used in all Risk Study examples)

	2014	2013	2012	2011	2010
Net Sales	$900	$800	$850	$750	$900
Operating Income	$150	$120	$130	$80	$140
Operating Margin	16.7% = $150/$900	15.0% = $120/$800	15.3% = $130/$850	10.7% = $80/$750	15.6% = $140/$900
Standard Deviation of Operating Margin	2.3%				
Average Operating Margin	**14.6%**				
Coefficient of Variation of Operating Margin	**15.8%**	= 2.3%/14.6%			

Exhibit 10.34: Subject Company Coefficient of Variation of ROE (used in all Risk Study examples)

	2014	2013	2012	2011	2010
Book Value	$820	$710	$630	$540	$500
Net Income before extraordinary items	$110	$80	$90	$40	$100
Return on Book Equity (ROE)	13.4% = $110/$820	11.3% = $80/$710	14.3% = $90/$630	7.4% = $40/$540	20.0% = $100/$500
Standard Deviation of ROE	4.6%				
Average ROE	13.3%				
Coefficient of Variation of ROE	**34.7%**	= 4.6%/13.3%			

The hypothetical subject company has an average operating margin of 14.6%, a coefficient of variation of operating margin of 15.8%, and a coefficient of variation of ROE of 34.7%, as summarized in Exhibit 10.35.

Exhibit 10.35: Subject Company Fundamental Risk Characteristics
(used in all Risk Study examples)

	Risk Measure	Appropriate Exhibit Buildup 3	Appropriate Exhibit Buildup 3-Unlevered
Average Operating Margin	14.6%	D-1	D-1
Coefficient of Variation of Operating Margin	15.8%	D-2	D-2
Coefficient of Variation of ROE	34.7%	D-3	D-3

Exhibit 10.35 also includes the data exhibits in which the appropriate risk premia for each of the size measures can be found. For example, for use in the build-up 3 method, risk premia over the risk-free rate (RP_{m+c}) for "coefficient of variation of operating margin" are found in Exhibit D-2. For use in the build-up 3-unlevered method, unlevered risk premia over the risk-free rate ($RP_{m+c,\ unlevered}$) for "coefficient of variation of operating margin" are *also* found in Exhibit D-2.

Risk Study Examples

Build-up 3

The build-up 3 method is an additive model used for calculating the required rate of return on equity capital. As the name implies, successive "building blocks" are summed, each representing the additional risk inherent to investing in alternative assets.

Examples of both the guideline portfolio method and the regression equation method follow, starting with the simpler guideline portfolio method. In general, the regression equation method is preferred because this method allows for interpolation between the individual guideline portfolios, although the guideline portfolio method is less complicated, and more direct.

Example 5a: Build-up 3 Method (using guideline portfolios)

The build-up 3 equation is:

$$k_{e\ build\text{-}up\ 3} = R_f + RP_{m+c} + ERP\ Adjustment$$

Note that the "ERP Adjustment" is a necessary adjustment when using Build-up 3. For a detailed discussion of the ERP Adjustment, see the section in Chapter 9 entitled, "Proper Application of the Equity Risk Premium (ERP) Adjustment".

To estimate the cost of equity capital (k_e) with the build-up 3 using the "guideline portfolio" method, three pieces of information are needed:

- Risk-free rate (R_f)
- Risk premium over the risk-free rate (RP_{m+c})
- Equity risk premium adjustment (*ERP* Adjustment)

We have assumed a risk-free rate of 4.0% for all examples, and the ERP Adjustment has been calculated as -0.1% in a previous example, so the only missing input is the risk premium over the risk-free rate (RP_{m+c}):

$k_{e\ build\text{-}up\ 3} = 4.0\% + RP_{m+c} + -0.1\%$

Gathering the RP_{m+c} premia is straightforward. Match the various fundamental risk measures of the subject company with the guideline portfolios composed of companies of similar size in Exhibits D-1, D-2, and D-3, and identify the corresponding *smoothed average risk premium.*

For example, according to Exhibit 10.35, our hypothetical subject company has an average operating margin of 14.6%, and the appropriate data exhibit is Exhibit C-1 (25 portfolios sorted by operating margin). An abbreviated version of Exhibit D-1 is shown in Exhibit 10.36. Of the 25 portfolios, the portfolio that has an average operating margin *closest* to the subject company's 14.6% is Portfolio 10 (14.35%). The corresponding *smoothed average risk premium* is 9.03% (9.0%, rounded).

Exhibit 10.36: Exhibit D-1 (abbreviated)
Companies Ranked by Operating Margin
Risk Premia over the Risk-Free Rate (RP_{m+c})
1963–2014

Portfolio Rank	Average Operating Margin	Log of Average Op Margin	Number as of 2014	Beta (SumBeta) Since '63	Arithmetic Average Risk Premium	Arithmetic Average Unlevered Risk Premium	*Smoothed Average Risk Premium*	Average Debt to Market Value of Equity
1	38.71%	-0.41	59	0.87	6.30%	5.35%	*5.54%*	*32.55%*
2	29.62%	-0.53	53	0.83	5.06%	4.06%	*6.48%*	*37.45%*
3	25.12%	-0.60	57	0.86	6.91%	5.92%	*7.06%*	*34.56%*
4	22.25%	-0.65	46	0.94	6.69%	5.74%	*7.49%*	*29.01%*
5	20.19%	-0.69	43	0.98	7.76%	6.89%	*7.83%*	*24.23%*
6	18.62%	-0.73	61	1.06	8.26%	7.42%	*8.12%*	*20.96%*
7	17.44%	-0.76	40	1.09	8.17%	7.27%	*8.35%*	*21.83%*
8	16.20%	-0.79	42	1.11	7.99%	7.05%	*8.61%*	*22.55%*
9	15.09%	-0.82	46	1.16	9.63%	8.62%	*8.85%*	*23.34%*
10	14.35%	-0.84	35	1.16	9.49%	8.43%	***9.03%***	*24.68%*

This process is continued for each of the fundamental risk characteristics that are available for the subject company. After all of the available fundamental risk measures for the subject company have been matched to the closest guideline portfolio in the appropriate exhibit and the corresponding *smoothed average risk premium* has been identified for each, the subject company's cost of equity capital can be estimated, as shown in Exhibit 10.37.

Exhibit 10.37: Build-up 3 Method Cost of Equity Capital Estimate (using guideline portfolios)

	Risk Measure	Appropriate Exhibit	Guideline Portfolio	Risk-Free Rate, R_f	Smoothed Premium Over Risk-Free Rate, RP_{m+c}	ERP Adjustment	Cost of Equity Capital k_e
Average Operating Margin	14.6%	D-1	10	4.0% +	9.0% +	-0.1% =	**12.9%**
Coefficient of Variation of Operating Margin	15.8%	D-2	13	4.0% +	9.8% +	-0.1% =	**13.7%**
Coefficient of Variation of ROE	34.7%	D-3	14	4.0% +	9.7% +	-0.1% =	13.6%
		Mean (average) values		4.0% +	9.5% +	-0.1% =	**13.4%**
		Median (typical) values		4.0% +	9.7% +	-0.1% =	**13.6%**

The hypothetical subject company in this example has an estimated cost of capital ranging from 12.9% to 13.7%, with a mean (average) and median (typical) cost of equity capital of 13.4% and 13.6%, respectively.

Example 5b: Build-up 3 Method (using regression equations)

The *only* difference between estimating cost of equity capital (k_e) using the build-up 3 method using "guideline portfolios" and using "regression equations" is how the risk premia over the risk-free rate (RP_{m+c}) are identified.

In the previous example, the smoothed risk premia over the risk-free rate *published* in the Risk Premium Report exhibits for the appropriate guideline portfolios were used to estimate cost of equity capital. In this example, however, the regression equations found in each of the data exhibits will be used to calculate "custom" interpolated smoothed risk premia, based upon the specific fundamental risk measures of the subject company.

This example utilizes the same long-term risk-free rate of 4.0%, ERP of 5.0%, and subject company fundamental risk factors as shown in Exhibit 10.35 that were used in the previous example, so the only missing input is the risk premium over the risk-free rate (RP_{m+c}). Again, according to Exhibit 10.35, our hypothetical subject company has an average operating margin of 14.6%, and the appropriate data exhibit is Exhibit D-1 (25 portfolios sorted by operating margin).

The regression equation provided in Exhibit D-1 is:

Smoothed Size Premium (RP_{m+c}) = *2.199% – 8.104% * Log (Operating Margin)*

To calculate an interpolated smoothed risk premium for the subject company's 14.6% operating margin, simply substitute the operating margin into the regression equation as follows:

Smoothed Size Premium (RP_{m+c}) *= 2.199% – 8.104% * Log (14.6%)*

The interpolated smoothed risk premium for "operating margin" is therefore 9.0%:

*9.0% = 2.199% – 8.104% * -0.835*

This process is continued for each of the three fundamental risk characteristics that are available for the subject company. Exhibit 10.38 shows the calculations for each of the three fundamental risk measure's custom interpolated smoothed risk premium (RP_{m+c}).

Exhibit 10.38: Build-up 3 Calculation of RP_{m+c} Premia (using regression equations)

	Risk Measure	Appropriate Exhibit	Appropriate Regression Equation		Smoothed Premium Over Risk-Free Rate, RP_{m+c}
Average Operating Margin	14.6%	D-1	Smoothed Premium = 2.199% – 8.104% * Log(Op. Margin)	=	9.0%
Coefficient of Variation of Operating Margin	15.8%	D-2	Smoothed Premium = 13.133% + 4.299% * Log(CV(Op. Margin))	=	9.7%
Coefficient of Variation of ROE	34.7%	D-3	Smoothed Premium = 10.545% + 1.915% * Log(CV(ROE))	=	9.7%

After the "custom" interpolated *smoothed average risk premia* have been calculated for all of the available fundamental risk measures, the subject company's cost of equity capital can be estimated, as shown in Exhibit 10.39.

Exhibit 10.39: Build-up 3 Method Cost of Equity Capital Estimate (using regression equations)

	Risk Measure	Appropriate Exhibit	Risk-Free Rate, R_f		Smoothed Premium Over Risk-Free Rate, RP_{m+c}		ERP Adjustment		Cost of Equity Capital k_e
Average Operating Margin	14.6%	D-1	4.0%	+	9.0%	+	-0.1%	=	**12.9%**
Coefficient of Variation of Operating Margin	15.8%	D-2	4.0%	+	9.7%	+	-0.1%	=	13.6%
Coefficient of Variation of ROE	34.7%	D-3	4.0%	+	9.7%	+	-0.1%	=	**13.6%**
		Mean (average) values	4.0%	+	9.5%	+	-0.1%	=	**13.4%**
		Median (typical) values	4.0%	+	9.7%	+	-0.1%	=	**13.6%**

The hypothetical subject company in this example has an estimated cost of capital ranging from 12.9% to 13.6%, with a mean (average) and median (typical) cost of equity capital of 13.4% and 13.6%, respectively.

Build-up 3-Unlevered

The build-up 3-unlevered method is an additive model used for calculating the required rate of return on equity capital. As the name implies, build-up-3 is used for estimating *unlevered* cost of equity capital (the cost of equity capital assuming a firm is financed 100% with equity and 0% debt).

Example 6: Build-up 3-Unlevered Method (using guideline portfolios)

The Build-up 3 equation is:

$$k_{e\ Build\text{-}up\ 3\text{-}unlevered} = R_f + RP_{m+c,\ unlevered} + ERP\ Adjustment$$

Note that the "ERP Adjustment" is a necessary adjustment when using Build-up 3-Unlevered method. For a detailed discussion of the ERP Adjustment, see the section in Chapter 9 entitled, "Proper Application of the Equity Risk Premium (ERP) Adjustment".

To estimate the cost of equity capital (k_e) with the build-up 3 using the "guideline portfolio" method, three pieces of information are needed:

- Risk-free rate (R_f)
- Unlevered Risk premium over the risk-free rate ($RP_{m+c,\ unlevered}$)
- Equity risk premium adjustment *(ERP Adjustment)*

We have assumed a risk-free rate of 4.0% for all examples, and the ERP Adjustment has been calculated as -0.1% in a previous example, so the only missing input is the unlevered risk premium over the risk-free rate ($RP_{m+c,\ unlevered}$):

$$k_{e\ Build\text{-}up\ 3\text{-}unlevered} = 4.0\% + RP_{m+c,\ unlevered} + -0.1\%$$

Gathering the $RP_{m+c,\ unlevered}$ premia is straightforward. Match the various fundamental risk measures of the subject company with the guideline portfolios composed of companies of similar size in Exhibits D-1, D-2, and D-3, and identify the corresponding *average unlevered risk premium*.

For example, according to Exhibit 10.35, our hypothetical subject company has an average operating margin of 14.6%, and the appropriate data exhibit is Exhibit D-1 (25 portfolios sorted by operating margin). An abbreviated version of Exhibit D-1 is shown in Exhibit 10.40. Of the 25 portfolios, the portfolio that has an average operating margin *closest* to the subject company's 14.6% is Portfolio 10 (14.35%). The corresponding *average unlevered risk premium* is 8.43% (8.4%, rounded).

Exhibit 10.40: Exhibit D-1 (abbreviated)
Companies Ranked by Operating Margin
Risk Premia over the Risk-Free Rate ($RP_{m+c,\ unlevered}$)
1963–2014

Portfolio Rank	Average Operating Margin	Log of Average Op Margin	Number as of 2014	Beta (SumBeta) Since '63	Arithmetic Average Unlevered Risk Premium	*Smoothed Average Risk Premium*	Average Debt to Market Value of Equity
1	38.71%	-0.41	59	0.87	5.35%	*5.54%*	*32.55%*
2	29.62%	-0.53	53	0.83	4.06%	*6.48%*	*37.45%*
3	25.12%	-0.60	57	0.86	5.92%	*7.06%*	*34.56%*
4	22.25%	-0.65	46	0.94	5.74%	*7.49%*	*29.01%*
5	20.19%	-0.69	43	0.98	6.89%	*7.83%*	*24.23%*
6	18.62%	-0.73	61	1.06	7.42%	*8.12%*	*20.96%*
7	17.44%	-0.76	40	1.09	7.27%	*8.35%*	*21.83%*
8	16.20%	-0.79	42	1.11	7.05%	*8.61%*	*22.55%*
9	15.09%	-0.82	46	1.16	8.62%	*8.85%*	*23.34%*
10	14.35%	-0.84	35	1.16	**8.43%**	*9.03%*	*24.68%*

This process is continued for each of the fundamental risk characteristics that are available for the subject company. After all of the available fundamental risk measures for the subject company have been matched to the closest guideline portfolio in the appropriate exhibit and the corresponding *average unlevered risk premium* has been identified for each, the subject company's unlevered cost of equity capital can be estimated, as shown in Exhibit 10.41.

Exhibit 10.41: Build-up 3 Method Unlevered Cost of Equity Estimate (using guideline portfolios)

	Risk Measure	Appropriate Exhibit	Guideline Portfolio	Risk-Free Rate, R_f	Unlevered Premium Over Risk-Free Rate, $RP_{m+c,\ unlevered}$	ERP Adjustment	Cost of Equity Capital k_e
Average Operating Margin	14.6%	D-1	10	4.0% +	8.4% +	-0.1% =	12.3%
Coefficient of Variation of Operating Margin	15.8%	D-2	13	4.0% +	7.4% +	-0.1% =	**11.3%**
Coefficient of Variation of ROE	34.7%	D-3	14	4.0% +	8.5% +	-0.1% =	**12.4%**
		Mean (average) values		4.0% +	8.1% +	-0.1% =	**12.0%**
		Median (typical) values		4.0% +	8.4% +	-0.1% =	**12.3%**

The hypothetical subject company in this example has an estimated unlevered cost of capital ranging from 11.3% to 12.4%, with a mean (average) and median (typical) cost of equity capital of 12.0% and 12.3%, respectively.

High-Financial-Risk Study

The Risk Premium Report exhibits are primarily designed to be used to develop cost of equity capital estimates for the majority of companies that are fundamentally healthy, and for which a "going concern" assumption is appropriate. A set of "high-financial-risk" companies is set aside and analyzed separately in the High-Financial- Risk Study.[10.33]

The companies analyzed in the High-Financial-Risk Study are identified in a two-step process. First, companies that are losing money, have high leverage, or are in bankruptcy are identified and eliminated from the base set of companies used in the Size Study and Risk Study.[10.34] It is possible to imagine companies that don't have any of these characteristics but could still be classified as high-financial-risk (i.e. "distressed"), and it is also possible to imagine companies which do have one or more of these characteristics but are not distressed.

For this reason, these companies are further scrutinized in a second test where they are ranked by the appropriate Altman z-Score (for "manufacturing" companies or for "service" companies).[10.35,10.36] Those companies identified as being in the "safe zone" (as defined by their z-Score) failed the first test, but passed the second test (z-Score), and are set aside and not used in any further analysis due to the inconclusive results. The remaining companies failed both the first test and the second test, and are placed in either the "gray" or "distressed" zone (as defined by their z-Score). The resulting base set of high-financial-risk companies is composed largely of companies whose financial condition is significantly inferior to the average, financially "healthy" public company. The results of the High-Financial-Risk Study are presented in the H exhibits. The H exhibits provide risk premia that may be used in both build-up and CAPM estimates of cost of equity capital if the individual analyst has determined that the subject company is "high-financial-risk".[10.37]

In cases in which the individual analyst has determined that the subject company is "high-financial-risk", the high-financial-risk premia reported in the H exhibits should be used instead of the returns reported in the Size Study, and not added to those returns.

10.33 For detailed information on the types of companies excluded from the Risk Premium Report Study's portfolios, see the section entitled "Risk Premium Report Portfolios" in Chapter 7, "The CRSP Decile Studies and the Risk Premium Report Studies – A Comparison".

10.34 The number of companies eliminated in this screen varies from year to year. These companies represented up to 25% of the data set in recent years, but less than 5% in 1963. Certain technical changes in methodology have resulted in a greater number of companies falling into the high-financial-risk database than in versions of this study published prior to 2000.

10.35 Altman z-Score is an accounting-data-based method designed to assess financial condition and developed originally for assessing the likelihood of bankruptcy. E. I. Altman, "Financial Ratios, Discriminant Analysis and the Prediction of Corporate Bankruptcy," *The Journal of Finance*, Vol. 23, No. 4 (Sep., 1968), pp. 589-609; "Predicting Financial Distress of Companies: Revisiting the z-Score and Zeta Models," July 2000; "Revisiting Credit Scoring Models in a Basel 2 Environment," May 2002

10.36 Service industry companies are those SIC codes: 7200, 7300, 7500, 7600, 8000, 8100, 8200, 8300, 8400, 8700. Manufacturing are all other SIC codes, with the exception of SICs beginning with "6" (financial institutions) or "9" (government). SIC 6 and SIC 9 are not included in the Report's analysis.

10.37 The decision to apply a high-financial-risk premium is ultimately dependent on the valuation analyst's professional judgment, based upon the analyst's detailed knowledge of the subject company.

The High-Financial-Risk "H" Exhibits

Exhibit H-A: The high-financial-risk equivalent of the A exhibits. "High-financial-risk premia over the risk-free rate" for use in the build-up method are found in the H-A exhibits. These premia can be added to the risk-free rate to estimate the cost of equity capital for a company that has been judged by the analyst to be high-financial-risk.

Exhibit H-B: The high-financial-risk equivalent of the B exhibits. "High-financial-risk premia over CAPM" (i.e. "size premia") for use with the CAPM method are found in the H-B exhibits. These premia can be used in the CAPM to estimate the cost of equity capital for a company that has been judged by the analyst to be high-financial-risk.

Exhibit H-C: The high-financial-risk equivalent of the C exhibits. The H-C exhibits can be used to *compare* the subject company's fundamental risk characteristics to the fundamental risk characteristics of portfolios made up of companies with similar z-Scores.

Why isn't there an H-D exhibit? In the Risk Premium Report D exhibits, operating margin and two other measures of risk are examined (coefficient of variation in operating margin and coefficient of variation in return on equity). Because the denominators of the latter two ratios are often negative for companies in the high-financial-risk portfolio (as a result of either negative earnings or negative book value of equity), developing comparable "high-financial-risk" premia for these frequently results in meaningless statistics.

Altman z-Score

Altman's z-Score was originally designed as a measure to predict the risk of failure up to two years prior to distress for a sample of manufacturing companies using financial data prepared according to the standards of the day. The accuracy of predicting the risk of failure diminished substantially as the lead time increased. The z-Score resulted from a statistical analysis of company data using the statistical technique of multiple discriminant analysis.

Altman has since offered improvements on the original z-Score, but the original z-Score is still frequently calculated as a convenient metric that captures within a single statistic a number of disparate financial ratios measuring liquidity, profitability, leverage, and asset turnover.[10.38]

Manufacturing Companies and z-Score

Z-Score ratios are not strictly comparable across industries or across time (for instance, one would expect large differences in asset turnover among an industrial company or a retailer), and as such, are not used here as a predictor of bankruptcy per se, but as mechanism for ranking the high-financial-risk companies by their relative levels of distress. The following z-Score model for publicly-traded "manufacturing" companies (i.e. excluding service industry companies) is used in preparing the analyses presented in the H-A, H-B, and H-C exhibits:

[10.38] In applying any of the z-Score equations cited here, express the ratios in terms of their decimal equivalents (e.g., x_1 = working capital / total assets = 0.083).

$z = 1.2x_1 + 1.4x_2 + 3.3x_3 + 0.6x_4 + 0.999x_5$

where:

z = Overall index

x_1 = Net working capital/total assets

x_2 = Retained earnings/total assets

x_3 = Earnings before interest and income taxes/total assets

x_4 = Market value of common equity/book value of total liabilities

x_5 = Sales/total assets

The companies are then sorted by z-Score into three portfolios:

$z > 2.99$ = "safe zone"

$1.80 < z < 2.99$ = "gray zone"

$z < 1.80$ = "distress zone"

Companies in the "safe" zone (z-Score greater than 2.99) are set aside and not used in any further analysis. Companies in the "gray" zone (z-Score between 1.80 and 2.99) and companies in the "distressed" zone (z-Score less than 1.80) are used to form the portfolios from which the statistics presented in H-A, H-B, and H-C exhibits are calculated. Portfolios are rebalanced annually (i.e. the companies are re-ranked and sorted at the beginning of each year). Portfolio rates of return were calculated using an equal-weighted average of the companies in the portfolio.

Service Companies and z"-Score

The following z"-Score model for publicly-traded "service" industry high-financial-risk companies is used in preparing the analyses presented in the H-A, H-B, and H-C exhibits:

$z'' = 6.56x_1 + 3.26x_2 + 6.72x_3 + 1.05x_4$

where:

z'' = Overall index

x_1 = Net working capital/total assets

x_2 = Retained earnings/total assets

x_3 = Earnings before interest and income taxes/total assets

x_4 = Book value of common equity/book value of total liabilities

The companies are then sorted by z"-Score into three portfolios:

z" > 2.60 = "safe zone"

1.10 < z" < 2.60 = "gray zone"

z" < 1.10 = "distress zone"

Companies in the "safe" zone (z"-Score greater than 2.60) are set aside and not used in any further analysis. Companies in the "gray" zone (z"-Score between 1.10 and 2.60) and companies in the "distressed" zone (z"-Score less than 1.10) are used to form the portfolios from which the statistics presented in H-A, H-B, and H-C exhibits are calculated. Portfolios are rebalanced annually (i.e. the companies are re-ranked and sorted at the beginning of each year). Portfolio rates of return were calculated using an equal-weighted average of the companies in the portfolio.

Again, in both cases (manufacturing and service), we are not using the z-Score or z"-Score as a predictor of bankruptcy. Rather, companies are ranked in the High-Financial-Risk Study based on their relative levels of distress, using z-Score and z"-Score as proxies for "distress".

Non-Public Companies and z'-Score

The traditional z-Score was developed using data for publicly traded companies, and one of the statistics utilizes stock price. This creates problems for application of the data to non-public companies. Altman developed a similar model using only the financial statement data for non-public companies. If the subject company is not publicly traded and not in the service industry, then the analyst can calculate a z-Score for non-public companies (the z'-Score) to compare with the data in the accompanying exhibits:

$z' = 0.717x_1 + 0.847x_2 + 3.107x_3 + 0.420x_4 + 0.998x_5$

where:

z' = Overall index

x_1 = Working capital/total assets

x_2 = Retained earnings/total assets

x_3 = Earnings before interest and income taxes/total assets

x_4 = Book value of common equity/book value of total liabilities

x_5 = Sales/total assets

The z'-Score's "zones of discrimination" loosely approximate the boundaries used to seperate the z-Score and z"-Score ranked companies into portfolios, and are as follows:

z' > 2.90 = "safe zone"

1.23 < z' < 2.90 = "gray zone"

z' < 1.23 = "distress zone"

While the H-A, H-B, and H-C exhibits are sorted by using the publically-traded company equations (z-Score for manufacturing companies and z"-Score for service companies) and are not strictly comparable to the z'-Score for non-public companies, the returns reported in these exhibits can be useful in developing cost of equity estimates based on the relative zones of discrimination.

Measurement of Historical Risk Premiums

As with the *2015 Valuation Handbook's* Risk Premium Report A, B, C, and D exhibits, the High-Financial-Risk Study's H exhibits report average historical risk premiums for the period 1963–2014 (1963 is the year that the Standard and Poor's *Compustat* database was inaugurated). A long-run average historical risk premium is often used as an indicator of the expected risk premium of a typical equity investor. Returns are based on dividend income plus capital appreciation and represents returns after corporate taxes (but before owner level taxes).

To estimate historical risk premiums, an average rate of return is first calculated for each portfolio over the sample period. Portfolios with fewer than six companies in any given year are excluded in the averages. Lastly, the average income return earned on long-term U.S. government bonds is subtracted from the portfolios' returns over the same period (using SBBI data) to arrive at an average historical risk premium for investments in equity.

The "H" Exhibits – Summary of Data Presented

Each of the exhibits H-A, H-B, and H-C displays one line of data for each of the z-Score- and z"-Score-ranked portfolios. These exhibits include the statistics outlined in Table 9. For comparative purposes, the average returns from the SBBI series for large companies (essentially the S&P 500 Index), small companies, and long-term government bond income returns for the period 1963 through the latest year are also reported on each exhibit.[10.39]

The H-A, H-B, and H-C exhibits include the statistics outlined in Exhibit 10.42.

[10.39] Source: Morningstar *Direct* database.

Exhibit 10.42: Statistics Reported for the z-Score- and z"-Score-ranked High-Financial-Risk Study's H-A, H-B, and H-C Exhibits

Exhibit H-A	Exhibit H-B	Exhibit H-C
• Beta calculated using the "sum beta" method applied to monthly returns for 1963 through 2014.	• Beta calculated using the "sum beta" method applied to monthly returns for 1963 through 2014.	• Arithmetic average historical risk premium over long-term Treasuries (average return on equity in excess of long-term Treasury bonds) since 1963 ($RP_{m+s,\ high\ financial\ risk}$).
• Standard deviation of annual historical equity returns.	• Arithmetic average historical equity return since 1963.	• Average carrying value of preferred stock plus long-term debt (including current portion) plus notes payable ("Debt") as a percent of MVIC since 1963.
• Geometric average historical equity return since 1963.	• Arithmetic average historical risk premium over long-term Treasuries (average return on equity in excess of long-term Treasury bonds) since 1963 ($RP_{m+s,\ high\ financial\ risk}$).	• Average debt to market value of equity.
• Arithmetic average historical equity return since 1963.	• Indicated CAPM premium, calculated as the beta of the portfolio multiplied by the average historical market risk premium since 1963 (measured as the difference between SBBI Large Stock total returns and SBBI income returns on long-term Treasury bonds).	• Beta calculated using the "sum beta" method applied to monthly returns for 1963 through 2014.
• Arithmetic average historical risk premium over long-term Treasuries (average return on equity in excess of long-term Treasury bonds) since 1963 ($RP_{m+s,\ high\ financial\ risk}$).	• Premium over CAPM, calculated by subtracting the "Indicated CAPM Premium" from the "Arithmetic Risk Premium" ($RP_{s,\ high\ financial\ risk}$).	• Operating Margin: The median operating income for the prior five years divided by the mean sales for the prior five years. Operating income is defined as sales minus cost of goods sold plus selling, general, and administrative expenses plus depreciation.
• Average carrying value of preferred stock plus long-term debt (including current portion) plus notes payable ("Debt") as a percent of MVIC since 1963.		

Overview of Methods Used to Estimate Cost of Equity Capital Using the High-Financial-Risk Study

The cost of equity capital estimation methods provided by the Risk Premium Report's High-Financial-Risk Study are summarized in Exhibit 10.43.

Exhibit 10.43: Methods of Estimating Cost of Equity Capital Using the Risk Premium Report's High-Financial-Risk Study

Method	Cost of Equity Capital Formula
Build-up 1-High-Financial-Risk	$k_e = R_f + RP_{m+s,\ high\text{-}financial\text{-}risk} + ERP\ Adjustment$
CAPM-High-Financial-Risk	$k_e = R_f + (\beta\ {*}ERP) + RP_{s,\ high\text{-}financial\text{-}risk}$

Note that the ERP Adjustment is a necessary adjustment when using the Build-up 1-High-Financial-Risk method. The ERP Adjustment is not necessary when using the CAPM-High-Financial-Risk method. For a detailed discussion of the ERP Adjustment, see the section in Chapter 9 entitled, "Proper Application of the Equity Risk Premium (ERP) Adjustment".

Hypothetical Subject Company Size Characteristics

The information in Exhibit 10.44 will be used to estimate cost of equity capital for a hypothetical non-service (i.e. "manufacturing") subject company.

Exhibit 10.44: Subject Company Characteristics (used in all examples)

	(in $millions)		(in $millions)
Market value of equity	$80	Sales	$250
Book value of equity	$100	Current assets	$75
Total assets	$300	Current liabilities	$50
Most recent year EBIT	-$5	Retained earnings	$75

The z-Score equation for a publicly-traded, non-service (i.e. "manufacturing") subject company is:

$z = 1.2x_1 + 1.4x_2 + 3.3x_3 + 0.6x_4 + 0.999x_5$

The inputs (x_1, x_2, x_3, x_4, and x_5) needed for the z-Score equation are calculated as shown in Exhibit 10.45.

Exhibit 10.45: z-Score Inputs Calculation

x_1	=	Net working capital / total assets	=	($75 current assets - $50 current liabilities) / ($300 total assets)	=	0.0833
x_2	=	Retained earnings / total assets	=	($75 retained earnings) / ($300 total assets)	=	0.2500
x_3	=	Earnings before interest and taxes / total assets	=	(-$5 EBIT) / ($300 total assets)	=	-0.0167
x_4	=	Market value of common equity / book value of total liabilities	=	($80 market value of equity) / ($300 total assets - $100 book value of equity)	=	0.4000
x_5	=	Sales / total assets	=	($250 sales) / ($300 total assets)	=	0.8333

Substituting these inputs into the z-Score equation yields a z-Score of 1.47:

$z = 1.2(0.0833) + 1.4(0.2500) + 3.3(-0.0167) + 0.6(0.4000) + 0.999(0.8333)$

$1.47 = 0.1000 + 0.3500 + (-0.0550) + 0.2400 + 0.8325$

Estimating Cost of Equity Capital Using the "Build-up 1-High-Financial-Risk" Method

The build-up 1-High-Financial-Risk equation is:

$k_{e\ build\text{-}up\ 1\text{-}HFR} = R_f + RP_{m+s,HFR} + ERP\ Adjustment$

This example utilizes the same long-term risk-free rate (4.0%) and ERP Adjustment (-0.1%) established in a previous example, so the only missing input is the high-financial-risk risk premium over the risk-free rate ($RP_{m+s,HFR}$):

$k_{e\ build\text{-}up\ 1\text{-}HFR} = 4.0\% + RP_{m+s,\ HFR} + -0.1\%$

The determination of the high-financial-risk premium in Exhibit H-A is a three-step process:

Step 1: Determine whether the characteristics of the subject company better match the characteristics of the companies included in Exhibits A-1 through A-8 (the 25 portfolios) or the characteristics of the high-financial-risk portfolios. The most straightforward way of doing this is to answer the following *five questions* about the subject company:[10.40]

- Is the subject company in bankruptcy or in liquidation?
- Is the subject company's "5-year average net income available to common equity" less than zero for the previous five years?
- Is the subject company's "5-year-average operating income" less than zero for the previous five years?
- Has the subject company had a negative book value of equity at any one of the company's previous five fiscal year-ends?
- Does the subject company have a debt-to-total capital ratio of more than 80%?

It is possible to imagine companies that don't have any of these characteristics, but could still be classified as high-financial-risk (i.e. "distressed"), and it is also possible to imagine companies which do have one or more of these characteristics but are not distressed.

If you answered "Yes" to one or more of the five questions, it may suggest that the subject company's characteristics are more like the companies that make up the "high-financial-risk" portfolios rather than like the "healthy" companies that make up the standard 25 portfolios, but not necessarily so. For example, a company may have a debt-to-total capital ratio greater than 80%, but this does not automatically imply that the company is in distress. A decision by the individual analyst that a company should be treated as "high-financial-risk" should be based on a detailed evaluation of the company's current financial condition and circumstances, and will generally involve more than a review of historical financial statistics and ratios. The decision to apply a high-financial-risk premium is ultimately dependent on the individual analyst's professional judgment and detailed knowledge of the subject company.

[10.40] These five questions mirror the five criteria by which high-financial-risk companies are identified in (and eliminated from) the universe of U.S. companies to form the base set of companies used in the Risk Premium Report's Size Study and Risk Study.

Step 2: If the individual analyst determines that the subject company's characteristics better match the characteristics of the companies comprising the high-financial-risk portfolios, calculate the z-Score of the subject company using the appropriate z-Score equation:[10.41]

- z-Score is for publicly-traded, non-service, (i.e. "manufacturing") companies[10.42]
- z"-Score is for publicly-traded, "service" companies
- z'-Score is non-public, non-service companies.

Step 3: Lastly, if the z-Score[10.43] of the subject company indicates that it is in the "gray zone" or "distress zone", match the z-Score of the subject company with the zone composed of companies with similar z-Scores in Exhibits H-A, and identify the corresponding average high-financial-risk premium over the risk-free rate ($RP_{m+s,\ HFR}$). For this example, the subject company is a manufacturing company with a z-Score of 1.47, placing it in the "distressed" zone (z-Scores <1.8) of Exhibit 10.46. The corresponding high-financial-risk arithmetic average risk premium is 16.56% (16.6% rounded).

Exhibit 10.46: Build-up 1-HFR Cost of Equity Input
Exhibit H-A, High-Financial-Risk Premia Over the Risk-Free Rate
Companies Ranked by z-Score
Historical Equity Risk Premium: Average Since 1963
High-Financial-Risk Company Data for Year Ending December 31, 2014

Portfolio	Beta (Sum Beta) Since '63	Standard Deviation of Returns	Geometric Average Return	Arithmetic Average Return	Arithmetic Average Risk Premium	Average Debt/ MVIC
Manufacturing (z-Score)						
1.8 to 2.99 *(gray zone)*	1.57	36.37%	16.42%	22.05%	15.44%	46.18%
< 1.8 *(distress zone)*	1.63	37.59%	16.41%	23.18%	**16.56%**	57.82%
Service (z"-Score)						
1.1 to 2.59 *(gray zone)*	1.58	43.23%	14.88%	27.89%	21.28%	40.95%
< 1.1 *(distress zone)*	1.71	45.11%	19.96%	34.21%	27.59%	47.81%

Estimate a high-financial-risk cost of equity for the subject company by adding the average high-financial -risk premium over the risk-free rate ($RP_{m+s,\ HFR}$) to the risk-free rate and the ERP Adjustment.

$$k_{e\ build\text{-}up\ 1\text{-}HFR} = R_f + RP_{m+s,HFR} + ERP\ Adjustment$$

20.5% = 4.0% + 16.6% + -0.1%

10.41 In all examples here, the z-Score for publicly-traded, non-service (i.e. "manufacturing") companies is used.

10.42 While the H-A, H-B, and H-C exhibits are ranked by z-Score and z"-Score and are not strictly comparable to the z'-Score for non-public companies, the returns reported in these exhibits can be useful in developing cost of equity estimates based on the relative zones of discrimination

10.43 Or, as appropriate, z"-Score or z'-Score

The "high-financial-risk" cost of equity capital estimate for the hypothetical subject company in this example is 20.5%.

Estimating Cost of Equity Capital Using the "CAPM-High-Financial-Risk" Method

The CAPM-High-Financial-Risk equation is:

$$k_{e,CAPM\text{-}HFR} = R_f + (\beta \times ERP) + RP_{s,HFR}$$

This example utilizes the same long-term risk-free rate (4.0%), ERP (5.0%), and beta (1.2) established in a previous example, so the only missing input is the high-financial-risk size premium ($RP_{s,HFR}$):

$$k_{e,CAPM\text{-}HFR} = 4.0\% + (1.2 \times 5.0\%) + RP_{s,HFR}$$

Note that the ERP Adjustment is *not* needed when estimating cost of equity capital using the Risk Premium Report exhibits' size premia.[10.44]

Determination of the high financial size premium ($RP_{s,\,HFR}$) in Exhibit H-B follows the same three-step process as was followed in the previous example:

Step 1: Ask the same *five questions* as were asked in the previous example to determine whether the characteristics of the subject company better match the characteristics of the companies included in Exhibits B-1 through B-8 (the 25 portfolios) or the characteristics of the high-financial-risk portfolios.

Step 2: If the individual analyst determines that the subject company's characteristics better match the characteristics of the companies comprising the high-financial-risk portfolios, calculate the z-Score of the subject company using the appropriate z-Score equation.

Step 3: Lastly, if the z-Score[10.45] of the subject company indicates that it is in the "gray zone" or "distress zone", match the z-Score of the subject company with the zone composed of companies with similar z-Scores in Exhibits H-B, and identify the corresponding high-financial-risk size premium ($RP_{s,\,HFR}$). For this example, the subject company is a manufacturing company with a z-Score of 1.47, placing it in the "distressed" zone (z-Scores < 1.8) of Exhibit 10.47. The corresponding high-financial-risk size premium is 8.33% (8.3% rounded).

[10.44] For a detailed discussion of the ERP Adjustment, see the section entitled "Proper Application of the Equity Risk Premium (ERP) Adjustment" in Chapter 9.

[10.45] Or, as appropriate, z"-Score or z'-Score.

Exhibit 10.47: CAPM-High-Financial-Risk Cost of Equity Capital Input
Exhibit H-B, High-Financial-Risk Premia Over CAPM (i.e. "High-Financial-Risk Size Premia") Companies Ranked by z-Score
Historical Equity Risk Premium: Average Since 1963
High-Financial-Risk Company Data for Year Ending December 31, 2014

Portfolio	Beta (Sum Beta) Since '63	Arithmetic Average Return	Arithmetic Average Risk Premium	Indicated CAPM Premium	Premium over CAPM
Manufacturing (z-Score)					
1.8 to 2.99 *(gray zone)*	1.57	22.05%	15.44%	7.92%	7.52%
< 1.8 *(distress zone)*	1.63	23.18%	16.56%	8.23%	**8.33%**
Service (z"-Score)					
1.1 to 2.59 *(gray zone)*	1.58	27.89%	21.28%	7.99%	13.29%
< 1.1 *(distress zone)*	1.71	34.21%	27.59%	8.64%	18.95%

Estimate a high-financial-risk cost of equity for the subject company by adding the average high-financial-risk premium over CAPM identified in Step 3 ($RP_{s, HFR}$) to the CAPM equation:

$$k_{e,CAPM\text{-}HFR} = R_f + (\beta \times ERP) + RP_{s,HFR}$$

$$18.3\% = 4.0\% + (1.2 \times 5.0\%) + 8.3\%$$

The "high-financial-risk" cost of equity capital estimate for the hypothetical subject company in this example is 18.3%.

Comparative Risk Study

Previously the Risk Premium Report's C exhibits were used in the calculation of "unlevered" cost of equity capital estimates. The C exhibits have another important capability, however. The C exhibits, when used in conjunction with the D exhibits, enable valuation analysts to potentially further refine their cost of equity estimate by gauging how "alike or different" the subject company is when compared to the companies that make up the Risk Premium Report's guideline portfolios in the A and B exhibits. These elements, used in tandem, form the basis of the "Comparative Risk Study".

The Risk Premium Report exhibits include information about the characteristics of the companies that make up the portfolios that are used to calculate the "risk premia over the risk-free rate" and the size premia. The Risk Premium Report's C exhibits can be used to gauge whether an increase or decrease adjustment to a risk premium or size premium (and thus, cost of equity capital) is indicated, based upon the "company-specific" differences of the subject company's fundamental risk and the average fundamental risk of companies that make up the portfolios from which the risk premia or size premia are derived.

Valuation is an Inherently Comparative Process

Just about any analysis boils down to trying to comparing one thing to another. For example, when "analyzing" the merits of a house we are thinking about purchasing, it's common to compare it to other houses with similar characteristics. While houses that are exactly the same may be available in certain instances, typically what we end up with is a "peer group" of comparable houses that may be similar in many respects, but may still have some differences. If the house we are looking at is the only one in the neighborhood without a swimming pool, we could probably make a pretty good argument that a downward adjustment in price is justified. On the other hand, if the house we are looking at has a two-car garage while all the other houses in the neighborhood have one-car garages, an upward adjustment in price may be unavoidable.

Just as we oftentimes make decisions based upon the alikeness (or difference) between alternatives, the use of a portfolio's average historical rate of return to estimate a discount rate for a subject company is also based upon the implicit assumption that the risks of the subject company are quantitatively similar to the risks of the average company in the portfolio. If the risks of the subject company differ materially from the average company in the portfolio, then the estimated discount rate may be less than (or greater than) the discount rate derived using the risk premium or size premium associated with the given portfolio.

Company-specific Risk

Using the term "company-specific" might be confusing for some readers, because another use of the term "company-specific" implies risks that in the theoretical sense can be diversified away.[10.46] Having said that, the intended meaning of the term "company-specific risk" can vary from person to person. For example, is a "company-specific" risk adjustment necessary in a hypothetical case in which the comparison peer group and the subject company are *identical* in every way? Many valuation analysts would contend that the answer to this question is "no" – although this answer probably has very little to do with the theoretical definition of company-specific risk. What is probably intended is that no further adjustment may be necessary because the peer group in this hypothetical case (being identical to the subject company) acts as a "perfect" proxy.

We see valuation analysts regularly make adjustments to cost of equity capital estimates made under the heading "company-specific" risk, including (but not limited to):

- Adjustments to cost of equity capital estimates derived from a sample of guideline public companies to account for a subject company having risk characteristics that differ from the peer group.
- Adjustments to cost of equity capital estimates to account for biased cash flow projections provided to the valuation analyst.
- Adjustments to cost of equity capital estimates to account for risks accepted by investors that may not hold diversified portfolios of investments.

The third case (the diversified versus undiversified investor) likely comes up often with valuators, since in many cases the owner of the asset being valued may be an investor who is otherwise "undiversified". Businesses and interests in businesses (any asset) sell in various markets made up of pools of likely buyers. The marginal investors in the pool of likely buyers set the market price. No market, other than possibly the pool of buyers for the smallest businesses, is comprised of fully undiversified investors. In preparing the *Cost of Capital* 5th ed., Pratt and Grabowski investigated the extent to which private equity investors have expanded the market for closely held businesses. The responses from interviews of business brokers was that private equity investors are active market participants for smaller businesses today than they were only several years earlier. For example, whenever the company for sale has EBITDA over $1 million, the pool of likely buyers includes private equity investors. These investors are surely diversified.

Risk of an investment and value must be developed based on the risks (and pricing) perceived by investors that comprise the pool of likely buyers for the subject asset—not based on the diversification or non-diversification of the current owner. As we noted in Chapter 1, "The cost of capital is a function of the investment, not the investor." The cost of capital should reflect the risk of the investment, not the cost of funds to a particular investor.

[10.46] The models used to estimate cost of equity generally assume that risks that can be "diversified away" are not compensable. This type of risk is properly called "unsystematic risk".

Using the C Exhibits to Refine Cost of Capital Estimates

The Risk Premium Report exhibits are designed to assist the valuation analyst in estimating the cost of equity capital for the subject company as if it were publicly traded. That is, the returns reflect the risks and the liquidity of publicly-traded stocks. However, discounting expected net cash flows for a closely held business using an "as if public" cost of capital may not be an accurate estimate of value to the extent that market participants consider other risks associated with investments in closely held businesses. In other words, when estimating the cost of equity capital for a subject company, the risks of the subject company more than likely differ in some respects from the risks of the sample of guideline public companies it is being compared to (i.e., the "peer group").

When we use the Risk Premium Report's risk premia over the risk-free rate from the A exhibits or the size premia from the B exhibits, the "peer group" is the guideline portfolio in which the subject company falls. Remember that the cost of equity capital estimates developed using the Risk Premium Report exhibits are still "as if public", even *after* using the C exhibits to gauge the company-specific differences of the subject company and the portfolio(s) to which the subject company is being compared. However, this refined estimate likely better reflects the risk of the subject company as if the stock of the company was publically traded, and had been discounted by the market's assessment of its company-specific risk characteristics (as measured by its accounting-based fundamental risk measures).

The C exhibits provide the following three comparative risk characteristics (i.e. "accounting-based fundamental risk measures") for each of the 25 portfolios and for each of the 8 size measures of size included on the A and B exhibits, each of which can be useful in assessing how "alike or different" the subject company is to the companies that make up the respective guideline portfolio:

- Average operating margin
- Average coefficient of variation of operating margin
- Average coefficient of variation of ROE

To calculate the statistics included in Exhibits C-1 through C-8, the fundamental risk characteristics are calculated for the same size-ranked portfolios that are created in the Size Study's A and B exhibits. For example, Exhibit A-1 is comprised of 25 portfolios ranked by market value of equity. To calculate the fundamental risk characteristics found in Exhibit C-1, the three fundamental risk measures used to rank the portfolios in the Risk Study (operating margin, coefficient of variation of operating margin, coefficient of variation of ROE) are calculated for *each* of the 25 (market-value-of-equity-ranked) portfolios in Exhibit A-1. These calculations are made in the same fashion for each of the 25 size-ranked portfolios created for Exhibits A-2 through A-8, (and thus for B-1 through B-8, since the portfolio composition in the B exhibits is identical to the portfolios composition in the A exhibits).

The C Exhibits – Summary of Data Presented

In addition to various statistical information repeated from the A and B exhibits, the C exhibits report the additional data points for each of the 25 portfolios described in Exhibit 10.48.

Exhibit 10.48: Statistics Reported for 25 Size-Ranked Portfolios in Exhibits C-1 through C-8 (and not otherwise reported in the A and B Exhibits)

- Average unlevered beta calculated using the "sum beta" method applied to monthly returns for 1963 through the 2014.
- Operating Margin: The mean operating income for the prior five years divided by the mean sales for the prior five years. Operating income is defined as sales minus cost of goods sold plus selling, general, and administrative expenses plus depreciation.
- Arithmetic average historical unlevered risk premium over long-term Treasuries (average return on equity in excess of long-term Treasury bonds) since 1963. *(RP m+s, unlevered)*
- Coefficient of Variation of Operating Margin: The standard deviation of operating margin over the prior five years divided by the average operating margin for the same years.
- "Smoothed" average historical unlevered risk premium: the fitted premium from a regression with the average historical unlevered risk premium as dependent variable and the logarithm of the average sorting criteria as independent variable *(RP m+s, unlevered)* (The coefficients and constants from this regression analysis are in the top right hand corner of the exhibits)
- Coefficient of Variation of Return on Book Value of Equity: The standard deviation of return on book equity for the prior five years divided by the mean return on book equity for the same years. Return on book equity is defined as net income before extraordinary items minus preferred dividends divided by book value of common equity.
- Average debt to market value of equity.

The "C" exhibits provides users of the Risk Premium Report the information they need to compare their subject company to the average company in the guideline portfolio in which their company falls in the A and B exhibits.

For example, the C exhibits report the operating margin of each of the 25 portfolios in the A and B exhibits. If the operating margin of the subject company is significantly *less* than the average operating margin of the companies that make up the A or B exhibit guideline portfolio, then (all things held the same) this may be an indication that the subject company is *riskier* than the average company in the guideline portfolio (and vice versa). This analysis may indicate the direction of an adjustment (increase or decrease), but not the magnitude of adjustment needed. Gauging the "magnitude" of the potential adjustment needed is easier said than done, simply because there is the potential for so much overlap between size risk and accounting-based fundamental risk factors (e.g., as size decreases, variability of earnings tends to increase, and vice versa (see Exhibits 10.30 and 10.31). For now, the best one might hope for is establishing a *range* in which the adjustment likely falls.

In this section two examples of using the Risk Premium Report's Comparative Risk Study to further refine a cost of equity capital estimate are provided. In the first example, the build-up method (and the A exhibits) is used, in the second example, the CAPM (and the B exhibits) is used.

The output of using the Comparative Risk Study is two-fold: (i) whether an adjustment (*upward* or *downward*) is indicated in the risk premium over the risk-free rate (RP_{m+s}) used in the build-up method or in the size premium (RP_s) used in the CAPM, and (ii) the *range* in which the adjustment likely falls.

In both examples *any* (or all) of the average fundamental risk measures (operating margin, coefficient of variation of operating margin, and coefficient of variation of ROE) of the companies that comprise *any* of the A and B exhibits' 25 portfolios can be are used. For simplicity, however, these examples use "operating margin" (for the build-up example) and then "coefficient of variation of operating margin" (for the CAPM example). In both examples, a *single* A exhibit and a *single* B exhibit are used (A-3 and B-3, which are 25 portfolios sorted by 5-year average net income).[10.47]

Using the Comparative Risk Study to Refine Build-up Method Estimates

Step 1: Identify the equivalent C *exhibit*, per Exhibit 10.49.

Exhibit A-3 (net income) is being used in this example, so the "equivalent C exhibit" is Exhibit C-3. Exhibit C-3 is where the fundamental risk characteristics of the companies that comprise the 25 portfolios in Exhibit A-3 are found.[10.48]

10.47 While these examples make use of only the fundamental risk measure "operating margin" and only a single A exhibit and B exhibit (i.e, only a single "size" measure, 5-year average net income), we suggest the valuation analyst use as many of the three fundamental risk measures that are available for the subject company, and as many of the size measures that are available for the subject company.

10.48 Alternatively, if we were using Exhibit A-1 in this example, you would go to Exhibit C-1 to find the average fundamental risk characteristics of the companies that comprise the 25 portfolios Exhibit A-1.

Exhibit 10.49: Identifying the Equivalent C Exhibit

	Build-up Method: Use A Exhibits		CAPM: Use B Exhibits		Equivalent: C Exhibit
Market Value of Equity	A-1	or	B-1	→	C-1
Book Value of Equity	A-2	or	B-2	→	C-2
5-Year Average Net Income	A-3	or	B-3	→	C-3
MVIC	A-4	or	B-4	→	C-4
Total Assets	A-5	or	B-5	→	C-5
5-Year Average EBITDA	A-6	or	B-6	→	C-6
Sales	A-7	or	B-7	→	C-7
Number of Employees	A-8	or	B-8	→	C-8

Step 2: Identify the fundamental risk characteristics (in this example, average "operating margin") of the equivalent *portfolio* in the equivalent C exhibit.

For example, say the subject company fell into portfolio 24 in Exhibit A-3. The smoothed average risk premium for portfolio 24 in Exhibit A-3 is 12.19% (12.2%, rounded). The "equivalent portfolio" in Exhibit C-3 is *also* portfolio 24.[10.49] We are using the fundamental risk measure "operating margin". The average operating margin reported for portfolio 24 in Exhibit C-3 is 7.77% (7.8%, rounded).

Step 3: Identify the guideline portfolio in the D-1 exhibit (25 portfolios sorted by operating margin) which has the most *similar* operating margin as was identified in Step 2 for portfolio 24 in Exhibit C-3 (7.8%).[10.50]

The portfolio in Exhibit D-1 that has the closest average operating margin to 7.8% is portfolio 19, which has an average operating margin of 7.57%. The smoothed average risk premium for portfolio 19 in Exhibit D-1 is 11.28% (11.3%, rounded).

Step 4: Identify the guideline portfolio in the D-1 exhibit (25 portfolios sorted by operating margin) which has the most *similar* operating margin to the subject company.

Say the subject company has an operating margin of 4.0%. The portfolio in Exhibit D-1 that has the closest average operating margin to 4.0% is portfolio 23, which has an average operating margin of 4.43%. The smoothed average risk premium for portfolio 23 in Exhibit D-1 is 13.16% (13.2%, rounded).

10.49 Alternatively, if the subject company fell into portfolio *22* in Exhibit A-3, the "equivalent portfolio" in Exhibit C-3 would then be portfolio *22*.

10.50 Exhibit D-1 is 25 portfolios sorted by average operating margin; Exhibit D-2 is 25 portfolios sorted by average coefficient of variation of operating margin; Exhibit D-3 is 25 portfolios sorted by average coefficient of variation of ROE.

Step 5: Apply an *upward* or *downward* adjustment to the risk premium over the risk-free rate (and thus the overall cost of equity capital) as indicated.

In this example, the subject company's net income most closely matched the average net income of portfolio 24 in Exhibit A-3 (25 portfolios sorted by net income). The "risk premium over the risk-free rate" for portfolio 24 in Exhibit A-3 is 12.2% (identified in Step 2).

An *upward* adjustment to the smoothed average "risk premium over the risk-free rate" of Exhibit A-3's portfolio 24 (12.2%) may be appropriate. The operating margin of the subject company (4.0%) is *lower* than the average operating margin of the companies that comprise Exhibit A-3's portfolio 24 (7.8%) (identified in Step 2). All things held the same, this suggests that the subject company may be *riskier* than the average company in Exhibit A-3's portfolio 24 (the *lower* the operating margin, the *riskier* the company may be, and vice versa).

The *upward* adjustment likely falls into a range of 0% to 1.9%, which is the difference between the smoothed average "risk premium over the risk-free rate" of Exhibit D-1's Portfolio 23 (13.2%) and the smoothed average "risk premium over the risk-free rate" of Exhibit D-1's Portfolio 19 (11.3%). [10.51]

Using the Comparative Risk Study to Refine CAPM Estimates

Step 1: Identify the equivalent C *exhibit*, per Exhibit 10.49.

Exhibit B-3 (net income) is being used in this example, so the "equivalent C exhibit" is Exhibit C-3. Exhibit C-3 is where the fundamental risk characteristics of the companies that comprise the 25 portfolios in Exhibit B-3 are found.[10.52]

Step 2: Identify the fundamental risk characteristics (in this example, average "coefficient of variation of operating margin") of the equivalent *portfolio* in the equivalent C exhibit.

For example, say the subject company fell into portfolio 22 in Exhibit B-3. The smoothed *size* premium for portfolio 22 in Exhibit B-3 is 4.98% (5.0%, rounded). The "equivalent portfolio" in Exhibit C-3 is *also* portfolio 22.[10.53] We are using the fundamental risk measure "coefficient of variation of operating margin". The average coefficient of variation of operating margin reported for portfolio 22 in Exhibit C-3 is 23.55% (23.6%, rounded).[10.54]

Step 3: Identify the guideline portfolio in the D-2 exhibit (25 portfolios sorted by coefficient of variation of operating margin) which has the most *similar* coefficient of variation of operating margin as was identified in Step 2 for portfolio 22 in Exhibit C-3 (23.6%).

10.51 (13.2% - 11.3%) = 1.9%. Thus the likely range of the adjustment is 0.0% to 1.9%.

10.52 Alternatively, if we were using Exhibit B-1 in this example, you would go to Exhibit C-1 to find the average fundamental risk characteristics of the companies that comprise the 25 portfolios Exhibit B-1. Etc.

10.53 Alternatively, if the subject company fell into portfolio 25 in Exhibit B-3, the "equivalent portfolio" in Exhibit C-3 would then be portfolio 25.

10.54 Exhibit D-1 is 25 portfolios sorted by average operating margin; Exhibit D-2 is 25 portfolios sorted by average coefficient of variation of operating margin; Exhibit D-3 is 25 portfolios sorted by average coefficient of variation of ROE.

The portfolio in Exhibit D-2 that has the closest average coefficient of variation of operating margin to 23.6% is portfolio 9, which has an average coefficient of variation of operating margin of 24.97%. The smoothed average risk premium for portfolio 9 in Exhibit D-2 is 10.54% (10.5%, rounded).

Step 4: Identify the guideline portfolio in the D-2 exhibit (25 portfolios sorted by coefficient of variation of operating margin) which has the most *similar* coefficient of variation of operating margin to the subject company.

Say the subject company has a coefficient of variation of operating margin of 15%. The portfolio in Exhibit D-2 that has the closest average coefficient of variation of operating margin to 15.0% is portfolio 14, which has an average coefficient of variation of operating margin of 15.04%. The smoothed average risk premium for portfolio 14 in Exhibit D-2 is 9.60% (9.6%, rounded).

Step 5: Apply an *upward* or *downward* adjustment to the size premium (and thus the overall cost of equity capital) as indicated.

In this example, the subject company's net income most closely matched the average net income of portfolio 22 in Exhibit B-3 (25 portfolios sorted by net income). The smoothed size premium for portfolio 22 in Exhibit B-3 is 5.0% (identified in Step 2).

A *downward* adjustment to the smoothed size premium of Exhibit B-3's portfolio 22 (5.0%) may be appropriate. The coefficient of variation of operating margin of the subject company (15.0%) is *lower* than the average coefficient of variation of operating margin of the companies that comprise Exhibit B-3's portfolio 22 (23.6%) (identified in Step 2). All things held the same, this suggests that the subject company may be *less* risky than the average company in Exhibit B-3's portfolio 22 (the *less* volatile operating margin is, the *less* risky the company may be, and vice versa).

The *downward* adjustment likely falls into a range of 0% to 0.9%, which is the difference between the smoothed average "risk premium over the risk-free rate" of Exhibit D-2's Portfolio 14 (9.6%) and the smoothed average "risk premium over the risk-free rate" of Exhibit D-2's Portfolio 9 (10.5%).[10.55]

[10.55] (9.6% - 10.5%) = –0.9%. Thus the *downward* adjustment likely falls in the range 0.0% to 0.9%.

Chapter 11
Real Estate

In this chapter, we introduce a discussion on real estate (i.e., real property) and associated rates of return.[11.1]

First, we present the reader with some factors to consider when evaluating the risks of individual real estate investments.

Second, the return and volatility characteristics of U.S. real estate as an asset class are compared to the return and volatility characteristics of other U.S. asset classes, followed by a brief discussion of real estate's changing correlation with (i) U.S. equities, and (ii) U.S. government bonds.[11.2]

Lastly, we provide a table of data that could be used as inputs in performing valuations of individual real property investments: (i) pre-tax yield (internal rate of return (IRR), discount rate), (ii) going-in (overall) capitalization rate, and (iii) terminal (residual) capitalization rate (see Exhibit 11.6). These data points are provided for the fourth quarter of 2014.[11.3]

Individual Real Estate Assets

Relative to say, stocks or bonds, direct investment in individual real estate assets can be highly illiquid, require intensive management, and have substantial investment risks that affect the cost of capital. Investors in real estate should be compensated for the additional investment risk over and above the risk-free rate for relative lack of liquidity, and for the additional management burden.[11.4]

11.1 Chapter 11 is significantly excerpted from Shannon P. Pratt and Roger J. Grabowski, *Cost of Capital: Applications and Examples* 5th edition (John Wiley & Sons, Inc., 2014), Chapter 40, "Cost of Capital of Real Property – Individual Assets", and Chapter 41, "Cost of Capital of Real Estate Entities". Chapter 11 herein is designed to be an introductory discussion of cost of capital as related to real estate. For a comprehensive, detailed discussion of valuing real estate, see Pratt & Grabowski.

11.2 *The Valuation Handbook – Guide to Cost of Capital* (this book) is based on U.S. company data, and so we limit our discussion to the U.S. real estate market in this chapter. The *International Valuation Handbook – Guide to Cost of Capital*, also authored by Duff & Phelps and published by Wiley, is based on global company data. The *International Valuation Handbook – Guide to Cost of Capital* includes country-level (i) equity risk premia, (ii) country risk premia, and (iii) relative volatility factors that can be used to estimate country-level cost of equity capital globally, for up to 188 countries, from the perspective of investors based in any one of up to 55 countries. To purchase the *International Valuation Handbook – Guide to Cost of Capital* and its Semi-annual Update, or other Duff & Phelps valuation data resources published by John Wiley & Sons, please go to www.wiley.com/go/ValuationHandbooks

11.3 In future editions of the *Valuation Handbook – Guide to Cost of Capital* we may consider expanding this coverage over a longer period of time. Source for Fourth Quarter 2014 data: RERC LLC, *RERC Real Estate Report, Valuation Rates and Metrics*, Winter 2015, Volume 43, No. 4, page 10. All rights reserved. Used with permission. RERC is a commercial real estate research, valuation and consulting firm with a national presence. RERC was recently acquired by Situs (a Ranieri Partners Company). To learn more about RERC, visit research.rerc.com

11.4 The discount for lack of marketability is built into the discount or capitalization rate, as it is in venture capital rates in business appraisals.

Real Estate Investment Trusts (REITs)

Real properties can be *directly* owned by individuals (i.e., sole proprietorship), partnerships, corporations (either subchapter C or subchapter S), limited liability company (LLC's) or trusts. An equity investment in real estate can also be made *indirectly* by purchasing shares of an entity holding real property interests. Real estate entities exist substantially for the purpose of holding, directly or indirectly, title to or beneficial interest in real property. The value of a real estate entity includes many components, such as land, buildings, furniture, fixtures and equipment, intangible assets, and often the business operation.

A REIT "is a company dedicated to owning, and in most cases, operating income producing real estate, such as apartments, shopping centers, offices and warehouses. Some REITs also engage in financing real estate."[11.5] REITs can be classified in three broad categories, (i) equity REITs, (ii) mortgage REITs, and (iii) hybrid REITs.[11.6]

Equity REITs mostly own and operate income-producing real estate. They increasingly have become real estate operating companies engaged in a wide range of real estate activities, including leasing, maintenance and development of real property and tenant services. One major distinction between equity REITs and other real estate companies is that a REIT must acquire and develop its properties primarily to operate them as part of its own portfolio rather than to resell them once they are developed.

Mortgage REITs mostly lend money directly to real estate owners and operators or extend credit indirectly through the acquisition of loans or mortgage-backed securities. Today's mortgage REITs generally extend mortgage credit only on existing properties. Many mortgage REITs also manage their interest rate and credit risks using securitized mortgage investments, dynamic hedging techniques and other accepted derivative strategies.

Hybrid REITs generally are companies that use the investment strategies of both equity REITs and mortgage REITs.

Structure of Real Estate Entities

Real properties are often owned directly (e.g., sole proprietorship) or by a pass-through entity. Pass-through entities (e.g., partnership, limited liability company, master limited partnerships) pay no entity-level income taxes but pass their income through to the investors, thereby avoiding double taxation (i.e., paying income taxes at the entity level and the owner/investor paying taxes on dividends received).

REITs are not technically pass-through entities, but have certain income tax characteristics that are beneficial to their investors. Under U.S. law, therequirements for REITs to maintain their status are quite specific:

11.5 Glossary of REIT Terms, National Association of Real Estate Investment Trusts (NAREIT), available at: https://www.reit.com/investing/reit-basics/reit-faqs/glossary-reit-terms. NAREIT is the worldwide representative voice for REITs and publicly traded real estate companies with an interest in U.S. real estate and capital markets.

11.6 Sources: The National Association of Real Estate Investment Trusts® (NAREIT) website at www.reit.com/nareit; SEC Office of Investor Education and Advocacy "Investor Bulletin: Real Estate Investment Trusts (REITs)", December 2011, available at: http://www.sec.gov/investor/alerts/reits.pdf.

For federal tax purposes, REITs are taxed as corporations. That technically means that REITs are taxed first at the entity level and then at the shareholder level. However, REITs are permitted to deduct dividends paid to shareholders from their corporate taxable income. And because REITs are required by U.S. law to distribute at least 90 percent of their taxable income to their shareholders each year, with most REITs distributing 100 percent of their taxable income, this means that REITs effectively pay very little, if any, corporate income tax at the federal level.

REITs will, however, be subject to corporate-level tax on what is left after their annual distributions. That is, if a REIT chooses to distribute 90 percent of its taxable income, it will become subject to corporate-level tax only on the remaining 10 percent.[11.7]

A portion of the dividends paid to a shareholder also may constitute a nontaxable return of capital, which is not considered income.

Treatment of REIT income at the state level is anything but simple. Some states follow the federal income-taxation rules, whereas other states (e.g., New Hampshire) impose an entity-level tax on REITs. Thus REITs can still be subject to at least some entity-level income taxation, even if profits are fully distributed.

In recent years, companies that were traditionally organized as C corporations have elected to convert to REITs to either mitigate double taxation at the investor level (i.e., to increase the net cash flow in the hands of the investors who invest in their stocks) or enhance shareholder returns in some other form. For example, American Tower, which owns, leases, and operates cellular towers, converted from a C corporation to a REIT.

Correlation of U.S. REITs Compared to Other U.S. Asset Classes

Diversification is "spreading a portfolio over many investments to avoid excessive exposure to any one source of risk".[11.8] Put simply, diversification is "not putting all your eggs in one basket". Diversification offers the potential of higher returns for the same level of risk, or lower risk for the same level of return.

In Exhibit 11.1, the correlation of U.S. REITs and (i) U.S. large company stocks and (ii) long-term U.S. government bonds is shown. Correlation is a measure of the how alternative investments "move" relative to each other, and is thus a measure of potential diversification benefit. The *higher* the correlation (the more investments "move" together), the *less* potential diversification benefit, whereas the *lower* the correlation (the less investments "move" together), the *greater* the potential diversification benefit. The thinking is that by holding a portfolio of assets that do not have high correlation with each other, as some investments decrease in value, others will increase (and vice versa), and thus potentially mitigate overall portfolio losses.

11.7 Cara Griffith, "Practical Tax Considerations for Working with REITs," State Tax Notes (October 31, 2011): 315–320, quoting Jennifer Weiss: 316. In 2009, the IRS issued guidance that indicates that the distributions may be in the form of cash or stock in certain instances.

11.8 Zvi Bodi, Alex Kane, and Alan J. Marcus, Investments (McGraw-Hill, 2002), page 981.

The correlation of U.S. REITs with both stocks and bonds declined during the 1990s, thus increasing the potential diversification benefit. Since the Financial Crisis, however the correlation of U.S. REITs with stocks has increased significantly, decreasing the potential diversification benefit between these two asset classes. In contrast, since the Financial Crisis the correlation of U.S. REITs with long-term U.S. government bonds decreased significantly, increasing the potential diversification benefit between these two asset classes.

Exhibit 11.1: Rolling 60-month Correlation of U.S. Equity REITs and (i) U.S. Large Company Stocks, and (ii) U.S. Long-term Government Bonds
December 1976–December 2014

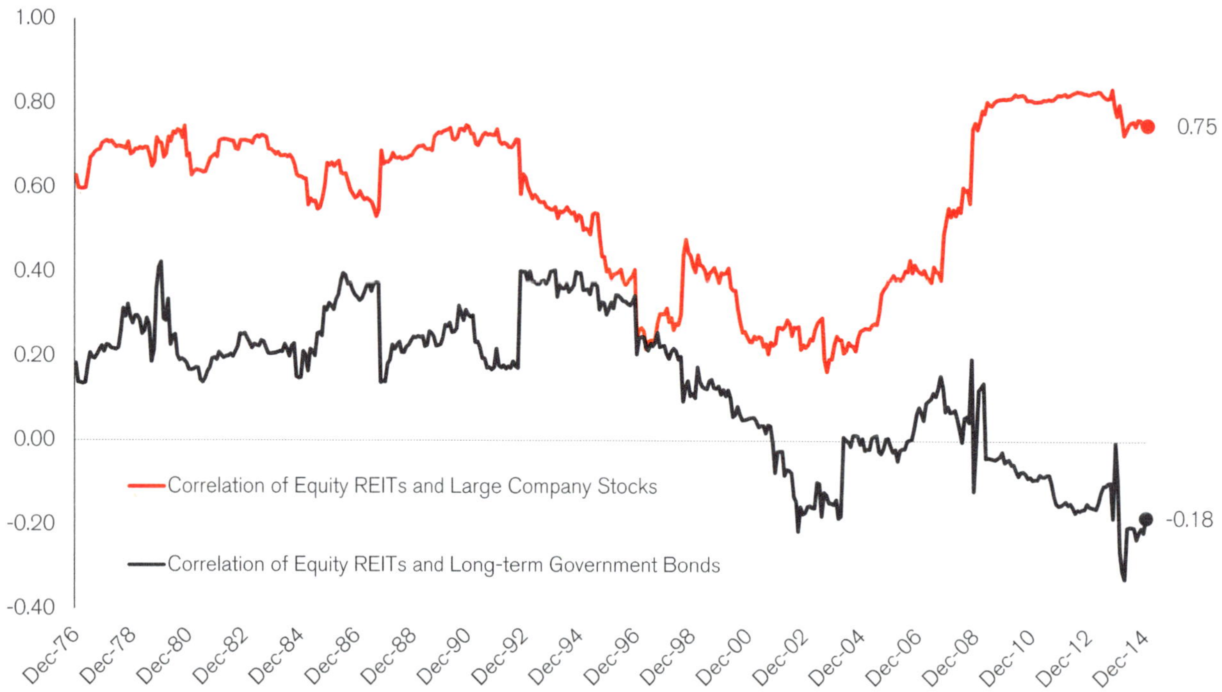

Sources of underlying data: (i) Equity REITs: The National Association of Real Estate Investment Trusts® (NAREIT) website at www.reit.com/nareit. Series used: FTSE NAREIT US Real Estate Index Series, "All Equity REITs" total return. All rights reserved. Used with permission. (ii) Stocks, Bonds, Bills, and Inflation (SBBI) total return series from the Morningstar *Direct* database. Series used: Large Company Stocks (IA SBBI US Large Stock TR USD Ext).The "SBBI US Large Stock" total return series is essentially the S&P 500 total return index; Long-term Gov't Bonds (IA SBBI US LT Govt TR USD). All rights reserved. Used with permission.

Summary Statistics of U.S. REITs Compared to Other U.S. Asset Classes

In this chapter, we utilize return data from the National Association of Real Estate Investment Trusts (NAREIT) to examine the performance of U.S. real estate relative to other broad U.S. asset classes, as well as inflation.

In Exhibit 11.2, summary statistics of the annual total returns for U.S. Equity REITs compared to other U.S. asset classes, plus inflation, over the time horizon 1972–2014 are presented. Over this time period, REITs outperformed all other asset classes shown, with the exception of small stocks.

Exhibit 11.2: Summary Statistics of Annual Returns of U.S. Equity REITs and Other U.S. Asset Classes, Plus Inflation
1972–2014

	Geometric Mean (%)	Arithmetic Mean (%)	Standard Deviation (%)
Equity REITs	12.2	13.8	18.3
Large Company Stocks	10.5	12.1	17.8
Small Company Stocks	13.4	15.8	23.0
Long-term Corp. Bonds	8.6	9.1	10.3
Long-term Gov't Bonds	8.6	9.3	12.5
Int.-term Gov't Bonds	7.4	7.6	6.5
T-Bills	5.0	5.1	3.4
Inflation	4.1	4.2	3.1

Source of underlying data: (i) Equity REITs: The National Association of Real Estate Investment Trusts® (NAREIT) website at www.reit.com/nareit. Series used: FTSE NAREIT US Real Estate Index Series, "All Equity REITs" total return. All rights reserved. Used with permission. (ii) Stocks, Bonds, Bills, and Inflation (SBBI) total return series from the Morningstar *Direct* database. Series used: Large Company Stocks (IA SBBI US Large Stock TR USD Ext).The "SBBI US Large Stock" total return series is essentially the S&P 500 total return index; Small Company Stocks (IA SBBI US Small Stock TR USD); Long-term Corp. Bonds (IA SBBI US LT Corp TR USD); Long-term Gov't Bonds (IA SBBI US LT Govt TR USD); Intermediate-term Gov't Bonds (IA SBBI US IT Govt TR USD); T-bills (IA SBBI US 30 Day TBill TR USD); Inflation (IA SBBI US Inflation). All rights reserved. Used with permission.

In Exhibit 11.3, the hypothetical growth of $1 over the time horizon 1972–2014 invested in each of the asset classes shown in Exhibit 11.2 is shown. The value of $1 invested in Equity REITs at the end of 1971 grew to $142.48 as of December 31, 2014.

Exhibit 11.3: Terminal Index Values of U.S. Equity REITs and Other U.S. Asset Classes, Plus Inflation; Index (Year-end 1971 = $1)
1972–2014

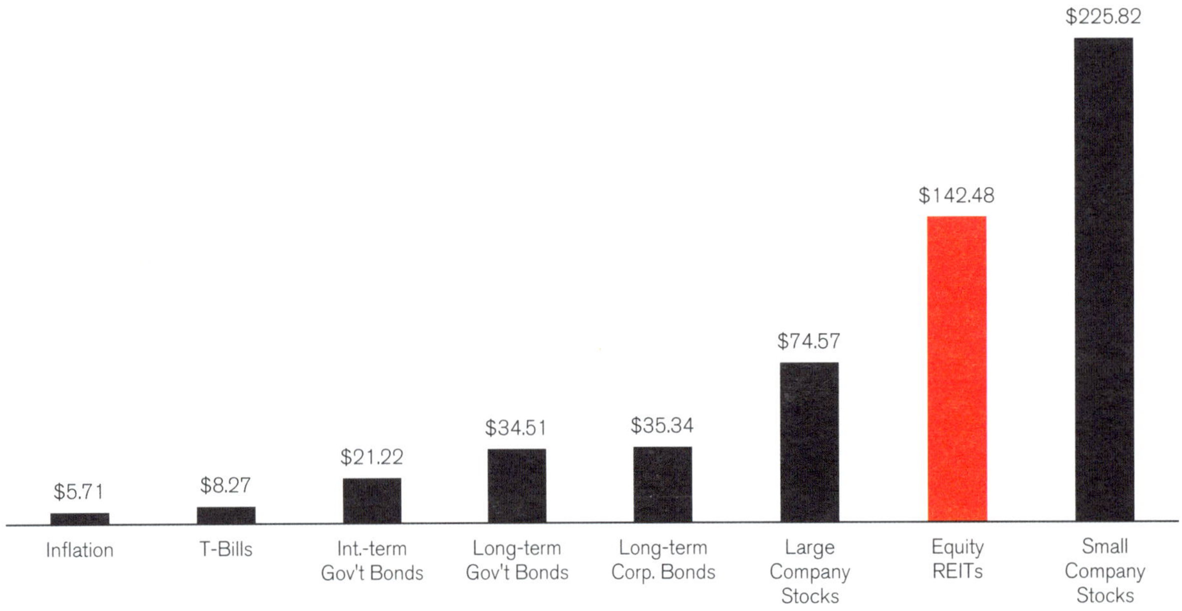

Sources of underlying data: (i) Equity REITs: The National Association of Real Estate Investment Trusts® (NAREIT) website at www.reit.com/nareit. Series used: FTSE NAREIT US Real Estate Index Series, "All Equity REITs" total return. All rights reserved. Used with permission. (ii) Stocks, Bonds, Bills, and Inflation (SBBI) total return series from the Morningstar *Direct* database. Series used: Large Company Stocks (IA SBBI US Large Stock TR USD Ext).The "SBBI US Large Stock" total return series is essentially the S&P 500 total return index; Small Company Stocks (IA SBBI US Small Stock TR USD); Long-term Corp. Bonds (IA SBBI US LT Corp TR USD); Long-term Gov't Bonds (IA SBBI US LT Govt TR USD); Int.-term Gov't Bonds (IA SBBI US IT Govt TR USD); T-bills (IA SBBI US 30 Day TBill TR USD); Inflation (IA SBBI US Inflation). All rights reserved. Used with permission.

Equity REITs can also categorized be categorized as sectors and subsectors. In Exhibit 11.4, summary statistics of the annual total returns for REIT property sectors Industrial/Office, Retail, Apartments, Health Care, and Lodging/Resorts over the time horizon 1994–2014 are presented. Over the 1994–2014 time horizon, the REIT sector Health Care had the highest average annual return (15.3%), while Lodging/Resorts had both the *lowest* average annual return (12.2%), and the *highest* standard deviation (33.2%).

Exhibit 11.4: Summary Statistics of Annual Returns of U.S. Equity REITs Property Sectors 1994–2014

	Geometric Mean (%)	Arithmetic Mean (%)	Standard Deviation (%)
Large Company Stocks	9.4	11.2	19.2
Industrial/Office	11.0	13.5	21.9
Retail	12.0	14.5	22.1
Apartments	12.2	14.1	20.7
Health Care	13.4	15.3	21.1
Lodging/Resorts	6.3	12.2	33.2

Source of underlying data: (i) Equity REITs: The National Association of Real Estate Investment Trusts® (NAREIT) website at www.reit.com/nareit. Series used: Industry/Office (FTSE NAREIT Equity Industrial/Office Index); Retail (which includes shopping centers and malls) (FTSE NAREIT Equity Retail Index); Apartments (FTSE NAREIT Equity Apartments Index); Health Care (FTSE NAREIT Equity Health Care Index); Lodging/Resorts (FTSE NAREIT Equity Lodging/Resorts Index). All rights reserved. Used with permission.

In Exhibit 11.5, the hypothetical growth of $1 over the time horizon 1994–2014 invested in each of the REIT property sectors shown in Exhibit 11.4 is shown. The value of $1 invested in the REIT sector Health Care sector at the end of 1993 grew to $13.93 as of December 31, 2014, while the value of $1 invested in the REIT sector Lodging/Resorts grew to $3.58.

Exhibit 11.5: Terminal Index Values of U.S. Equity REITs Property Sectors, and U.S. Large Company Stocks 1994–2014

Source of underlying data: (i) Equity REITs: The National Association of Real Estate Investment Trusts® (NAREIT) website at www.reit.com/nareit. Series used: Industry/Office (FTSE NAREIT Equity Industrial/Office Index); Retail (which includes shopping centers and malls) (FTSE NAREIT Equity Retail Index); Apartments (FTSE NAREIT Equity Apartments Index); Health Care (FTSE NAREIT Equity Health Care Index); Lodging/Resorts (FTSE NAREIT Equity Lodging/Resorts Index). All rights reserved. Used with permission.

Real Estate Property Valuation Inputs

The income and cost of capital associated with the ownership of real property are the focus of this section. This is different from the income and cost of capital that might be earned (or required) by a business enterprise operating on the property, such as a marina, hotel, fitness club, or restaurant, or a portfolio of properties, such as a real estate operating company or a REIT.

At the end of this section we will provide examples of data inputs that can be used to estimate the value of real estate property interests, using one of the following methods:

1) Direct Capitalization Method

2) Discounted Cash Flow Method

The following is a brief discussion of each of these methods; our objective is not to provide an all-encompassing guide on real estate valuation and associated discount rates. Rather, it attempts to provide a context for the data exhibits presented at the end of this chapter.[11.9]

Direct Capitalization Method

In real property valuation, direct capitalization is defined as:

A method used to convert an estimate of a single year's income expectancy into an indication of value in one direct step, either by dividing the income estimate by an appropriate rate or by multiplying the income estimate by an appropriate factor.

A capitalization technique employs capitalization rates and multipliers extracted from sales. Only the first year's income is considered. Yield and value change are implied, but not identified.[11.10]

Embedded in a market-derived overall capitalization rate are the market-oriented assumptions concerning the future income expectations or the performance of similar properties. The market-oriented assumptions result in changes in projected income and value over time. The expected annual compound rate of change in income and value can be added to the overall capitalization rate to indicate the property yield or discount rate.

[11.9] This discussion is excerpted in part from Pratt Grabowski, Chapter 40, "Cost of Capital of Real Property Individual Assets".
[11.10] Brueggeman and Fisher, Real Estate Finance and Investment. op.cit.

Overall Direct Capitalization

In real property valuation, the direct capitalization formula is generally expressed as:

Formula 11.1

$$PV_p = \frac{I_p}{c_p}$$

where:

PV_p = Overall value or present value of the property

I_p = Overall income to the property, measured before debt service, income taxes, and depreciation

c_p = Overall property capitalization rate

This basic formula can be modified to analyze the financial, physical, or legal interests in real property, provided the appropriate income stream can be estimated. Multipliers are a derivative of the direct capitalization overall rate. The net income multiplier is the reciprocal of the overall rate. Multipliers can be applied to the potential gross income, effective gross income, net operating income, or the equity cash flow. If income factors or multipliers are applied, the formulas generally are used to produce an indication of the property's value. It is of critical importance to adequately define the type of income being estimated in order to employ the correct techniques to estimate proper value. A description of such income relationships is beyond the scope of this chapter.

The property yield rate can be estimated at stabilized occupancy if the long-term growth in cash flow and value are stable, as shown in Formula 11.2:

Formula 11.2

$$c = k - g$$

where:

c = Capitalization rate

k = Discount or yield rate

g = Expected long-term sustainable growth rate in the cash flow available to subject investment

Formula 11.2 uses variable names and terminology as is used earlier in this book. This formula is quite similar to the formula presented in real estate textbooks, which is presented in Formula 11.3:[11.11]

Formula 11.3

$$c = k - A$$

where:

c = Capitalization rate

k = Discount or yield rate

A = Expected change in income and value (adjustment factor)

The variable A represents the relative change in value and (often expressed as Δ_a). To calculate A, a periodic adjustment factor representing the appropriate time period is multiplied by the total change in value. Subscripts are used to indicate the applicable rates to the various components, such as equity and debt.

Estimating the Capitalization Rate

Any real property interest that produces an income stream can be valued using the direct capitalization method. Several approaches are available to estimate the appropriate capitalization rate for the specific real property interest being valued. The approach that is most applicable depends on the quantity, quality, and reliability of the available market information. More than one approach may be necessary to develop the appropriate capitalization rate.

Potential buyers determine the assumptions that are utilized to estimate the transaction price to be paid for real property interests. There are various published surveys indicating the overall rates that are being applied to estimate value.

Actual transactions provide a clear indication of the market interaction between buyers and sellers. The "going-in" capitalization rate can be extracted from the sale information. The going-in capitalization rate is obtained by dividing a property's expected net operating income (NOI) for the first year after purchase by the sale price of the property.[11.12]

Recent comparable sales provide excellent support for market-derived capitalization rates, if the information has been confirmed by the participants involved in the transaction. The comparable sales must represent a competitive investment with similar risk characteristics to the property that is being evaluated.

[11.11] Charles B. Akerson, *Capitalization Theory and Techniques Study Guide* (Chicago: Appraisal Institute, 1984), 59.

[11.12] *The Dictionary of Real Estate Appraisal*, 5th ed. (Chicago: Appraisal Institute, 2010)

The method that should be used to develop the overall rate is based on a number of factors, and the analyst must realize that each approach has certain strengths and weaknesses. More than one method should be employed, whenever possible. The methods applied to develop the overall rate must be supportable and defensible. Market value is estimated based on the actions of typically informed and knowledgeable investors. Therefore, the most appropriate method is the method that reflects the typical actions of the most probable investors. The quantity and quality of data is important to provide support for the indicated overall rate. The information collected must also be reliable.

Discounted Cash Flow Method

The overall value of the property is equal to the present value of the income stream plus the present value of the reversion of the property at the end of the projection period, which is shown in Formula 11.4:

Formula 11.4

$$PV_p = \frac{CF_1}{(1+k_p)} + \frac{CF_2}{(1+k_p)^2} + \frac{CF_3}{(1+k_p)^3} + \ldots \frac{CF_n}{(1+k_p)^n} + \frac{\{(NOI_{n+1} / c_n) - [(NOI_{n+1} / c_n) \times SC\%]\}}{(1+k_p)^n}$$

where:

PV_p = Present Value

CF = Cash flow for a specific period

k_p = Overall rate of return or discount rate for property (property yield rate)

NOI_{n+1} = Net operating income in the year following the projection term

c_n = Terminal or residual or going-out capitalization rate in final year n used to capitalize NOI_{n+1}

$SC\%$ = Cost of sale

The last term is the reversion (i.e., proceeds) from the sale of the property. The net operating income is capitalized by the terminal capitalization rate or the so-called "going-out" capitalization rate. The terminal capitalization rate is usually, but not always, greater than the going-in capitalization rate. It is reasonable to assume that this rate will be greater because the improvements are older and the economic life may be reduced accordingly. In addition, there is more risk in forecasting the net operating income in the future. Ideally, the building is stabilized at that point in time. If not, adjustments may be required. The costs associated with selling the property must be deducted from the proceeds of sale at the end of the projection period.

The cash flow and the reversion from the sale of the property are developed before deduction for interest, taxes, depreciation, and amortization. These items are considered if the analyst's objective is to estimate investment value, not market value.

Semiannual, quarterly, or monthly discounting and capitalization are not typically used in estimating the market value of real property. Application of different time periods can affect the analysis. These conventions were used during the late 1970s when the inflation rate and the returns on money market accounts were quite high in comparison to historical averages. The proper approach would be market oriented, in which case most real property investors expect to receive the cash flows annually. For development properties, a shorter time period is often used.

Different discount rates may be applied to the cash flows and the property reversion. If the real property is leased on a long-term basis to a creditworthy tenant, the risks associated with collecting the related cash flows may be low and warrant a discount rate that might be comparable to the yield on the bonds that are available for a similar time period. The future sale price of the property may be quite speculative and will warrant a substantially higher discount rate to reflect the risk differential. The discount rate is also the weighted average of the yields associated with both components of the cash flow, from operations and the sale of the property.

Estimating the Property Discount Rate

The property (overall) rate of return or discount rate (sometimes called property yield rate) is defined as:

The rate of return on the total capital invested, including both debt and equity. Generally, if the objective is to estimate market value, the real property is analyzed on a before-tax basis. The overall yield rate takes into consideration changes in net income over the investment period and net reversion at the end of the holding period. It is applied to cash flow before debt service.[11.13]

The property discount rate is forward looking and, therefore, cannot be abstracted from current comparable sales information without confirmation of the assumptions employed by the buyer to determine the price that was paid for an asset. The discount rate incorporates the investor's compensation for the apparent risks, associated with a specific investment as discussed previously.

In theory, the property discount rate should be the sum of its parts: the real rate of return plus the expected inflation rate plus the risk premium (known as the build-up or summation method). The risk premium adjustment includes a variety of risk factors (e.g. market risk, environmental risk, legislative risk, etc.) that are difficult to quantify. Many consider it almost impossible to build up a discount rate by measuring the risks of each component.

The property yield rate can be developed by the "band of investment" method, provided that the assumptions used are market supported.[11.14] The discount rate is the weighted average return on the financial components, equity, and debt. The basic formula is shown below:

11.13 Peter F. Korpacz, "The Illusive Cap Rate," *Valuation Briefs* (RICS Americas: January 14, 2010).

11.14 The "band of investment method" is not discussed in detail herein. For a detailed discussion of the band of investment method, see Shannon P. Pratt and Roger J. Grabowski, *Cost of Capital: Applications and Examples* 5th edition (John Wiley & Sons, Inc., 2014), Chapter 40.

Formula 11.5

$$k_p = \left[\left(F_d / PV_p \right) \times k_m \right] + \left[1 - \left(F_d / PV_p \right) \times k_e \right]$$

where:

k_p	=	Property yield discount rate
k_m	=	Mortgage interest rate
k_e	=	Rate of return on equity investment and all other variables defined in Formula 11.4
$1 - (F_d / PV_p)$	=	Equity to value ratio
$F_d \; / \; PV_p$	=	Loan to value ratio

Formula 11.5 can be modified to include multiple equity investments and mortgages, such as mezzanine loans. The total weights must equal 100%. The typical real property investment includes debt, which provides support for this approach to develop the discount rate. The property discount rate provides for the required return on the mortgage and the expected return on the equity invested.

This method provides only an indication of the property discount rate during the first period. During subsequent periods, the equity component is increasing as the mortgage is amortized. The equity investor is seeking the same yield on the additional equity each year. This approach is widely used despite its shortcomings, which become obvious when interest rates are increasing or decreasing and the terms of any refinancing assumptions are changed.

The property discount rate can be estimated from overall capitalization rates if the anticipated changes in income and property value are known. Overall rates can be obtained from recent transactions. If the buyers are interviewed, the assumptions concerning the future changes in value and income can be established. If the income and value are expected to increase at a constant compound rate of growth, the formula to estimate the discount rate is derived from Formula 11.3, which we rearrange here in Formula 11.6:

Formula 11.6

$$k = c + A$$

where all variables are as defined in Formula 11.3.

Formula 11.6 can be altered to accommodate level, increasing, or decreasing annuities. The property discount rates and the equity dividend capitalization rates can be extracted from comparable sales if the assumptions developed by the purchaser to prepare the expected cash flows prior to acquisition have been verified.

Discount rates can also be estimated by surveying market participants. Published surveys summarizing the expectations and experience of investors are generally available for purchase or subscription. For example, Exhibit 11.6 shows information obtained from RERC's Winter 2015 Real Estate Report (data through fourth quarter 2014).

This and other similar surveys provide benchmarks that can be used along with other market information to support the discount rate. The discount rates reported can be compared to 10-year U.S. government bonds over time to provide an indication of the risk premium associated with a real estate investment in a central business district (CBD), for example. A wide range is often indicated, and further research is required to support the final selection of an appropriate discount rate.

Cost to Capital Valuation Inputs

Exhibit 11.6 presents data sourced from RERC that can be used as inputs in performing valuations of individual real property investments as of the fourth quarter of 2014.

RERC surveys some of the nation's leading commercial real estate valuation experts each quarter to get their views about the most critical valuation-related trends affecting commercial real estate and then analyzes and interprets their responses and reports them in the quarterly RERC Real Estate Report. According to RERC, most of these experts have been through several recessions and business cycles, have worked through several commercial real estate crises, and their independent observations, knowledge, and insights are worth noting.

The primary data points presented in Exhibit 11.6 reflect ex-ante required returns, or goals, of investors contemplating acquisitions, and are defined as follows:

- **Pre-tax Yield (IRR, Discount Rate):** The pre-tax yield is the rate of interest that discounts the pre-income tax cash flows received on an investment back to a present value that is exactly equal to the amount of the original equity investment. (It is in effect a time-weighted average return on equity and, as used here, is synonymous with the term "yield.")

- **Going-In (Overall) Capitalization Rate:** The first-year NOI divided by price or value.

- **Terminal (Residual) Capitalization Rate:** Terminal cap rate is the rate used to estimate resale or reversion value at the end of the holding period. Typically, it is the NOI in the year following the last year of the holding period that is capitalized. Similar to the going-in capitalization rate, but applied at the end of the holding investment period.

The discussion in the preceding sub-section presented a number of methods where these discount and capitalization rates can be used. The RERC rates in Exhibit 11.6 were based on a survey conducted in October, November, and December 2014 and reflect expected returns for fourth quarter 2014 investments by main property type: Office, Industrial, Retail, Apartment, and Hotel.[11.15]

[11.15] As defined by RERC in the quarterly *RERC Real Estate Report*, winter 2015 issue, based on 4q 2014 investment criteria and analysis, Scope and Methodology, page 70.

Exhibit 11.6: Required Return Expectations by Property Type – 4Q 2014

Pre-tax Yield Rate (IRR) (%)

	Office		**Industrial**			**Retail**					
	CBD*	Suburban	Warehouse	R&D**	Flex***	Regional Mall	Power Center	Neigh/ Comm	**Apartment**	**Hotel**	**Average All Types**
Range	6.0 - 9.7	6.3 - 9.9	5.5 - 9.5	6.5 - 9.5	6.3 - 9.5	5.5 - 9.0	6.0 - 9.1	6.3 - 9.6	5.8 - 9.0	7.0 - 10.0	5.5 - 10.0
Average	7.5	8.1	7.4	8.1	8.2	7.1	7.4	7.6	7.1	9.0	7.8
Weighted Average	7.8		7.5			7.3			7.1	9.0	7.8

Going-In Cap Rate (%)

	Office		**Industrial**			**Retail**					
	CBD	Suburban	Warehouse	R&D	Flex	Regional Mall	Power Center	Neigh/ Comm	**Apartment**	**Hotel**	**Average All Types**
Range	4.5 - 7.5	5.0 - 8.0	4.8 - 7.3	5.5 - 8.0	6.0 - 8.5	4.0 - 7.5	5.0 - 8.0	5.0 - 8.0	3.5 - 6.0	5.0 - 8.5	3.5 - 8.5
Average	5.6	6.6	6.0	6.9	6.9	5.4	6.3	6.2	5.0	6.8	6.2
Weighted Average	6.0		6.1			5.8			5.0	6.8	6.2

Terminal Cap Rate (%)

	Office		**Industrial**			**Retail**					
	CBD	Suburban	Warehouse	R&D	Flex	Regional Mall	Power Center	Neigh/ Comm	**Apartment**	**Hotel**	**Average All Types**
Range	4.8 - 8.0	5.8 - 8.8	5.5 - 7.8	6.0 - 8.5	6.5 - 9.0	4.5 - 8.3	5.5 - 8.5	5.5 - 8.5	4.3 - 6.8	6.0 - 9.0	4.3 - 9.0
Average	6.3	7.3	6.6	7.4	7.5	6.0	6.8	6.8	5.7	7.5	6.8
Weighted Average	6.7		6.7			6.4			5.7	7.5	6.8

*CBD: Central Business District ** R&D: Research and Development *** Flex: Can be used for industrial or office space.

Source of underlying data: RERC LLC, *RERC Real Estate Report, Valuation Rates and Metrics*, Winter 2015, Volume 43, No. 4, page 10. All rights reserved. Used with permission. RERC, a Situs company, is a nationally-recognized commercial real estate research, valuation and consulting firm that provides valuation management and fiduciary services, appraisal and litigation services, and research, analytics and publications for 10 major property types on an institutional, regional, and metro-level basis. Current and historical required pre-tax yield rates, required going-in capitalization rates, and required terminal capitalization rates and other investment criteria are available from RERC. To learn more about RERC, visit research.rerc.com

Key Things to Remember about Real Property Valuation

This section introduced some methods utilized to develop the appropriate returns on individual, income producing, real property investments. The basic concepts are quite similar to business valuation concepts, but additional factors must be considered in the analysis of income-producing real estate and the consideration of external and explicit financial funding.

Furthermore, data used in real estate valuations differ from the traditional sources used to derive discount rates when performing business valuations.

Chapter 12
Answers to Commonly Asked Questions

The authors decided to add this chapter in 2015 in order to share some of the many thoughtful questions received from valuation analysts about the *Valuation Handbook – Guide to Cost of Capital*.[12.1] Reader comments, questions, and suggestions are an important source of information for helping us to constantly improve the *Valuation Handbook* (and our related valuation data resources).[12.2]

The questions in this chapter are a sampling of some of the questions we received throughout the 2014 calendar year, and thus most refer to information found specifically in last year's *2014 Valuation Handbook*. However, the concepts and ideas the questions address apply equally to the *2015 Valuation Handbook*.

Question 1: Are the data and methodologies used in the *2015 Valuation Handbook* the same as those that were used in the (now discontinued) Morningstar/Ibbotson *SBBI Valuation Yearbook*?

Response: This is an important question. The short answer is yes, the historical equity risk premia and size premia data published in the *2015 Valuation Handbook* is the same exact equity risk premia and size premia data that was published in the former *SBBI Valuation Yearbook*. This continuity is important in any case, but may be especially important in cases when similar valuation analysis is done over a number of years.

The premia in the *2015 Valuation Handbook* were calculated using the same exact methodology as the former *SBBI Valuation Yearbook*. And, the premia were calculated using the same exact data sources: (i) Standard and Poor's, (ii) the Center for Research in Security Prices at the University of Chicago Booth School of Business (CRSP) and (iii) Morningstar – the actual "SBBI" data series are used in our calculations in the *2015 Valuation Handbook*.

12.1 This chapter is somewhat analogous to the section entitled "Advice to Practitioners" in Shannon P. Pratt and Roger J. Grabowski, *Cost of Capital: Applications and Examples 5th edition*, where the authors and contributing authors provide their thoughts and insights on handling challenging questions they have received in regards to client engagements, across a *wide* spectrum of valuation topics. Unlike the "Advice to Practitioners" section therein, Chapter 12 herein focuses on questions that we have received concerning the data and methodology specific to the *Valuation Handbook – Guide to Cost of Capital*.

12.2 Other valuation data resources authored by Duff & Phelps, and published by Wiley include: (i) the *Valuation Handbook – Industry Cost of Capital*, which provides the same type of rigorous industry-level analyses of U.S. industries previously published in the green-cover Morningstar/ Ibbotson Cost of Capital Yearbook (discontinued in 2013), and (ii) *International Valuation Handbook – Guide to Cost of Capital*, which provides country-level equity risk premia (ERPs), relative volatility (RV) factors, and country risk premia (CRPs) which can be used to estimate country-level cost of equity capital globally, for up to 188 countries, from the perspective of investors based in any one of up to 55 countries (depending on data availability). In Fall 2015, Duff & Phelps expects to publish a fourth book, *International Valuation Handbook – Industry Cost of Capital,* which will provide *global* industry analyses. To purchase these valuation data resources, please go to www.wiley.com/go/ValuationHandbooks

Question 2: In last year's *2014 Valuation Handbook* I could not find the summary statistics of annual returns by asset class that was previously found in Table 2-1 *2013 SBBI Valuation Yearbook* (see page 23 of that book). Will the *2015 Valuation Handbook* contain information on the income return and capital appreciation components for large-, mid-, and low-cap stocks, or for long-term and intermediate-term government bonds that was previously available in this table?

Response: Yes. Over the course of 2014 we received a number requests to add this information to the *2015 Valuation Handbook*, and Morningstar graciously granted us permission to use the additional SBBI series needed to produce this table in the *2015 Valuation Handbook*. This information is found in Exhibit 2.3 on page 2-4, "Summary Statistics of Total Returns, Income Returns, and Capital Appreciation Returns of Basic U.S. Asset Classes 1926–2014".

Question 3: According to the Board of Governors of the Federal Reserve website, the risk-free rate of the 20-year U.S. government (constant-maturity) bond yield as of December 31, 2014 is 2.47% (daily rates), whereas the *2015 Valuation Handbook* reports 2.40%. Why is there a difference?[12.3]

Response: For the long-term (20-year) U.S. government bond yield, the *2015 Valuation Handbook* uses the same SBBI data that was used in the previously-published Morningstar/Ibbotson *SBBI Valuation Yearbooks*.[12.4]

The *2015 Valuation Handbook's* Appendix 3, which is the direct equivalent of the former "back page" of the *SBBI Valuation Yearbook*, includes all of the critical valuation data (equity risk premia, size premia, etc.) previously published in the *SBBI Valuation Yearbook*, using (i) the same underlying data (S&P, CRSP, and SBBI data), and (ii) using the same methodology, including the risk-free rate information.

For example, in last year's *2014 Valuation Handbook*, we reported in Appendix 3 that the (SBBI) long-term (20-year) U.S. government bond yield was 3.67%, which is the identical value that was reported in the Morningstar/Ibbotson *2014 SBBI Classic Yearbook*.[12.5] It is the same data, and the same data source.

This is not to say that there are not differences between the "SBBI" long-term (20-year) government bond series yields and the long-term yields reported by say, the Federal Reserve Bank or the U.S. Treasury websites. These differences are due to slight methodological differences, and are not material. The correlation between these series is 0.999. In other words, the series are nearly identical, and overlap to a very high degree, as illustrated in Exhibit 12.1.

12.3 This question was originally asked in regards to last year's *2014 Valuation Handbook – Guide to Cost of Capital* (data through December 2013), and has been updated with year-end 2014 data.

12.4 For a description of the construction of the SBBI indices, see the *2014 SBBI Classic Yearbook* (Morningstar, Chicago, 2014) Chapter 3, "Description of the Basic Series". The *SBBI Classic Yearbook* is an analysis of the relative performance of various asset classes in the U.S. and does *not* provide extensive valuation data or methodology.

12.5 Source: *2014 SBBI Classic Yearbook* (Morningstar, Chicago, 2014), Table A-9, "Long-Term Government Bonds: Yields", pages 212–213. Morningstar continues to publish the *SBBI Classic Yearbook*. The *SBBI Classic Yearbook* is an analysis of the relative performance of various asset classes in the U.S. and does *not* provide extensive valuation data or methodology.

Exhibit 12.1: 20-year (constant maturity) U.S. Government Bond Yields from the Board of Governors of the Federal Reserve Website Compared to the SBBI Long-term (20-year) U.S. Government Bond Yield October 1993–December 2014

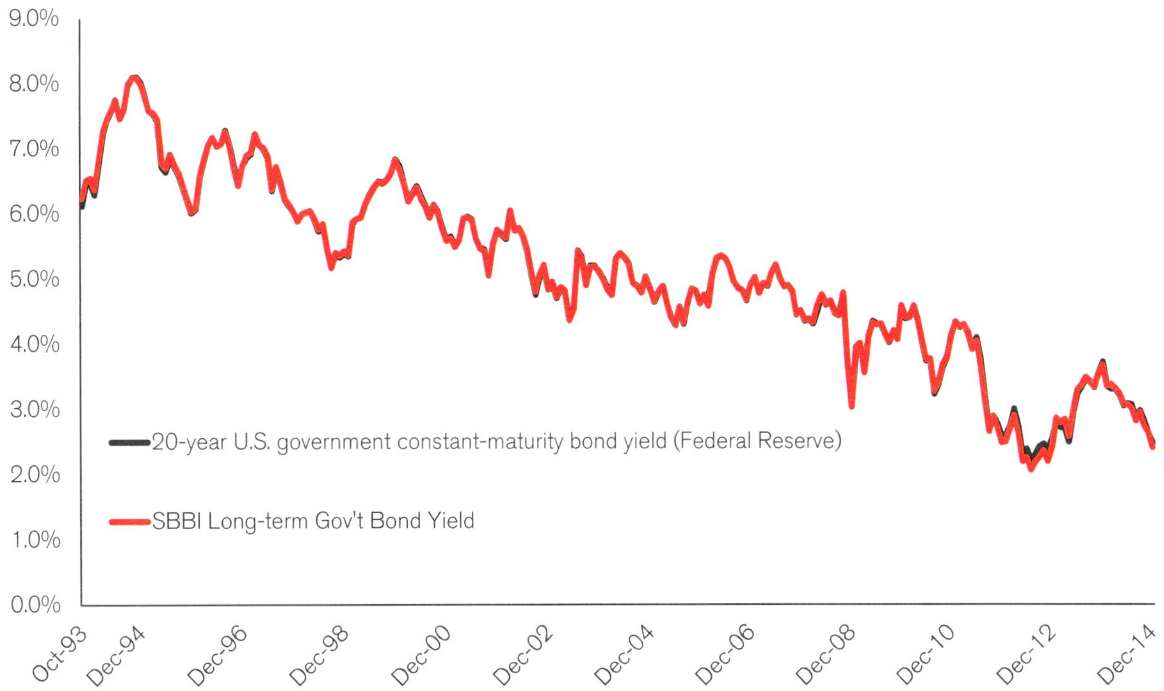

Sources of underlying data: (i) Stocks, Bonds, Bills, and Inflation (SBBI) series from the Morningstar *Direct* database. Series used: SBBI Long-term Gov't Bonds (IA SBBI US LT Govt Yld USD). All rights reserved. Used with permission. (ii) Yields from the Board of Governors of the Federal Reserve website at http://www.federalreserve.gov/releases/h15/data.htm. Series used: Market yield on U.S. Treasury securities at 20-year constant maturity, quoted on investment basis (Unique Identifier: H15/H15/RIFLGFCY20_N.B).

Duff & Phelps went to great lengths and cost to secure the same exact underlying data for the *2015 Valuation Handbook* that was previously used to produce the *Ibbotson SBBI Valuation Yearbook*, including the actual "SBBI" series. This continuity is important in any case, but may be especially important in cases when similar valuation analysis is done over a number of years.

Question 4: In future editions of the *Valuation Handbook*, is it possible to include in Exhibit 4.7 the market capitalizations of the smallest and the largest company in each of the deciles, since market capitalizations change over time (at least they did in the *Ibbotson SBBI Valuation Yearbooks*)?

Response: The market caps of the companies with the smallest and largest market capitalization can be found in Appendix 3 of the *2014 Valuation Handbook* (Appendix 3 is the equivalent of the former "back page" of the *SBBI Valuation Yearbook*). This information is also published in the *2015 Valuation Handbook*. Exhibit 4.7, which is in both the 2014 and 2015 books, has a different purpose. Exhibit 4.7 is a demonstration of how size premia can differ, based on what type of beta is used (OLS beta, Annual beta, or Sum beta).

And yes, you are correct, the smallest and largest companies in the CRSP portfolios *do* change over time (CRSP refers to these as "breakpoints"). The compositions of the CRSP portfolios are reset each quarter, and thus the market caps of the smallest and largest companies in each of the CRSP portfolios can *also* change over time.

Question 5: In last year's *2014 Valuation Handbook*, page 2-3, last paragraph, second sentence, states that "The CML is defined as a line used in the capital asset pricing model..." I always thought that the Security Market Line (SML) is used in CAPM. It plots beta on the x-axis. What am I missing?

Response: The Capital Market Line (CML) as referenced in the *2014 Valuation Handbook* is correct, as is the graph shown in last year's book Exhibit 2.3. However, we can see how someone could have a literal interpretation and focus on the fact that the CAPM equation is based on the Security Market Line (SML).

Both the CML and SML are linear relationships (or equations) defined by the CAPM theory.

The CML depicts the expected relationship of risk (as defined by expected standard deviation of returns) and expected return of portfolios. The point where the CML is tangent to the efficient frontier of the opportunity set of portfolios of investments is denoted as *M*, the market portfolio. Only efficient portfolios that consist of combinations of risk-free assets and the market portfolio can lie on the CML. The expected returns of *portfolios* are a linear function of portfolios' standard deviation of returns.[12.6]

An individual security's risk will consist not only of the systematic risk of portfolios along the CML, but will also contain unsystematic risk. Thus, all individual assets must be more risky than the points on the CML. Individual securities (as opposed to portfolios) will be located *within* the opportunity set instead of directly on the CML.

The SML shows a relationship between covariance (between individual security and the market) and expected return. The expected return of a security is a positive linear function of the security's covariance with the market (increasing function of its systematic risk as measured by covariance).

In equilibrium, every individual security's expected return and risk observation will lie on the SML and off of the CML. But, in equilibrium, portfolios' (rather than individual securities) expected returns and standard deviations will lie on the CML and the SML. Thus, CAPM, the Sharpe/Lintner/Mossin extension of the Markowitz capital market theory of the two-parameter-model, is a function of the CML for portfolios.

Obviously, we can define the SML in terms of the familiar beta (covariance with the market) on the "x" axis.

Exhibit 2.3 is simply a plot of "what happened". It depicts the historical annual returns of certain asset classes, along with their associated "risk" (as measured by standard deviation). It is a depiction of the realized returns versus risk along the observed CML. But historical data play no role in the theory itself.

[12.6] This explanation is drawn from a great reference book, Jack Clarke Francis and Stephen H. Archer, *Portfolio Analysis* (Prentice Hall, 1971).

Question 6: On page 3-14 of last year's *2014 Valuation Handbook,* Exhibit 3.6, "Realized Equity Risk Premiums: Stock Market Returns Minus U.S. Government Bonds Through 2013", shows that the 20-year arithmetic average (1994–2013) historical ERP was 6.06%. In contrast, on page 59 of Morningstar's *2013 Ibbotson SBBI Valuation Yearbook,* Table 5-5, "Stock Market Return and Equity Risk Premium Over Time" shows the 20-year arithmetic average (1993–2012) historical ERP was 4.7%.

Why is the difference between the two books so large? If they are comparable sources, any thoughts on how a 20-year average historical ERP increased so significantly when only a single year had passed?

Response: Exhibit 3.6 of last year's *2014 Valuation Handbook* and Table 5-5 of the previous year's *2013 Ibbotson Valuation Yearbook* compare the realized equity risk premium (ERP) over various time periods using the same data and methodology. The two ERP measurements refer to the 20-year period ending December 2012 (1993–2012) in the *2013 SBBI Valuation Yearbook*, and the 20-year period ending 2013 (1994–2013) in last year's *2014 Valuation Handbook.*

The short answer is that the 4.7% (as reported in the *2013 SBBI Valuation*) and the 6.06% (as reported in the *2014 Valuation Handbook*) are indeed comparable, and both are correct.

The longer answer is summarized in Exhibit 12.2, which includes the average returns used to calculate both the 4.7% (in the *2013 SBBI Valuation Yearbook*) and the 6.06% (in last year's *2014 Valuation Handbook*). The 6.06% reported in the *2014 Valuation Handbook* is the difference between the average annual S&P 500 total return index return over the 20-year period from 1994–2013 and the average annual income return of long-term U.S. government bonds over the same period (11.13% – 5.07%). Likewise, the 4.7% (rounded from 4.73%) reported in the *2013 SBBI Valuation Yearbook* is the difference between the average annual S&P 500 total return index return over the 20-year period 1993–2012 and the average annual income return of long-term U.S. government bonds over the same period (10.01% – 5.28%).

The main driver of the increase in ERP as measured over these two (different) time periods is the unusually large increase in the S&P 500 total return index in 2013 (32.39%). With the time frame being only 20 years, this large increase acted to significantly *increase* the average total return for "stocks" by 1.12% over the measurement period (from 10.01% to 11.13%). At the same time, the average income return of long-term government bonds *decreased* by 0.21% (from 5.28% to 5.07%). The cumulative effect of these differences (1.12% + 0.21% = 1.33%) accounts for the difference in the ERP as measured over these two periods (6.06% –4.73% = 1.33%).

Exhibit 12.2: Summary of Average Returns Used to Calculate Equity Risk Premia Over the 1993–2012 and 1994–2013 Periods

	***2013 Valuation Yearbook* (Table 5-5)** 20-year period ending 2012 (1993-2012)	***2014 Valuation Handbook* (Exhibit 3.6)** 20-year period ending 2013 (1994-2013)
S&P 500 Index Total Returns	10.01%	11.13%
Minus: Long-term Government Bond Income Returns	–5.28%	–5.07%
Equals: ERP Over 20-year Period	= 4.73%	= 6.06%

Question 7: Why were the size premia calculated for the standard CRSP deciles and size groupings in last year's Morningstar/Ibbotson *2014 SBBI Classic Yearbook*[12.7] slightly different than those published in last year's *2014 Valuation Handbook*?

Response: The *differences* in reported size premia for the CRSP deciles between last year's *2014 Valuation Handbook* and last year's *2014 SBBI Classic Yearbook* are summarized in Exhibit 12.3.[12.8]

12.7 Morningstar continues to publish the *SBBI Classic Yearbook* in 2015. The *SBBI Classic Yearbook* is an analysis of the relative performance of various asset classes in the U.S., and does *not* provide extensive valuation data or methodology.

12.8 Differences in the two publications' size premia are measured in Exhibit II as: (*2014 SBBI Classic Yearbook* size premia – *2014 Valuation Handbook* size premia). Source: *2014 SBBI Classic Yearbook* (Morningstar, 2014), page 109; *2014 Valuation Handbook – Guide to Cost of Capital* (Duff & Phelps, 2014), Appendix 3.

Exhibit 12.3: Size Premia (differences only); *Morningstar 2014 Classic Yearbook* versus *2014 Valuation Handbook*
As of December 31, 2013

As of December 31, 2013	Size Premia (differences)
Mid-Cap (3-5)	0.04%
Low-Cap (6-8)	-0.11%
Micro-Cap (9-10)	-0.03%
Breakdown of CRSP Deciles 1–10	
Decile 1	0.04%
Decile 2	0.05%
Decile 3	0.07%
Decile 4	0.03%
Decile 5	-0.02%
Decile 6	-0.10%
Decile 7	-0.20%
Decile 8	0.12%
Decile 9	-0.05%
Decile 10	0.03%

For example, in Exhibit 12.3, the size premium for Decile 10 published in the *2014 SBBI Classic Yearbook* was approximately 0.03% *greater* than the size premium for Decile 10 published in the *2014 Valuation Handbook*. Similarly, the size premium for Decile 7 in the *Classic Yearbook* was 0.20% *less* than Decile 7's size premium in the *2014 Valuation Handbook.*

While these differences are relatively minor in nature, it is nonetheless important to examine and understand the likely source of these differences.

Let's start with what we know. The same two primary data sources were used to calculate the size premia in both the *2014 Valuation Handbook* and in the *2014 Classic Yearbook:*

- SBBI Series from Morningstar's *EnCorr* database[12.9]

- The Center for Research in Security Prices (CRSP) market-cap-based NYSE/NYSE MKT/NASDAQ indices

[12.9] In 2014, Morningstar discontinued the *EnCorr* database, and transitioned all SBBI series over to the Morningstar *Direct* database. To learn more about the Morningstar *Direct* database, visit corporate.morningstar.com

The specific inputs from these two sources used to calculate the size premia published in the *2014 Valuation Handbook* and the *2014 Classic Yearbook* are:[12.10]

1. S&P 500 total return index

2. 30-day U.S. T-Bill total return series

3. Long-term income return of 20-year U.S. government bonds

4. CRSP NYSE/NYSE AMEX/NASDAQ Market Capitalization Deciles 1–10 total return indices

To calculate the size premia in the *2014 Valuation Handbook* and the *2014 SBBI Classic Yearbook*, the following summarizes the elements that are common to both:

- **Identical Market Benchmark:** The *2014 SBBI Classic Yearbook* and the *2014 Valuation* Handbook both used the S&P 500 total return index as the "market benchmark" when calculating the betas for each of the CRSP deciles and size groupings.[12.11] These betas are important inputs needed to calculate size premia over CAPM.

- **Identical 30-day U.S.** Treasury Bill series: The *2014 SBBI Classic Yearbook* and the *2014 Valuation Handbook* calculated the CRSP deciles' betas as monthly return data in excess of the same exact 30-day U.S. Treasury bill total return series over the period January 1926–December 2013.[12.12]

- **Identical Long-Term Equity Risk Premium:** The *2014 SBBI Classic Yearbook* and the *2014 Valuation Handbook* calculated (and used) the same exact values for the arithmetic annual return of the S&P 500 total return index and the long-term income return of 20-year U.S. government bonds over the1926–2013 time horizon (12.05% and 5.09%, respectively; these two values are used to calculate the long-term equity risk premium, which is an important input needed to calculate size premia).[12.13]

- Identical Methodology: Finally, both the *2014 SBBI Classic Yearbook* and the *2014 Valuation Handbook* use the same methodology to calculate the size premia for the CRSP deciles:

12.10 Source of inputs 1, 2, and 3 in last year's *2014 Valuation Handbook – Guide to Cost of Capital* : Morningstar *EnCorr* database. In 2014, Morningstar discontinued the *EnCorr* database, and transitioned all SBBI series over to the Morningstar *Direct* database. To learn more about the Morningstar *Direct* database, visit corporate.morningstar.com. Source of input 4: CRSP U.S. Stock Database and CRSP U.S. Indices Database © 2014 Center for Research in Security Prices (CRSP®), University of Chicago Booth School of Business. To learn more about the Center for Research in Security Prices (CRSP) at the University of Chicago Booth School of Business, visit www.crsp.com

12.11 The specific series used in the *2014 SBBI Classic Yearbook* and *2014 Valuation Handbook – Guide to Cost of Capital* as the market benchmark when calculating betas for the CRSP deciles and size groupings is "S&P 500 TR (IA Extended)". Source: Morningstar *EnCorr* database. In 2014, Morningstar discontinued the *EnCorr* database, and transitioned all SBBI series over to the Morningstar *Direct* database. To learn more about the Morningstar *Direct* database, visit corporate.morningstar.com.

12.12 See *2014 SBBI Classic Yearbook* (Morningstar, 2014), page 109; *2014 Valuation Handbook – Guide to Cost of Capital* (Duff & Phelps, 2014), page 4-10.

12.13 See *2014 SBBI Classic Yearbook* (Morningstar, 2014), page 109; *2014 Valuation Handbook – Guide to Cost of Capital* (Duff & Phelps, 2014), page 4-10.

Size premium = (the excess returns that *actually happened* – the excess returns that CAPM *predicted* would happen)

So, what is different? The *only* set of inputs that we have not examined thus far is the total returns for the CRSP NYSE/NYSE MKT/NASDAQ Market Capitalization Deciles 1–10. Exhibit 12.4 is a summary of the average annual return of each of the standard CRSP deciles over the 1926–2013 period, as published in (i) the *2014 SBBI Classic Yearbook* and (ii) the *2014 Valuation Handbook*.[12.14] To be clear, note that the "Difference" column in Exhibit 12.4 is not the same as the "Size Premia (differences)" column found in Exhibit 12.3 (even though some of figures may coincide). The latter is adjusted by the beta of each portfolio.

Exhibit 12.4: Average Annual Total Returns of the CRSP NYSE/NYSE MKT/NASDAQ Market Capitalization Deciles 1–10 as Published in the *2014 SBBI Classic Yearbook* and *2014 Valuation Handbook*
1926–2013

	As published in: *2014 SBBI Classic Yearbook*	As published in: *2014 Valuation Handbook*	Difference
Size Grouping	Arithmetic Annual Average Return (1926–2013)	Arithmetic Annual Average Return (1926–2013)	Classic *minus* Handbook
Mid-Cap (3-5)	14.02%	14.01%	0.02%
Low-Cap (6-8)	15.51%	15.57%	-0.07%
Micro-Cap (9-10)	18.38%	18.41%	-0.03%
Breakdown of CRSP Deciles 1–10			
Decile 1	11.13%	11.10%	0.03%
Decile 2	13.09%	13.04%	0.05%
Decile 3	13.68%	13.64%	0.04%
Decile 4	14.12%	14.09%	0.03%
Decile 5	14.88%	14.92%	-0.03%
Decile 6	15.11%	15.12%	-0.01%
Decile 7	15.48%	15.68%	-0.20%
Decile 8	16.62%	16.55%	0.07%
Decile 9	17.23%	17.27%	-0.04%
Decile 10	20.88%	20.85%	0.04%

The slightly different size premia values reported in the *2014 SBBI Classic Yearbook* and the *2014 Valuation Handbook* are traceable to the slightly different CRSP decile total returns used by the two publications.[12.15] For example, the average annual return of CRSP Decile 7 over the 1926–2013 period as reported in the *2014 SBBI Classic Yearbook* is 15.48%, while the average annual return of Decile 7

[12.14] Source of underlying data in Exhibit 12.4: CRSP U.S. Stock Database and CRSP U.S. Indices Database © 2014 Center for Research in Security Prices (CRSP®), University of Chicago Booth School of Business. See *2014 SBBI Classic Yearbook* (Morningstar, 2014), Table 7-6, page 109; *2014 Valuation Handbook – Guide to Cost of Capital* (Duff & Phelps, 2014), Exhibit 7.3, page 7-10.

[12.15] Eight decimals were used in the calculation of the differences in Exhibit12.4; these results were then rounded to two decimals.

as reported in the *2014 Valuation Handbook* is 15.68%, a difference of -0.20% (15.48% – 15.68%). Note that this difference (-0.20%) is the same as the difference in the size premia reported for Decile 7 in the *2014 SBBI Classic Yearbook* and *2014 Valuation Handbook* in Exhibit 12.3, although as mentioned earlier the size premiums in Exhibit 12.3 are beta adjusted, whereas the differences in Exhibit 12.4 are not.[12.16]

Which Size Premia are Correct?

In Exhibit 12.5, the values that $1.00 invested as of December 31, 1925 in each of the CRSP standard market-capitalization-weighted deciles (and three size groupings) would have grown to as of December 31, 2013 are calculated in three alternative ways: (i) by CRSP itself, using their official returns database,[12.17] (ii) using the CRSP returns that were used to calculate the size premia published in the *2014 Valuation Handbook*, and (iii) as published in the *2014 SBBI Classic Yearbook*.[12.18]

Exhibit 12.5: Terminal Index Values for the CRSP NYSE/NYSE MKT/NASDAQ Market Capitalization Deciles as of December 31, 2013 (i) Calculated by CRSP, (ii) Calculated Using the CRSP Returns Used to Calculate the Size Premia Published in the *2014 Valuation Handbook*, and (iii) as Published in the *2014 SBBI Classic Yearbook*.
December 31, 1925 = $1.00

Size Grouping/ Decile	Calculated by CRSP	Calculated using the CRSP returns used to calculate the size premia published in the *2014 Valuation Handbook*	Published in the 2014 *SBBI Classic Yearbook*
Mid-Cap (3-5)	$11,419	$11,419	$11,728
Low-Cap (6-8)	$17,514	$17,514	$16,606
Micro-Cap (9-10)	$27,771	$27,771	$29,190
Decile 1	$2,510	$2,510	$2,589
Decile 2	$7,704	$7,704	$7,769
Decile 3	$9,846	$9,846	$10,635
Decile 4	$10,606	$10,606	$10,514
Decile 5	$17,141	$17,141	$16,189
Decile 6	$16,115	$16,115	$15,955
Decile 7	$17,175	$17,175	$15,347
Decile 8	$19,675	$19,675	$18,600
Decile 9	$17,440	$17,440	$19,294
Decile 10	$68,670	$68,670	$62,843

12.16 The *largest* contributing factor to the differences in the size premia reported in the *2014 SBBI Classic Yearbook* and *2014 Valuation Handbook – Guide to Cost of Capital* is the difference in the average annual return over the 1926–2013 period (this accounted for 79.8% of the variation). Differences in the betas calculated for each of the deciles was (to a significantly *lesser* degree) a contributing factor to the differences in size premia (this accounted for 20.2% of the variation). However, both the average annual return input and the beta input are a function of the raw monthly annual CRSP returns, and thus the *root* cause is the difference in returns.

12.17 Source: Document "qtr201312.q", prepared by the Center for Research in Security Prices (CRSP), Jan-16-2014/201312 Copyright © 2014

12.18 Source: *2014 SBBI Classic Yearbook* (Morningstar 2014), Table 7-3, pages 103–104, Table 7-4, pages 105–106. Values have been rounded to nearest dollar.

Looking to Exhibit 12.5, the following observations can be made:

- The terminal index values calculated by CRSP using their official database match the terminal index values calculated using the CRSP returns used to produce the size premia in the *2014 Valuation Handbook*, and

- The terminal index values of the CRSP deciles reported in *2014 SBBI Classic Yearbook* do not match CRSP's own calculations.

All other things held the same, the terminal index values in Exhibit 12.5 are dependent on the January 1926–December 2013 monthly returns used to calculate them: if the returns *change*, the terminal index values *change*. The conclusion of this analysis is therefore straightforward:

- The CRSP decile returns used to calculate the size premia in the Morningstar/Ibbotson *2014 SBBI Classic Yearbook* (data through December 31, 2013) do not match the returns in CRSP's own official database as of December 31, 2013, and

- The CRSP decile returns used to calculate the size premia in the *2014 Valuation Handbook* (data through December 31, 2013) match the returns in CRSP's own official database as of December 31, 2013.

In the *2015 Valuation Handbook* (this book), we again worked carefully with CRSP to ensure that the size premia in the *2015 Valuation Handbook* are based upon the exact monthly total return values in CRSP's official database as of December 31, 2014 for the time horizon January 1926–December 2014.

In Exhibit 12.6, the values that $1.00 invested as of December 31, 1925 in each of the CRSP standard market-capitalization-weighted deciles (and three size groupings) would have grown to as of December 31, 2014 are calculated again in two alternative ways: (i) by CRSP itself, using their official returns database,[12.19] and (ii) using the CRSP returns that were used to calculate the size premia published in the *2015 Valuation Handbook*. The terminal index values again *exactly* match. The conclusion of this analysis is thus again straightforward:

- The CRSP decile returns used to calculate the size premia in the 2015 *Valuation Handbook* (this book) match the returns in CRSP's own official database as of December 31, 2014.

[12.19] Source: Document "qtr201412.q", prepared by the Center for Research in Security Prices (CRSP), Jan-16-2015/201412 Copyright © 2015.

Exhibit 12.6: Terminal Index Values for the CRSP NYSE/NYSE MKT/NASDAQ Market Capitalization Deciles as of December 31, 2014 (i) Calculated by CRSP, (ii) Calculated Using the CRSP Returns Used to Calculate the Size Premia Published in the *2015 Valuation Handbook*
December 31, 1925 = $1.00

Size Grouping/ Decile	Calculated by CRSP	Calculated using the CRSP returns used to calculate the size premia published in the *2015 Valuation Handbook*
Mid-Cap (3-5)	$12,887	$12,887
Low-Cap (6-8)	$17,801	$17,801
Micro-Cap (9-10)	$29,972	$29,972
Decile 1	$2,899	$2,899
Decile 2	$8,240	$8,240
Decile 3	$12,021	$12,021
Decile 4	$10,850	$10,850
Decile 5	$18,407	$18,407
Decile 6	$16,372	$16,372
Decile 7	$18,135	$18,135
Decile 8	$18,883	$18,883
Decile 9	$18,030	$18,030
Decile 10	$81,406	$81,406

Question 8: Can you provide guidance on applying a size premium for a small regulated utility company?

Unlike small companies operating in a non-regulated environment, the small regulated utility company is assured of a certain income stream, and typically operates in a monopoly environment. This would arguably remove a great deal of risk that a typical small company might otherwise face. Furthermore, some of our appraisal firms have concluded that the small electric company could have less risk than their larger counterpart. This could partly be due to the fact that the small utility is often a pure play business, whereas the bigger utilities sometimes venture into areas that are considered riskier.

Given this background, should a small regulated utility company have a similar risk premium to that of a typical small company?

Response: Size premia data are calculated based on a measure of central tendency (i.e., a measure of mid-point) for the sample of firms that comprise a specific size portfolio. Accordingly, the size premia data are reported for the mid-point of the companies included in each of the portfolios. Companies within that same size portfolio can have different risk profiles and, consequently, should have a different cost of capital. The *2015 Valuation Handbook* provides additional data to help understand risk differences among companies.

For example, let us examine the data in Exhibit B-5 of the *2015 Valuation Handbook*, Appendix 4. This Exhibit presents size premia data (over CAPM), where size is measured by Total Assets.

Assume that the subject small regulated utility has $1 billion in total assets placing it in Portfolio 21 in Exhibit B-5. The corresponding smoothed size premium (over CAPM) is shown as 4.53%.

Now, let's further examine the characteristics of the companies that comprise Portfolio 21 of Exhibit B-5. For that information, we turn to the Comparative Risk Characteristics presented in the C Exhibits. The matching Exhibit to Exhibit B-5 is Exhibit C-5.

Upon examination of Exhibit C-5, we observe that the average operating margin of the companies within Portfolio 21 (i.e., the companies comprising that size grouping) equals 8.80% and the average coefficient of variation in operating margin (i.e., how much does the operating margin vary over time) equals 22.26%.

To the extent that a subject company's operating margin was *less* than 8.80%, the risk of that business is likely *greater* than that of the typical company comprising Portfolio 21. Conversely, to the extent that a subject company's operating margin was *greater* than 8.80%, the risk of that business is likely *less* than that of the typical company comprising Portfolio 21.

Now, let's look at Exhibit D-1. Exhibit D-1 is the same companies that are in the A, B, and C exhibits, but instead of being sorted from largest to smallest according to size, the companies are sorted by "operating margin". There is a general relationship between these metrics, such that as operating margin *decreases*, the cost of capital (risk) typically *increases*.

Also, to the extent that a subject company's *variability* of operating margin (as measured by coefficient of variation) is *greater* than 22.26%, the risk of that business is likely *greater* than that of the companies comprising Portfolio 21 (see Exhibit D-2). Alternatively, to the extent that a subject company's variability of operating margin was *less* than 22.26%, the risk of that business is likely *less* than that of the companies comprising Portfolio 21. The relationship in Exhibit D-2 shows that as the coefficient of variation of operating margin decreases, the cost of capital (risk) typically decreases.

Exhibits D-1 and D-2 can help quantify how much less or more from the typical size premium should be the cost of capital for the subject company. For a detailed example of how one might make such an adjustment, consider reviewing The section entitled "Comparative Risk Study" on pages 10-64 to 10-71 in the *2015 Valuation Handbook*.

The authors believe that the cost of capital needs to reflect the risk characteristics of the subject company, rather than the risks exhibited by the typical firm. The data in the *2015 Valuation Handbook* will help you make such adjustments.

Question 9: When discussing the Buildup-3 method using the D Exhibits, page 10-47 indicates that the smoothed arithmetic average premiums in the D exhibits are "unlevered". Is this correct? By contrast, the "Unlevered Buildup-3" discussion on page 10-50 makes no mention of smoothed premiums, and does not use the regression equation method.

Response: The Risk Premium Report D Exhibits include both levered and unlevered risk premiums for each portfolio (see columns labeled respectively "Arithmetic Average Risk Premium" and "Arithmetic Average Unlevered Risk Premium"). However, the *2015 Valuation Handbook* only includes smoothed premiums for levered risks premiums (see column labeled "Smoothed Average Risk Premium"), but does not provide smoothed unlevered risk premiums.

Question 10: I downloaded the full list of companies included in last year's *2014 Valuation Handbook* industry risk premia (Exhibit 5.7). I noticed that certain SIC codes had the exact *same* listing of companies, but *different* industry risk premia. For example, SIC codes 805 and 8051 were comprised of the same companies, but had different industry risk premia. Same for SIC codes 807 and 8071. Why would this be?

Response: Industry risk premia (RP_i) in the *2014 Valuation Handbook* (and the *2015 Valuation Handbook*) are full-information betas that have been adjusted so that they can be added as a simple "up or down" adjustment in the build-up method. The full-information betas (FIB) published in last year's *2014 Valuation Handbook* of the SIC codes that the question references are as follows:

SIC 805, FIB = 1.93
SIC 8051 FIB = 1.87
SIC 807, FIB = 0.65
SIC 8071, FIB = 0.66

The short answer is that SIC 805 and SIC 8051, and SIC 807 and SIC 8071, are (by definition) different "industries". How they come out of the full-information beta calculation in *relation* to all the other industries will likely vary. Full-information betas are designed to measure the *relative* impact on the betas of companies in an industry based on the *relative* exposure (as measured by sales) each company has within the industry.

In Exhibit 12.7, hypothetical values are used in a simplified two-company universe to illustrate how SIC 805 and SIC 8051 can be comprised of *exactly the same companies* (Company ABC and Company DEF), but have *different* industry exposures (vis-à-vis "Sales"), and therefore potentially different full-information betas (and thus different industry risk premia).

Exhibit 12.7: Company Exposure to an Industry ("Sales to SIC") for a Hypothetical Two-Company Universe

	SIC'	**Sales to SIC'**	**SIC"**	**Sales to SIC"**
Company ABC	805	$1.00	8051	$0.50
Company ABC	805	–	8052	$0.50
Company DEF	805	$2.00	8051	$2.00
Total Sales		$3.00		$3.00

SIC 8051 and SIC 8052 both "roll up into" SIC 805. Also:

- SIC 805 is comprised *solely* of Company ABC and Company DEF.
- SIC 8051 is comprised *solely* of Company ABC and Company DEF.

However, note that Company ABC also has exposure to SIC 8052, which makes the relationship between Company ABC and Company DEF within the context of SIC 805 *different* than the relationship between Company ABC and Company DEF within the context of SIC 8051.[12.20] This can (and likely will) result in different full-information betas for SIC 805 and SIC 8051.

Question 11: Exhibit 5.7 ("*Industry Risk Premia* (RP_i) *Through Year-end 2013*") in last year's *2014 Valuation Handbook* does not include an industry risk premium for SIC 0251 (Broiler, Fryer, and Roaster Chickens). What do I do if an industry risk premium is not listed for my industry?

Response: You are correct, an industry risk premium for SIC 0251 (Broiler, Fryer, and Roaster Chickens) is not included in Exhibit 5.7 in last year's *2014 Valuation Handbook*.[12.21] The reason for this is that there were not enough publicly-traded companies available to meet the minimum criteria for calculating an industry risk premium (minimum 10).

To answer the broader question of what to do if an industry risk premium is not listed for your industry, there are generally two possible solutions.

The first solution is the easier of the two: use the industry risk premium for the "next level up" SIC code. For example, an industry risk premium is *not* published in Exhibit 5.7 of last year's *2014 Valuation Handbook* for SIC 5141 (Groceries, General Line). However, there *is* an industry risk premium published for SIC 514 (Groceries and Related Products), which is the "next level up" SIC code.[12.22] Note that as you move from 4-digit SICs to 3-digit SICs to 2-digit SICs, the industries become *less* specific (i.e., broader),

[12.20] For example, Company ABC's revenues derived from SIC 805 *relative to* Company DEF's revenues derived from SIC 805 is 0.5 ($1.00 / $2.00); Company ABC's revenues derived from SIC 8051 *relative to* Company DEF's revenues derived from SIC 8051 is 0.25 ($0.50 / $2.00).

[12.21] An industry risk premium for SIC 0251 does not appear to have been published in *any* edition of the *SBBI Valuation Yearbook* either, from 2000–2013. The *SBBI Valuation Yearbook* was published from 1999–2013; industry risk premia were first published in the 2000 edition.

[12.22] "One level up" from SIC 5141 is SIC 514; "one level up" from SIC 514 is SIC 51).

so it is recommended that the analyst examine the full industry descriptions of the SIC codes and make a determination if the SIC code is a suitable proxy for the given subject company.[12.23]

The second solution is to identify a sample of public companies that have comparable risks to the subject company, calculate a custom peer group beta, and then use that peer group beta to calculate a custom industry risk premia. This can be accomplished by applying Formula 5.5 on page 5-13 herein.

Question 12: I downloaded the "Industry Risk Premia Company List" document that is provided at www.duffandphelps.com/CostofCapital, and noticed that there are companies in some of the SICs that look out of place. For example, 3M Company is listed in SIC 26 ("Paper and Allied Products"), SIC 36 ("Electronic and Other Electrical Equipment and Components, Except Computer Equipment"), and SIC 384 ("Surgical, Medical, and Dental Instruments and Supplies").

Response: The "Industry Risk Premia Company List" document lists all of the companies used in the calculation of each of the industry risk premium in Exhibit 5.7 of the *Valuation Handbook*. The full-information beta analysis employed to form the industry risk premia provided in Exhibit 5.7 uses a cross-sectional regression in which a company's exposure to an industry (as defined by SIC code) is based on a sales-based weighted methodology. Any given company's exposure vis-à-vis "sales" to any given industry can vary from less than 1.0% to 100.0%. The full-information beta approach enables the inclusion of these companies' participation in the industry in the beta calculation.[12.24]

Ideally, one would like to have a sampling of betas from many "pure play" guideline public companies when estimating a proxy beta. "Pure play" companies are companies with say, at least 75.0% of revenue from a single Standard Industrial Classification (SIC) code. In some industries the *largest* participants may be conglomerates for which participation in the given industry is a *small* part of their overall revenues. For example, as of December 2013 (the "data through" date of last year's *2014 Valuation Handbook*) the percentage of General Electric's sales in SIC 351 (Engines and Turbines) was less than 20.0% of the company's overall sales, so in a strictly pure-play beta analysis General Electric would be excluded. However, General Electric was arguably the *dominant* participant in this industry, with 55.6% of all sales.[12.25] Companies that have exposure a given industry (even if limited) can be included in the analysis when full-information beta methodology is employed.

12.23 A source of information on SIC codes and their descriptions is the United States Department of Labor Occupational Safety & Health Administration (OSHA) website at: https://www.osha.gov/pls/imis/sicsearch.html

12.24 The full-information betas published in the *2014 Valuation Handbook* (and in the former *SBBI Valuation Yearbook*) are based on an article by Paul D. Kaplan and James D. Peterson: "Full-Information Industry Betas", *Financial Management*, Summer 1998.

12.25 As of the most recently completed fiscal year as of last year's *2014 Valuation Handbook*, and in the context of the 3,435 U.S. companies included in the full information beta analysis used to create Exhibit 5.7 in the *2014 Valuation Handbook*. Source: Standard and Poor's *Research Insight* database.

To be clear: The companies included in the full-information beta analysis used to create the industry risk premia in the *Valuation Handbook* are *not* necessarily "pure play" companies:

- You many notice companies included in each industry that may seem *out of place*. However, these companies only impact the full-information betas (and thus the industry risk premia) by the weighted sales exposure the company has to the given industry.

- You may also notice companies listed in *multiple* industries. For example, General Electric was a participant in SIC 351 (Engines and Turbines), but was also a participant in SIC 363 (Household Appliances), and SIC 384 (Surgical, Medical, And Dental Instruments and Supplies).

To learn more, see Chapter 5, "Basic Building Blocks of the Cost of Equity Capital – Betas and Industry Risk Premia" herein.

Question 13: In Exhibit 5.7 ("Industry Risk Premia") in last year's *2014 Valuation Handbook*, there are fewer companies in some of the SIC 6xxx codes than there are in the subsequent March, June, and September 2014 quarterly updates to this table.[12.26]

Response: A significant number of SIC 6xxx companies were excluded from the analysis in the full-information beta analysis which is used to calculate the industry risk premia provided in Exhibit 5.7 for last year's *2014 Valuation Handbook*. In the quarterly updates to Exhibit 5.7, these excluded companies were added back. The primary result of the exclusions were that certain SIC 6xxx codes were not reported in the December 31, 2013 analysis (i.e., the *2014 Valuation Handbook*), but are reported in the subsequent 2014 quarterly updates. For the SIC 6xxx codes that were reported in *both* the December 31, 2013 analysis (i.e., the *2014 Valuation Handbook*) and the subsequent 2014 quarterly updates, the industry risk premia calculated are not significantly different.

Question 14: What caused the significant volatility in the industry risk premium (IRP) for SIC 78 *Motion Pictures*? I note that most IRPs are relatively stable from period to period, but some appear to be somewhat instable from period to period.

Response: IRPs are a special form of beta that has been adjusted so that it can be employed as a simple up or down adjustment in the build-up method of estimating cost of equity capital. Just like the betas that they are based upon, industry risk premia change from period to period.

All things held the same, however, the *smaller* the number of companies included in the calculations of an IRP for an SIC ("industry") code, the *greater* the chance of variability from period to period. Specifically, in regards to SIC 78, the IRPs calculated using the historical 1926-present ERP over the last 16 years (2000–2015) have been relatively unstable (see Exhibit 12.8).

12.26 The "Industry Risk Premia Quarterly Updates" includes March, June, and September updates to the approximately 250 U.S. industry risk premia that are published in the *Valuation Handbook's* Exhibit 5.7. Industry risk premia are a necessary cost of capital input that can be used within the context of the build-up method to estimate the cost of equity capital. The industry risk premia in the *Valuation Handbook* and in these quarterly updates are the equivalent of the industry risk premia formerly published in the Morningstar/Ibbotson *SBBI Valuation Yearbook's* Table 3-5.

Exhibit 12.8: SIC 78 (Motion Pictures) Industry Risk Premium (IRP) as Published in the *2000–2013 SBBI Valuation Yearbook*, and the *2014 and 2015 Valuation Handbook*

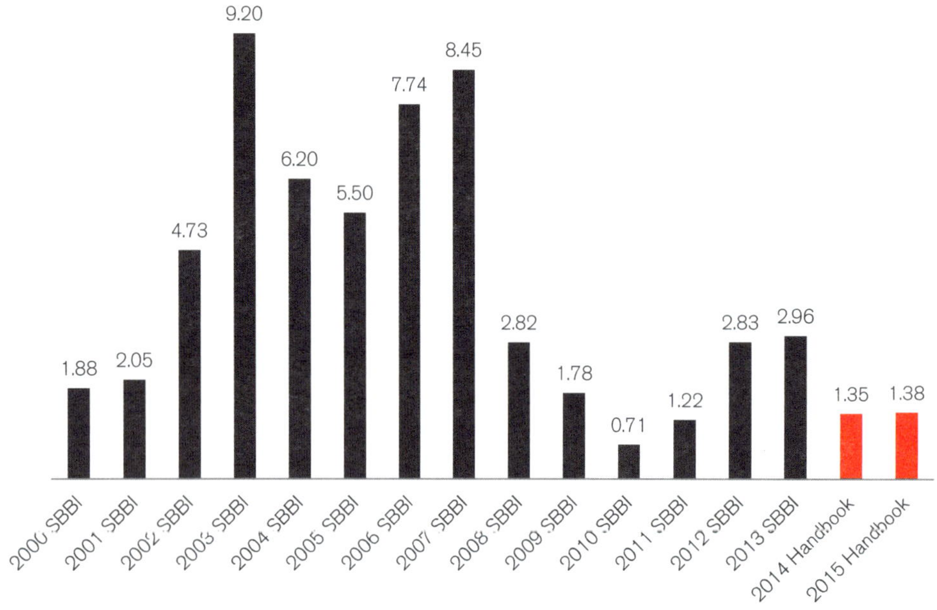

Note that for the comparison across time to be "apples to apples", the IRPs in Exhibit 12.8 are calculated using a long-term historical ERP. For example, the 1.35% industry risk premium published in the *2014 Valuation Handbook* and the 1.38% published in the 2015 *Valuation Handbook* are calculated in the same fashion in this regard as the 2.96% premia reported in the *Ibbotson SBBI* 2013 *Valuation Yearbook*.[12.27]

The methodology used to calculate the full information betas (and thus the industry risk premia) in the *2014 and 2015 Valuation Handbooks'* Exhibit 5.7 was nearly identical with how they were calculated in the former *SBBI*.[12.28] However, there are some differences with the *2014 and 2015 Valuation Handbooks'* methodology for calculating industry risk premia compared to the former *SBBI Valuation Yearbook's* methodology that were implemented to *increase* the statistical quality and the stability of the IRPs.

First, instead of requiring that each company had to have "36 months of [return] data in the previous 60 months", we required "36 months of *contiguous* return data, ending December 31, 2013" in the *2014 Handbook* (and December 31, 2014 in the *2015 Valuation Handbook*). The goal of our more stringent criteria was to *lessen* the threshold for excluding companies that had "spotty" data, and thus *increase* the data quality of the overall set.

12.27 All industry risk premia published in the *2000–2013 SBBI Valuation Yearbooks* were calculated using only the long-term "historical" ERP. In the *Valuation Handbook*, industry risk premia are also calculated using the long-term "historical" ERP, but are *also* calculated using the supply side ERP and the Duff & Phelps recommended "conditional" ERP.

12.28 The full-information betas published in the *2014 Valuation Handbook* (and in the former *SBBI Valuation Yearbook*) are based on an article by Paul D. Kaplan and James D. Peterson: "Full-Information Industry Betas", *Financial Management*, Summer 1998.

Second, the minimum number of companies participating in an industry (by SIC code) required in order to be included in the full-information beta regression analysis. We required a minimum of 10 participants in each industry; the former SBBI required 5 participants. The goal of this more stringent requirement was to eliminate SICs that have few participant companies, and are prone to high volatility from period to period.

Question 15: I purchased the *2015 Valuation Handbook – Guide to Cost of Capital.* Why would I also need the new *2015 Valuation Handbook – Industry Cost of Capital?*

Response: The *2015 Valuation Handbook – Guide to Cost of Capital* provides the key year-end data previously published in (i) the Morningstar/Ibbotson *SBBI Valuation Yearbook* and (ii) the Duff & Phelps *Risk Premium Report*, and can be used to develop cost of equity capital estimates for an *individual* business, business ownership interest, security, or intangible asset.

Valuation is an inherently comparative process – just about any analysis boils down to trying to compare one thing to another. For example, once the valuation practitioner has developed his or her own custom cost of equity estimate for the subject company, a natural first question *is "How does my own analysis of the subject company compare to the subject company's peers (i.e., the industry)?"* It is a normal and prudent step in *any* analysis is to perform some benchmarking as a "reasonableness" test.

The *2015 Valuation Handbook – Industry Cost of Capital* includes cost of capital estimates (equity capital, debt capital, and WACC) for over 200 U.S. industries, plus a host of detailed statistics that can be used for benchmarking purposes.

The industry-level statistics in the *2015 Valuation Handbook – Industry Cost of Capital* do not replace the valuation practitioner's own custom analyses of the subject company, business ownership interest, security, or intangible asset. However, the valuation analyst will likely find the statistics presented to be a useful indicator for (i) benchmarking, (ii) augmenting, and (iii) providing additional support for his or her own custom analyses of the industry in which a subject business, business ownership interest, security, or intangible asset resides.[12.29]

Question 16: In Appendix 3 ("*CRSP Deciles Size Premia Study: Key Variables*") of the *2015 Valuation Handbook,* there are small gaps in the market caps between the deciles.[12.30]

For example, the *upper* boundary of decile 10 is $300.725 million, but the *lower* boundary of decile 9 is $300.752 million. This also occurs in the Mid-, Low-, and Micro-Cap size groupings. For example, the *upper* boundary of the Low-cap size grouping is $2,542.913 million, but the *lower* boundary of Mid-Cap size grouping is $2,552.441 million. While these gaps aren't material, we are doing a fairly vigorous valuation exercise where this question could come up. Can you explain why these gaps exist?

12.29 To purchase the *2015 Valuation Handbook – Industry Cost of Capital*, or other valuation data resources authored by Duff & Phelps, and published by Wiley, please go to www.wiley.com/go/ValuationHandbooks.

12.30 Appendix 3 of the *Valuation Handbook* includes the "key variables in estimating the cost of capital" that were previously published in the Morningstar/Ibbotson *Stocks, Bonds, Bills and Inflation (SBBI) Valuation Yearbook.*

Response: The breakpoints of the deciles and size groupings in Appendix 3 of the *2015 Valuation Handbook* are the *actual* market caps of *actual* companies, as of the time of portfolio formation. The upper and lower boundaries of these portfolios are determined by the Center for Research in Security Prices at the University of Chicago Booth School Of Business (CRSP). CRSP creates these portfolios, and reports the boundaries to us. These gaps have always existed between the CRSP portfolios (e.g., the gaps were also present in the former Morningstar/Ibbotson *SBBI Valuation Yearbook*).

The way to handle this is demonstrated with an example, using the upper and lower market caps of the Mid-, Low-, and Micro-cap size groupings shown in Exhibit 12.9 (Exhibit 12.9 is an excerpt of Appendix 3 from the *2015 Valuation Handbook*).

Exhibit 12.9: Largest and Smallest Companies in CRSP Standard Market-Cap-Weighted Size Groupings Mid-Cap, Low-Cap, and Micro-Cap (size premia not shown)

CRSP Deciles Size Premium

Decile	Market Capitalization of Smallest Company (in millions)		Market Capitalization of Largest Company (in millions)	Size Premium (Return in Excess of CAPM)
Mid-Cap 3-5	$2,552.441	–	$10,105.622	1.07%
Low-Cap 6-8	549.056	–	2,542.913	1.80%
Micro-Cap 9-10	3.037	–	548.839	3.74%

To identify which of the size groupings the subject falls in:

- Large-capitalization companies have equity capitalizations greater than $10,105.622 million.
- Mid-capitalization companies have equity capitalizations *equal* to or *less* than $10,105.622 million, but *greater* than $2,542.913 million.
- Low-capitalization companies have equity capitalizations *equal* to or *less* than $2,542.913 million, but *greater* than $548.839 million.
- Micro-capitalization companies have equity capitalizations *equal* to or *less* than $548.839 million.

The same regimen can be applied to any of the other CRSP portfolios 1-10 and 10th decile sub-deciles as well.

Question 17: We have been using the CAPM to estimate the cost of capital for each division annually. We search for "pure play" companies to estimate a beta. For some divisions we find no "pure play" betas and end up guessing. Any suggestions?

Response: Yes. One option would be to use the "full-information" industry betas from Exhibit 5.7 in the *2015 Valuation Handbook*.

Ideally, one would like to have a sampling of betas from many "pure play" guideline public companies when estimating a proxy beta. In some industries, however, the *largest* participants may be conglomerates for which participation in the given industry is a *small* part of their overall revenues. In a strictly pure-play analysis, these companies would be *excluded*, even though they may be the dominant participant in the industry. The full-information beta approach enables the inclusion of these companies' participation in the industry in the beta calculation.

Another option is to refer to the *Valuation Handbook – Industry Cost of Capital*.[12.31, 12.32] For example, in the *2014 Valuation Handbook – Industry Cost of Capital*, which provides industry and peer group betas for over 200 U.S. industries.

In addition to industry and peer group betas (both levered and unlevered), the *Valuation Handbook – Industry Cost of Capital* provides eight (8) cost of equity capital estimates for each of the industries covered in the book (depending on data availability), cost of debt capital and weighted average cost of capital (WACC) estimates, plus capital structure, valuation multiples, industry betas, and more. The analyst can use this information to (i) benchmark, (ii) supplement, and (iii) strengthen his or her own custom cost of capital analysis.[12.33]

12.311 The *2014 Valuation Handbook – Industry Cost of Capital* (with data through March 2014) was published in October 2014 by Duff and Phelps. The 2015 version of the "industry" book is scheduled for release in late May 2015 (with data through March 2015), and will be published by John Wiley and Sons. The *Valuation Handbook – Industry Cost of Capital* provides the same type of rigorous industry-level analysis previously published in the green-cover Morningstar/ Ibbotson *Cost of Capital Yearbook* (discontinued in 2013). Like the previous Morningstar/Ibbotson *Cost of Capital Yearbook*, the *Valuation Handbook – Industry Cost of Capital* is published with data through March, and includes three intra-year quarterly updates (June, September, and December; updates are not sold separately, and only as a group). And, like the previous Morningstar/Ibbotson *Cost of Capital Yearbook*, the new *Valuation Handbook – Industry Cost of Capital* analyzes over 200 U.S. industries identified by their Standard Industrial Classification (SIC) code. To order copies of the *Valuation Handbook - Industry Cost of Capital* and its quarterly updates, please go to www.wiley.com/go/ValuationHandbooks

12.32 See Exhibit 1.4 herein for a sample industry analysis page from the *2014 Valuation Handbook – Industry Cost of Capital*.

12.33 A normal and prudent step in any analysis is to perform some benchmarking as a "reasonableness" test. The information in the *Valuation Handbook – Industry Cost of Capital* helps the analyst answer the question, "How does my own analysis of the subject company compare to the subject company's peers (i.e., the industry)?"

Question 18: My question is about the Risk Premium Report exhibits in the *2015 Valuation Handbook*.[12.34] I noticed that the smoothed "risk premium over the risk-free rate" seemed to have changed since last year. For example, the smoothed risk premium over the risk-free rate for portfolio 25 in Exhibit A-1 decreased from 14.17% to 13.92%?

Response: Changes in the premia published in the Risk Premium Report exhibits from one year to the next is not unusual (it would actually be *more* unusual if they did *not* change). This is true for both "risk premium over the risk-free rate" (RP_{m+s}), and also "risk premia over CAPM", which are otherwise known as size premia (RP_s).

In Exhibit 12.10, the RP_{m+s} values are shown for portfolio 25 (comprised of the smallest companies) for both Exhibit A-1 (size measure = market capitalization) and Exhibit A-3 (size measure = 5-year average net income). Note that the premia vary over time.[12.35]

Exhibit 12.10: Risk Premia Over the Risk-free Rate for Exhibit A-1 (size measure = market capitalization) and Exhibit A-3 (size measure = 5-year average net income)
1996 *Risk Premium Report* – 2015 *Risk Premium Report*

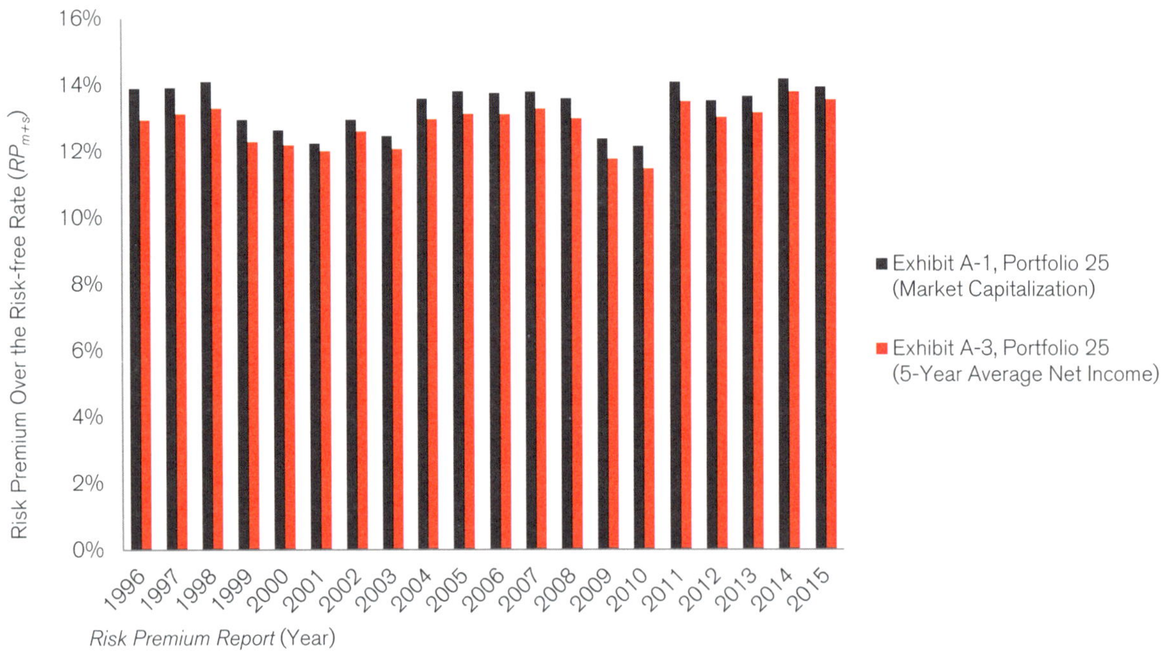

The Risk Premium Report exhibits' size premia (see Exhibits B-1 through B-8) *also* vary over time, as do the CRSP Deciles Size Study exhibits' size premia (see Exhibit 4.6 in the *2015 Valuation Handbook*, which shows the size premium for CRSP decile 10, from year-end 1962 to year-end 2014).

12.34 The Risk Premium Report Exhibits are in Appendix 4 of the *2015 Valuation Handbook*. The Duff & Phelps Risk *Premium Report* is no longer published as a stand-alone publication. The *Risk Premium Report* data is included in the new *2015 Valuation Handbook*, along with the data previously available in the former Morningstar/Ibbotson *SBBI Valuation Yearbook*.

12.35 Over the 1996–2015 period, the risk premium over the risk-free rate for portfolio 25 in Exhibit A-1 and Exhibit A-3 have varied 2.03% (max 14.17% - min 12.14%) and 2.32% (max 13.77% - min 11.45%), respectively.

Glossary

Altman z-Score
Widely used formula used to predict the probability that a firm will go into bankruptcy. In the Risk Premium Report's "High-Financial-Risk Study", companies are ranked based on the relative levels of distress, using z-Score as a proxy for "distress".

Arbitrage Pricing Theory
A multivariate model for estimating the cost of equity capital, which incorporates several systematic risk factors.

Asset Based Approach
A method of indicating the value of a business, business or business interest based on a summation of the net value of the individual assets and liabilities. Since each of the assets and liabilities will have been valued using either the market, income or cost approaches, it is not a distinct valuation approach.

Beta
A measure of systemic risk of a stock; the tendency of a stock's price to correlate with changes in a specific index.

Capital Appreciation Return
The return resulting from a price change of an investment over a given period.

Capital Asset Pricing Model (CAPM)
A model in which the cost of capital for any stock or portfolio of stocks equals a risk-free rate plus a risk premium that is proportionate to the systematic risk of the stock or portfolio.

Capital Structure
The composition of the invested capital of a business enterprise; the mix of debt and equity financing.

Company-Specific-Risk
Company-specific risk may have different meanings to different people. Oftentimes valuation analysts think of company-specific risk as an adjustment made to account for the differences between the subject company and the peer group to which it is being compared. In this sense, company-specific risk is differentiated from idiosyncratic risk (also known as "unsystematic" risk), which specifically refers to the uncertainty of expected returns arising from factors other than those factors correlated with the investment market as a whole.

Cost of Capital
The expected rate of return that the market requires in order to attract funds to a particular investment.

Discount Cash Flow Method
A method within the income approach in which a discount rate is applied to future expected income streams to estimate the present value.

Enterprise Value
The total value of the equity in a business plus the value of its debt or debt-related liabilities, minus any cash or cash equivalents available to meet those liabilities.

Equity Risk Premium (ERP)
The ERP is the rate of return added to a risk-free rate to reflect the additional risk of equity instruments over risk-free instruments. Also known as the market risk premium.

Going Concern
Business enterprise that is expected to continue operations for the foreseeable future.

Idiosyncratic Risk

Idiosyncratic risk (also known as "unsystematic" risk) refers to the uncertainty of expected returns arising from factors other than those factors correlated with the investment market as a whole. In this sense, idiosyncratic risk is differentiated from "company-specific" risk, which valuation analysts oftentimes think of as an adjustment made to account for the differences between the subject company and the peer group to which it is being compared.

Income Return

That portion of total return attributable to periodic cash flows (e.g., dividends).

Industry Risk Premium (RP_i)

A measure of beta (market) risk scaled around 0. Industry risk premia are appropriately used in "build-up" methods of estimating cost of equity that do not otherwise have a measure of beta. Industry risk premia are not appropriate for use in the CAPM model.

Inflation

The overall general upward price movement of goods and services in an economy. In the U.S., usually measured as change in the Consumer Price Index (CPI).

Levered Beta

A beta reflecting a capital structure that includes debt.

Liquidity

A measure of the ease with which an asset may be converted into cash. A highly liquid asset can be easily converted into cash; an illiquid asset is difficult to convert into cash.

Market Approach

A valuation approach which provides an indication of value by comparing the subject asset with identical or similar assets for which price information is available.

Market Value of Invest Capital (MVIC)

The sum of equity and debt in a business enterprise. Debt can be either (i) all interest-bearing debt or (ii) long-term, interest-bearing debt. When the term is used, it should be supplemented by the appropriate qualifying words.

Net Present Value

The value, as of a specified date, of future cash inflows less all cash outflows (including the cost of investment) calculated using an appropriate discount rate.

Portfolio Premium

The historical observed return over the risk-free rate (i.e. "excess return") earned by a given portfolio.

Reinvestment Return

That portion of total return attributable to the reinvestment of dividends, interest and capital gains. It is usually assumed that the reinvestment is in the same asset.

Risk Premia Over CAPM (i.e., size premium) (RP_s)

The difference between historical (observed) excess return and the excess return predicted by the CAPM. Because the difference between the historical excess return and CAPM-predicted excess return of portfolios comprised of *smaller* companies is typically *greater* than the difference between the historical excess return and CAPM-predicted excess return of portfolios comprised of *larger* companies, this difference is commonly referred to as a "beta-adjusted size premium".

Risk Premia Over Risk-Free Rate (RP_{m+s})

Risk premia over the risk-free rate" represent the difference between the historical (observed) return of equities over the risk-free rate. This difference is a measure of risk in terms of the combined effect of market risk and size risk.

Risk-Free Rate
The return available, as of the valuation date, on a security that the market generally regards as free of the risk of default.

Risk Study
The *Risk Study* analyzes the relationship between three fundamental measures of risk (operating margin, coefficient of variation on operating margin, and coefficient of variation on ROE) and return. The *Risk Study* finds that as risk increases, required returns tend to increase.

Size Premium
The difference in historical excess returns observed and the excess returns otherwise predicted by CAPM. *See "Risk Premia Over CAPM"*.

Size Study
The *Size Study* analyzes the relationship between size and return using 25 size-ranked portfolios using eight alternate measures of company size (market value of equity, book value of equity, 5 year average net income, MVIC, total assets, 5 year average EBITDA, sales, number of employees). The *Size Study* finds as size decreases, required return tend to increase.

Smoothed Premia
"Smoothed" premia is generally the most appropriate indicator for most of the portfolio groups when using the Risk Premium Report exhibits. Smoothing the premia essentially averages out the somewhat scattered nature of the raw average premia. Smoothed Premia is calculated using regression analysis. The CRSP Deciles Size Premia are not presently smoothed.

Subject Company
The subject company is the entity being valued.

Supply-side Model
Adapted by Roger Ibbotson and Peng Chen to estimate a forward-looking, long-term equity risk premium. The model analyzes historical equity return into the following factors; inflation, earnings, dividends, P/E, dividend payout ratio, book value of equity, return on equity, and GDP per capita. The model normalizes the growth in P/E ratio that is embedded in historical returns deeming it unsustainable and is removed for the model.

Systematic Risk
Risk that affects an entire market and not just a specific company or asset. Within the framework of the CAPM and other cost of capital estimation models, systematic risk is the only risk that is compensable because (unlike "unsystematic" risk) it cannot be "diversified away".

Unlevered Beta
An *unlevered beta* is the beta a company would have if it had no debt (i.e., financed only with equity capital). Also known as an "asset" beta.

Unsystematic Risk
Function of uncertainty of future returns due to the characteristics of the industry, the individual company, and the type of investment interest, and is unrelated to a variation of returns in the market as a whole. Within the framework of the CAPM and other cost of capital estimation models, unsystematic risk is not compensable because (unlike "systematic" risk) it can be "diversified away".

Valuation Date
The date on which the opinion of value applies. The valuation date shall also include the time at which it applies if the value of the type of asset can change materially in the course of a single day.

Weighted Average Cost of Capital (WACC)
A discount rate estimated by the weighted average, at market values, of the cost of all financing sources in a business enterprise's capital structure.

Yield
In terms of a bond, yield is the rate of return that equates future expected cash flows to the bond's market price.

Index

Appendix 1
Definitions of Standard and Poor's *Compustat* Data Items Used to Calculate the Risk Premium Report Exhibits[A.1]

Current Assets – Total: Data Item A4, Units: Millions of dollars

This item represents cash, and other assets which, in the next 12 months, are expected to be realized in cash or used in the production of revenue. This item is the sum of:

1. Cash and Short-Term Investments
2. Current Assets – Other
3. Inventories – Total
4. Receivables – Total

Current Liabilities – Total: Data Item A5, Units: Millions of dollars

This item represents liabilities due within one year, including the current portion of long-term debt. This item is the sum of:

1. Accounts Payable
2. Current Liabilities – Other
3. Debt in Current Liabilities
4. Income Taxes

Assets – Total: Data Item A6, Units: Millions of dollars

This item represents current assets plus net property, plant, and equipment plus other noncurrent assets (including intangible assets, deferred items and investments and advances). Total liabilities and stockholders' equity represents current liabilities plus long-term debt plus other long-term liabilities plus stockholders' equity.

Long-Term Debt – Total: Data Item A9, Units: Millions of dollars

The item represents debt obligations due more than one year from the company's balance sheet date.

This item includes

1. Purchase obligations and payments to officers (when listed as long-term liabilities)
2. Notes payable, due within one year and to be refunded by long-term debt when carried as a non-current liability
3. Long-term lease obligations (capitalized lease obligations)
4. Industrial revenue bonds
5. Advances to finance construction
6. Loans on insurance policies
7. Indebtedness to affiliates
8. Bonds, mortgages, and similar debt
9. All obligations that require interest payments
10. Publishing companies' royalty contracts payable
    1. Timber contracts for forestry and paper
    2. Extractive industries' advances for exploration and development
    3. Production payments and advances for exploration and development

This item excludes

1. Subsidiary preferred stock (included in Minority Interest)
2. The current portion of long-term debt (included in Current Liabilities)
3. Accounts payable due after one year (included in Liabilities – Other)

[A.1] Source: Standard & Poor's Research Insight *Compustat* North America Data Guide

4. Accrued interest on long-term debt (included in Liabilities – Other)

5. Customers' deposits on bottles, kegs and cases (included in Liabilities – Other)

6. Deferred compensation

Long-term debt should be reported net of premium or discount. Standard and Poor's *Compustat* will collect the net figure.

Sales (Net): Data Item A12, Units: Millions of dollars

This item represents gross sales (the amount of actual billings to customers for regular sales completed during the period) reduced by cash discounts, trade discounts, and returned sales and allowances for which credit is given to customers. This item is scaled in millions. For example the 1999 annual sales for GM is 173215.000 (or 173 billion, 215 million dollars).

This item includes

1. Any revenue source that is expected to continue for the life of the company
2. Other operating revenue
3. Installment sales
4. Franchise sales (when corresponding expenses are available) Special cases (by industry) include

Special cases (by industry) include

1. Royalty income when considered operating income (such as, oil companies, extractive industries, publishing companies, etc.)
2. Retail companies' sales of leased departments when corresponding costs are available and included in expenses (if costs are not available, the net figure is included in Nonoperating Income [Expense])
3. Shipping companies' operating differential subsidies and income on reserve fund securities when shown separately
1. Airline companies, net mutual aid assistance and federal subsidies
2. Cigar, cigarette, oil, rubber, and liquor companies' net sales are after deducting excise taxes
3. Income derived from equipment rental is considered part of operating revenue
4. Utilities' net sales are total current operating revenue
5. Advertising companies' net sales are commissions earned, not gross billings
6. Franchise operations' franchise and license fees
7. Hospitals' sales net of provision for contractual allowances (will sometimes include doubtful accounts)

This item excludes

1. Nonoperating income
2. Interest income (included in Nonoperating Income ([Expense])
3. Equity in earnings of unconsolidated subsidiaries (included in Nonoperating Income [Expense])
4. Other income (included in Nonoperating Income [Expense])
5. Rental income (included in Nonoperating Income [Expense])
6. Gain on sale of securities or fixed assets (included in Special Items)
7. Discontinued operations (included in Special Items)
8. Excise taxes (excluded from sales and also deducted from Cost of Goods Sold)
9. Royalty income (included in Nonoperating Income [Expense])

Operating Income Before Depreciation: Data Item A13, Units: Millions of dollars

This item represents Net Sales less Cost of Goods Sold and Selling, General, and Administrative Expenses before deducting Depreciation, Depletion and Amortization.This item includes the effects of adjustments for Cost of Goods Sold and Selling, General, and Administrative Expenses. A partial listing of items which comprise Cost of Goods Sold and Selling, General, And Administrative Expenses is as follows:

This item includes

1. Cost of Goods Sold
   - Rent and royalty expense
   - General taxes (other than income taxes)
   - Profit sharing contributions
   - Pension costs, including past service pension costs (except when written off in one year)
   - Motion picture and entertainment companies' amortization of film costs
1. Selling General, and Administrative Expense
   - Research and development expense
   - Strike expense
   - Bad debt expense (provisions for doubtful accounts)
   - Exploration expense
   - Parent company charges for administrative service

The following items, when separately listed, are treated as Nonoperating Income (Expense) rather than as operating expenses:

1. Moving expenses
2. Recurring foreign exchange adjustments
3. Idle plant expenses
4. Profit on sales of properties (except for securities, etc.) for the companies in the oil, coal, airline, and other industries where these transactions are considered a normal part of doing business

5. Amortization of negative intangibles

The current year's results of discontinued operations are not considered operating expenses and are shown as an extraordinary item.

Income Before Extraordinary Items: Data Item A18, Units: Millions of dollars

This item represents the income of a company after all expenses, including special items, income taxes, and minority interest – but before provisions for common and/or preferred dividends. This item does not reflect discontinued operations (appearing below taxes) or extraordinary items.

This item includes (when reported below taxes):

1. Amortization of intangibles
2. Equity in earnings of unconsolidated subsidiaries
3. Gain or loss on the sale of securities when they are a regular part of a company's operations
4. Shipping companies' operating differential subsidies (current and prior years)

Cash Dividends – Preferred: Data Item A19, Units: Millions of dollars

This item represents the total amount of the preferred dividend requirement on cumulative preferred stock and dividends paid on noncumulative preferred stock of the company during the year.

1. The amount of dividend requirements used by the company in calculating Available for Common
1. Preferred dividends of a merged company accounted for by the pooling of interest method are included for the year of the merger, unless the preferred stock was exchanged for common stock of the acquiring company (included in Cash Dividends – Common)

Utility companies' subsidiary preferred dividends are included

This item excludes

1. Preferred dividends deducted only for that portion of the year the stock was outstanding, if an entire issuance of convertible preferred stock is converted into common during the year
2. The dividends on the old preferred stock treated as common dividends, if common stock is issued by the company in exchanges for preferred stock of another company
3. Subsidiary preferred dividends (included in Minority Interest)

Price – Calendar Year – Close: Data Item A24, Units: Dollars and cents

This item represents the absolute close transactions during the year for companies on national stock exchanges and bid prices for over-the-counter issues. Prices are reported on a calendar-year basis. Prices are adjusted for all stock splits and stock dividends that occurred in the fiscal year, except for 06-11 fiscal year companies which have declared stock splits and stock dividends between the end of their fiscal year and the end of the calendar year. In those instances, that stated prices are not adjusted. When a 01-05 fiscal year company has a stock split or a stock dividend after the calendar yearend but before the fiscal year-end, prices will be adjusted. If a company suspends trading, the close price of the stock will be presented as of the last trading day.

Common Shares Outstanding – Company: Data Item A25, Units: Millions

This item represents the net number of all common shares outstanding at yearend, excluding treasury shares and scrip.

Common treasury shares carried on the asset side of the balance sheet are netted against the number of common shares issued.

Common shares paid in stock dividends are included when the ex-dividend date falls within the year and the payment date the next year.

Common shares will be excluded when a company nets shares held by a consolidated subsidiary against the capital account.

Employees: Data Item A29, Units: Thousands

This item represents the number of company workers as reported to shareholders. This is reported by some firms as an average number of employees and by some as the number of employees at year-end. No attempt has been made to differentiate between these bases of reporting. If both are given, the year-end figure is used.

This item, for banks always represents the number of year-end employees.

This item includes:

1. All part-time and seasonal employees
2. All employees of consolidated subsidiaries, both domestic and foreign

This item excludes:

1. Contract workers
2. Consultants
3. Employees of unconsolidated subsidiaries

Debt Due in 1st Year: Data Item A44, Units: Millions of dollars

This item represents the current portion of long-term debt (included in Current Liabilities).

This item includes

1. The installments son a loan
2. The sinking fund payments
3. The current portion of any item defined as long-term debt (for example, the current portion of a long-term lease obligation)

Common Equity – Total: Data Item A60, Units: Millions of dollars
This item represents the common shareholders' interest in the company.
This item includes

1. Common stock outstanding (including treasury stock adjustments)
2. Capital surplus
3. Retained earnings
4. Treasury stock adjustments for both common and non-redeemable preferred tock

This figure is not adjusted for excess liquidating value over carrying value of preferred stock or for intangibles.

Nonoperating Income (Expense): Data Item A61, Units: Millions of dollars
This item represents any income or expense items resulting from secondary business-related activities, excluding those considered part of the normal operations of the business. Nonoperating income and expense will be reported as a net figure with nonoperating income treated as a positive number and nonoperating expense treated as a negative number.
This item includes

1. Income
    - Discount on debt reacquired
    - Dividend income
    - Equity in earnings of a nonconsolidated subsidiary
    - Franchise income when corresponding expenses are not included in the Income Statement
    - Interest charged to construction (interest capitalized)
    - Leased department income when corresponding expenses are not included in the Income Statement
    - Other income, Rental income, Royalty income, Interest income
2. Expense
    - Amortization of deferred credit
    - Amortization of negative intangibles
    - Foreign exchange adjustments
    - Idle plant expense
    - Miscellaneous expense
    - Moving expense
    - Other expense

Preferred Stock: Data Item A130, Units: Millions of dollars
This item represents the net number of preferred shares at year-end multiplied by the par or stated value per share as presented in the company's Balance Sheet.
This item includes

1. Preferred stock subscriptions
2. Utilities subsidiary preferred stock
3. Redeemable preferred stock
    1. Preference stock
    2. Receivables on preferred stock

This item excludes

1. Preferred stock sinking funds reported in current liabilities
2. Secondary classes of common stock
3. Subsidiary preferred stock

This item is reduced by the effects of

1. Par or carrying value of nonredeemable preferred treasury stock which was nettled against this item prior to annual and quarterly fiscal periods of 1982 and 1986, 1st quarter, respectively
2. Cost of redeemable preferred treasury stock which is netted against Preferred Stock – Redeemable

Operating Income After Depreciation: Data Item A178, Units: Millions of dollars
This item represents the operating income of a company after deducting expenses for cost of goods sold, selling, general, and administrative expenses, and depreciation.

Liabilities – Total: Data Item A181, Units: Millions of dollars
This item represents the sum of:

1. Current Liabilities – Total
2. Deferred Taxes and Investment Tax Credit (Balance Sheet)
3. Liabilities – Other
4. Long-Term Debt – Total
5. Minority Interest (Balance Sheet)

Notes Payable: Data Item A206, Units: Millions of dollars

This item represents the total amount of short-term notes.

This item includes

1. Bank acceptances
2. Bank overdrafts
3. Loans payable to officers of the company
4. Loans payable to parents, and consolidated and unconsolidated subsidiaries
    1. Loans payable to stockholders
    2. Notes payable – banks, others
    3. Telephone companies' interim notes payable and advances from parent company
    4. Commercial paper

This item excludes

1. Current portion of long-term notes payable (included in Debt Due in One Year)
2. Due to factor (included in Current Liabilities – Other) This item is not available for utilities.

Appendix 2
Changes to the Risk Premium Report Over Time

Now in its 19th year of publication, the Risk Premium Report Study continues to be at the forefront in providing comprehensive valuation methodology and data.

The most significant recent change to the Risk Premium Report Study is its incorporation into the *Valuation Handbook – Guide to Cost of Capital* in 2014, along with the CRSP Deciles Size Premia Study. The CRSP Deciles Size Premia Study is the valuation data previously published in the (now discontinued) Morningstar/Ibbotson *SBBI Valuation Yearbook* from 1999–2013. The Risk Premium Report Study, previously published as the Duff & Phelps Risk Premium Report, will no longer be published as a stand-alone publication. Both the Risk Premium Report Study data set and CRSP Deciles Size Premia Study data set (the former SBBI data) now published in the *Valuation Handbook* by Wiley & Sons.

The development of the online *Risk Premium Toolkit* by Business Valuation Resources (BVR) in 2011 (originally introduced as the "*Risk Premium Calculator*" in 2011; renamed the "*Risk Premium Toolkit*" in 2015) remains an important milestone. The online *Risk Premium Toolkit* is a web-based application that makes using the *Valuation Handbook's* Risk Premium Report Study data and CRSP Deciles Size Premia Data even easier.[A.1] The Risk Premium Toolkit instantly delivers a fully customizable "Executive Summary" in Microsoft Word format that includes sourcing, key inputs, and a concluded range of cost of equity capital estimates using both the buildup and CAPM methods. In addition, a detailed record of all inputs, outputs, and calculations is exported to a "Support and Detail" Microsoft Excel workbook.[A.2]

ValuSource has also developed an online companion application to the *Valuation Handbook – Guide to Cost of Capital*, the online "*Cost of Capital Analyzer*". The *Cost of Capital Analyzer* is also designed to help the valuation analyst use the *2015 Valuation Handbook's* data as efficiently as possible. Both the CRSP Deciles Size Premia Studies and the Risk Premium Report Studies data are included in the *Cost of Capital Analyzer*. The *Cost of Capital Analyzer* can be used by Excel users and will download directly in ValuSource valuation software, including *ValuSource Pro*, *Business Valuation Manager Pro* and *Express Business Valuation*.[A.3]

Readers may be interested in the difference between the data presented herein and analogous data published in articles that appeared in1996 and 1997 (cited above), a 1995 article ("The Size Effect and Equity Returns", *Business Valuation Review*, June 1995), as well as annual updates previously published on the Morningstar (formerly Ibbotson Associates) website from 1998–2012. These changes over time are summarized in the following sections.

Changes from Previously Published Versions of the Risk Premium Report's Size Study

- The 1995 article reported 30-year historical averages. We currently report averages since 1963.
- The 1995 article looked only at the market value of equity as a measure of size. We currently look at eight alternate measures of size.
- The current report includes Total Assets as one of the measures of size. This replaces a Book Value of Invested Capital measure that appeared in the 1996 and 1997 articles.
- The current report excludes newly listed companies, places many companies into a separate high-financial-risk database, includes AMEX and NASDAQ companies, and includes only companies covered by *Compustat*. The 1995 article used all operating NYSE companies found in the CRSP database.
- The 1995 article used market-weighted averaging to calculate the portfolio rates of return. The current report uses equal-weighted averaging.
- The 1995 article used natural logarithms, while the current report uses base-10 logarithms. This makes no difference in the calculation of the "smoothed" premiums, but we have found that base-10 logs are easier to explain than natural logs.

A.1 The CRSP Deciles Size Premia Study data was added to the online Risk Premium Toolkit in mid-2014.

A.2 The online "Risk Premium Toolkit" is available from BVR at www.BVResources.com/DuffPhelps or by calling 1 (503) 291-7963 ext 2. The "Cost of Capital Analyzer" is available from ValuSource at www.valusource.com/vhb or by calling 1 (800) 825-8763.

- The 1995 and 1996 articles included financial companies. The current report excludes financial companies (though in our currently published versions of prior years' reports we exclude financial companies).

- The current report corrects for possible "delisting bias" in the CRSP database. The 1995, 1996, and 1997 articles did not make this adjustment (though in our currently published versions of prior years' reports we include this correction).

- The current report includes tables showing "Premiums over CAPM". Versions of this study before 2000 did not include these tables (though our currently published versions of prior years' reports include these data).

- Certain revisions in methodology (made for technical reasons) expanded the number of companies categorized as high-financial -risk relative to versions published before 2000 (though our currently published versions of prior years' reports incorporate this changed methodology).

- The current report changes the method of using financial data such that no data is considered for fiscal years ending less than three months before the formation of portfolios. Versions of this study prior to 2001 allowed use of financial data through the previous month end (though our currently published versions of prior years' reports incorporate this changed methodology).

- The current report uses the "sum beta" method applied to monthly returns to estimate portfolio betas. Versions before 2003 estimated betas using ordinary least squares with annual data (though our currently published versions of prior years' reports incorporate the "sum beta" methodology).

- The current report includes un-levered average risk premiums and sum betas for each portfolio. Versions of this study prior to 2005 as originally published did not include this data (though our currently published versions of prior years' reports include these data). The Reports through 2007 used an un-levering formula commonly referred to as the Hamada formula. The current report uses the un-levering formula commonly referred to as the Harris-Pringle formula. See Chapter 12 in *Cost of Capital: Applications and Examples* 5th ed. by Shannon Pratt and Roger Grabowski, Wiley (April, 2014). In the current report the methodology and assumptions for un-levering risk premiums reported in Exhibits C-1 through C-8 were updated. Exhibits C-1 through C-8 for the prior report (2010) were also updated using the updated un-levering methodology.

- The current report incorporates various corrections and other changes that have affected the CRSP and *Compustat* databases since the data in the earlier articles was generated. We now use CRSP as the source for all stock prices and number of shares outstanding.

- The current report is the result of a complete reprogramming of the software used in the analyses and may result in differences from prior versions.

- The current report includes information about the size of the companies that comprise Portfolio 25 by percentile (5th, 25th, 50th, 75th, and 95th percentiles) for each of the eight size measures. In the 2013 Report, we started reporting the *smallest* and *largest* companies' size characteristics as well.

- The current report the methodology and assumptions for un-levering risk premiums reported in Exhibits C-1 through C-8 were updated. Exhibits C-1 through C-8 for the prior report (2010) were also updated using the updated un-levering methodology.

- In the 2013 Report, an expanded section about using the Report to value small companies was added. This new section provides a listing of the smallest and largest companies in "Portfolio 25" (Portfolio 25 is comprised of the smallest companies) for each of the eight size measures (see Table 2 on page 22). This was added to give the valuation analyst greater capability to gauge the size characteristics of his or her subject company relative to the size characteristics of companies that comprise Portfolio 25, and also provides support for adjustments to premia made by utilizing the "regression equation method" to estimate custom "interpolated" risk premia or size premia.

Changes from Previously Published Versions of the Risk Study

- Versions of our study published after 1999 have included the three separate measures of risk described in Part II of this report and presented in Exhibits C-1 through C-8 and Exhibits D-1 through D-3 (our currently published versions of prior years' reports include these data).

- Various changes in methodology over the last several years have affected the underlying database, and these are summarized at the end of Part I.

- In the current version of Exhibits D-1 through D-3, we report averages of the sorting criteria for the most recent year, while versions before 2003 reported the average of the averages for all years since 1963 (though our currently published versions of prior years' reports incorporate this change).

- The current report incorporates various corrections and other changes that have affected the CRSP and Compustat databases since the data in the earlier articles was generated. We now use CRSP as the source for all stock prices and number of shares outstanding.
- The current report is the result of a complete reprogramming of the software used in the analyses and may result in differences from prior versions.

- The current report the methodology and assumptions for unlevering risk premiums reported in Exhibits C-1 through C-8 were updated; these updated methodologies were used to add average unlevered risk premia over the risk-free rate to the D exhibits.

Changes from Previously Published Versions of the High-Financial-Risk Study

- In reports before 2008 we presented data on the high-financial-risk companies as a single portfolio.

- We first published the data on high-financial-risk companies ranked by z-Score as a Supplemental Report to the Risk Premium Report 2009. We also published characteristics of the companies comprising the high-financial-risk portfolios.

- This is the first time we are publishing data for high-financial-risk service industry companies separated from all other high-financial- risk companies. We also exclude from the averages and the returns for any years in which the portfolio of high-financial-risk companies is fewer than 6 companies.

- In the current report's H exhibits, "safe zone" statistics are not reported. "Safe zone" companies are companies which were classified as "high-financial-risk" in an initial screen, but were not classified as "high-financial-risk" in the second (z-Score) screen. These companies are set aside and not considered in any further analysis due to the inconclusive testing. In the current report "Gray zone " and "distressed zone" statistics are reported; in previous reports "safe zone", "gray zone", and "distressed zone" were reported.

Appendix 3
CRSP Deciles Size Premia Study: Key Variables

Appendix 3 includes the "key variables in estimating the cost of capital" that were previously published in the *Ibbotson Stocks, Bonds, Bills and Inflation (SBBI) Valuation Yearbook*.[A3.1]

The equity risk premium, size premium, and other valuation data reported in Appendix 3 of the *2015 Valuation Handbook*:

- Was calculated using the same data sources that were used to calculate the equity risk premium, size premium, and other valuation data previously published in the former *SBBI Valuation Yearbook*, and

- Was calculated using the same methodology that was used to calculate the equity risk premium, size premium, and other valuation data previously published in the former *SBBI Valuation Yearbook*.

For detailed examples of using the equity risk premium, size premium, and other valuation data reported in Appendix 3 to estimate cost of equity capital using the capital asset pricing model (CAPM) and the build-up method, see Chapter 8, "CRSP Deciles Size Premia Examples".

[A3.1] The *Ibbotson SBBI Valuation Yearbook* was previously published by Morningstar, Inc. (Chicago). The *SBBI Valuation Yearbook* was discontinued in 2013.

CRSP Deciles Size Premia Study: Key Variables

Yield (Risk-free Rate)[1]

Long-term (20-year) U.S. Treasury Coupon Bond Yield	2.40%

Equity Risk Premium[2]

Long-horizon expected equity risk premium (historical): large company stock total returns minus long-term government bond income returns	7.00
Long-horizon expected equity risk premium (supply-side): historical equity risk premium minus price-to-earnings ratio calculated using three-year average earnings	6.21
Duff & Phelps recommended equity risk premium (conditional): The Duff & Phelps recommended ERP was developed in relation to (and should be used in conjunction with) a 4.0% "normalized" risk-free rate.[3]	5.00

CRSP Deciles Size Premium[4]

Decile	Market Capitalization of Smallest Company (in millions)		Market Capitalization of Largest Company (in millions)	Size Premium (Return in Excess of CAPM)
Mid-Cap 3-5	$2,552.441	–	$10,105.622	1.07%
Low-Cap 6-8	549.056	–	2,542.913	1.80
Micro-Cap 9-10	3.037	–	548.839	3.74
Breakdown of CRSP Deciles 1-10				
1-Largest	$24,428.848	–	$591,015.721	-0.36%
2	10,170.746	–	24,272.837	0.63
3	5,864.266	–	10,105.622	0.91
4	3,724.624	–	5,844.592	1.06
5	2,552.441	–	3,724.186	1.60
6	1,688.895	–	2,542.913	1.74
7	1,011.278	–	1,686.860	1.71
8	549.056	–	1,010.634	2.15
9	300.752	–	548.839	2.69
10-Smallest	3.037	–	300.725	5.78
Breakdown of CRSP 10th Decile				
10a	$190.860	–	$300.725	4.22%
10w	231.975	–	300.725	3.18
10x	190.860	–	231.840	5.54
10b	$3.037	–	$190.529	8.94%
10y	116.330	–	190.529	7.51
10z	3.037	–	115.920	11.98

[1] As of December 31, 2014.

[2] See Chapter 3 for complete methodology.

[3] See Exhibit 3.15.

[4] See Chapter 7 for complete methodology.

Note: Examples on how these variables can be used are found in Chapter 8.

Sources of underlying data: 1.) CRSP U.S. Stock Database and CRSP U.S. Indices Database Calculations performed by Duff & Phelps LLC.

Appendix 4
Risk Premium Report Study Exhibits

The Risk Premium Report exhibits include the Size Study, the Risk Study, the High-Financial-Risk Study, and the Comparative Risk Study.

- **Size Study:** Comprised of Exhibits A-1 through A-8 (used in the build-up method) and Exhibits B-1 through B-8 (used in CAPM). Analyzes the relationship between equity returns and company size, using eight measures of company size.

- **Risk Study:** Comprised of Exhibits D-1, D-2, and D-3 (fundamental measures of risk based on accounting data). Analyzes the relationship between equity returns and three accounting-based fundamental risk measures.

- **High-Financial-Risk Study:** Comprised of Exhibits H-A, H-B, and H-C. Exhibit H-A is the high-financial-risk equivalent to the A exhibits, Exhibit H-B is the high-financial-risk equivalent to the B exhibits, and Exhibit H-C is the high-financial-risk equivalent to the C exhibits. Analyzes the relationship between equity returns and high-financial-risk, as measured by the Altman z-Score.

- **Comparative Risk Study:** Comprised of the C exhibits, when used in conjunction with the D exhibits. The C Exhibits can help valuation analysts further refine their cost of equity capital estimates by comparing their subject company's fundamental risk factors to the fundamental risk factors of the companies that comprise the 25 Size Study portfolios.

For detailed examples of using the valuation data reported in Appendix 4 to estimate cost of equity capital using the capital asset pricing model (CAPM) and various build-up methods, see Chapter 9, "Risk Premium Report Exhibits – General Information" and Chapter10, "Risk Premium Report Exhibits – Examples".

Risk Premium Report – Exhibits A-1 through A-8 Premia Over the Risk-Free Rate (RP_{m+s})

Risk premia over the risk-free rate reflect risk in terms of the combined effect of *market* risk and size risk in excess of the risk-free rate. These premia are added to the risk-free rate, within the context of the build-up method. An ERP Adjustment is required when using the A exhibits.

The A Exhibits are used in the following method to estimate a cost of equity capital:

- Build-up 1

Size Measures:

A-1: Market value of equity

A-2: Book value of equity

A-3: 5-year average net income

A-4: Market value of invested capital (MVIC)

A-5: Total assets

A-6: 5-year average EBITDA

A-7: Sales

A-8: Number of employees

Companies Ranked by Market Value of Equity | **Premia Over the Risk-Free Rate (RP_{m+s})** | **Exhibit A-1**

Historical Equity Risk Premium: Average Since 1963

Data for Year Ending December 31, 2014

Portfolio Rank by Size	Average Mkt. Value (in $millions)	Log of Average Mkt. Value	Number as of 2014	Beta (Sum Beta) Since '63	Standard Deviation of Returns	Geometric Average Return	Arithmetic Average Return	Arithmetic Average Risk Premium	*Smoothed Average Risk Premium*	Average Debt/ MVIC
1	178,744	5.25	39	0.83	16.01%	10.90%	12.13%	5.52%	*3.22%*	14.12%
2	53,009	4.72	36	0.96	16.87%	9.77%	11.15%	4.54%	*5.02%*	19.00%
3	32,537	4.51	29	0.92	15.58%	10.43%	11.66%	5.04%	*5.75%*	20.61%
4	24,601	4.39	28	0.94	16.45%	11.55%	12.86%	6.25%	*6.16%*	22.57%
5	17,777	4.25	33	0.99	16.97%	10.98%	12.37%	5.76%	*6.64%*	23.16%
6	13,745	4.14	33	1.02	17.43%	11.38%	12.89%	6.27%	*7.02%*	22.54%
7	11,640	4.07	36	1.01	18.36%	11.98%	13.55%	6.94%	*7.27%*	23.43%
8	9,409	3.97	40	1.06	19.02%	12.95%	14.64%	8.03%	*7.59%*	22.15%
9	7,894	3.90	34	1.10	18.35%	13.98%	15.55%	8.94%	*7.85%*	22.62%
10	6,698	3.83	34	1.11	19.51%	13.51%	15.29%	8.68%	*8.09%*	22.81%
11	5,692	3.76	32	1.10	19.93%	12.89%	14.75%	8.14%	*8.33%*	22.78%
12	4,950	3.69	34	1.11	19.51%	12.20%	14.02%	7.40%	*8.54%*	22.87%
13	4,383	3.64	36	1.12	19.16%	13.23%	14.93%	8.32%	*8.72%*	23.31%
14	3,880	3.59	35	1.15	19.98%	13.35%	15.26%	8.65%	*8.90%*	23.20%
15	3,358	3.53	39	1.14	20.35%	15.45%	17.38%	10.77%	*9.12%*	23.26%
16	2,785	3.44	46	1.16	20.45%	14.72%	16.64%	10.02%	*9.39%*	23.67%
17	2,323	3.37	47	1.19	21.94%	13.70%	15.89%	9.28%	*9.66%*	22.35%
18	1,954	3.29	54	1.22	20.51%	13.06%	15.11%	8.49%	*9.92%*	23.32%
19	1,651	3.22	61	1.21	22.56%	14.44%	16.76%	10.15%	*10.17%*	23.33%
20	1,324	3.12	55	1.21	22.46%	13.85%	16.15%	9.53%	*10.50%*	24.07%
21	1,084	3.03	67	1.25	22.71%	14.62%	16.96%	10.35%	*10.79%*	23.97%
22	868	2.94	82	1.23	23.73%	14.92%	17.48%	10.87%	*11.12%*	24.64%
23	639	2.81	59	1.26	23.23%	14.66%	17.05%	10.43%	*11.58%*	24.06%
24	412	2.62	88	1.24	24.96%	16.72%	19.45%	12.84%	*12.23%*	24.78%
25	132	2.12	267	1.28	29.92%	19.09%	22.92%	16.31%	*13.92%*	27.48%
Large Stocks (Ibbotson SBBI data)						10.27%	11.66%	5.05%		
Small Stocks (Ibbotson SBBI data)						13.77%	16.47%	9.86%		
Long-Term Treasury Income (Ibbotson SBBI data)						6.58%	6.61%			

Equity Risk Premium Study: Data through December 31, 2014

Data Smoothing with Regression Analysis

Dependent Variable: Arithmetic Average Risk Premium

Independent Variable: Log of Average Market Value of Equity

Regression Output:	
Constant	21.167%
Standard Error of Y Estimate	1.035%
R Squared	85%
No. of Observations	25
Degrees of Freedom	23
X Coefficient(s)	-3.418%
Standard Error of Coefficient	0.302%
t-Statistic	-11.32

*Smoothed Premium = 21.167% - 3.418% * Log(Market Value)*

Smoothed Premium vs. Arithmetic Premium

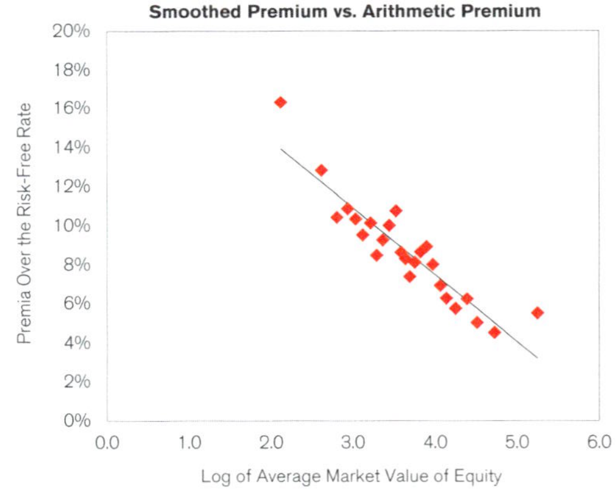

Sources of underlying data: 1.) Calculations performed by Duff & Phelps LLC.

Historical Equity Risk Premium: Average Since 1963
Data for Year Ending December 31, 2014

Portfolio Rank by Size	Average Book Val. (in $millions)	Log of Average Book Val.	Number as of 2014	Beta (Sum Beta) Since '63	Standard Deviation of Returns	Geometric Average Return	Arithmetic Average Return	Arithmetic Average Risk Premium	*Smoothed Average Risk Premium*	Average Debt/ MVIC
1	55,457	4.74	35	0.81	15.54%	10.97%	12.37%	5.76%	*5.04%*	23.36%
2	18,036	4.26	29	0.87	16.26%	10.94%	12.41%	5.80%	*6.27%*	27.49%
3	11,882	4.07	32	0.90	16.17%	11.97%	13.48%	6.87%	*6.73%*	28.44%
4	7,797	3.89	33	0.92	16.71%	11.95%	13.49%	6.87%	*7.20%*	28.09%
5	5,773	3.76	31	1.03	18.21%	11.69%	13.55%	6.94%	*7.53%*	26.19%
6	4,551	3.66	32	1.01	17.93%	12.06%	13.83%	7.22%	*7.79%*	26.19%
7	3,798	3.58	34	1.05	19.69%	12.27%	14.34%	7.73%	*7.99%*	24.81%
8	3,217	3.51	31	1.08	18.88%	12.49%	14.42%	7.81%	*8.18%*	24.66%
9	2,695	3.43	36	1.12	20.24%	12.30%	14.50%	7.89%	*8.37%*	24.65%
10	2,271	3.36	36	1.07	18.74%	13.05%	14.91%	8.30%	*8.56%*	25.47%
11	1,932	3.29	36	1.09	19.81%	13.20%	15.32%	8.71%	*8.74%*	25.86%
12	1,665	3.22	35	1.08	20.13%	14.53%	16.65%	10.03%	*8.90%*	25.38%
13	1,463	3.17	31	1.12	20.81%	13.84%	16.17%	9.55%	*9.04%*	24.62%
14	1,305	3.12	37	1.14	20.90%	12.80%	15.01%	8.40%	*9.17%*	23.64%
15	1,172	3.07	36	1.11	20.38%	14.58%	16.78%	10.16%	*9.29%*	23.61%
16	1,055	3.02	47	1.23	26.05%	15.24%	18.41%	11.80%	*9.41%*	23.79%
17	913	2.96	39	1.19	22.23%	13.87%	16.41%	9.80%	*9.56%*	22.90%
18	794	2.90	47	1.19	21.41%	14.25%	16.64%	10.03%	*9.72%*	23.17%
19	664	2.82	66	1.24	21.33%	12.72%	15.13%	8.52%	*9.92%*	23.20%
20	534	2.73	71	1.21	21.54%	13.73%	16.14%	9.53%	*10.16%*	22.64%
21	440	2.64	54	1.21	20.82%	14.93%	17.23%	10.62%	*10.37%*	23.03%
22	338	2.53	80	1.24	22.83%	14.29%	17.03%	10.42%	*10.66%*	23.02%
23	264	2.42	77	1.25	23.05%	14.69%	17.39%	10.77%	*10.94%*	23.17%
24	185	2.27	108	1.27	24.72%	15.00%	18.14%	11.53%	*11.32%*	22.66%
25	65	1.81	251	1.26	25.67%	15.55%	18.89%	12.28%	*12.49%*	23.27%
Large Stocks (Ibbotson SBBI data)						10.27%	11.66%	5.05%		
Small Stocks (Ibbotson SBBI data)						13.77%	16.47%	9.86%		
Long-Term Treasury Income (Ibbotson SBBI data)						6.58%	6.61%			

Equity Risk Premium Study: Data through December 31, 2014
Data Smoothing with Regression Analysis
Dependent Variable: Arithmetic Average Risk Premium
Independent Variable: Log of Average Book Value of Equity

Regression Output:	
Constant	17.084%
Standard Error of Y Estimate	0.763%
R Squared	83%
No. of Observations	25
Degrees of Freedom	23
X Coefficient(s)	-2.540%
Standard Error of Coefficient	0.238%
t-Statistic	-10.69

*Smoothed Premium = 17.084% - 2.540% * Log(Book Value)*

Smoothed Premium vs. Arithmetic Premium

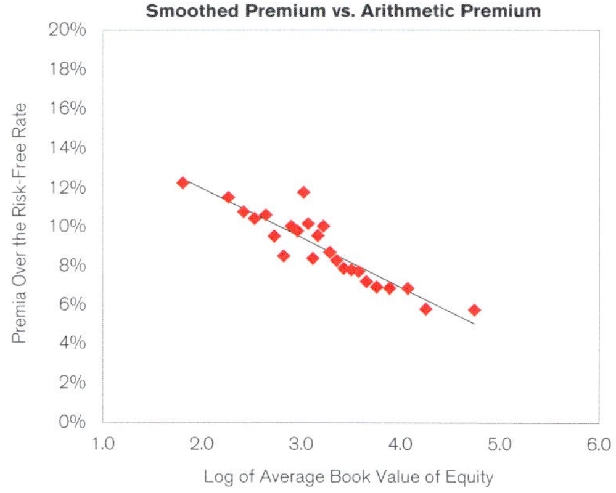

Sources of underlying data: 1.) © 201502 CRSP®, Center for Research in Security Prices. University of Chicago Booth School of Business used with permission. All rights reserved. 2.) Morningstar *Direct* database. Used with permission. All rights reserved. Calculations performed by Duff & Phelps LLC.

Companies Ranked by 5-Year Average Net Income | **Premia Over the Risk-Free Rate (RP_{m+s})** | **Exhibit A-3**

Historical Equity Risk Premium: Average Since 1963

Data for Year Ending December 31, 2014

Portfolio Rank by Size	Average Net Inc. (in $millions)	Log of Average Net Inc.	Number as of 2014	Beta (Sum Beta) Since '63	Standard Deviation of Returns	Geometric Average Return	Arithmetic Average Return	Arithmetic Average Risk Premium	*Smoothed Average Risk Premium*	Average Debt/ MVIC
1	8,922	3.95	35	0.77	15.92%	12.11%	13.32%	6.71%	*4.51%*	20.08%
2	2,422	3.38	32	0.87	15.57%	11.20%	12.35%	5.74%	*6.01%*	24.43%
3	1,540	3.19	29	0.87	15.82%	12.58%	13.75%	7.14%	*6.53%*	26.21%
4	1,066	3.03	29	0.90	15.95%	12.21%	13.42%	6.81%	*6.95%*	26.56%
5	760	2.88	36	0.95	16.95%	11.71%	13.08%	6.47%	*7.34%*	26.07%
6	566	2.75	35	0.99	18.16%	11.93%	13.42%	6.81%	*7.68%*	24.25%
7	441	2.64	34	1.05	18.02%	12.16%	13.72%	7.11%	*7.96%*	24.55%
8	354	2.55	31	1.09	18.94%	13.05%	14.73%	8.12%	*8.21%*	24.11%
9	297	2.47	33	1.04	17.51%	12.36%	13.83%	7.22%	*8.42%*	23.70%
10	255	2.41	32	1.06	18.17%	13.50%	15.02%	8.41%	*8.59%*	23.90%
11	218	2.34	40	1.08	19.43%	13.74%	15.48%	8.86%	*8.77%*	23.62%
12	182	2.26	33	1.08	19.92%	14.33%	16.18%	9.57%	*8.98%*	24.14%
13	159	2.20	33	1.06	18.80%	14.72%	16.35%	9.74%	*9.13%*	23.57%
14	136	2.13	35	1.16	20.25%	12.81%	14.77%	8.16%	*9.31%*	23.96%
15	122	2.09	38	1.12	21.75%	13.49%	15.64%	9.03%	*9.44%*	23.52%
16	106	2.02	39	1.12	20.10%	14.92%	16.80%	10.19%	*9.60%*	22.86%
17	90	1.95	47	1.20	21.30%	13.78%	15.89%	9.28%	*9.79%*	22.73%
18	76	1.88	46	1.21	20.75%	15.24%	17.25%	10.64%	*9.98%*	22.75%
19	58	1.77	75	1.25	22.05%	13.78%	16.07%	9.45%	*10.29%*	23.25%
20	44	1.65	56	1.23	22.10%	16.12%	18.33%	11.72%	*10.60%*	23.82%
21	35	1.54	68	1.22	22.05%	15.12%	17.32%	10.70%	*10.89%*	24.51%
22	25	1.40	76	1.22	23.32%	14.53%	17.07%	10.46%	*11.24%*	23.82%
23	18	1.27	86	1.26	24.62%	16.31%	18.91%	12.30%	*11.61%*	22.84%
24	11	1.05	126	1.25	24.78%	15.97%	18.68%	12.07%	*12.19%*	23.76%
25	3	0.54	220	1.32	29.02%	17.68%	21.43%	14.82%	*13.53%*	24.99%
Large Stocks (Ibbotson SBBI data)						10.27%	11.66%	5.05%		
Small Stocks (Ibbotson SBBI data)						13.77%	16.47%	9.86%		
Long-Term Treasury Income (Ibbotson SBBI data)						6.58%	6.61%			

Equity Risk Premium Study: Data through December 31, 2014

Data Smoothing with Regression Analysis

Dependent Variable: Arithmetic Average Risk Premium

Independent Variable: Log of Average Net Income

Regression Output:	
Constant	14.953%
Standard Error of Y Estimate	0.859%
R Squared	85%
No. of Observations	25
Degrees of Freedom	23
X Coefficient(s)	-2.644%
Standard Error of Coefficient	0.229%
t-Statistic	-11.56

*Smoothed Premium = 14.953% - 2.644% * Log(Net Income)*

Smoothed Premium vs. Arithmetic Premium

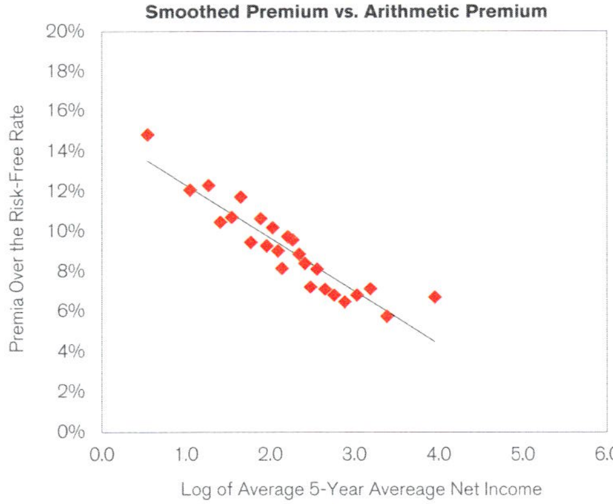

Companies Ranked by Market Value of Invested Capital | **Premia Over the Risk-Free Rate (RP_{m+s})** | **Exhibit A-4**

Historical Equity Risk Premium: Average Since 1963

Data for Year Ending December 31, 2014

Portfolio Rank by Size	Average MVIC (in $millions)	Log of Average MVIC	Number as of 2014	Beta (Sum Beta) Since '63	Standard Deviation of Returns	Geometric Average Return	Arithmetic Average Return	Arithmetic Average Risk Premium	*Smoothed Average Risk Premium*	Average Debt/ MVIC
1	210,749	5.32	39	0.80	15.90%	10.89%	12.10%	5.49%	*3.55%*	18.79%
2	66,082	4.82	33	0.87	15.72%	10.20%	11.41%	4.80%	*5.20%*	25.22%
3	41,570	4.62	29	0.90	15.81%	10.49%	11.72%	5.11%	*5.86%*	26.83%
4	31,430	4.50	29	0.94	17.12%	11.20%	12.62%	6.01%	*6.26%*	26.76%
5	24,299	4.39	30	0.98	16.18%	11.73%	12.99%	6.37%	*6.63%*	26.10%
6	18,313	4.26	32	1.01	16.47%	11.30%	12.65%	6.03%	*7.03%*	25.98%
7	14,818	4.17	32	0.99	17.71%	12.83%	14.26%	7.65%	*7.33%*	23.89%
8	12,250	4.09	41	1.05	19.53%	12.35%	14.14%	7.53%	*7.61%*	24.02%
9	10,109	4.00	37	1.10	19.01%	12.59%	14.32%	7.71%	*7.88%*	24.53%
10	8,722	3.94	35	1.11	19.44%	13.82%	15.57%	8.96%	*8.09%*	24.10%
11	7,509	3.88	31	1.11	19.20%	13.31%	15.09%	8.48%	*8.30%*	25.25%
12	6,429	3.81	35	1.06	19.16%	13.53%	15.21%	8.59%	*8.52%*	24.85%
13	5,617	3.75	31	1.15	19.48%	13.13%	14.90%	8.29%	*8.72%*	25.03%
14	4,848	3.69	36	1.18	21.03%	13.36%	15.45%	8.84%	*8.93%*	23.68%
15	4,248	3.63	38	1.17	21.60%	13.61%	15.77%	9.16%	*9.12%*	24.24%
16	3,558	3.55	46	1.19	21.34%	14.90%	17.01%	10.40%	*9.37%*	23.28%
17	3,005	3.48	42	1.23	21.96%	14.29%	16.56%	9.95%	*9.61%*	24.01%
18	2,551	3.41	51	1.17	20.84%	15.22%	17.21%	10.60%	*9.84%*	23.58%
19	2,059	3.31	63	1.21	22.14%	12.70%	14.96%	8.34%	*10.15%*	23.85%
20	1,678	3.22	60	1.25	21.88%	13.88%	16.11%	9.50%	*10.44%*	25.01%
21	1,335	3.13	63	1.27	23.23%	13.93%	16.40%	9.78%	*10.77%*	24.32%
22	1,060	3.03	82	1.24	22.07%	14.99%	17.18%	10.57%	*11.09%*	24.17%
23	813	2.91	63	1.26	24.98%	15.92%	18.69%	12.07%	*11.47%*	23.73%
24	526	2.72	94	1.24	24.78%	15.71%	18.40%	11.78%	*12.09%*	24.33%
25	157	2.20	272	1.27	28.94%	18.66%	22.28%	15.67%	*13.81%*	22.60%
Large Stocks (Ibbotson SBBI data)						10.27%	11.66%	5.05%		
Small Stocks (Ibbotson SBBI data)						13.77%	16.47%	9.86%		
Long-Term Treasury Income (Ibbotson SBBI data)						6.58%	6.61%			

Equity Risk Premium Study: Data through December 31, 2014

Data Smoothing with Regression Analysis

Dependent Variable: Arithmetic Average Risk Premium

Independent Variable: Log of Average MVIC

Regression Output:

Constant	21.024%
Standard Error of Y Estimate	0.878%
R Squared	88%
No. of Observations	25
Degrees of Freedom	23
X Coefficient(s)	-3.282%
Standard Error of Coefficient	0.255%
t-Statistic	-12.85

*Smoothed Premium = 21.024% - 3.282% * Log(MVIC)*

Smoothed Premium vs. Arithmetic Premium

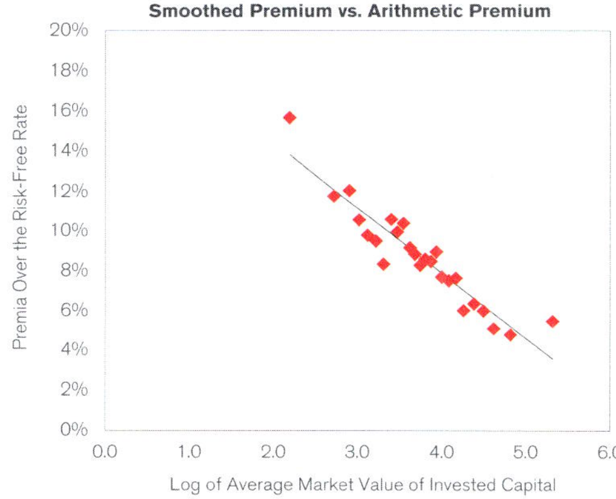

Sources of underlying data: 1.) © 201502 CRSP®, Center for Research in Security Prices. University of Chicago Booth School of Business used with permission. 2.) Morningstar *Direct* database. Used with permission. Calculations performed by Duff & Phelps LLC.

Companies Ranked by Total Assets **Premia Over the Risk-Free Rate (RP_{m+s})** **Exhibit A-5**

Historical Equity Risk Premium: Average Since 1963
Data for Year Ending December 31, 2014

Portfolio Rank by Size	Average Total Assets (in $millions)	Log of Average Assets	Number as of 2014	Beta (Sum Beta) Since '63	Standard Deviation of Returns	Geometric Average Return	Arithmetic Average Return	Arithmetic Average Risk Premium	*Smoothed Average Risk Premium*	Average Debt/ MVIC
1	149,065	5.17	33	0.80	16.05%	10.89%	12.58%	5.97%	*4.78%*	28.15%
2	47,360	4.68	32	0.84	15.46%	10.20%	12.55%	5.93%	*6.12%*	33.52%
3	33,350	4.52	30	0.93	16.76%	10.49%	13.37%	6.76%	*6.53%*	31.08%
4	24,076	4.38	28	0.91	17.11%	11.20%	13.06%	6.45%	*6.92%*	30.52%
5	16,808	4.23	29	0.94	17.18%	11.73%	14.53%	7.92%	*7.34%*	29.55%
6	12,901	4.11	35	0.95	16.24%	11.30%	14.39%	7.78%	*7.65%*	27.97%
7	10,303	4.01	30	1.05	18.80%	12.83%	14.83%	8.21%	*7.91%*	27.06%
8	8,789	3.94	27	1.04	17.77%	12.35%	14.04%	7.42%	*8.10%*	27.03%
9	7,296	3.86	29	1.11	20.25%	12.59%	14.34%	7.73%	*8.32%*	27.94%
10	6,312	3.80	35	1.10	18.83%	13.82%	13.92%	7.31%	*8.49%*	27.11%
11	5,399	3.73	35	1.13	20.77%	13.31%	14.91%	8.30%	*8.67%*	27.60%
12	4,475	3.65	35	1.10	20.52%	13.53%	15.44%	8.82%	*8.89%*	25.71%
13	3,859	3.59	37	1.14	19.81%	13.13%	16.02%	9.41%	*9.06%*	25.87%
14	3,338	3.52	34	1.12	20.62%	13.36%	15.68%	9.07%	*9.25%*	25.18%
15	2,881	3.46	35	1.15	19.29%	13.61%	15.72%	9.11%	*9.41%*	25.54%
16	2,457	3.39	38	1.18	21.14%	14.90%	16.77%	10.16%	*9.59%*	24.02%
17	2,041	3.31	47	1.19	19.99%	14.29%	17.29%	10.67%	*9.81%*	24.23%
18	1,729	3.24	58	1.22	22.88%	15.22%	17.57%	10.96%	*10.00%*	24.86%
19	1,429	3.15	45	1.23	21.72%	12.70%	16.31%	9.70%	*10.25%*	24.91%
20	1,199	3.08	53	1.24	23.57%	13.88%	16.35%	9.74%	*10.43%*	24.00%
21	937	2.97	88	1.24	21.68%	13.93%	16.23%	9.62%	*10.72%*	23.71%
22	745	2.87	64	1.25	23.15%	14.99%	17.13%	10.52%	*10.99%*	22.91%
23	585	2.77	66	1.25	23.14%	15.92%	18.18%	11.57%	*11.27%*	22.59%
24	392	2.59	117	1.25	24.32%	15.71%	18.13%	11.52%	*11.74%*	21.63%
25	132	2.12	284	1.27	27.85%	18.66%	21.21%	14.60%	*13.02%*	19.03%
Large Stocks (Ibbotson SBBI data)						10.27%	11.66%	5.05%		
Small Stocks (Ibbotson SBBI data)						13.77%	16.47%	9.86%		
Long-Term Treasury Income (Ibbotson SBBI data)						6.58%	6.61%			

Equity Risk Premium Study: Data through December 31, 2014
Data Smoothing with Regression Analysis
Dependent Variable: Arithmetic Average Risk Premium
Independent Variable: Log of Total Assets

Regression Output:	
Constant	18.743%
Standard Error of Y Estimate	0.708%
R Squared	88%
No. of Observations	25
Degrees of Freedom	23
X Coefficient(s)	-2.699%
Standard Error of Coefficient	0.207%
t-Statistic	-13.06

*Smoothed Premium = 18.743% - 2.699% * Log(Assets)*

Smoothed Premium vs. Arithmetic Premium

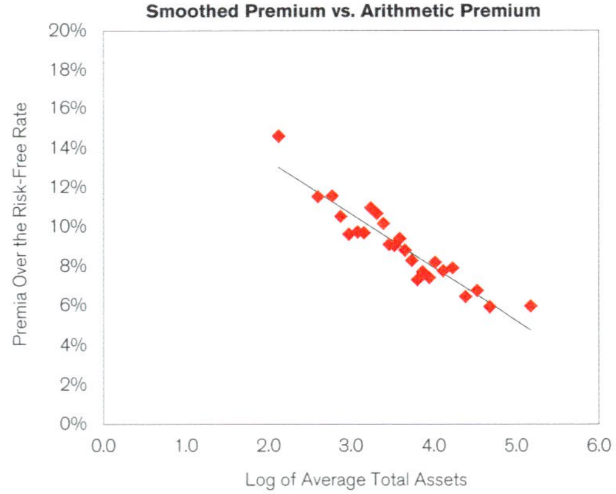

Sources of underlying data: 1.) © 201502 CRSP®, Center for Research in Security Prices. University of Chicago Booth School of Business used with permission. All rights reserved. 2.) Morningstar *Direct* database. Used with permission. All rights reserved. Calculations performed by Duff & Phelps LLC.

Companies Ranked by 5-Year Average EBITDA | **Premia Over the Risk-Free Rate (RP_{m+s})** | **Exhibit A-6**

Historical Equity Risk Premium: Average Since 1963

Data for Year Ending December 31, 2014

Portfolio Rank by Size	Average EBITDA (in $millions)	Log of Average EBITDA	Number as of 2014	Beta (Sum Beta) Since '63	Standard Deviation of Returns	Geometric Average Return	Arithmetic Average Return	Arithmetic Average Risk Premium	*Smoothed Average Risk Premium*	Average Debt/MVIC
1	22,068	4.34	32	0.79	15.80%	11.74%	12.92%	6.31%	*4.70%*	22.87%
2	6,070	3.78	31	0.84	15.76%	11.64%	12.83%	6.22%	*6.21%*	28.55%
3	3,983	3.60	28	0.89	15.94%	12.19%	13.41%	6.80%	*6.70%*	28.89%
4	2,947	3.47	30	0.91	15.96%	12.21%	13.38%	6.77%	*7.05%*	28.53%
5	2,106	3.32	34	0.99	18.09%	12.15%	13.72%	7.11%	*7.44%*	27.63%
6	1,540	3.19	33	0.93	16.27%	13.09%	14.35%	7.73%	*7.81%*	27.89%
7	1,234	3.09	31	1.02	18.49%	12.67%	14.21%	7.60%	*8.06%*	25.67%
8	1,036	3.02	30	1.06	17.55%	13.15%	14.63%	8.02%	*8.27%*	25.00%
9	883	2.95	34	1.11	19.46%	11.68%	13.45%	6.84%	*8.45%*	24.84%
10	754	2.88	33	1.09	18.87%	12.46%	14.11%	7.50%	*8.64%*	25.62%
11	643	2.81	37	1.01	18.53%	13.85%	15.46%	8.84%	*8.83%*	24.58%
12	530	2.72	32	1.09	20.68%	14.03%	16.09%	9.48%	*9.05%*	25.67%
13	446	2.65	38	1.08	19.97%	14.53%	16.39%	9.78%	*9.25%*	25.85%
14	388	2.59	32	1.16	20.37%	14.94%	16.83%	10.21%	*9.41%*	23.98%
15	341	2.53	33	1.15	21.03%	13.13%	15.30%	8.69%	*9.56%*	24.50%
16	296	2.47	38	1.17	20.29%	14.27%	16.21%	9.60%	*9.73%*	23.77%
17	260	2.41	42	1.18	21.88%	15.24%	17.42%	10.80%	*9.88%*	24.33%
18	222	2.35	46	1.20	22.53%	14.92%	17.19%	10.58%	*10.07%*	24.81%
19	184	2.26	54	1.24	20.95%	14.89%	16.96%	10.35%	*10.29%*	24.46%
20	150	2.18	70	1.25	21.96%	13.73%	15.99%	9.38%	*10.52%*	24.67%
21	113	2.05	71	1.22	23.35%	15.08%	17.46%	10.85%	*10.86%*	23.99%
22	87	1.94	69	1.23	22.21%	16.02%	18.25%	11.64%	*11.16%*	23.53%
23	66	1.82	65	1.23	23.70%	15.70%	18.23%	11.61%	*11.49%*	23.36%
24	46	1.66	110	1.26	24.47%	15.73%	18.42%	11.81%	*11.90%*	23.07%
25	15	1.16	291	1.30	28.19%	17.18%	20.67%	14.06%	*13.24%*	21.89%
Large Stocks (Ibbotson SBBI data)						10.27%	11.66%	5.05%		
Small Stocks (Ibbotson SBBI data)						13.77%	16.47%	9.86%		
Long-Term Treasury Income (Ibbotson SBBI data)						6.58%	6.61%			

Equity Risk Premium Study: Data through December 31, 2014

Data Smoothing with Regression Analysis

Dependent Variable: Arithmetic Average Risk Premium

Independent Variable: Log of Average EBITDA

Regression Output:

Constant	16.366%
Standard Error of Y Estimate	0.730%
R Squared	88%
No. of Observations	25
Degrees of Freedom	23
X Coefficient(s)	-2.685%
Standard Error of Coefficient	0.209%
t-Statistic	-12.88

*Smoothed Premium = 16.366% - 2.685% * Log(EBITDA)*

Smoothed Premium vs. Arithmetic Premium

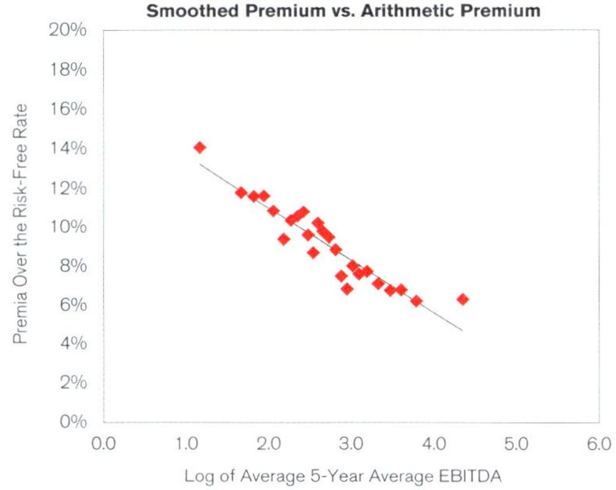

Sources of underlying data: 1.) © 201502 CRSP®, Center for Research in Security Prices. University of Chicago Booth School of Business used with permission. All rights reserved. 2.) Morningstar *Direct* database. Used with permission. All rights reserved. Calculations performed by Duff & Phelps LLC.

Companies Ranked by Sales **Premia Over the Risk-Free Rate (RP_{m+s})** **Exhibit A-7**

Historical Equity Risk Premium: Average Since 1963
Data for Year Ending December 31, 2014

Portfolio Rank by Size	Average Sales (in $millions)	Log of Average Sales	Number as of 2014	Beta (Sum Beta) Since '63	Standard Deviation of Returns	Geometric Average Return	Arithmetic Average Return	Arithmetic Average Risk Premium	*Smoothed Average Risk Premium*	Average Debt/ MVIC
1	120,333	5.08	32	0.89	17.23%	11.79%	13.25%	6.63%	*6.09%*	23.34%
2	40,618	4.61	30	0.97	18.17%	11.88%	13.46%	6.85%	*7.08%*	24.58%
3	22,774	4.36	31	0.99	16.88%	12.11%	13.44%	6.82%	*7.61%*	26.60%
4	16,014	4.20	31	1.00	16.55%	13.85%	15.14%	8.52%	*7.93%*	27.16%
5	12,063	4.08	31	1.02	18.00%	13.90%	15.41%	8.80%	*8.19%*	28.26%
6	9,580	3.98	31	1.02	18.19%	13.48%	15.03%	8.42%	*8.40%*	27.53%
7	8,000	3.90	28	1.08	19.51%	13.79%	15.51%	8.90%	*8.56%*	25.60%
8	6,681	3.82	34	1.05	19.05%	12.63%	14.34%	7.73%	*8.73%*	26.58%
9	5,886	3.77	35	1.10	20.14%	12.94%	14.78%	8.17%	*8.84%*	26.24%
10	4,987	3.70	36	1.13	20.24%	13.15%	15.05%	8.44%	*8.99%*	26.11%
11	4,261	3.63	34	1.10	18.93%	13.98%	15.68%	9.07%	*9.14%*	26.09%
12	3,584	3.55	38	1.11	21.04%	14.56%	16.59%	9.98%	*9.29%*	26.22%
13	2,975	3.47	38	1.21	21.00%	15.79%	17.90%	11.29%	*9.46%*	26.18%
14	2,594	3.41	36	1.13	20.88%	14.59%	16.56%	9.95%	*9.59%*	26.18%
15	2,310	3.36	38	1.12	19.29%	14.82%	16.50%	9.89%	*9.70%*	25.34%
16	2,064	3.31	41	1.15	20.40%	13.13%	15.12%	8.51%	*9.80%*	25.35%
17	1,770	3.25	47	1.14	21.53%	15.25%	17.37%	10.76%	*9.94%*	26.02%
18	1,506	3.18	39	1.20	21.69%	14.63%	16.83%	10.22%	*10.09%*	25.98%
19	1,314	3.12	52	1.24	21.03%	12.45%	14.57%	7.95%	*10.21%*	25.68%
20	1,064	3.03	64	1.16	21.93%	15.24%	17.43%	10.82%	*10.40%*	25.79%
21	860	2.93	61	1.18	23.14%	14.51%	16.89%	10.28%	*10.60%*	24.62%
22	711	2.85	61	1.25	22.39%	15.06%	17.34%	10.73%	*10.77%*	24.65%
23	552	2.74	87	1.24	24.68%	15.10%	17.79%	11.18%	*11.00%*	23.79%
24	371	2.57	111	1.24	23.84%	14.98%	17.60%	10.99%	*11.37%*	22.38%
25	120	2.08	278	1.25	25.58%	16.96%	19.89%	13.28%	*12.40%*	19.82%
Large Stocks (Ibbotson SBBI data)						10.27%	11.66%	5.05%		
Small Stocks (Ibbotson SBBI data)						13.77%	16.47%	9.86%		
Long-Term Treasury Income (Ibbotson SBBI data)						6.58%	6.61%			

Equity Risk Premium Study: Data through December 31, 2014
Data Smoothing with Regression Analysis
Dependent Variable: Arithmetic Average Risk Premium
Independent Variable: Log of Average Sales

Regression Output:	
Constant	16.769%
Standard Error of Y Estimate	0.840%
R Squared	75%
No. of Observations	25
Degrees of Freedom	23
X Coefficient(s)	-2.103%
Standard Error of Coefficient	0.256%
t-Statistic	-8.20

*Smoothed Premium = 16.769% - 2.103% * Log(Sales)*

Smoothed Premium vs. Arithmetic Premium

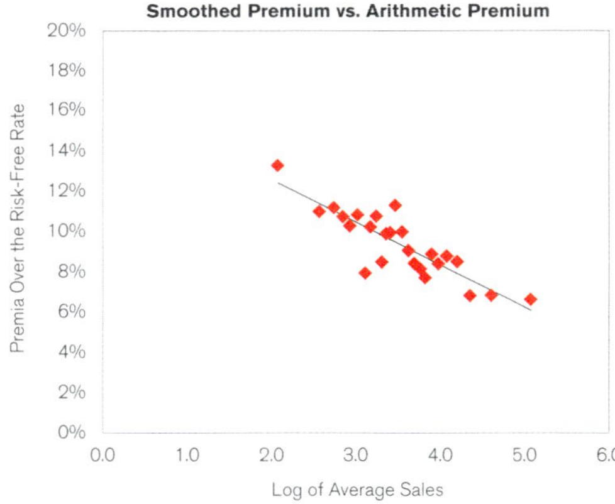

Historical Equity Risk Premium: Average Since 1963

Data for Year Ending December 31, 2014

Portfolio Rank by Size	Average Number of Employees	Log of Number of Employees	Number as of 2014	Beta (Sum Beta) Since '63	Standard Deviation of Returns	Geometric Average Return	Arithmetic Average Return	Arithmetic Average Risk Premium	*Smoothed Average Risk Premium*	Average Debt/ MVIC
1	314,558	5.50	30	0.99	18.66%	11.60%	13.24%	6.63%	*6.28%*	24.01%
2	99,492	5.00	37	1.03	18.03%	12.11%	13.64%	7.03%	*7.29%*	23.12%
3	61,721	4.79	30	1.06	18.96%	12.66%	14.37%	7.75%	*7.70%*	24.41%
4	46,474	4.67	35	1.11	19.95%	13.37%	15.23%	8.62%	*7.95%*	23.35%
5	35,103	4.55	36	1.09	19.41%	13.46%	15.21%	8.60%	*8.19%*	24.79%
6	27,449	4.44	29	1.12	20.47%	13.99%	15.88%	9.27%	*8.41%*	23.39%
7	21,991	4.34	39	1.07	20.37%	12.33%	14.24%	7.63%	*8.60%*	24.22%
8	18,164	4.26	34	1.07	17.72%	12.86%	14.37%	7.76%	*8.77%*	24.92%
9	15,432	4.19	35	1.16	21.15%	13.92%	16.00%	9.39%	*8.91%*	26.34%
10	13,384	4.13	39	1.14	21.61%	14.11%	16.18%	9.57%	*9.04%*	25.01%
11	11,642	4.07	37	1.17	21.12%	14.82%	16.86%	10.25%	*9.16%*	25.31%
12	10,185	4.01	33	1.10	20.50%	14.88%	16.77%	10.16%	*9.27%*	25.31%
13	9,052	3.96	38	1.13	19.77%	13.67%	15.57%	8.96%	*9.38%*	25.88%
14	7,625	3.88	50	1.15	19.63%	12.62%	14.51%	7.90%	*9.53%*	26.39%
15	6,354	3.80	48	1.18	21.70%	14.46%	16.67%	10.06%	*9.69%*	26.69%
16	5,598	3.75	46	1.13	20.94%	13.65%	15.68%	9.07%	*9.80%*	26.60%
17	4,911	3.69	41	1.20	20.77%	13.29%	15.35%	8.74%	*9.91%*	26.12%
18	4,080	3.61	46	1.19	20.13%	15.12%	17.07%	10.45%	*10.07%*	26.43%
19	3,358	3.53	64	1.15	21.67%	14.10%	16.21%	9.60%	*10.24%*	25.31%
20	2,721	3.43	64	1.17	21.45%	13.36%	15.51%	8.90%	*10.43%*	24.59%
21	2,235	3.35	65	1.18	23.11%	15.43%	17.86%	11.25%	*10.60%*	24.78%
22	1,755	3.24	50	1.18	21.43%	15.33%	17.41%	10.80%	*10.81%*	24.93%
23	1,277	3.11	97	1.21	23.40%	15.17%	17.71%	11.10%	*11.09%*	24.12%
24	831	2.92	84	1.20	23.39%	16.18%	18.69%	12.08%	*11.46%*	23.63%
25	287	2.46	237	1.23	24.89%	17.29%	20.03%	13.42%	*12.39%*	20.47%
Large Stocks (Ibbotson SBBI data)						10.27%	11.66%	5.05%		
Small Stocks (Ibbotson SBBI data)						13.77%	16.47%	9.86%		
Long-Term Treasury Income (Ibbotson SBBI data)						6.58%	6.61%			

Equity Risk Premium Study: Data through December 31, 2014

Data Smoothing with Regression Analysis

Dependent Variable: Arithmetic Average Risk Premium

Independent Variable: Log of Average Employees

Regression Output:	
Constant	17.329%
Standard Error of Y Estimate	0.823%
R Squared	74%
No. of Observations	25
Degrees of Freedom	23
X Coefficient(s)	-2.010%
Standard Error of Coefficient	0.246%
t-Statistic	-8.17

*Smoothed Premium = 17.329% - 2.010% * Log(Employees)*

Smoothed Premium vs. Arithmetic Premium

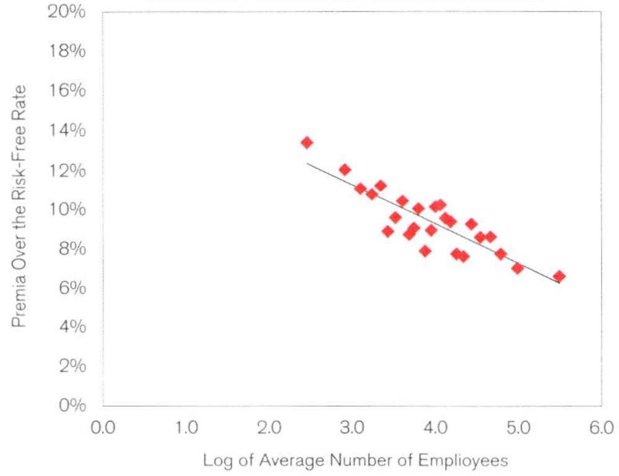

Sources of underlying data: 1.) © 201502 CRSP®, Center for Research in Security Prices. University of Chicago Booth School of Business used with permission. 2.) Morningstar *Direct* database. Used with permission. Calculations performed by Duff & Phelps LLC.

Risk Premium Report – Exhibits B-1 through B-8 Premia Over CAPM (RP_s)

Premia over CAPM (commonly referred to as "size premia") represent the difference between historical (observed) excess return and the excess return predicted by the capital asset pricing model (CAPM). Size premia can be added to cost of capital estimation models as an adjustment for the additional risk of small companies relative to large companies.

The B Exhibits are used in the following method to estimate a cost of equity capital:

- CAPM
- Build-up 2

Size Measures:

B-1: Market value of equity

B-2: Book value of equity

B-3: 5-year average net income

B-4: Market value of invested capital (MVIC)

B-5: Total assets

B-6: 5-year average EBITDA

B-7: Sales

B-8: Number of employees

Companies Ranked by Market Value of Equity | **Premia over CAPM (Size Premia, RP_s)** | **Exhibit B-1**

Historical Equity Risk Premium: Average Since 1963
Data for Year Ending December 31, 2014

Equity Risk Premium Study: Data through December 31, 2014
Data Smoothing with Regression Analysis
Dependent Variable: Premium over CAPM
Independent Variable: Log of Average Market Value of Equity

Portfolio Rank by Size	Average Mkt. Value (in $millions)	Log of Average Mkt. Value	Beta (Sum Beta) Since '63	Arithmetic Average Return	Arithmetic Average Risk Premium	Indicated CAPM Premium	Premium over CAPM	*Smoothed Premium over CAPM*
1	178,744	5.25	0.83	12.13%	5.52%	4.21%	1.31%	*-1.07%*
2	53,009	4.72	0.96	11.15%	4.54%	4.84%	-0.30%	*0.29%*
3	32,537	4.51	0.92	11.66%	5.04%	4.67%	0.38%	*0.84%*
4	24,601	4.39	0.94	12.86%	6.25%	4.77%	1.48%	*1.16%*
5	17,777	4.25	0.99	12.37%	5.76%	5.00%	0.76%	*1.52%*
6	13,745	4.14	1.02	12.89%	6.27%	5.17%	1.10%	*1.81%*
7	11,640	4.07	1.01	13.55%	6.94%	5.12%	1.81%	*2.00%*
8	9,409	3.97	1.06	14.64%	8.03%	5.36%	2.67%	*2.23%*
9	7,894	3.90	1.10	15.55%	8.94%	5.56%	3.37%	*2.43%*
10	6,698	3.83	1.11	15.29%	8.68%	5.59%	3.08%	*2.62%*
11	5,692	3.76	1.10	14.75%	8.14%	5.56%	2.58%	*2.80%*
12	4,950	3.69	1.11	14.02%	7.40%	5.62%	1.78%	*2.96%*
13	4,383	3.64	1.12	14.93%	8.32%	5.64%	2.68%	*3.09%*
14	3,880	3.59	1.15	15.26%	8.65%	5.82%	2.82%	*3.23%*
15	3,358	3.53	1.14	17.38%	10.77%	5.74%	5.02%	*3.39%*
16	2,785	3.44	1.16	16.64%	10.02%	5.87%	4.16%	*3.60%*
17	2,323	3.37	1.19	15.89%	9.28%	6.04%	3.24%	*3.80%*
18	1,954	3.29	1.22	15.11%	8.49%	6.16%	2.33%	*4.00%*
19	1,651	3.22	1.21	16.76%	10.15%	6.13%	4.02%	*4.19%*
20	1,324	3.12	1.21	16.15%	9.53%	6.11%	3.43%	*4.44%*
21	1,084	3.03	1.25	16.96%	10.35%	6.33%	4.02%	*4.66%*
22	868	2.94	1.23	17.48%	10.87%	6.21%	4.67%	*4.91%*
23	639	2.81	1.26	17.05%	10.43%	6.36%	4.08%	*5.25%*
24	412	2.62	1.24	19.45%	12.84%	6.27%	6.57%	*5.74%*
25	132	2.12	1.28	22.92%	16.31%	6.47%	9.84%	*7.03%*
Large Stocks (Ibbotson SBBI data)				11.66%	5.05%			
Small Stocks (Ibbotson SBBI data)				16.47%	9.86%			
Long-Term Treasury Income (Ibbotson SBBI data)				6.61%				

Regression Output:	
Constant	12.505%
Standard Error of Y Estimate	1.105%
R Squared	74%
No. of Observations	25
Degrees of Freedom	23
X Coefficient(s)	-2.585%
Standard Error of Coefficient	0.322%
t-Statistic	-8.02

*Smoothed Premium = 12.505% - 2.585% * Log(Market Value)*

Smoothed Premium vs. Unadjusted Premium

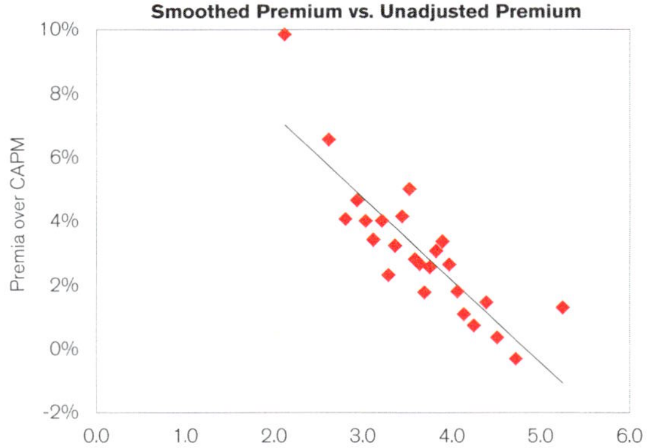

Sources of underlying data: 1.) © 201502 CRSP®, Center for Research in Security Prices. University of Chicago Booth School of Business used with permission. All rights reserved. 2.) Morningstar *Direct* database. Used with permission. All rights reserved. Calculations performed by Duff & Phelps LLC.

Historical Equity Risk Premium: Average Since 1963
Data for Year Ending December 31, 2014

Equity Risk Premium Study: Data through December 31, 2014
Data Smoothing with Regression Analysis
Dependent Variable: Premium over CAPM
Independent Variable: Log of Average Book Value of Equity

Portfolio Rank by Size	Average Book Val. (in $millions)	Log of Average Book Val.	Beta (Sum Beta) Since '63	Arithmetic Average Return	Arithmetic Average Risk Premium	Indicated CAPM Premium	Premium over CAPM	*Smoothed Premium over CAPM*
1	55,457	4.74	0.81	12.37%	5.76%	4.10%	1.66%	*0.88%*
2	18,036	4.26	0.87	12.41%	5.80%	4.38%	1.42%	*1.66%*
3	11,882	4.07	0.90	13.48%	6.87%	4.57%	2.30%	*1.95%*
4	7,797	3.89	0.92	13.49%	6.87%	4.67%	2.21%	*2.24%*
5	5,773	3.76	1.03	13.55%	6.94%	5.19%	1.75%	*2.45%*
6	4,551	3.66	1.01	13.83%	7.22%	5.10%	2.12%	*2.62%*
7	3,798	3.58	1.05	14.34%	7.73%	5.33%	2.40%	*2.74%*
8	3,217	3.51	1.08	14.42%	7.81%	5.46%	2.35%	*2.86%*
9	2,695	3.43	1.12	14.50%	7.89%	5.68%	2.21%	*2.98%*
10	2,271	3.36	1.07	14.91%	8.30%	5.38%	2.92%	*3.10%*
11	1,932	3.29	1.09	15.32%	8.71%	5.50%	3.21%	*3.21%*
12	1,665	3.22	1.08	16.65%	10.03%	5.46%	4.57%	*3.32%*
13	1,463	3.17	1.12	16.17%	9.55%	5.68%	3.87%	*3.41%*
14	1,305	3.12	1.14	15.01%	8.40%	5.74%	2.67%	*3.49%*
15	1,172	3.07	1.11	16.78%	10.16%	5.60%	4.56%	*3.56%*
16	1,055	3.02	1.23	18.41%	11.80%	6.24%	5.56%	*3.63%*
17	913	2.96	1.19	16.41%	9.80%	6.04%	3.76%	*3.73%*
18	794	2.90	1.19	16.64%	10.03%	5.99%	4.04%	*3.83%*
19	664	2.82	1.24	15.13%	8.52%	6.24%	2.28%	*3.96%*
20	534	2.73	1.21	16.14%	9.53%	6.11%	3.42%	*4.11%*
21	440	2.64	1.21	17.23%	10.62%	6.12%	4.49%	*4.24%*
22	338	2.53	1.24	17.03%	10.42%	6.24%	4.18%	*4.42%*
23	264	2.42	1.25	17.39%	10.77%	6.33%	4.45%	*4.60%*
24	185	2.27	1.27	18.14%	11.53%	6.41%	5.13%	*4.84%*
25	65	1.81	1.26	18.89%	12.28%	6.36%	5.92%	*5.57%*
Large Stocks (Ibbotson SBBI data)				11.66%	5.05%			
Small Stocks (Ibbotson SBBI data)				16.47%	9.86%			
Long-Term Treasury Income (Ibbotson SBBI data)				6.61%				

Regression Output:

Constant	8.469%
Standard Error of Y Estimate	0.764%
R Squared	66%
No. of Observations	25
Degrees of Freedom	23
X Coefficient(s)	-1.599%
Standard Error of Coefficient	0.238%
t-Statistic	-6.73

*Smoothed Premium = 8.469% - 1.599% * Log(Book Value)*

Smoothed Premium vs. Unadjusted Premium

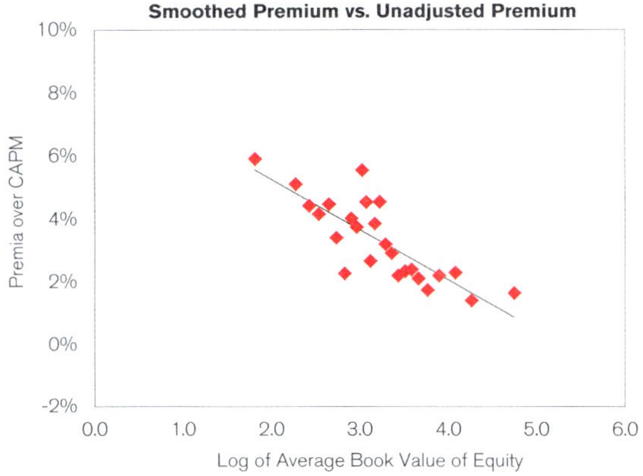

Sources of underlying data: 1.) © 201502 CRSP®, Center for Research in Security Prices. University of Chicago Booth School of Business used with permission. All rights reserved. 2.) Morningstar *Direct* database. Used with permission. All rights reserved. Calculations performed by Duff & Phelps LLC.

Companies Ranked by 5-Year Average Net Income | **Premia over CAPM (Size Premia, RP_s)** | **Exhibit B-3**

Historical Equity Risk Premium: Average Since 1963
Data for Year Ending December 31, 2014

Portfolio Rank by Size	Average Net Inc. (in $millions)	Log of Average Net Inc.	Beta (Sum Beta) Since '63	Arithmetic Average Return	Arithmetic Average Risk Premium	Indicated CAPM Premium	Premium over CAPM	*Smoothed Premium over CAPM*
1	8,922	3.95	0.77	13.32%	6.71%	3.91%	2.80%	*0.54%*
2	2,422	3.38	0.87	12.35%	5.74%	4.39%	1.35%	*1.53%*
3	1,540	3.19	0.87	13.75%	7.14%	4.38%	2.76%	*1.87%*
4	1,066	3.03	0.90	13.42%	6.81%	4.57%	2.24%	*2.15%*
5	760	2.88	0.95	13.08%	6.47%	4.81%	1.66%	*2.41%*
6	566	2.75	0.99	13.42%	6.81%	4.98%	1.83%	*2.63%*
7	441	2.64	1.05	13.72%	7.11%	5.30%	1.81%	*2.82%*
8	354	2.55	1.09	14.73%	8.12%	5.52%	2.60%	*2.98%*
9	297	2.47	1.04	13.83%	7.22%	5.27%	1.95%	*3.12%*
10	255	2.41	1.06	15.02%	8.41%	5.35%	3.05%	*3.23%*
11	218	2.34	1.08	15.48%	8.86%	5.48%	3.39%	*3.35%*
12	182	2.26	1.08	16.18%	9.57%	5.47%	4.10%	*3.49%*
13	159	2.20	1.06	16.35%	9.74%	5.37%	4.37%	*3.59%*
14	136	2.13	1.16	14.77%	8.16%	5.84%	2.31%	*3.71%*
15	122	2.09	1.12	15.64%	9.03%	5.66%	3.37%	*3.79%*
16	106	2.02	1.12	16.80%	10.19%	5.64%	4.55%	*3.90%*
17	90	1.95	1.20	15.89%	9.28%	6.04%	3.24%	*4.02%*
18	76	1.88	1.21	17.25%	10.64%	6.11%	4.53%	*4.15%*
19	58	1.77	1.25	16.07%	9.45%	6.34%	3.12%	*4.35%*
20	44	1.65	1.23	18.33%	11.72%	6.19%	5.53%	*4.56%*
21	35	1.54	1.22	17.32%	10.70%	6.18%	4.52%	*4.75%*
22	25	1.40	1.22	17.07%	10.46%	6.15%	4.31%	*4.98%*
23	18	1.27	1.26	18.91%	12.30%	6.36%	5.94%	*5.22%*
24	11	1.05	1.25	18.68%	12.07%	6.31%	5.77%	*5.61%*
25	3	0.54	1.32	21.43%	14.82%	6.67%	8.15%	*6.49%*

	Arithmetic Average Return	Arithmetic Average Risk Premium
Large Stocks (Ibbotson SBBI data)	11.66%	5.05%
Small Stocks (Ibbotson SBBI data)	16.47%	9.86%
Long-Term Treasury Income (Ibbotson SBBI data)	6.61%	

Equity Risk Premium Study: Data through December 31, 2014
Data Smoothing with Regression Analysis
Dependent Variable: Premium over CAPM
Independent Variable: Log of Average Net Income

Regression Output:	
Constant	7.428%
Standard Error of Y Estimate	0.937%
R Squared	68%
No. of Observations	25
Degrees of Freedom	23
X Coefficient(s)	-1.743%
Standard Error of Coefficient	0.250%
t-Statistic	-6.98

*Smoothed Premium = 7.428% - 1.743% * Log(Net Income)*

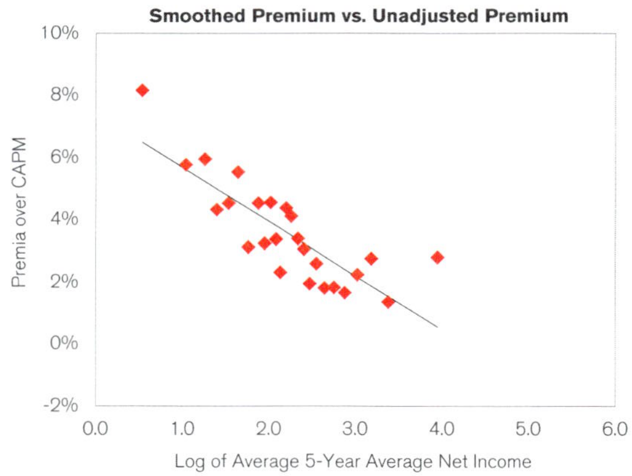

Sources of underlying data: 1.) © 201502 CRSP®, Center for Research in Security Prices. University of Chicago Booth School of Business used with permission. All rights reserved. 2.) Morningstar *Direct* database. Used with permission. All rights reserved. Calculations performed by Duff & Phelps LLC.

Companies Ranked by Market Value of Invested Capital — **Premia over CAPM (Size Premia, RP_s)** — **Exhibit B-4**

Historical Equity Risk Premium: Average Since 1963
Data for Year Ending December 31, 2014

Equity Risk Premium Study: Data through December 31, 2014
Data Smoothing with Regression Analysis
Dependent Variable: Premium over CAPM
Independent Variable: Log of Average MVIC

Portfolio Rank by Size	Average MVIC (in $millions)	Log of Average MVIC	Beta (Sum Beta) Since '63	Arithmetic Average Return	Arithmetic Average Risk Premium	Indicated CAPM Premium	Premium over CAPM	*Smoothed Premium over CAPM*
1	210,749	5.32	0.80	12.10%	5.49%	4.04%	1.45%	*-0.60%*
2	66,082	4.82	0.87	11.41%	4.80%	4.39%	0.41%	*0.59%*
3	41,570	4.62	0.90	11.72%	5.11%	4.55%	0.57%	*1.06%*
4	31,430	4.50	0.94	12.62%	6.01%	4.77%	1.24%	*1.35%*
5	24,299	4.39	0.98	12.99%	6.37%	4.95%	1.43%	*1.61%*
6	18,313	4.26	1.01	12.65%	6.03%	5.08%	0.95%	*1.90%*
7	14,818	4.17	0.99	14.26%	7.65%	5.01%	2.64%	*2.12%*
8	12,250	4.09	1.05	14.14%	7.53%	5.32%	2.21%	*2.31%*
9	10,109	4.00	1.10	14.32%	7.71%	5.56%	2.15%	*2.51%*
10	8,722	3.94	1.11	15.57%	8.96%	5.59%	3.36%	*2.66%*
11	7,509	3.88	1.11	15.09%	8.48%	5.62%	2.85%	*2.81%*
12	6,429	3.81	1.06	15.21%	8.59%	5.34%	3.25%	*2.97%*
13	5,617	3.75	1.15	14.90%	8.29%	5.79%	2.50%	*3.11%*
14	4,848	3.69	1.18	15.45%	8.84%	5.96%	2.88%	*3.26%*
15	4,248	3.63	1.17	15.77%	9.16%	5.90%	3.26%	*3.39%*
16	3,558	3.55	1.19	17.01%	10.40%	6.03%	4.37%	*3.57%*
17	3,005	3.48	1.23	16.56%	9.95%	6.19%	3.76%	*3.75%*
18	2,551	3.41	1.17	17.21%	10.60%	5.90%	4.69%	*3.91%*
19	2,059	3.31	1.21	14.96%	8.34%	6.13%	2.22%	*4.13%*
20	1,678	3.22	1.25	16.11%	9.50%	6.30%	3.20%	*4.34%*
21	1,335	3.13	1.27	16.40%	9.78%	6.40%	3.38%	*4.58%*
22	1,060	3.03	1.24	17.18%	10.57%	6.29%	4.28%	*4.81%*
23	813	2.91	1.26	18.69%	12.07%	6.37%	5.70%	*5.08%*
24	526	2.72	1.24	18.40%	11.78%	6.28%	5.51%	*5.53%*
25	157	2.20	1.27	22.28%	15.67%	6.42%	9.25%	*6.76%*
Large Stocks (Ibbotson SBBI data)				11.66%	5.05%			
Small Stocks (Ibbotson SBBI data)				16.47%	9.86%			
Long-Term Treasury Income (Ibbotson SBBI data)				6.61%				

Regression Output:

Constant	11.936%
Standard Error of Y Estimate	0.966%
R Squared	75%
No. of Observations	25
Degrees of Freedom	23
X Coefficient(s)	-2.355%
Standard Error of Coefficient	0.281%
t-Statistic	-8.38

*Smoothed Premium = 11.936% - 2.355% * Log(MVIC)*

Smoothed Premium vs. Unadjusted Premium

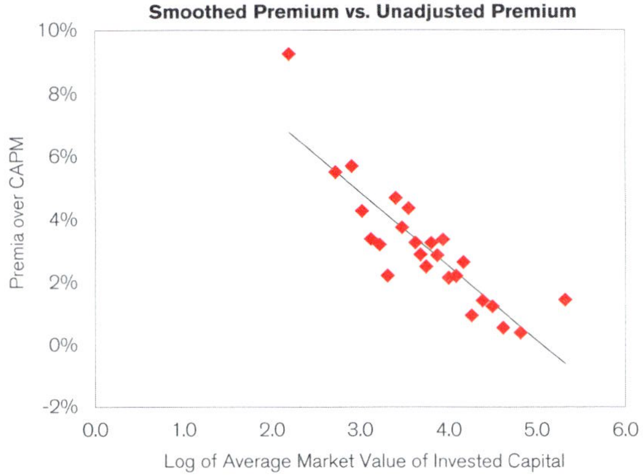

Premia over CAPM (Size Premia, RP_s)

Historical Equity Risk Premium: Average Since 1963

Data for Year Ending December 31, 2014

Portfolio Rank by Size	Average Total Assets (in $millions)	Log of Average Assets	Beta (Sum Beta) Since '63	Arithmetic Average Return	Arithmetic Average Risk Premium	Indicated CAPM Premium	Premium over CAPM	*Smoothed Premium over CAPM*
1	149,065	5.17	0.80	12.58%	5.97%	4.03%	1.94%	*0.71%*
2	47,360	4.68	0.84	12.55%	5.93%	4.23%	1.70%	*1.57%*
3	33,350	4.52	0.93	13.37%	6.76%	4.68%	2.08%	*1.84%*
4	24,076	4.38	0.91	13.06%	6.45%	4.57%	1.87%	*2.08%*
5	16,808	4.23	0.94	14.53%	7.92%	4.76%	3.16%	*2.35%*
6	12,901	4.11	0.95	14.39%	7.78%	4.81%	2.97%	*2.55%*
7	10,303	4.01	1.05	14.83%	8.21%	5.30%	2.91%	*2.72%*
8	8,789	3.94	1.04	14.04%	7.42%	5.26%	2.17%	*2.84%*
9	7,296	3.86	1.11	14.34%	7.73%	5.59%	2.14%	*2.98%*
10	6,312	3.80	1.10	13.92%	7.31%	5.53%	1.78%	*3.09%*
11	5,399	3.73	1.13	14.91%	8.30%	5.69%	2.61%	*3.21%*
12	4,475	3.65	1.10	15.44%	8.82%	5.55%	3.27%	*3.35%*
13	3,859	3.59	1.14	16.02%	9.41%	5.78%	3.63%	*3.46%*
14	3,338	3.52	1.12	15.68%	9.07%	5.68%	3.39%	*3.57%*
15	2,881	3.46	1.15	15.72%	9.11%	5.82%	3.28%	*3.68%*
16	2,457	3.39	1.18	16.77%	10.16%	5.98%	4.18%	*3.80%*
17	2,041	3.31	1.19	17.29%	10.67%	5.99%	4.68%	*3.94%*
18	1,729	3.24	1.22	17.57%	10.96%	6.15%	4.80%	*4.07%*
19	1,429	3.15	1.23	16.31%	9.70%	6.21%	3.48%	*4.21%*
20	1,199	3.08	1.24	16.35%	9.74%	6.27%	3.47%	*4.34%*
21	937	2.97	1.24	16.23%	9.62%	6.27%	3.35%	*4.53%*
22	745	2.87	1.25	17.13%	10.52%	6.29%	4.22%	*4.70%*
23	585	2.77	1.25	18.18%	11.57%	6.31%	5.25%	*4.88%*
24	392	2.59	1.25	18.13%	11.52%	6.33%	5.19%	*5.19%*
25	132	2.12	1.27	21.21%	14.60%	6.44%	8.17%	*6.01%*
Large Stocks (Ibbotson SBBI data)				11.66%	5.05%			
Small Stocks (Ibbotson SBBI data)				16.47%	9.86%			
Long-Term Treasury Income (Ibbotson SBBI data)				6.61%				

Equity Risk Premium Study: Data through December 31, 2014

Data Smoothing with Regression Analysis

Dependent Variable: Premium over CAPM

Independent Variable: Log of Average Total Assets

Regression Output:	
Constant	9.690%
Standard Error of Y Estimate	0.805%
R Squared	70%
No. of Observations	25
Degrees of Freedom	23
X Coefficient(s)	-1.736%
Standard Error of Coefficient	0.235%
t-Statistic	-7.39

*Smoothed Premium = 9.690% - 1.736% * Log(Total Assets)*

Smoothed Premium vs. Unadjusted Premium

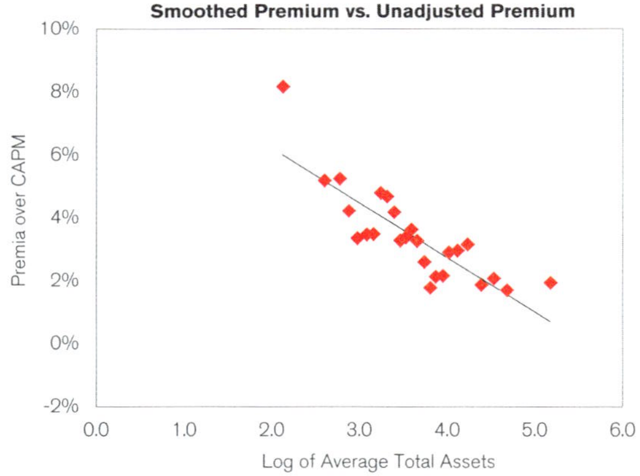

Sources of underlying data: 1.) © 201502 CRSP®, Center for Research in Security Prices. University of Chicago Booth School of Business used with permission. All rights reserved. 2.) Morningstar *Direct* database. Used with permission. All rights reserved. Calculations performed by Duff & Phelps LLC.

Historical Equity Risk Premium: Average Since 1963
Data for Year Ending December 31, 2014

Portfolio Rank by Size	Average EBITDA (in $millions)	Log of Average EBITDA	Beta (Sum Beta) Since '63	Arithmetic Average Return	Arithmetic Average Risk Premium	Indicated CAPM Premium	Premium over CAPM	*Smoothed Premium over CAPM*
1	22,068	4.34	0.79	12.92%	6.31%	3.98%	2.33%	*0.76%*
2	6,070	3.78	0.84	12.83%	6.22%	4.25%	1.97%	*1.72%*
3	3,983	3.60	0.89	13.41%	6.80%	4.48%	2.31%	*2.04%*
4	2,947	3.47	0.91	13.38%	6.77%	4.58%	2.18%	*2.26%*
5	2,106	3.32	0.99	13.72%	7.11%	5.02%	2.09%	*2.51%*
6	1,540	3.19	0.93	14.35%	7.73%	4.69%	3.05%	*2.75%*
7	1,234	3.09	1.02	14.21%	7.60%	5.15%	2.45%	*2.91%*
8	1,036	3.02	1.06	14.63%	8.02%	5.34%	2.67%	*3.04%*
9	883	2.95	1.11	13.45%	6.84%	5.61%	1.22%	*3.16%*
10	754	2.88	1.09	14.11%	7.50%	5.52%	1.98%	*3.28%*
11	643	2.81	1.01	15.46%	8.84%	5.11%	3.73%	*3.40%*
12	530	2.72	1.09	16.09%	9.48%	5.49%	3.98%	*3.55%*
13	446	2.65	1.08	16.39%	9.78%	5.45%	4.33%	*3.67%*
14	388	2.59	1.16	16.83%	10.21%	5.85%	4.37%	*3.78%*
15	341	2.53	1.15	15.30%	8.69%	5.82%	2.87%	*3.88%*
16	296	2.47	1.17	16.21%	9.60%	5.94%	3.66%	*3.98%*
17	260	2.41	1.18	17.42%	10.80%	5.99%	4.82%	*4.08%*
18	222	2.35	1.20	17.19%	10.58%	6.07%	4.51%	*4.20%*
19	184	2.26	1.24	16.96%	10.35%	6.25%	4.09%	*4.34%*
20	150	2.18	1.25	15.99%	9.38%	6.31%	3.06%	*4.49%*
21	113	2.05	1.22	17.46%	10.85%	6.17%	4.68%	*4.71%*
22	87	1.94	1.23	18.25%	11.64%	6.20%	5.44%	*4.90%*
23	66	1.82	1.23	18.23%	11.61%	6.21%	5.40%	*5.11%*
24	46	1.66	1.26	18.42%	11.81%	6.37%	5.43%	*5.38%*
25	15	1.16	1.30	20.67%	14.06%	6.57%	7.49%	*6.23%*

	Arithmetic Average Return	Arithmetic Average Risk Premium
Large Stocks (Ibbotson SBBI data)	11.66%	5.05%
Small Stocks (Ibbotson SBBI data)	16.47%	9.86%
Long-Term Treasury Income (Ibbotson SBBI data)	6.61%	

Equity Risk Premium Study: Data through December 31, 2014
Data Smoothing with Regression Analysis
Dependent Variable: Premium over CAPM
Independent Variable: Log of Average EBITDA

Regression Output:

Constant	8.239%
Standard Error of Y Estimate	0.823%
R Squared	70%
No. of Observations	25
Degrees of Freedom	23
X Coefficient(s)	-1.723%
Standard Error of Coefficient	0.235%
t-Statistic	-7.32

*Smoothed Premium = 8.239% - 1.723% * Log(EBITDA)*

Smoothed Premium vs. Unadjusted Premium

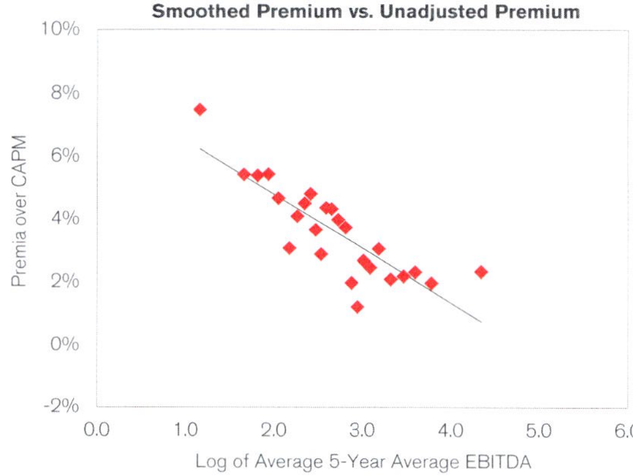

Sources of underlying data: 1.) © 201502 CRSP®, Center for Research in Security Prices. University of Chicago Booth School of Business used with permission. All rights reserved. 2.) Morningstar *Direct* database. Used with permission. All rights reserved. Calculations performed by Duff & Phelps LLC.

Companies Ranked by Sales

Premia over CAPM (Size Premia, RP_s)

Historical Equity Risk Premium: Average Since 1963

Data for Year Ending December 31, 2014

Portfolio Rank by Size	Average Sales (in $millions)	Log of Average Sales	Beta (Sum Beta) Since '63	Arithmetic Average Return	Arithmetic Average Risk Premium	Indicated CAPM Premium	Premium over CAPM	*Smoothed Premium over CAPM*
1	120,333	5.08	0.89	13.25%	6.63%	4.51%	2.13%	*1.52%*
2	40,618	4.61	0.97	13.46%	6.85%	4.88%	1.96%	*2.18%*
3	22,774	4.36	0.99	13.44%	6.82%	5.00%	1.82%	*2.54%*
4	16,014	4.20	1.00	15.14%	8.52%	5.04%	3.49%	*2.75%*
5	12,063	4.08	1.02	15.41%	8.80%	5.17%	3.62%	*2.93%*
6	9,580	3.98	1.02	15.03%	8.42%	5.17%	3.25%	*3.07%*
7	8,000	3.90	1.08	15.51%	8.90%	5.45%	3.45%	*3.18%*
8	6,681	3.82	1.05	14.34%	7.73%	5.31%	2.42%	*3.29%*
9	5,886	3.77	1.10	14.78%	8.17%	5.57%	2.60%	*3.36%*
10	4,987	3.70	1.13	15.05%	8.44%	5.69%	2.75%	*3.46%*
11	4,261	3.63	1.10	15.68%	9.07%	5.58%	3.49%	*3.56%*
12	3,584	3.55	1.11	16.59%	9.98%	5.60%	4.39%	*3.67%*
13	2,975	3.47	1.21	17.90%	11.29%	6.10%	5.19%	*3.78%*
14	2,594	3.41	1.13	16.56%	9.95%	5.69%	4.25%	*3.86%*
15	2,310	3.36	1.12	16.50%	9.89%	5.65%	4.24%	*3.93%*
16	2,064	3.31	1.15	15.12%	8.51%	5.82%	2.68%	*4.00%*
17	1,770	3.25	1.14	17.37%	10.76%	5.77%	4.99%	*4.10%*
18	1,506	3.18	1.20	16.83%	10.22%	6.09%	4.13%	*4.20%*
19	1,314	3.12	1.24	14.57%	7.95%	6.28%	1.68%	*4.28%*
20	1,064	3.03	1.16	17.43%	10.82%	5.88%	4.94%	*4.41%*
21	860	2.93	1.18	16.89%	10.28%	5.98%	4.30%	*4.54%*
22	711	2.85	1.25	17.34%	10.73%	6.30%	4.42%	*4.65%*
23	552	2.74	1.24	17.79%	11.18%	6.25%	4.93%	*4.81%*
24	371	2.57	1.24	17.60%	10.99%	6.24%	4.74%	*5.05%*
25	120	2.08	1.25	19.89%	13.28%	6.30%	6.98%	*5.74%*
Large Stocks (Ibbotson SBBI data)				11.66%	5.05%			
Small Stocks (Ibbotson SBBI data)				16.47%	9.86%			
Long-Term Treasury Income (Ibbotson SBBI data)				6.61%				

Equity Risk Premium Study: Data through December 31, 2014

Data Smoothing with Regression Analysis

Dependent Variable: Premium over CAPM

Independent Variable: Log of Average Sales

Regression Output:

Constant	8.662%
Standard Error of Y Estimate	0.885%
R Squared	54%
No. of Observations	25
Degrees of Freedom	23
X Coefficient(s)	-1.405%
Standard Error of Coefficient	0.270%
t-Statistic	-5.20

*Smoothed Premium = 8.662% - 1.405% * Log(Sales)*

Smoothed Premium vs. Unadjusted Premium

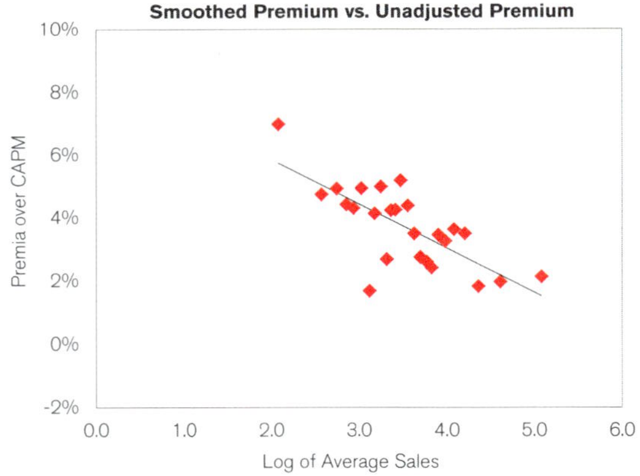

Sources of underlying data: 1.) © 201502 CRSP®, Center for Research in Security Prices. University of Chicago Booth School of Business used with permission. All rights reserved. 2.) Morningstar *Direct* database. Used with permission. All rights reserved. Calculations performed by Duff & Phelps LLC.

Historical Equity Risk Premium: Average Since 1963
Data for Year Ending December 31, 2014

Equity Risk Premium Study: Data through December 31, 2014
Data Smoothing with Regression Analysis
Dependent Variable: Premium over CAPM
Independent Variable: Log of Average Employees

Portfolio Rank by Size	Average Number of Employees	Log of Average Employees	Beta (Sum Beta) Since '63	Arithmetic Average Return	Arithmetic Average Risk Premium	Indicated CAPM Premium	Premium over CAPM	*Smoothed Premium over CAPM*
1	314,558	5.50	0.99	13.24%	6.63%	5.01%	1.62%	*1.15%*
2	99,492	5.00	1.03	13.64%	7.03%	5.22%	1.81%	*1.96%*
3	61,721	4.79	1.06	14.37%	7.75%	5.34%	2.42%	*2.29%*
4	46,474	4.67	1.11	15.23%	8.62%	5.63%	2.99%	*2.49%*
5	35,103	4.55	1.09	15.21%	8.60%	5.50%	3.10%	*2.68%*
6	27,449	4.44	1.12	15.88%	9.27%	5.67%	3.60%	*2.86%*
7	21,991	4.34	1.07	14.24%	7.63%	5.41%	2.22%	*3.01%*
8	18,164	4.26	1.07	14.37%	7.76%	5.42%	2.33%	*3.15%*
9	15,432	4.19	1.16	16.00%	9.39%	5.84%	3.54%	*3.26%*
10	13,384	4.13	1.14	16.18%	9.57%	5.75%	3.81%	*3.36%*
11	11,642	4.07	1.17	16.86%	10.25%	5.93%	4.31%	*3.46%*
12	10,185	4.01	1.10	16.77%	10.16%	5.58%	4.58%	*3.55%*
13	9,052	3.96	1.13	15.57%	8.96%	5.73%	3.22%	*3.63%*
14	7,625	3.88	1.15	14.51%	7.90%	5.83%	2.07%	*3.75%*
15	6,354	3.80	1.18	16.67%	10.06%	5.98%	4.08%	*3.88%*
16	5,598	3.75	1.13	15.68%	9.07%	5.73%	3.33%	*3.97%*
17	4,911	3.69	1.20	15.35%	8.74%	6.06%	2.68%	*4.06%*
18	4,080	3.61	1.19	17.07%	10.45%	6.03%	4.43%	*4.19%*
19	3,358	3.53	1.15	16.21%	9.60%	5.80%	3.81%	*4.33%*
20	2,721	3.43	1.17	15.51%	8.90%	5.93%	2.97%	*4.47%*
21	2,235	3.35	1.18	17.86%	11.25%	5.96%	5.29%	*4.61%*
22	1,755	3.24	1.18	17.41%	10.80%	5.97%	4.83%	*4.78%*
23	1,277	3.11	1.21	17.71%	11.10%	6.12%	4.98%	*5.00%*
24	831	2.92	1.20	18.69%	12.08%	6.06%	6.02%	*5.30%*
25	287	2.46	1.23	20.03%	13.42%	6.22%	7.20%	*6.05%*
Large Stocks (Ibbotson SBBI data)				11.66%	5.05%			
Small Stocks (Ibbotson SBBI data)				16.47%	9.86%			
Long-Term Treasury Income (Ibbotson SBBI data)				6.61%				

Regression Output:	
Constant	10.011%
Standard Error of Y Estimate	0.802%
R Squared	66%
No. of Observations	25
Degrees of Freedom	23
X Coefficient(s)	-1.612%
Standard Error of Coefficient	0.240%
t-Statistic	-6.73

*Smoothed Premium = 10.011% - 1.612% * Log(Employees)*

Smoothed Premium vs. Unadjusted Premium

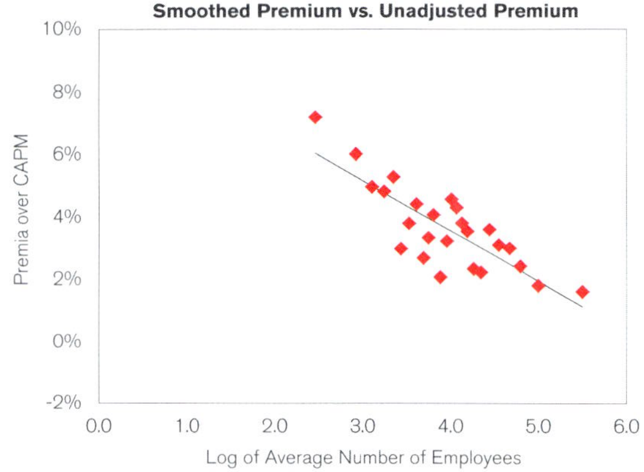

Sources of underlying data: 1.) © 201502 CRSP®, Center for Research in Security Prices. University of Chicago Booth School of Business used with permission. All rights reserved. 2.) Morningstar *Direct* database. Used with permission. All rights reserved. Calculations performed by Duff & Phelps LLC.

Risk Premium Report – Exhibits C-1 through C-8

The "C" exhibits provide information about the companies that comprise the 25 portfolios that are used to create the various risk premia and size premia published in the Report. The "C" exhibits provide the following three comparative risk characteristics (i.e. "accounting-based fundamental risk measures") for each of the 25 portfolios and for each of the 8 size measures of size, each of which can be useful in assessing how "alike or different" the subject company is to the companies that make up the respective guideline portfolio:

- Operating Margin
- Coefficient of variation in operating income margin
- Coefficient of variation in return on book equity

The C Exhibits are used in the following method to estimate an unlevered cost of equity capital:

- Build-up 1-Unlevered

Size Measures:

C-1: Market value of equity

C-2: Book value of equity

C-3: 5-year average net income

C-4: Market value of invested capital (MVIC)

C-5: Total assets

C-6: 5-year average EBITDA

C-7: Sales

C-8: Number of employees

Companies Ranked by Market Value of Equity

Data for Year Ending December 31, 2014

Comparative Risk Characteristics **Exhibit C-1**

Data Smoothing with Regression Analysis

Dependent Variable: Average Unlevered Risk Premium

Independent Variable: Log of Average Market Value of Equity

Constant	18.810%
X Coefficient(s)	-3.094%

*Smoothed Unlevered Premium = 18.810% - 3.094% * Log(Market Value)*

Portfolio Rank by Size	Average Mkt. Value (in $millions)	Log of Average Mkt. Value	Number of Firms	Arithmetic Average Risk Premium	Average Debt to MVIC	Average Debt to Market Value of Equity	Average Unlevered Risk Premium[1]	*Smoothed Average Unlevered Risk Premium*	Beta (Sum Beta) Since '63	Average Unlevered Beta	Average Operating Margin	Average CV(Operating Margin)	Average CV(ROE)
1	178,744	5.25	39	5.52%	14.12%	16.44%	4.99%	*2.56%*	0.83	0.73	16.51%	9.63%	16.35%
2	53,009	4.72	36	4.54%	19.00%	23.45%	3.72%	*4.19%*	0.96	0.79	14.11%	10.95%	20.19%
3	32,537	4.51	29	5.04%	20.61%	25.96%	4.19%	*4.85%*	0.92	0.75	13.35%	11.32%	19.23%
4	24,601	4.39	28	6.25%	22.57%	29.16%	5.28%	*5.22%*	0.94	0.75	13.20%	12.10%	20.93%
5	17,777	4.25	33	5.76%	23.16%	30.14%	4.72%	*5.66%*	0.99	0.78	12.42%	12.60%	20.27%
6	13,745	4.14	33	6.27%	22.54%	29.10%	5.22%	*6.00%*	1.02	0.81	12.76%	13.67%	21.33%
7	11,640	4.07	36	6.94%	23.43%	30.61%	5.85%	*6.23%*	1.01	0.80	12.95%	13.12%	20.27%
8	9,409	3.97	40	8.03%	22.15%	28.45%	6.95%	*6.51%*	1.06	0.85	12.99%	14.24%	23.51%
9	7,894	3.90	34	8.94%	22.62%	29.23%	7.79%	*6.75%*	1.10	0.87	12.36%	14.25%	22.86%
10	6,698	3.83	34	8.68%	22.81%	29.56%	7.52%	*6.97%*	1.11	0.88	11.64%	14.73%	24.50%
11	5,692	3.76	32	8.14%	22.78%	29.50%	6.99%	*7.19%*	1.10	0.87	11.88%	15.07%	25.11%
12	4,950	3.69	34	7.40%	22.87%	29.65%	6.23%	*7.38%*	1.11	0.88	12.08%	14.45%	22.20%
13	4,383	3.64	36	8.32%	23.31%	30.39%	7.12%	*7.54%*	1.12	0.88	11.66%	15.18%	23.09%
14	3,880	3.59	35	8.65%	23.20%	30.21%	7.41%	*7.70%*	1.15	0.91	10.82%	16.79%	24.83%
15	3,358	3.53	39	10.77%	23.26%	30.32%	9.55%	*7.90%*	1.14	0.90	10.99%	17.11%	24.23%
16	2,785	3.44	46	10.02%	23.67%	31.01%	8.75%	*8.15%*	1.16	0.91	10.52%	17.60%	25.75%
17	2,323	3.37	47	9.28%	22.35%	28.78%	8.04%	*8.39%*	1.19	0.95	10.45%	18.28%	25.83%
18	1,954	3.29	54	8.49%	23.32%	30.42%	7.17%	*8.63%*	1.22	0.96	9.79%	20.13%	28.25%
19	1,651	3.22	61	10.15%	23.33%	30.42%	8.83%	*8.85%*	1.21	0.95	9.26%	21.38%	30.31%
20	1,324	3.12	55	9.53%	24.07%	31.69%	8.19%	*9.15%*	1.21	0.94	9.14%	23.29%	31.29%
21	1,084	3.03	67	10.35%	23.97%	31.52%	8.95%	*9.42%*	1.25	0.98	8.92%	24.22%	34.03%
22	868	2.94	82	10.87%	24.64%	32.70%	9.47%	*9.72%*	1.23	0.95	8.53%	25.02%	35.04%
23	639	2.81	59	10.43%	24.06%	31.68%	9.03%	*10.13%*	1.26	0.98	7.94%	26.19%	37.99%
24	412	2.62	88	12.84%	24.78%	32.95%	11.41%	*10.72%*	1.24	0.96	7.80%	30.40%	41.31%
25	132	2.12	267	16.31%	27.48%	37.90%	14.67%	*12.25%*	1.28	0.96	6.11%	43.01%	58.93%

CV(X) = Standard deviation of X divided by mean of X, calculated over 5 fiscal years.

[1] Unlevered risk premiums and unlevered betas are calculated using methodology described in Chapter 10 with an average assumed debt beta = 0.1.

Sources of underlying data: 1.) © 201502 CRSP®, Center for Research in Security Prices. University of Chicago Booth School of Business used with permission. All rights reserved. 2.) Morningstar *Direct* database. Used with permission. All rights reserved. Calculations performed by Duff & Phelps LLC.

Companies Ranked by Book Value

Data for Year Ending December 31, 2014

Comparative Risk Characteristics

Data Smoothing with Regression Analysis
Dependent Variable: Average Unlevered Risk Premium
Independent Variable: Log of Average Book Value

Constant	15.386%
X Coefficient(s)	-2.397%

*Smoothed Unlevered Premium = 15.386% - 2.397% * Log(Book Value)*

Portfolio Rank by Size	Average Book Value (in $millions)	Log of Average Book Value	Number of Firms	Arithmetic Average Risk Premium	Average Debt to MVIC	Average Debt to Market Value of Equity	Average Unlevered Risk Premium[1]	*Smoothed Average Unlevered Risk Premium*	Beta (Sum Beta) Since '63	Average Unlevered Beta	Average Operating Margin	Average CV(Operating Margin)	Average CV(ROE)
1	55,457	4.74	35	5.76%	23.36%	30.48%	4.92%	*4.01%*	0.81	0.64	13.71%	12.46%	20.99%
2	18,036	4.26	29	5.80%	27.49%	37.92%	4.74%	*5.18%*	0.87	0.66	13.65%	12.77%	19.95%
3	11,882	4.07	32	6.87%	28.44%	39.74%	5.71%	*5.62%*	0.90	0.68	12.12%	12.95%	22.76%
4	7,797	3.89	33	6.87%	28.09%	39.07%	5.70%	*6.06%*	0.92	0.69	11.85%	13.61%	23.10%
5	5,773	3.76	31	6.94%	26.19%	35.49%	5.71%	*6.37%*	1.03	0.78	12.61%	13.56%	23.93%
6	4,551	3.66	32	7.22%	26.19%	35.48%	6.01%	*6.62%*	1.01	0.77	12.31%	13.91%	24.26%
7	3,798	3.58	34	7.73%	24.81%	33.00%	6.53%	*6.80%*	1.05	0.82	12.07%	14.39%	25.38%
8	3,217	3.51	31	7.81%	24.66%	32.73%	6.59%	*6.98%*	1.08	0.84	11.59%	15.28%	25.69%
9	2,695	3.43	36	7.89%	24.65%	32.71%	6.61%	*7.16%*	1.12	0.87	11.79%	14.72%	23.32%
10	2,271	3.36	36	8.30%	25.47%	34.18%	7.06%	*7.34%*	1.07	0.82	11.30%	14.68%	23.85%
11	1,932	3.29	36	8.71%	25.86%	34.87%	7.42%	*7.51%*	1.09	0.83	11.95%	14.78%	25.28%
12	1,665	3.22	35	10.03%	25.38%	34.01%	8.78%	*7.66%*	1.08	0.83	10.97%	15.02%	23.28%
13	1,463	3.17	31	9.55%	24.62%	32.66%	8.28%	*7.80%*	1.12	0.87	11.21%	15.43%	23.54%
14	1,305	3.12	37	8.40%	23.64%	30.95%	7.17%	*7.92%*	1.14	0.89	10.91%	16.70%	24.76%
15	1,172	3.07	36	10.16%	23.61%	30.91%	8.96%	*8.03%*	1.11	0.87	10.51%	17.23%	23.88%
16	1,055	3.02	47	11.80%	23.79%	31.22%	10.43%	*8.14%*	1.23	0.96	10.05%	18.83%	26.99%
17	913	2.96	39	9.80%	22.90%	29.70%	8.53%	*8.29%*	1.19	0.94	9.89%	18.68%	27.48%
18	794	2.90	47	10.03%	23.17%	30.16%	8.76%	*8.43%*	1.19	0.93	9.89%	19.10%	28.44%
19	664	2.82	66	8.52%	23.20%	30.21%	7.19%	*8.62%*	1.24	0.97	9.61%	19.71%	29.81%
20	534	2.73	71	9.53%	22.64%	29.26%	8.26%	*8.85%*	1.21	0.96	9.26%	21.08%	31.53%
21	440	2.64	54	10.62%	23.03%	29.93%	9.32%	*9.05%*	1.21	0.96	8.81%	22.51%	33.34%
22	338	2.53	80	10.42%	23.02%	29.90%	9.10%	*9.32%*	1.24	0.97	8.52%	24.83%	34.73%
23	264	2.42	77	10.77%	23.17%	30.16%	9.42%	*9.58%*	1.25	0.99	8.26%	25.46%	37.59%
24	185	2.27	108	11.53%	22.66%	29.30%	10.20%	*9.95%*	1.27	1.00	8.30%	26.68%	38.20%
25	65	1.81	251	12.28%	23.27%	30.33%	10.91%	*11.05%*	1.26	0.99	7.36%	38.66%	53.02%

CV(X) = Standard deviation of X divided by mean of X, calculated over 5 fiscal years.

[1] Unlevered risk premiums and unlevered betas are calculated using methodology described in Chapter 10 with an average assumed debt beta = 0.1.

Sources of underlying data: 1.) © 201502 CRSP®, Center for Research in Security Prices. University of Chicago Booth School of Business used with permission. All rights reserved. 2.) Morningstar *Direct* database. Used with permission. All rights reserved. Calculations performed by Duff & Phelps LLC.

Companies Ranked by Net Income

Data for Year Ending December 31, 2014

Comparative Risk Characteristics

Data Smoothing with Regression Analysis

Dependent Variable: Average Unlevered Risk Premium

Independent Variable: Log of Average Net Income

Constant	13.286%
X Coefficient(s)	-2.433%

*Smoothed Unlevered Premium = 13.286% - 2.433% * Log(Net Income)*

Portfolio Rank by Size	Average Net Inc. (in $millions)	Log of Average Net Inc.	Number of Firms	Arithmetic Average Risk Premium	Average Debt to MVIC	Average Debt to Market Value of Equity	Average Unlevered Risk Premium[1]	*Smoothed Average Unlevered Risk Premium*	Beta (Sum Beta) Since '63	Average Unlevered Beta	Average Operating Margin	Average CV(Operating Margin)	Average CV(ROE)
1	8,922	3.95	35	6.71%	20.08%	25.12%	6.03%	*3.67%*	0.77	0.64	15.85%	10.06%	16.54%
2	2,422	3.38	32	5.74%	24.43%	32.34%	4.79%	*5.05%*	0.87	0.68	14.38%	10.37%	17.60%
3	1,540	3.19	29	7.14%	26.21%	35.52%	6.12%	*5.53%*	0.87	0.67	12.86%	11.78%	18.63%
4	1,066	3.03	29	6.81%	26.56%	36.17%	5.73%	*5.92%*	0.90	0.69	12.83%	11.52%	18.18%
5	760	2.88	36	6.47%	26.07%	35.27%	5.35%	*6.28%*	0.95	0.73	12.43%	13.06%	21.15%
6	566	2.75	35	6.81%	24.25%	32.02%	5.72%	*6.59%*	0.99	0.77	12.90%	12.60%	20.57%
7	441	2.64	34	7.11%	24.55%	32.53%	5.94%	*6.85%*	1.05	0.82	12.72%	12.72%	20.42%
8	354	2.55	31	8.12%	24.11%	31.78%	6.91%	*7.08%*	1.09	0.85	12.66%	13.55%	21.66%
9	297	2.47	33	7.22%	23.70%	31.06%	6.09%	*7.27%*	1.04	0.82	12.09%	14.24%	22.77%
10	255	2.41	32	8.41%	23.90%	31.41%	7.25%	*7.43%*	1.06	0.83	12.21%	13.91%	21.87%
11	218	2.34	40	8.86%	23.62%	30.93%	7.69%	*7.60%*	1.08	0.85	11.77%	14.79%	21.90%
12	182	2.26	33	9.57%	24.14%	31.82%	8.37%	*7.79%*	1.08	0.84	11.79%	14.96%	21.99%
13	159	2.20	33	9.74%	23.57%	30.84%	8.59%	*7.93%*	1.06	0.84	11.28%	15.72%	22.18%
14	136	2.13	35	8.16%	23.96%	31.51%	6.88%	*8.09%*	1.16	0.90	11.30%	14.37%	21.17%
15	122	2.09	38	9.03%	23.52%	30.75%	7.82%	*8.21%*	1.12	0.88	10.76%	15.33%	22.89%
16	106	2.02	39	10.19%	22.86%	29.64%	9.01%	*8.36%*	1.12	0.88	10.85%	16.44%	24.04%
17	90	1.95	47	9.28%	22.73%	29.41%	8.02%	*8.53%*	1.20	0.95	10.48%	18.21%	26.55%
18	76	1.88	46	10.64%	22.75%	29.46%	9.36%	*8.71%*	1.21	0.96	10.19%	18.79%	25.87%
19	58	1.77	75	9.45%	23.25%	30.29%	8.10%	*8.99%*	1.25	0.99	9.53%	19.76%	26.36%
20	44	1.65	56	11.72%	23.82%	31.26%	10.36%	*9.28%*	1.23	0.96	9.31%	21.23%	29.94%
21	35	1.54	68	10.70%	24.51%	32.48%	9.31%	*9.54%*	1.22	0.95	9.00%	22.89%	30.60%
22	25	1.40	76	10.46%	23.82%	31.27%	9.12%	*9.87%*	1.22	0.95	8.88%	23.55%	32.72%
23	18	1.27	86	12.30%	22.84%	29.61%	10.96%	*10.21%*	1.26	0.99	8.53%	26.53%	36.56%
24	11	1.05	126	12.07%	23.76%	31.17%	10.69%	*10.74%*	1.25	0.98	7.77%	29.68%	41.72%
25	3	0.54	220	14.82%	24.99%	33.31%	13.28%	*11.98%*	1.32	1.01	5.85%	51.32%	71.98%

CV(X) = Standard deviation of X divided by mean of X, calculated over 5 fiscal years.

[1] Unlevered risk premiums and unlevered betas are calculated using methodology described in Chapter 10 with an average assumed debt beta = 0.1.

Sources of underlying data: 1.) © 201502 CRSP®, Center for Research in Security Prices. University of Chicago Booth School of Business used with permission. All rights reserved. 2.) Morningstar *Direct* database. Used with permission. All rights reserved. Calculations performed by Duff & Phelps LLC.

Companies Ranked by Market Value of Invested Capital (MVIC) | **Comparative Risk Characteristics** | **Exhibit C-4**

Data for Year Ending December 31, 2014

Data Smoothing with Regression Analysis

Dependent Variable: Average Unlevered Risk Premium

Independent Variable: Log of Average MVIC

Constant	19.000%
X Coefficient(s)	-3.073%

*Smoothed Unlevered Premium = 19.000% - 3.073% * Log(MVIC)*

Portfolio Rank by Size	Average MVIC (in $millions)	Log of Average MVIC	Number of Firms	Arithmetic Average Risk Premium	Average Debt to MVIC	Average Debt to Market Value of Equity	Average Unlevered Risk Premium[1]	*Smoothed Average Unlevered Risk Premium*	Beta (Sum Beta) Since '63	Average Unlevered Beta	Average Operating Margin	Average CV(Operating Margin)	Average CV(ROE)
1	210,749	5.32	39	5.49%	18.79%	23.14%	4.82%	*2.64%*	0.80	0.67	16.61%	9.96%	17.08%
2	66,082	4.82	33	4.80%	25.22%	33.73%	3.82%	*4.19%*	0.87	0.67	15.43%	11.43%	20.06%
3	41,570	4.62	29	5.11%	26.83%	36.67%	4.03%	*4.80%*	0.90	0.68	14.41%	11.59%	19.69%
4	31,430	4.50	29	6.01%	26.76%	36.54%	4.87%	*5.18%*	0.94	0.72	12.89%	11.82%	20.65%
5	24,299	4.39	30	6.37%	26.10%	35.31%	5.22%	*5.52%*	0.98	0.75	12.36%	12.05%	21.76%
6	18,313	4.26	32	6.03%	25.98%	35.09%	4.85%	*5.90%*	1.01	0.77	12.41%	13.25%	24.03%
7	14,818	4.17	32	7.65%	23.89%	31.40%	6.57%	*6.18%*	0.99	0.78	12.87%	13.70%	21.61%
8	12,250	4.09	41	7.53%	24.02%	31.61%	6.37%	*6.44%*	1.05	0.82	12.55%	13.88%	22.26%
9	10,109	4.00	37	7.71%	24.53%	32.51%	6.47%	*6.69%*	1.10	0.85	12.07%	14.29%	23.31%
10	8,722	3.94	35	8.96%	24.10%	31.75%	7.73%	*6.89%*	1.11	0.86	12.53%	14.26%	24.35%
11	7,509	3.88	31	8.48%	25.25%	33.78%	7.18%	*7.09%*	1.11	0.86	12.16%	15.11%	23.68%
12	6,429	3.81	35	8.59%	24.85%	33.06%	7.39%	*7.30%*	1.06	0.82	11.80%	14.59%	23.02%
13	5,617	3.75	31	8.29%	25.03%	33.39%	6.97%	*7.48%*	1.15	0.88	11.98%	15.67%	24.60%
14	4,848	3.69	36	8.84%	23.68%	31.02%	7.55%	*7.67%*	1.18	0.92	11.22%	15.95%	24.58%
15	4,248	3.63	38	9.16%	24.24%	32.00%	7.86%	*7.85%*	1.17	0.91	10.29%	17.09%	26.69%
16	3,558	3.55	46	10.40%	23.28%	30.35%	9.11%	*8.09%*	1.19	0.94	10.06%	18.28%	25.50%
17	3,005	3.48	42	9.95%	24.01%	31.59%	8.59%	*8.31%*	1.23	0.96	10.08%	18.73%	27.50%
18	2,551	3.41	51	10.60%	23.58%	30.85%	9.32%	*8.53%*	1.17	0.92	9.62%	19.13%	26.83%
19	2,059	3.31	63	8.34%	23.85%	31.31%	7.00%	*8.82%*	1.21	0.95	9.22%	20.81%	29.07%
20	1,678	3.22	60	9.50%	25.01%	33.35%	8.05%	*9.09%*	1.25	0.96	9.16%	21.89%	31.22%
21	1,335	3.13	63	9.78%	24.32%	32.14%	8.35%	*9.39%*	1.27	0.98	8.94%	23.21%	33.37%
22	1,060	3.03	82	10.57%	24.17%	31.87%	9.17%	*9.70%*	1.24	0.97	8.50%	25.70%	36.00%
23	813	2.91	63	12.07%	23.73%	31.12%	10.68%	*10.06%*	1.26	0.99	8.17%	25.65%	36.57%
24	526	2.72	94	11.78%	24.33%	32.16%	10.38%	*10.64%*	1.24	0.96	7.66%	29.02%	39.91%
25	157	2.20	272	15.67%	22.60%	29.20%	14.33%	*12.25%*	1.27	1.01	6.44%	42.65%	55.55%

CV(X) = Standard deviation of X divided by mean of X, calculated over 5 fiscal years.

[1] Unlevered risk premiums and unlevered betas are calculated using methodology described in Chapter 10 with an average assumed debt beta = 0.1.

Sources of underlying data: 1.) © 201502 CRSP®, Center for Research in Security Prices. University of Chicago Booth School of Business used with permission. All rights reserved. 2.) Morningstar *Direct* database. Used with permission. All rights reserved. Calculations performed by Duff & Phelps LLC.

Exhibit C-5

Companies Ranked by Total Assets

Data for Year Ending December 31, 2014

Comparative Risk Characteristics

Data Smoothing with Regression Analysis

Dependent Variable: Average Unlevered Risk Premium

Independent Variable: Log of Average Total Assets

Constant	17.274%
X Coefficient(s)	-2.653%

*Smoothed Unlevered Premium = 17.274% - 2.653% * Log(Assets)*

Portfolio Rank by Size	Average Total Assets (in $millions)	Log of Average Total Assets	Number of Firms	Arithmetic Average Risk Premium	Average Debt to MVIC	Average Debt to Market Value of Equity	Average Unlevered Risk Premium[1]	*Smoothed Average Unlevered Risk Premium*	Beta (Sum Beta) Since '63	Average Unlevered Beta	Average Operating Margin	Average CV(Operating Margin)	Average CV(ROE)
1	149,065	5.17	33	5.97%	28.15%	39.18%	4.98%	*3.55%*	0.80	0.60	13.79%	12.76%	20.90%
2	47,360	4.68	32	5.93%	33.52%	50.42%	4.69%	*4.87%*	0.84	0.59	13.76%	13.44%	22.33%
3	33,350	4.52	30	6.76%	31.08%	45.09%	5.46%	*5.27%*	0.93	0.67	12.20%	13.31%	22.13%
4	24,076	4.38	28	6.45%	30.52%	43.93%	5.20%	*5.65%*	0.91	0.66	12.55%	11.63%	20.54%
5	16,808	4.23	29	7.92%	29.55%	41.95%	6.66%	*6.06%*	0.94	0.69	11.19%	12.53%	23.67%
6	12,901	4.11	35	7.78%	27.97%	38.83%	6.57%	*6.37%*	0.95	0.71	12.26%	13.40%	24.85%
7	10,303	4.01	30	8.21%	27.06%	37.10%	6.92%	*6.63%*	1.05	0.79	11.62%	14.45%	26.23%
8	8,789	3.94	27	7.42%	27.03%	37.05%	6.14%	*6.81%*	1.04	0.79	11.71%	14.04%	22.73%
9	7,296	3.86	29	7.73%	27.94%	38.76%	6.31%	*7.02%*	1.11	0.83	11.56%	14.89%	25.98%
10	6,312	3.80	35	7.31%	27.11%	37.19%	5.95%	*7.19%*	1.10	0.83	11.69%	15.05%	25.28%
11	5,399	3.73	35	8.30%	27.60%	38.13%	6.87%	*7.37%*	1.13	0.84	11.32%	15.34%	23.99%
12	4,475	3.65	35	8.82%	25.71%	34.61%	7.53%	*7.59%*	1.10	0.84	10.71%	15.93%	24.25%
13	3,859	3.59	37	9.41%	25.87%	34.90%	8.04%	*7.76%*	1.14	0.87	11.13%	16.21%	25.12%
14	3,338	3.52	34	9.07%	25.18%	33.66%	7.76%	*7.92%*	1.12	0.87	10.71%	16.89%	25.82%
15	2,881	3.46	35	9.11%	25.54%	34.30%	7.75%	*8.09%*	1.15	0.88	10.01%	17.26%	26.63%
16	2,457	3.39	38	10.16%	24.02%	31.61%	8.85%	*8.28%*	1.18	0.92	9.43%	17.35%	25.98%
17	2,041	3.31	47	10.67%	24.23%	31.98%	9.34%	*8.49%*	1.19	0.92	10.07%	18.56%	26.24%
18	1,729	3.24	58	10.96%	24.86%	33.09%	9.55%	*8.68%*	1.22	0.94	9.44%	18.80%	27.29%
19	1,429	3.15	45	9.70%	24.91%	33.17%	8.27%	*8.90%*	1.23	0.95	9.60%	19.57%	28.28%
20	1,199	3.08	53	9.74%	24.00%	31.59%	8.36%	*9.10%*	1.24	0.97	9.48%	20.40%	29.31%
21	937	2.97	88	9.62%	23.71%	31.08%	8.25%	*9.39%*	1.24	0.97	8.80%	22.26%	32.12%
22	745	2.87	64	10.52%	22.91%	29.72%	9.19%	*9.65%*	1.25	0.98	8.60%	24.70%	35.16%
23	585	2.77	66	11.57%	22.59%	29.18%	10.26%	*9.93%*	1.25	0.99	8.36%	25.93%	36.13%
24	392	2.59	117	11.52%	21.63%	27.60%	10.26%	*10.39%*	1.25	1.00	8.21%	27.19%	37.66%
25	132	2.12	284	14.60%	19.03%	23.51%	13.47%	*11.65%*	1.27	1.05	7.50%	38.97%	50.11%

CV(X) = Standard deviation of X divided by mean of X, calculated over 5 fiscal years.

[1] Unlevered risk premiums and unlevered betas are calculated using methodology described in Chapter 10 with an average assumed debt beta = 0.1.

Sources of underlying data: 1.) © 201502 CRSP®, Center for Research in Security Prices. University of Chicago Booth School of Business used with permission. All rights reserved. 2.) Morningstar *Direct* database. Used with permission. All rights reserved. Calculations performed by Duff & Phelps LLC.

Companies Ranked by 5-Year Average EBITDA

Data for Year Ending December 31, 2014

Comparative Risk Characteristics

Exhibit C-6

Data Smoothing with Regression Analysis

Dependent Variable: Average Unlevered Risk Premium

Independent Variable: Log of Average EBITDA

Constant	14.699%
X Coefficient(s)	-2.532%

*Smoothed Unlevered Premium = 14.699% - 2.532% * Log(EBITDA)*

Portfolio Rank by Size	Average EBITDA (in $millions)	Log of Average EBITDA	Number of Firms	Arithmetic Average Risk Premium	Average Debt to MVIC	Average Debt to Market Value of Equity	Average Unlevered Risk Premium[1]	*Smoothed Average Unlevered Risk Premium*	Beta (Sum Beta) Since '63	Average Unlevered Beta	Average Operating Margin	Average CV(Operating Margin)	Average CV(ROE)
1	22,068	4.34	32	6.31%	22.87%	29.65%	5.52%	*3.70%*	0.79	0.63	14.70%	11.37%	19.26%
2	6,070	3.78	31	6.22%	28.55%	39.96%	5.15%	*5.12%*	0.84	0.63	13.99%	12.25%	22.08%
3	3,983	3.60	28	6.80%	28.89%	40.63%	5.65%	*5.58%*	0.89	0.66	12.83%	11.57%	19.34%
4	2,947	3.47	30	6.77%	28.53%	39.93%	5.60%	*5.91%*	0.91	0.68	11.96%	11.71%	21.13%
5	2,106	3.32	34	7.11%	27.63%	38.17%	5.86%	*6.28%*	0.99	0.75	12.00%	13.08%	23.72%
6	1,540	3.19	33	7.73%	27.89%	38.67%	6.57%	*6.63%*	0.93	0.70	12.42%	12.80%	23.10%
7	1,234	3.09	31	7.60%	25.67%	34.54%	6.41%	*6.87%*	1.02	0.78	12.35%	13.10%	21.38%
8	1,036	3.02	30	8.02%	25.00%	33.33%	6.81%	*7.06%*	1.06	0.82	12.13%	14.06%	22.76%
9	883	2.95	34	6.84%	24.84%	33.04%	5.57%	*7.24%*	1.11	0.86	12.16%	14.57%	24.69%
10	754	2.88	33	7.50%	25.62%	34.45%	6.21%	*7.41%*	1.09	0.84	12.26%	15.06%	23.45%
11	643	2.81	37	8.84%	24.58%	32.59%	7.71%	*7.59%*	1.01	0.79	11.26%	14.96%	23.12%
12	530	2.72	32	9.48%	25.67%	34.53%	8.20%	*7.80%*	1.09	0.83	11.56%	15.19%	23.69%
13	446	2.65	38	9.78%	25.85%	34.86%	8.50%	*7.99%*	1.08	0.83	11.41%	15.80%	24.98%
14	388	2.59	32	10.21%	23.98%	31.55%	8.93%	*8.14%*	1.16	0.90	10.81%	16.33%	24.34%
15	341	2.53	33	8.69%	24.50%	32.45%	7.39%	*8.29%*	1.15	0.89	10.73%	16.01%	23.34%
16	296	2.47	38	9.60%	23.77%	31.19%	8.30%	*8.44%*	1.17	0.92	10.41%	16.58%	23.17%
17	260	2.41	42	10.80%	24.33%	32.16%	9.47%	*8.58%*	1.18	0.92	9.94%	17.79%	26.83%
18	222	2.35	46	10.58%	24.81%	33.00%	9.20%	*8.76%*	1.20	0.93	9.91%	18.73%	27.84%
19	184	2.26	54	10.35%	24.46%	32.38%	8.94%	*8.97%*	1.24	0.96	9.52%	18.98%	26.73%
20	150	2.18	70	9.38%	24.67%	32.75%	7.94%	*9.19%*	1.25	0.97	9.30%	21.02%	28.31%
21	113	2.05	71	10.85%	23.99%	31.57%	9.49%	*9.50%*	1.22	0.95	9.24%	22.01%	30.84%
22	87	1.94	69	11.64%	23.53%	30.78%	10.30%	*9.79%*	1.23	0.96	8.79%	22.98%	31.37%
23	66	1.82	65	11.61%	23.36%	30.48%	10.28%	*10.10%*	1.23	0.97	8.27%	26.28%	36.06%
24	46	1.66	110	11.81%	23.07%	29.99%	10.45%	*10.49%*	1.26	0.99	8.03%	29.35%	38.42%
25	15	1.16	291	14.06%	21.89%	28.03%	12.73%	*11.75%*	1.30	1.04	6.63%	43.91%	55.45%

CV(X) = Standard deviation of X divided by mean of X, calculated over 5 fiscal years.

[1] Unlevered risk premiums and unlevered betas are calculated using methodology described in Chapter 10 with an average assumed debt beta = 0.1.

Sources of underlying data: 1.) © 201502 CRSP®, Center for Research in Security Prices. University of Chicago Booth School of Business used with permission. All rights reserved. 2.) Morningstar *Direct* database. Used with permission. All rights reserved. Calculations performed by Duff & Phelps LLC.

Companies Ranked by Sales

Data for Year Ending December 31, 2014

Comparative Risk Characteristics

Data Smoothing with Regression Analysis

Dependent Variable: Average Unlevered Risk Premium

Independent Variable: Log of Average Sales

Constant	15.105%
X Coefficient(s)	-2.001%

*Smoothed Unlevered Premium = 15.105% - 2.001% * Log(Sales)*

Portfolio Rank by Size	Average Sales (in $millions)	Log of Average Sales	Number of Firms	Arithmetic Average Risk Premium	Average Debt to MVIC	Average Debt to Market Value of Equity	Average Unlevered Risk Premium[1]	*Smoothed Average Unlevered Risk Premium*	Beta (Sum Beta) Since '63	Average Unlevered Beta	Average Operating Margin	Average CV(Operating Margin)	Average CV(ROE)
1	120,333	5.08	32	6.63%	23.34%	30.44%	5.70%	*4.94%*	0.89	0.71	9.26%	12.87%	21.46%
2	40,618	4.61	30	6.85%	24.58%	32.58%	5.77%	*5.88%*	0.97	0.75	8.61%	13.81%	22.69%
3	22,774	4.36	31	6.82%	26.60%	36.24%	5.63%	*6.38%*	0.99	0.75	9.53%	13.77%	23.14%
4	16,014	4.20	31	8.52%	27.16%	37.28%	7.29%	*6.69%*	1.00	0.75	10.78%	12.37%	20.67%
5	12,063	4.08	31	8.80%	28.26%	39.39%	7.48%	*6.94%*	1.02	0.76	10.04%	14.72%	24.71%
6	9,580	3.98	31	8.42%	27.53%	37.99%	7.14%	*7.14%*	1.02	0.77	10.43%	15.05%	25.30%
7	8,000	3.90	28	8.90%	25.60%	34.40%	7.63%	*7.29%*	1.08	0.83	10.21%	14.27%	23.70%
8	6,681	3.82	34	7.73%	26.58%	36.20%	6.45%	*7.45%*	1.05	0.80	9.82%	15.19%	22.41%
9	5,886	3.77	35	8.17%	26.24%	35.58%	6.84%	*7.56%*	1.10	0.84	9.78%	14.92%	25.68%
10	4,987	3.70	36	8.44%	26.11%	35.34%	7.09%	*7.70%*	1.13	0.86	9.69%	16.20%	24.23%
11	4,261	3.63	34	9.07%	26.09%	35.31%	7.74%	*7.84%*	1.10	0.84	10.09%	15.41%	24.75%
12	3,584	3.55	38	9.98%	26.22%	35.53%	8.65%	*7.99%*	1.11	0.84	10.08%	16.80%	24.92%
13	2,975	3.47	38	11.29%	26.18%	35.46%	9.82%	*8.15%*	1.21	0.92	9.74%	17.27%	26.08%
14	2,594	3.41	36	9.95%	26.18%	35.46%	8.59%	*8.27%*	1.13	0.86	9.78%	17.71%	26.43%
15	2,310	3.36	38	9.89%	25.34%	33.93%	8.59%	*8.37%*	1.12	0.86	10.10%	17.68%	25.27%
16	2,064	3.31	41	8.51%	25.35%	33.95%	7.16%	*8.47%*	1.15	0.89	10.14%	17.65%	26.72%
17	1,770	3.25	47	10.76%	26.02%	35.18%	9.39%	*8.61%*	1.14	0.87	10.23%	18.08%	27.08%
18	1,506	3.18	39	10.22%	25.98%	35.11%	8.77%	*8.75%*	1.20	0.92	10.13%	19.08%	27.90%
19	1,314	3.12	52	7.95%	25.68%	34.55%	6.47%	*8.86%*	1.24	0.95	9.48%	20.98%	33.45%
20	1,064	3.03	64	10.82%	25.79%	34.76%	9.44%	*9.05%*	1.16	0.89	9.54%	20.92%	30.10%
21	860	2.93	61	10.28%	24.62%	32.66%	8.93%	*9.23%*	1.18	0.92	10.10%	21.57%	32.18%
22	711	2.85	61	10.73%	24.65%	32.72%	9.30%	*9.40%*	1.25	0.96	9.71%	22.70%	33.19%
23	552	2.74	87	11.18%	23.79%	31.22%	9.81%	*9.62%*	1.24	0.97	9.89%	23.78%	34.65%
24	371	2.57	111	10.99%	22.38%	28.83%	9.70%	*9.96%*	1.24	0.98	9.25%	27.13%	37.97%
25	120	2.08	278	13.28%	19.82%	24.71%	12.13%	*10.95%*	1.25	1.02	8.81%	39.79%	51.45%

CV(X) = Standard deviation of X divided by mean of X, calculated over 5 fiscal years.

[1] Unlevered risk premiums and unlevered betas are calculated using methodology described in Chapter 10 with an average assumed debt beta = 0.1.

Sources of underlying data: 1.) © 201502 CRSP®, Center for Research in Security Prices. University of Chicago Booth School of Business used with permission. All rights reserved. 2.) Morningstar *Direct* database. Used with permission. All rights reserved. Calculations performed by Duff & Phelps LLC.

Companies Ranked by Number of Employees

Data for Year Ending December 31, 2014

Comparative Risk Characteristics

Exhibit C-8

Data Smoothing with Regression Analysis

Dependent Variable: Average Unlevered Risk Premium

Independent Variable: Log of Average Employees

Constant	15.689%
X Coefficient(s)	-1.924%

*Smoothed Unlevered Premium = 15.689% - 1.924% * Log(Employees)*

Portfolio Rank by Size	Average Number of Employees	Log of Average Employees	Number of Firms	Arithmetic Average Risk Premium	Average Debt to MVIC	Average Debt to Market Value of Equity	Average Unlevered Risk Premium[1]	*Smoothed Average Unlevered Risk Premium*	Beta (Sum Beta) Since '63	Average Unlevered Beta	Average Operating Margin	Average CV(Operating Margin)	Average CV(ROE)
1	314,558	5.50	30	6.63%	24.01%	31.60%	5.54%	*5.11%*	0.99	0.78	8.51%	12.34%	20.73%
2	99,492	5.00	37	7.03%	23.12%	30.07%	5.94%	*6.07%*	1.03	0.82	8.77%	12.27%	21.45%
3	61,721	4.79	30	7.75%	24.41%	32.28%	6.58%	*6.47%*	1.06	0.82	9.35%	13.21%	23.10%
4	46,474	4.67	35	8.62%	23.35%	30.46%	7.42%	*6.71%*	1.11	0.88	9.42%	14.65%	25.22%
5	35,103	4.55	36	8.60%	24.79%	32.97%	7.36%	*6.95%*	1.09	0.84	9.55%	14.59%	23.30%
6	27,449	4.44	29	9.27%	23.39%	30.53%	8.06%	*7.15%*	1.12	0.88	9.41%	14.44%	24.05%
7	21,991	4.34	39	7.63%	24.22%	31.95%	6.44%	*7.34%*	1.07	0.84	9.49%	14.30%	23.19%
8	18,164	4.26	34	7.76%	24.92%	33.19%	6.53%	*7.50%*	1.07	0.83	9.80%	15.30%	24.54%
9	15,432	4.19	35	9.39%	26.34%	35.77%	7.98%	*7.63%*	1.16	0.88	9.90%	16.38%	27.39%
10	13,384	4.13	39	9.57%	25.01%	33.35%	8.25%	*7.75%*	1.14	0.88	9.70%	17.11%	26.08%
11	11,642	4.07	37	10.25%	25.31%	33.88%	8.87%	*7.87%*	1.17	0.90	9.60%	17.86%	25.81%
12	10,185	4.01	33	10.16%	25.31%	33.89%	8.87%	*7.98%*	1.10	0.85	9.74%	16.94%	25.19%
13	9,052	3.96	38	8.96%	25.88%	34.92%	7.60%	*8.08%*	1.13	0.87	9.85%	17.04%	26.80%
14	7,625	3.88	50	7.90%	26.39%	35.85%	6.50%	*8.22%*	1.15	0.88	9.74%	17.80%	27.75%
15	6,354	3.80	48	10.06%	26.69%	36.41%	8.60%	*8.37%*	1.18	0.89	9.38%	18.63%	27.65%
16	5,598	3.75	46	9.07%	26.60%	36.24%	7.67%	*8.48%*	1.13	0.86	9.85%	18.99%	28.75%
17	4,911	3.69	41	8.74%	26.12%	35.35%	7.29%	*8.59%*	1.20	0.91	9.62%	20.66%	29.98%
18	4,080	3.61	46	10.45%	26.43%	35.93%	8.99%	*8.74%*	1.19	0.90	9.42%	21.23%	31.72%
19	3,358	3.53	64	9.60%	25.31%	33.89%	8.26%	*8.91%*	1.15	0.88	9.60%	21.83%	31.06%
20	2,721	3.43	64	8.90%	24.59%	32.61%	7.57%	*9.08%*	1.17	0.91	9.95%	21.74%	32.09%
21	2,235	3.35	65	11.25%	24.78%	32.94%	9.90%	*9.25%*	1.18	0.91	10.74%	21.97%	32.61%
22	1,755	3.24	50	10.80%	24.93%	33.20%	9.44%	*9.45%*	1.18	0.91	10.27%	23.55%	35.21%
23	1,277	3.11	97	11.10%	24.12%	31.79%	9.75%	*9.71%*	1.21	0.94	9.71%	26.89%	38.60%
24	831	2.92	84	12.08%	23.63%	30.94%	10.77%	*10.07%*	1.20	0.94	9.86%	30.38%	42.29%
25	287	2.46	237	13.42%	20.47%	25.74%	12.25%	*10.96%*	1.23	1.00	9.22%	39.79%	50.58%

CV(X) = Standard deviation of X divided by mean of X, calculated over 5 fiscal years.

[1] Unlevered risk premiums and unlevered betas are calculated using methodology described in Chapter 10 with an average assumed debt beta = 0.1.

Sources of underlying data: 1.) © 201502 CRSP®, Center for Research in Security Prices. University of Chicago Booth School of Business used with permission. All rights reserved. 2.) Morningstar *Direct* database. Used with permission. All rights reserved. Calculations performed by Duff & Phelps LLC.

Risk Premium Report – Exhibits D-1 through D-3

The D exhibits used in the *Risk Study* present 25 portfolios ranked by three fundamental accounting measures: five-year average operating income margin, the coefficient of variation in operating income margin, and the coefficient of variation in return on book equity. Use of fundamental accounting measures of risk allows for direct assessment of the riskiness of the subject company.

The D Exhibits are used in the following method to estimate a cost of equity capital:

- Build-up 3
- Build-up 3-Unlevered

Risk Measures:

D-1: Operating Margin

D-2: Coefficient of variation in operating income margin

D-3: Coefficient of variation in return on book equity

Companies Ranked by Operating Margin **Exhibit D-1**

Historical Equity Risk Premium: Average Since 1963

Data for Year Ending December 31, 2014

Portfolio Rank	Average Operating Margin	Log of Average Op Margin	Number as of 2014	Beta (Sum Beta) Since '63	Average Unlevered Beta	Standard Deviation of Returns	Geometric Average Return	Arithmetic Average Return	Arithmetic Average Risk Premium	Arithmetic Average Unlevered Risk Premium	*Smoothed Average Risk Premium*	Average Debt to Market Value of Equity	Average Debt/ MVIC
1	38.71%	-0.41	59	0.87	0.68	16.77%	11.63%	12.91%	6.30%	5.35%	*5.54%*	32.55%	24.56%
2	29.62%	-0.53	53	0.83	0.63	17.22%	10.28%	11.68%	5.06%	4.06%	*6.48%*	37.45%	27.25%
3	25.12%	-0.60	57	0.86	0.66	17.33%	12.11%	13.52%	6.91%	5.92%	*7.06%*	34.56%	25.68%
4	22.25%	-0.65	46	0.94	0.75	16.69%	11.94%	13.30%	6.69%	5.74%	*7.49%*	29.01%	22.49%
5	20.19%	-0.69	43	0.98	0.81	17.96%	12.86%	14.37%	7.76%	6.89%	*7.83%*	24.23%	19.50%
6	18.62%	-0.73	61	1.06	0.89	17.80%	13.39%	14.87%	8.26%	7.42%	*8.12%*	20.96%	17.32%
7	17.44%	-0.76	40	1.09	0.92	18.60%	13.16%	14.78%	8.17%	7.27%	*8.35%*	21.83%	17.92%
8	16.20%	-0.79	42	1.11	0.93	19.74%	12.81%	14.60%	7.99%	7.05%	*8.6[illegible]%*	22.55%	18.40%
9	15.09%	-0.82	46	1.16	0.96	19.33%	14.53%	16.24%	9.63%	8.62%	*8.85%*	23.34%	18.92%
10	14.35%	-0.84	35	1.16	0.95	20.47%	14.20%	16.10%	9.49%	8.43%	*9.03%*	24.68%	19.79%
11	13.54%	-0.87	50	1.16	0.95	20.76%	13.07%	15.02%	8.41%	7.33%	*9.24%*	25.19%	20.12%
12	12.53%	-0.90	55	1.18	0.96	20.13%	13.40%	15.27%	8.65%	7.50%	*9.5[illegible]%*	26.74%	21.10%
13	11.67%	-0.93	50	1.20	0.97	20.73%	13.36%	15.39%	8.77%	7.64%	*9.76%*	25.91%	20.58%
14	11.00%	-0.96	52	1.19	0.95	21.90%	14.03%	16.37%	9.76%	8.58%	*9.97%*	27.13%	21.34%
15	10.30%	-0.99	57	1.24	0.99	23.31%	15.16%	17.59%	10.98%	9.70%	*10.20%*	28.45%	22.15%
16	9.52%	-1.02	47	1.19	0.93	21.89%	16.30%	18.49%	11.88%	10.58%	*10.48%*	30.95%	23.63%
17	8.92%	-1.05	45	1.25	0.97	23.23%	14.95%	17.45%	10.84%	9.41%	*10.7[illegible]%*	32.73%	24.66%
18	8.31%	-1.08	49	1.23	0.96	24.42%	16.00%	18.71%	12.10%	10.70%	*10.95%*	32.35%	24.45%
19	7.57%	-1.12	52	1.28	0.97	24.46%	15.48%	18.25%	11.64%	10.12%	*11.28%*	34.47%	25.63%
20	6.77%	-1.17	67	1.26	0.94	23.73%	16.12%	18.70%	12.08%	10.48%	*11.67%*	37.59%	27.32%
21	6.11%	-1.21	58	1.27	0.95	24.50%	17.81%	20.43%	13.82%	12.19%	*12.04%*	38.19%	27.64%
22	5.28%	-1.28	58	1.23	0.91	25.00%	16.44%	19.23%	12.62%	11.02%	*12.55%*	39.07%	28.09%
23	4.43%	-1.35	76	1.30	0.95	26.02%	17.13%	20.24%	13.63%	11.84%	*13.16%*	41.81%	29.48%
24	3.32%	-1.48	64	1.28	0.93	25.63%	16.90%	19.88%	13.27%	11.48%	*14.1[illegible]%*	42.70%	29.92%
25	2.09%	-1.68	82	1.28	0.94	28.41%	17.21%	20.76%	14.14%	12.39%	*15.81%*	41.62%	29.39%

	Geometric Average Return	Arithmetic Average Return	Arithmetic Average Risk Premium
Large Stocks (Ibbotson SBBI data)	10.27%	11.66%	5.05%
Small Stocks (Ibbotson SBBI data)	13.77%	16.47%	9.86%
Long-Term Treasury Income (Ibbotson SBBI data)	6.58%	6.61%	

Equity Risk Premium Study: Data through December 31, 2014

Data Smoothing with Regression Analysis

Dependent Variable: Arithmetic Average Risk Premium

Independent Variable: Log of Average Operating Margin

Regression Output:	
Constant	2.199%
Standard Error of Y Estimate	0.888%
R Squared	89%
No. of Observations	25
Degrees of Freedom	23
X Coefficient(s)	-8.104%
Standard Error of Coefficient	0.606%
t-Statistic	-13.38

*Smoothed Premium = 2.199% - 8.104% * Log(Operating Margin)*

Smoothed Premium vs. Arithmetic Premium

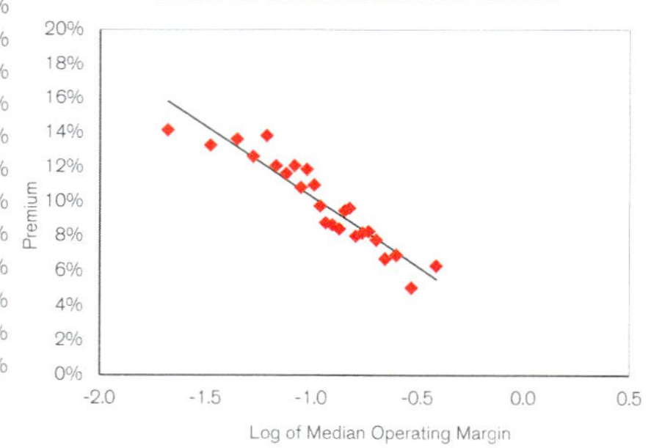

Sources of underlying data: 1.) © 201502 CRSP®, Center for Research in Security Prices. University of Chicago Booth School of Business used with permission. All rights reserved. 2.) Morningstar *Direct* database. Used with permission. All rights reserved. Calculations performed by Duff & Phelps LLC.

Companies Ranked by CV(Operating Margin) **Exhibit D-2**

Historical Equity Risk Premium: Average Since 1963

Data for Year Ending December 31, 2014

Portfolio Rank	Average CV(Op Margin)	Log of Average CV(Op Margin)	Number as of 2014	Beta (Sum Beta) Since '63	Average Unlevered Beta	Standard Deviation of Returns	Geometric Average Return	Arithmetic Average Return	Arithmetic Average Risk Premium	Arithmetic Average Unlevered Risk Premium	*Smoothed Average Risk Premium*	Average Debt to Market Value of Equity	Average Debt/ MVIC
1	182.26%	0.26	117	1.46	1.14	30.56%	16.97%	21.02%	14.41%	12.81%	*14.25%*	30.34%	23.28%
2	88.42%	-0.05	67	1.38	1.05	27.95%	16.74%	20.15%	13.54%	11.88%	*12.90%*	34.53%	25.67%
3	68.33%	-0.17	65	1.34	1.01	25.09%	14.00%	16.89%	10.28%	8.65%	*12.42%*	35.34%	26.11%
4	53.30%	-0.27	83	1.34	1.02	25.79%	14.79%	17.86%	11.25%	9.60%	*11.96%*	35.51%	26.21%
5	43.02%	-0.37	64	1.27	0.98	25.00%	15.62%	18.51%	11.90%	10.42%	*11.56%*	33.56%	25.13%
6	37.21%	-0.43	53	1.27	0.97	25.45%	14.57%	17.45%	10.83%	9.29%	*11.29%*	35.15%	26.01%
7	32.19%	-0.49	64	1.27	0.97	23.88%	15.19%	17.86%	11.25%	9.75%	*11.02%*	33.94%	25.34%
8	28.11%	-0.55	61	1.26	0.97	23.24%	15.24%	17.75%	11.14%	9.68%	*10.76%*	33.16%	24.90%
9	24.97%	-0.60	55	1.18	0.92	22.44%	16.08%	18.45%	11.83%	10.50%	*10.54%*	32.44%	24.50%
10	22.04%	-0.66	56	1.16	0.90	22.25%	15.64%	17.85%	11.24%	9.94%	*10.31%*	31.97%	24.23%
11	19.84%	-0.70	56	1.15	0.90	20.87%	15.07%	17.03%	10.42%	9.14%	*10.11%*	31.90%	24.18%
12	18.17%	-0.74	48	1.14	0.88	20.09%	15.13%	16.97%	10.36%	9.06%	*9.95%*	32.86%	24.73%
13	16.38%	-0.79	49	1.12	0.88	19.14%	13.51%	15.27%	8.66%	7.45%	*9.76%*	30.53%	23.39%
14	15.04%	-0.82	39	1.11	0.88	20.43%	14.91%	16.80%	10.19%	9.01%	*9.60%*	30.02%	23.09%
15	13.82%	-0.86	45	1.09	0.86	19.18%	14.74%	16.45%	9.84%	8.68%	*9.44%*	29.97%	23.06%
16	12.52%	-0.90	44	1.07	0.85	20.30%	13.59%	15.48%	8.87%	7.73%	*9.25%*	30.29%	23.25%
17	11.72%	-0.93	43	1.01	0.80	18.53%	14.54%	16.09%	9.48%	8.42%	*9.13%*	30.01%	23.08%
18	10.49%	-0.98	45	1.02	0.81	19.00%	14.49%	16.14%	9.53%	8.48%	*8.92%*	29.27%	22.64%
19	9.26%	-1.03	37	0.99	0.79	18.14%	13.66%	15.21%	8.60%	7.55%	*8.69%*	30.07%	23.12%
20	8.51%	-1.07	33	0.98	0.79	17.48%	13.89%	15.33%	8.72%	7.77%	*8.53%*	27.42%	21.52%
21	7.47%	-1.13	47	0.91	0.73	16.63%	12.85%	14.14%	7.53%	6.61%	*8.29%*	28.89%	22.42%
22	6.41%	-1.19	49	0.89	0.71	15.49%	12.63%	13.75%	7.14%	6.23%	*8.00%*	29.92%	23.03%
23	5.54%	-1.26	38	0.89	0.71	16.93%	12.74%	14.08%	7.47%	6.54%	*7.73%*	30.09%	23.13%
24	4.44%	-1.35	42	0.85	0.68	16.48%	12.45%	13.71%	7.10%	6.25%	*7.32%*	28.81%	22.37%
25	2.82%	-1.55	44	0.81	0.67	15.41%	12.11%	13.25%	6.64%	5.89%	*6.47%*	26.18%	20.75%
Large Stocks (Ibbotson SBBI data)							10.27%	11.66%	5.05%				
Small Stocks (Ibbotson SBBI data)							13.77%	16.47%	9.86%				
Long-Term Treasury Income (Ibbotson SBBI data)							6.58%	6.61%					

Equity Risk Premium Study: Data through December 31, 2014
Data Smoothing with Regression Analysis
Dependent Variable: Arithmetic Average Risk Premium
Independent Variable: Log of Average CV(Operating Margin)

Regression Output:

Constant	13.133%
Standard Error of Y Estimate	0.743%
R Squared	86%
No. of Observations	25
Degrees of Freedom	23
X Coefficient(s)	4.299%
Standard Error of Coefficient	0.355%
t-Statistic	12.10

*Smoothed Premium = 13.133% + 4.299% * Log(CV Op. Inc.)*

Smoothed Premium vs. Arithmetic Premium

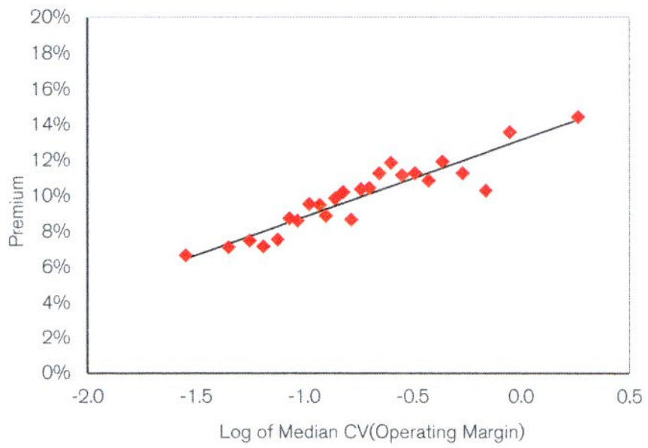

Sources of underlying data: 1.) Calculations performed by Duff & Phelps LLC.

Companies Ranked by CV(ROE)

Exhibit D-3

Historical Equity Risk Premium: Average Since 1963
Data for Year Ending December 31, 2014

Portfolio Rank	Average CV(ROE)	Log of Average CV(ROE)	Number as of 2014	Beta (Sum Beta) Since '63	Average Unlevered Beta	Standard Deviation of Returns	Geometric Average Return	Arithmetic Average Return	Arithmetic Average Risk Premium	Arithmetic Average Unlevered Risk Premium	*Smoothed Average Risk Premium*	Average Debt to Market Value of Equity	Average Debt/ MVIC
1	1818.47%	1.26	52	1.45	1.02	30.56%	15.07%	19.56%	12.94%	10.80%	*12.96%*	46.13%	31.57%
2	460.26%	0.66	71	1.42	1.03	27.71%	15.95%	19.70%	13.09%	11.14%	*11.81%*	41.28%	29.22%
3	256.56%	0.41	52	1.37	1.01	26.50%	14.19%	17.69%	11.08%	9.28%	*11.33%*	39.17%	28.14%
4	173.54%	0.24	64	1.32	0.98	25.58%	14.15%	17.49%	10.87%	9.17%	*11.00%*	38.23%	27.66%
5	133.67%	0.13	69	1.29	0.98	25.66%	14.74%	18.02%	11.41%	9.81%	*10.79%*	36.00%	26.47%
6	110.32%	0.04	52	1.27	0.97	23.67%	14.48%	17.32%	10.71%	9.18%	*10.63%*	34.66%	25.74%
7	94.45%	-0.02	43	1.27	0.97	23.96%	13.33%	16.22%	9.61%	8.10%	*10.50%*	34.47%	25.63%
8	81.26%	-0.09	65	1.23	0.96	22.47%	13.46%	16.08%	9.47%	8.09%	*10.37%*	31.74%	24.09%
9	69.00%	-0.16	67	1.22	0.95	21.88%	13.97%	16.47%	9.86%	8.51%	*10.24%*	31.30%	23.84%
10	60.00%	-0.22	49	1.17	0.92	22.47%	13.01%	15.64%	9.03%	7.79%	*10.12%*	29.97%	23.06%
11	52.85%	-0.28	78	1.16	0.92	20.82%	15.09%	17.40%	10.79%	9.57%	*10.01%*	29.47%	22.76%
12	45.24%	-0.34	43	1.14	0.90	21.11%	14.10%	16.39%	9.77%	8.59%	*9.89%*	29.21%	22.61%
13	41.10%	-0.39	46	1.15	0.92	19.31%	13.60%	15.63%	9.02%	7.85%	*9.81%*	28.16%	21.97%
14	35.85%	-0.45	56	1.10	0.88	20.16%	14.07%	16.22%	9.60%	8.50%	*9.69%*	27.93%	21.83%
15	31.37%	-0.50	58	1.12	0.90	20.55%	14.79%	17.04%	10.43%	9.30%	*9.58%*	27.82%	21.76%
16	28.09%	-0.55	60	1.07	0.86	19.49%	14.04%	16.10%	9.49%	8.41%	*9.49%*	28.26%	22.03%
17	25.05%	-0.60	45	1.04	0.84	19.20%	13.24%	15.26%	8.65%	7.64%	*9.39%*	26.85%	21.17%
18	22.46%	-0.65	52	1.04	0.84	18.86%	14.53%	16.43%	9.82%	8.79%	*9.30%*	27.58%	21.62%
19	20.34%	-0.69	41	0.98	0.79	19.92%	14.45%	16.53%	9.92%	8.96%	*9.22%*	27.56%	21.61%
20	18.50%	-0.73	46	0.95	0.77	18.19%	13.47%	15.29%	8.68%	7.78%	*9.14%*	26.52%	20.96%
21	16.20%	-0.79	45	0.96	0.78	18.26%	13.58%	15.41%	8.80%	7.89%	*9.03%*	26.57%	20.99%
22	14.35%	-0.84	39	0.93	0.75	18.23%	14.49%	16.35%	9.74%	8.84%	*8.93%*	27.29%	21.44%
23	12.41%	-0.91	42	0.89	0.72	16.53%	13.86%	15.39%	8.78%	7.93%	*8.81%*	27.20%	21.38%
24	9.21%	-1.04	57	0.85	0.70	17.30%	14.38%	16.05%	9.44%	8.69%	*8.56%*	24.63%	19.76%
25	6.20%	-1.21	52	0.82	0.68	16.44%	12.95%	14.44%	7.83%	7.13%	*8.23%*	23.84%	19.25%
Large Stocks (Ibbotson SBBI data)							10.27%	11.66%	5.05%				
Small Stocks (Ibbotson SBBI data)							13.77%	16.47%	9.86%				
Long-Term Treasury Income (Ibbotson SBBI data)							6.58%	6.61%					

Equity Risk Premium Study: Data through December 31, 2014
Data Smoothing with Regression Analysis
Dependent Variable: Arithmetic Average Risk Premium
Independent Variable: Log of Average CV(ROE)

Regression Output:	
Constant	10.545%
Standard Error of Y Estimate	0.664%
R Squared	73%
No. of Observations	25
Degrees of Freedom	23
X Coefficient(s)	1.915%
Standard Error of Coefficient	0.242%
t-Statistic	7.92

*Smoothed Premium = 10.545% + 1.915% * Log(CV ROE)*

Smoothed Premium vs. Arithmetic Premium

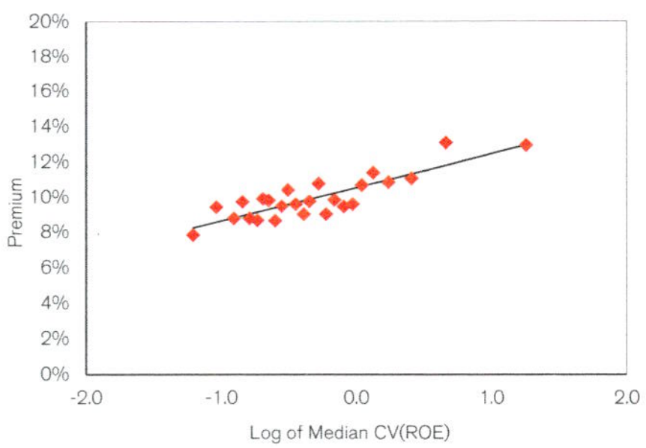

Sources of underlying data: 1.) © 201502 CRSP®, Center for Research in Security Prices. University of Chicago Booth School of Business used with permission. All rights reserved. 2.) Morningstar *Direct* database. Used with permission. All rights reserved. Calculations performed by Duff & Phelps LLC.

Risk Premium Report – Exhibits H-A through H-C

The High-Financial-Risk Study includes Exhibits H-A, H-B, and H-C. The companies in the H exhibits are companies that are losing money, have high leverage, or are in bankruptcy. These companies were eliminated from the base set of companies used in the *Size Study* and *Risk Study*. The H exhibits provide risk premia that may be used in both build-up and CAPM estimates of cost of equity capital.

The H Exhibits are used in the following method to estimate a cost of equity capital:

- Build-up 1-High-Financial-Risk
- CAPM-High-Financial-Risk

Historical Equity Risk Premium: Average Since 1963
High-Financial-Risk Company Data for Year Ending December 31, 2014

Portfolio	Beta (Sum Beta) Since '63	Standard Deviation of Returns	Geometric Average Return	Arithmetic Average Return	Arithmetic Average Risk Premium	Average Debt/ MVIC
Manufacturing (z-Score)						
1.8 to 2.99 *(gray zone)*	1.57	36.37%	16.42%	22.05%	15.44%	46.18%
< 1.8 *(distress zone)*	1.63	37.59%	16.41%	23.18%	16.56%	57.82%
Service (z''-Score)						
1.1 to 2.59 *(gray zone)*	1.58	43.23%	14.88%	27.89%	21.28%	40.95%
< 1.1 *(distress zone)*	1.71	45.11%	19.96%	34.21%	27.59%	47.81%
Large Stocks (Ibbotson SBBI data)			10.27%	11.66%	5.05%	
Small Stocks (Ibbotson SBBI data)			13.77%	16.47%	9.86%	
Long-Term Treasury Income (Ibbotson SBBI data)			6.58%	6.61%		

Sources of underlying data: 1.) © 201502 CRSP®, Center for Research in Security Prices. University of Chicago Booth School of Business used with permission. All rights reserved. 2.) Morningstar *Direct* database. Used with permission. All rights reserved. Calculations performed by Duff & Phelps LLC.

Companies Ranked by z-Score | **Premia Over CAPM ($RP_{s,\ high\text{-}financial\text{-}risk}$)** | **Exhibit H-B**

Historical Equity Risk Premium: Average Since 1963
High-Financial-Risk Company Data for Year Ending December 31, 2014

Portfolio	Beta (Sum Beta) Since '63	Arithmetic Average Return	Arithmetic Average Risk Premium	Indicated CAPM Premium	Premium over CAPM
Manufacturing (z-Score)					
1.8 to 2.99 *(gray zone)*	1.57	22.05%	15.44%	7.92%	7.52%
< 1.8 *(distress zone)*	1.63	23.18%	16.56%	8.23%	8.33%
Service (z"-Score)					
1.1 to 2.59 *(gray zone)*	1.58	27.89%	21.28%	7.99%	13.29%
< 1.1 *(distress zone)*	1.71	34.21%	27.59%	8.64%	18.95%
Large Stocks (Ibbotson SBBI data)		11.66%	5.05%		
Small Stocks (Ibbotson SBBI data)		16.47%	9.86%		
Long-Term Treasury Income (Ibbotson SBBI data)		6.61%			

Sources of underlying data: 1.) © 201502 CRSP®, Center for Research in Security Prices. University of Chicago Booth School of Business used with permission. All rights reserved. 2.) Morningstar *Direct* database. Used with permission. All rights reserved. Calculations performed by Duff & Phelps LLC.

Companies Ranked by z-Score **Premia Over the Risk-Free Rate ($RP_{m+s,\ high\text{-}financial\text{-}risk}$)** **Exhibit H-C**

Historical Equity Risk Premium: Average Since 1963
High-Financial-Risk Company Data for Year Ending December 31, 2014

Portfolio	Arithmetic Average Risk Premium	Average Debt to MVIC	Average Debt to Market Value of Equity	Beta (Sum Beta) Since '63	Average Operating Margin
Manufacturing (z-Score)					
1.8 to 2.99 *(gray zone)*	15.44%	46.18%	85.82%	1.57	4.23%
< 1.8 *(distress zone)*	16.56%	57.82%	137.10%	1.63	3.81%
Service (z"-Score)					
1.1 to 2.59 *(gray zone)*	21.28%	40.95%	69.34%	1.58	6.80%
< 1.1 *(distress zone)*	27.59%	47.81%	91.62%	1.71	1.36%

Sources of underlying data: 1.) © 201502 CRSP®, Center for Research in Security Prices. University of Chicago Booth School of Business used with permission. All rights reserved. 2.) Morningstar *Direct* database. Used with permission. All rights reserved. Calculations performed by Duff & Phelps LLC.